W9-AMT-071

FLORIDA STATE
UNIVERSITY LIBRARIES

APR 15 1999

TALLAHASSEE, FLORIDA

Québec

WORLD BIBLIOGRAPHICAL SERIES

General Editors:
Robert G. Neville (Executive Editor)
John J. Horton

Robert A. Myers   Hans H. Wellisch
Ian Wallace   Ralph Lee Woodward, Jr.

John J. Horton is Deputy Librarian of the University of Bradford and was formerly Chairman of its Academic Board of Studies in Social Sciences. He has maintained a longstanding interest in the discipline of area studies and its associated bibliographical problems, with special reference to European Studies. In particular he has published in the field of Icelandic and of Yugoslav studies, including the two relevant volumes in the World Bibliographical Series.

Robert A. Myers is Associate Professor of Anthropology in the Division of Social Sciences and Director of Study Abroad Programs at Alfred University, Alfred, New York. He has studied post-colonial island nations of the Caribbean and has spent two years in Nigeria on a Fulbright Lectureship. His interests include international public health, historical anthropology and developing societies. In addition to *Amerindians of the Lesser Antilles: a bibliography* (1981), *A Resource Guide to Dominica, 1493-1986* (1987) and numerous articles, he has compiled the World Bibliographical Series volumes on *Dominica* (1987), *Nigeria* (1989) and *Ghana* (1991).

Ian Wallace is Professor of German at the University of Bath. A graduate of Oxford in French and German, he also studied in Tübingen, Heidelberg and Lausanne before taking teaching posts at universities in the USA, Scotland and England. He specializes in contemporary German affairs, especially literature and culture, on which he has published numerous articles and books. In 1979 he founded the journal *GDR Monitor*, which he continues to edit under its new title *German Monitor*.

Hans H. Wellisch is Professor emeritus at the College of Library and Information Services, University of Maryland. He was President of the American Society of Indexers and was a member of the International Federation for Documentation. He is the author of numerous articles and several books on indexing and abstracting, and has published *The Conversion of Scripts and Indexing and Abstracting: an International Bibliography*, and *Indexing from A to Z*. He also contributes frequently to *Journal of the American Society for Information Science*, *The Indexer* and other professional journals.

Ralph Lee Woodward, Jr. is Professor of History at Tulane University, New Orleans. He is the author of *Central America, a Nation Divided*, 2nd ed. (1985), as well as several monographs and more than seventy scholarly articles on modern Latin America. He has also compiled volumes in the World Bibliographical Series on *Belize* (1980), *El Salvador* (1988), *Guatemala* (Rev. Ed.) (1992) and *Nicaragua* (Rev. Ed.) (1994). Dr. Woodward edited the Central American section of the *Research Guide to Central America and the Caribbean* (1985) and is currently associate editor of Scribner's *Encyclopedia of Latin American History*.

VOLUME 211

Québec

Alain-G. Gagnon

Compiler

CLIO PRESS

OXFORD, ENGLAND · SANTA BARBARA, CALIFORNIA
DENVER, COLORADO

© Copyright 1998 by ABC-CLIO Ltd.

All rights reserved. No part of this publication may be reproduced, stored in any retrieval system, or transmitted in any form or by any means, electronic, mechanical, photocopying or otherwise, without the prior permission in writing of the publishers.

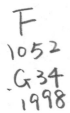

British Library Cataloguing in Publication Data

Gagnon, Alain-G., 1954-
Québec. – (World bibliographical series; v. 211)
1. Québec (Province) – Bibliography
I. Title
016.9'714

ISBN 1-85109-290-0

ABC-CLIO Ltd.,
Old Clarendon Ironworks,
35A Great Clarendon Street,
Oxford OX2 6AT, England.

—————

ABC-CLIO Inc.,
130 Cremona Drive,
Santa Barbara,
CA 93117, USA.

Designed by Bernard Crossland.
Typeset by Columns Design Ltd., Reading, England.
Printed in Great Britain by print in black, Midsomer Norton.

THE WORLD BIBLIOGRAPHICAL SERIES

This series, which is principally designed for the English speaker, will eventually cover every country (and some of the world's principal regions and cities), each in a separate volume comprising annotated entries on works dealing with its history, geography, economy and politics; and with its people, their culture, customs, religion and social organization. Attention will also be paid to current living conditions – housing, education, newspapers, clothing, etc. – that are all too often ignored in standard bibliographies; and to those particular aspects relevant to individual countries. Each volume seeks to achieve, by use of careful selectivity and critical assessment of the literature, an expression of the country and an appreciation of its nature and national aspirations, to guide the reader towards an understanding of its importance. The keynote of the series is to provide, in a uniform format, an interpretation of each country that will express its culture, its place in the world, and the qualities and background that make it unique. The views expressed in individual volumes, however, are not necessarily those of the publisher.

VOLUMES IN THE SERIES

Contents

Contents

Contents

Contents

Introduction

For several years Québec has been the focus of particular attention among specialists from different national political communities such as the Catalans, the Scottish, the Flemish, and the Walloons. The Québec Referendum of October 1995, proposing Québec sovereignty, as well as the active participation of Québec in the promotion of North American free trade agreements, have contributed to propel this member state of the Canadian federation onto the international scene. The interest was all the greater since nationalism and free trade have traditionally been perceived as antagonistic realities: nationalism signifying in the eyes of numerous observers withdrawal and protectionism; and liberalization of markets suggesting a greater opening to the world and the end of partitioning.

The interest in studying Québec society lies precisely in the fact that there exists both an important nationalist climate and a substantial support for the liberalization of markets and a decompartmentalization of the nation state for the benefit of the wider region. At the present time, when there is a double process of internationalization, on one hand, and a search for local identities, on the other, Québec is a particularly useful model for federated states with ambitions to intervene on the international scene in the name of specific regional economic objectives.

Aware that important decisions extend beyond the confines of the nation state, Quebecers aspire to be in a position to participate in economically oriented international forums in order to ensure their interests will be adequately represented. Québec's considerable human and economic capital allows it to act at the international level. Moreover, Québec has endowed itself with a first-rate bureaucracy.

The Québec situation is particularly significant because it challenges the pertinence of continuing the Canadian federal experience. Whether Québec's political future lies within Canada or not, it undoubtedly possesses the characteristics of a modern nation: it is a modern liberal society where citizenship is essentially defined according to a territorial and civic basis. Having been associated for a long time with conservative ideology, Québec nationalism is now characterized by liberalism and pluralism, as the work of renowned philosophers such as Charles Taylor (McGill University) and Guy Laforest (Université Laval) attests.

Québec is distinguished by its culture, language, history, and civilian tradition, among other elements. Therefore, to study Québec merely as another Canadian province would be simplistic and would hardly allow for an understanding of the degree to which this community, while sharing numerous common values with Canadians outside of Québec, differentiates itself in many respects.

This annotated bibliography will allow readers to better comprehend the Québec reality and to grasp the extent to which Québec constitutes a fundamentally different entity on the North American continent. This reality has evolved continuously over the last half-century. Numerous modern currents, such as pluralism and liberalism, have gradually traversed the rural and traditional Québec that the American Everett Hughes studied at the beginning of the 1940s. Québec remains a theatre of diverse opinions, competing political options and multiple religious values.

Principal historic landmarks

Jacques Cartier, the French explorer, took possession of Canada in the name of the King of France, François I, in 1534. Numerous commercial expeditions were established with the objective of exploiting the area's abundant fish and fur resources. France's involvement in Europe's religious wars halted emigration to New France. Colonial administration was therefore left to private companies who undertook settling the colony in exchange for an exclusive monopoly over natural resources.

Québec City was founded in 1608 by Samuel de Champlain. The cities of Trois-Rivières and Hochelaga (which later became Montréal) were founded in 1634 and 1642 respectively. Gradually, New France was taking form. Population growth was stifled, however, by the private companies' incapacity to entice settlers to North American soil. Just over two centuries after the arrival of the first French settlers, the population of New France lagged far behind that of the New England states (55,000 compared with 1,500,000 respectively).

Living conditions remained precarious throughout the French regime from 1534 to 1759. Successive governors and intendants, appointed by the kings of France, attempted to diversify the local economy. However, their efforts to develop the agriculture sector, and to establish cheese dairies, butter dairies, flour mills, and other enterprises, as well as their attempts to find markets for these products merely revealed the inherent weaknesses of colonization as well as France's own financial difficulties.

The development of New France was directly affected by the wars that France launched in England and, in a lesser capacity, in Holland. The French territory in North America diminished at various times over the 17th and 18th centuries. The outcome of the Seven Year War (1756-63) marked the end of the French administration in North America. Québec and Montréal surrendered in 1759 and 1760 respectively, and the Transfer of New France to England was confirmed by the Royal Proclamation of 1763. The English Conquest shattered the lives of the inhabitants of New France. Several members of the religious and administrative elite returned to France and the inhabitants were obligated to submit to English authorities who imposed new cultural and religious practices upon them for a certain time.

The desire of the British to impose their traditions gradually resolved itself as the threats of an uprising of the southern colonies materialized. In the hope of ensuring Canadian inhabitants' loyalty, England ratified the Québec Act in 1774 which repealed some of the more egregious clauses contained in the Royal Proclamation of 1763. Civil law was reinforced, freedom of religion was re-established for Catholics, and the use of the French language was authorized. In addition, Canadians were allowed to participate in the government of the colony.

Following the victory of the republican forces during the War of Independence (1775-83), Canada became an important refuge for British Loyalists. Concentrated in Upper Canada (Ontario), Loyalists demanded the establishment of a Legislative Assembly in which they could occupy a majority position. England responded favourably to their demand by adopting the Constitution Act of 1791 which divided the colony into two entities: Lower Canada (now Québec) whose majority was francophones, and Upper Canada, populated mainly by anglophones. The two entities were both equipped with an elected House of Assembly that exercised minimal powers compared with the unelected Executive Council which controlled the destinies of the inhabitants as it pleased.

The integration of Lower Canada's economy into that of the British Empire at the beginning of the 19th century brought about an increased commercialization of agricultural production and natural resources already under the control of established English merchants in Montréal. Small merchants and members of the liberal professions acted as intermediaries between the inhabitants and the large English merchants.

A series of political events drove the inhabitants of Lower Canada (as in Upper Canada) to revolt against the established powers. This was the rebellion of the Patriots of 1837-38. A serious political crisis thus broke out between the Executive Council, controlled by the English merchants, and the House of Assembly, composed mainly of members of the francophone middle class whose locus was the Patriot Party. The members of the House of Assembly demanded, among other things, responsible government in order to control administrative appointments and the militia. This battle was one between two elites who were seeking to take control of an emerging state.

Following London's refusal to comply with the Patriots' demands, armed revolts broke out in the Richelieu Valley and in several villages along the Ottawa River. Poorly armed and outnumbered by the British militia, the Patriots were victims of a repression that precipitated the hanging of twelve men and the deportation of fifty-eight others.

The consequences of this defeat were politically, socially and economically significant for the inhabitants of Lower Canada. The British Government then appointed Lord Durham to carry out an investigation of the rebellion and mandated him to produce a report on the necessary reforms needed to ensure the maintenance of peace and order in British North America. In his 1839 report, Lord Durham asserted that only the assimilation of French Canadians could ensure proper order among a people considered to be 'without history and without literature'. He proposed the unification of Upper and Lower Canada into one political entity, each one having identical representation despite the numerical superiority of French Canadians concentrated in Lower Canada. Durham believed that the anglophones from Upper and Lower Canada would easily control the House of Assembly.

The British Government followed up on the principal recommendation of the Durham report by adopting the Union Act in 1840, which united the two political entities. Responsible government was accorded to the colony in 1848. The defeat of the Patriots contributed to discrediting the liberal forces associated with the leaders of the rebellion of 1837-38, and ensured the Catholic Church, which had condemned the uprising of the people, a near monopoly of power as the main mouthpiece of French Canadians throughout the century to come.

Even if they were seriously weakened following the flight of the Patriots, the republican and liberal forces, Les Rouges (the Reds) in particular, continued to denounce the controlling role of the Church in several areas, including those related to education and health services.

In 1867, the shadow of the American Civil War and signs of a potential future American invasion convinced French Canadians and English Canadians of the benefits of a confederative alliance uniting the provinces of Ontario (Upper Canada), Québec (Lower Canada), New Brunswick, and Nova Scotia. Each of these entities decided, on the one hand, to share powers and, on the other hand, to retain specific responsibilities.

The British devolved more economic power to the central government in response to the consequences of the American decision to end reciprocity with the British colonies north of the 49th parallel. The member states of the new Canadian federation found themselves entrusted with important responsibilities in cultural and social areas.

Fortified by an expanding internal market, the economic future of Canada looked promising. The economic elite quickly planned to profit from the captive Canadian market. A pan-Canadian policy of economic integration was officially launched in 1879. It comprised three aims: the construction of a pan-Canadian railway system; the colonization of Western Canada through immigration; and the establishment of a tariff policy aiming to offer Canadian manufacturers a net advantage over foreign competitors.

It must be emphasized that while the Canadian federation constitutes a great historical compromise between francophones and anglophones, it also represents the beginning of an enduring misunderstanding. Members of Parliament, journalists and citizens who interpreted the Canadian Confederation as a pact between two founding peoples (one of which was concentrated in Québec and represented by the Legislative Assembly of the province) were quickly disillusioned when Prime Minister John A. Macdonald imposed a hierarchical and imperial conception of relations between the central state and the member states. Macdonald, who was Prime Minister of Canada from 1867 to 1873 and again from 1878 to 1891, disapproved, among other things, of several laws adopted by the Québec Legislative Assembly. Macdonald's centralist tendencies served as a catalyst for an emerging provincial autonomy movement spearheaded by both the Ontario and Québec governments. Moreover, this movement provided an impetus for a French Canadian nationalism based on defending the confederative pact as many had originally interpreted it in 1867.

Subsequent events in the late 19th century, perceived by many as threats to the survival of French-speaking Canada, acted as catalysts in the further development of French Canadian nationalism. Among these events were: the hanging of Louis Riel; the closing of French-language schools in Manitoba and Ontario; and the decisions of the Canadian Government to serve Great Britain during the Boer War and the two world wars, with the consequent imposition of military conscription. The two world conflicts, therefore, were loci for major confrontations between French Canadian and English Canadian elites. At the time, French Canadian nationalists promoted Canada's political independence from Great Britain. More recently, Québec's place within the

Canadian federation was further weakened in 1982 when Québec's consent was conspicuously absent from the repatriation of the Canadian Constitution from Great Britain.

The turn of the century corresponds to a period of great economic change in Québec. Technological progress and a rapid increase in industrial production contributed to the province's economic growth and to Québec's gradual integration into the North American economy. These changes contributed to Montréal's status as Canada's economic metropolis. At this time, Montréal was home to the largest railway industries in America, to a financial network of the highest importance, and to principal members of the Canadian upper class.

In Québec City, the headquarters of Québec's parliamentary institutions, successive Liberal governments, from those of Simon-Napoléon Parent and Jean-Lomer Gouin to that of Louis-Alexandre Taschereau, adopted a laissez-faire economic policy. This policy facilitated increased American ownership (attracted by the abundance of natural resources) within the Québec economy. Before the beginning of the century, the agricultural sector was no longer the main employer among French Canadians and, according to the 1921 census, the Québec population was already beyond fifty per cent urban. Nevertheless, the myth of a rural and pre-industrial Québec endured in the Canadian imagination until the beginning of the 1960s.

The opening of the American market to Canadian products favoured the industrial development of the province and certain elements of the English Canadian middle class. During this time, living conditions remained particularly difficult for the working classes: the infant mortality rate was high among francophones; the unemployment rate reached unparalleled levels during the Depression in the 1930s; and social inequalities continued to increase. As one of the premier defenders of the French Canadian nation, the Catholic Church became heavily involved in the effort to contain working-class discontent through the creation and support of local union movements. These unions were established for two reasons: to prevent foreign unions from taking root in Québec; and to cultivate corporatist labour relations structures in the province. Inspired by the rapid development of the welfare state in Europe, several Québec intellectuals such as André Laurendeau, Marcel Rioux, and Charles Taylor, proposed massive state intervention to regulate economic fluctuations.

Maurice Duplessis' reign as Québec's Premier, from 1936 to 1939 and again from 1944 to 1959, failed to provide a favourable climate for state intervention. Autonomist, nationalist, anti-communist, and allied with ecclesiastical forces, Duplessis opposed, in the name of provincial autonomy and provincial rights, interventionist social policies developed by the central government. He opposed state intervention in the name of free enterprise and anti-communism. This period was also marked by the reinforcement of both conservative ideology and the Church's pre-eminent role in society. Québec's dependence on the American economy was therefore accelerated. This extensive integration, moreover, marked the beginning of the decline of Montréal's economy as Canada's principal pillar of development. The US economy's westward shift ultimately favoured the development of Toronto; the city is in close proximity to America's large industrial and financial centres, namely Chicago and Detroit. The predominance of conservative ideology frequently led to major coercive measures against workers, unions, and intellectuals.

Several social scientists have highlighted the growing gulf between the dominant discourse of the post-war period and Québec's rapidly modernizing society. Workers were organizing themselves, defending their rights and liberating themselves from the influence of the clergy; artists were turning towards the major trends sweeping Europe for inspiration at the expense of religion; women were being integrated into the labour market; and the North American lifestyle was invading Québec. French Canadian nationalism, initially defensive and conservative, no longer corresponded with the expectations of a generation of men and women who believed that the establishment of progressive social and economic policies was the best way of defending the interests of a poor and uneducated population deprived of control over the province's economic levers. This widening gap between the conservative leadership of traditional elites and the emerging social movements contributed to the significant political and social upheavals of the 1960s. Moreover, these upheavals eventually led to the creation of innovative institutions and to new ways of perceiving the world.

From the Quiet Revolution to the present

Jean Lesage's PLQ (Parti libéral du Québec), which came to power in June 1960, was the first government to adopt state intervention in Québec. The size of the Québec governmental system increased considerably throughout the 1960s and particularly from 1960 to 1966, the period popularly known as the Quiet Revolution. This intensified state intervention soon provoked a modification of power relationships within the province as well as among the member states of the Canadian federation.

One consequence of the Quiet Revolution and the considerable public sector expansion was the reinforcement of the technocratic middle class. This new group of civil servants and intellectuals played an important role in the evolution of modern Québec. They influenced the development of linguistic and constitutional policies and had a key role to play in the first mass mobilization of the independence movement. Ironically, it was the middle class of technocrats, the first supporters of the Parti québécois, which was founded in 1968, who turned their back on the party in 1980 following attempts to tone down the party's plan for Québec sovereignty.

While combating the effects of the province's economic peripheralization, massive state intervention in Québec also contributed to the establishment of a link between the Parti québécois and its most fervent supporters: the new technocratic middle class and private and public sector unions. However, towards the beginning of the 1980s, the effects of the global economic crisis combined with Québec's economic peripheralization could no longer be ignored. It was increasingly obvious that Québec could no longer support an enormous governmental system in an increasingly difficult economic context.

The limits of state capitalism appeared towards the end of the 1970s, raising growing conflicts between the Parti québécois and the sectors that, from the beginning, had been its most devoted partisans. Government policies finally changed significantly: from state capitalism emerged a new middle class based in the private sector and controlling sufficient power to compete with the new technocratic middle class.

Responding to this new reality, the Parti québécois Government, identified with the economic approach of state control, gradually converted to the idea that the market constituted the most effective distributor of economic resources. From 1980, market forces and laissez-faire policies regained their past supremacy.

Shifting alliances and power struggles are shaping Québec's current political landscape. These two factors help explain not only the rise and fall in the fortunes of political parties, but also the decline of the new technocratic middle class (a considerable political force during the 1960s and 1970s) and the vitality of the francophone private sector. Moreover, class alliances within Québec have been considerably modified by changes in the global economy and a restructuring of capitalist ties brought on by the new international division of labour.

Québec today

The national question currently occupies an important place in Québec as it does in other modern states. At a time when the impermeability of borders and state intervention are increasingly being challenged, the national question appears difficult to resolve. A paradox results: the very conditions that favour the emergence of new nation states also present significant obstacles to the ability of these new nation states to maintain their integrity. Moreover, the trends that underlie the process of internationalization suggest that globalization forces states to harmonize their public policies: this levelling process makes it increasingly difficult for individual states to pursue interventionist policies whose goal is the creation of a more egalitarian society increasingly unlikely.

Some commentators feel that English-speaking Canada's pursuit of homogenization obliges Québec either to fall into rank or to free itself from the yoke of 1982 and therefore maintain its national attributes. It has also been argued that the central Canadian government still presides over a federation, but its brand of federalism has degenerated in favour of unitarianism, which is precipitating the country's break-up. Only a political system open to deep diversity, to plurinationalism rather than multiculturalism, would seem to be able to release Canada from the current impasse.

The challenges and responsibilities Québec will face are intensified inasmuch as it constitutes one of the rare cases where secessionist forces have a real chance of democratically attaining the status of nation state. The October 1995 referendum, which saw no less than 94 per cent of registered voters exercise their right to vote, constitutes a fine lesson in democracy. Once the votes were counted, slightly more than 50,000 votes separated the 'Yes' and 'No' forces: 49.4 per cent voted for the sovereignty proposals, and 50.6 per cent opposed them.

In the years since the 1995 referendum, no real progress has been made to resolve the Québec-Canada situation. The two main groups remain entrenched in their positions: the Québec sovereignty forces are witnessing a new surge of support for the emergence of a new nation state between now and the year 2000; Canadian unitarianist forces remain unwilling to make concessions for fear they will compromise the collective identity of the country.

About the bibliography

Writing and publishing in Québec have flourished despite Lord Durham's fiery challenge in 1840 that Québec was without a literature or history. Since then, and especially since 1950, Québec's writers, researchers and novelists have manifested a decidedly extroverted desire to share their experiences and research with the world while winning international acclaim and praise at the same time.

Selection of titles

This volume deals with a selection of 1,400 titles in 1,056 annotated entries from among hundreds of thousands of publications on Québec.

Consistent with the standard format and objectives of the World Biblio-graphical Series, this work strives for accessibility and manageability while including those titles which provide an accurate and objective portrait of Québec's distinct place in the world. We have limited this bibliography to published books, and have deliberately excluded articles, primary sources, university theses, and other non-printed material such as audio-visual works. The inclusion of such titles would have lengthened the book considerably. Government publications have, as a rule, been avoided. The only exceptions to this rule are federal or provincial titles which are released periodically and which provide information of significant or crucial importance to certain themes such as population, immigration, and emigration. The importance of constitutional matters has also necessitated the inclusion of certain government commission reports that are indispensable to their thematic sections.

Contemporary newspapers, magazines, and scholarly journals, in addition to their indexes, have also been listed in order to provide the reader with a substantial number of additional sources from which to broaden bibliographic searches. Again, in keeping with the series' objectives, we have tried to include only those periodicals that remain in publication.

The significant role of literature and the arts in Québec's historical development is evident by the number of titles that are included in these sections. These sections will direct readers to the important works that have shaped Québec's cultural and literary landscape.

Emphasis was placed on: 1) books published since 1960; and 2) books that focus exclusively on Québec. Exceptions to the first criterion were made for older works where contemporary titles were unavailable, and for seminal works which have withstood the test of time. Regard-ing the second criterion, we were especially keen to avoid duplicating the work already published in the *Canada* volume of the series (WBS, volume 62). Moreover, the inclusion of French titles in this biblio-graphy has produced a unique and separate entity that should not be regarded merely as a supplement to the *Canada* volume.

Accessibility of titles

Mindful of the international readership of this series, we have attempted to ensure that titles included in every thematic section are widely available. However, the reader will undoubtedly come across titles that are hard to obtain, even among those that have been recently published. As Québec's lingua franca is French, the majority of titles included are in French. This might restrict the availability of these titles in countries where French is not a major language. It would be impossible to gain a wide-ranging perspective of certain themes such as history and politics without including French publications. Rather, the mere fact that the majority of these items are in French reflects one of Québec's most important and essential characteristics. We have made efforts in the annotations to indicate publications which are in English and French.

Each entry is descriptive, indicating the topics discussed, conclusions, and, if appropriate, the reading level of each title. Where we have judged it useful, a summary evaluation of the work and its importance has also been included. Bibliographical entries are classified according to the author's surname and then by title. In cases where authorship was indeterminable, entries were classified according to the first word (disregarding non-articles) in the title.

Acknowledgements

The preparation of such an important work required the participation of several people over the past three years.

I would first of all like to emphasize the work of Rémy Gagnon and Sarah Fortin, doctoral candidates in the Department of Political Science at McGill University, who actively participated in setting up the project and in putting together the first selection of titles. There was also the work of Ève Bézaire-Dussault, Jeff Heynen, Pamela Lipson, Damion Stodola, and Luc Turgeon, who tirelessly itemized, summarized, and verified the entries included in the present bibliography. Additional thanks go to Pamela Lipson for her help in translation. In particular, I would like to thank Damion Stodola, who put together the three indexes, and who contributed exceptionally to making this bibliography an accessible research tool.

This project would not have been made possible without the financial support of the Ministère des relations internationales du Québec (Québec Ministry of International Relations) who, through the incumbent, Mr. Sylvain Simard, allocated very significant financial assistance to the Québec Studies Program at McGill University. This assistance has been essential to the preparation of this bibliography on Québec and to its integration in the World Bibliographical Series, published by ABC-CLIO.

Alain-G. Gagnon, Director
Québec Studies Program
McGill University
Montréal
13 June 1998

Glossary

Action française	French Action
Action libérale nationale	National Liberal Action Party
Action nationale	National Action
Assemblée nationale	National Assembly
Association canadienne-française pour l'avancement des sciences	French Canadian Association for the Advancement of Science
Bloc populaire	Popular Bloc
Bloc québécois	Québec Bloc
Bulletin Populaire	Popular Bulletin
Caisse de dépôt et placement du Québec	Québec Deposit and Investment Fund
Caisses populaires	Credit Unions
Centrale de l'enseignement du Québec	Québec Teachers' Union
Centres locaux de services communautaires	Local Community Service Centres
Confédération des syndicats nationaux	Confederation of National Unions
Conseil du patronat	Employers' Association
Cité Libre	Free City
Le Devoir	The Duty

Glossary

Fédération des travailleuses et des travailleurs du Québec	Québec Federation of Labour
Front de libération du Québec	Québec Liberation Front
Mouvement Desjardins	Desjardins Movement
Parti libéral du Québec	Québec Liberal Party
Parti Pris	Fixed Opinion
Parti québécois	Québec Party
La Presse	The Press
Québec Presse	Québec Press
La Relève	The New Guard
Union nationale	National Union Party

Québec and Its People

1   **Québec today.**
Paule Beaugrand-Champagne, Sylvie Fontaine, Geneviève Pelletier.
Québec: Ministère des Relations internationales, 1988. 69p.

Published by the Ministry of International Affairs, this booklet provides a snapshot of Québec and its distinguishing traits. Brief synopses of Québec's regions, cities, culture, industries and economy are concisely presented.

2   **Le Québec en chiffres de 1850 à nos jours.** (Québec in numbers from 1850 to today.)
Gérald Bernier, Robert Boily, Daniel Salée.   Montréal: Association canadienne-française pour l'Avancement des Sciences, 1986. 398p.

A compilation of socio-demographic, economic, political and social statistics which traces Québec's development. The reader will appreciate the frequent comparisons made with Ontario which help to place trends in perspective. Moreover, this research tool is particularly useful in bringing empirical data to the trends which have marked Québec's historical development. Aside from academic specialists and students, the public at large, unions and other organizations will find this guide useful as it regroups information from many disparate sources.

3   **Le Québec Statistique.** (Statistical Québec.)
Bureau statistique du Québec.   Québec: Les Publications du Québec, 1914- . annual.

An annual publication providing a comprehensive statistical portrait of Québec. This invaluable book provides general statistics on economic, demographic, social and cultural characteristics of Québec. Statistics indicate general trends and each chapter is preceded by an analysis of the statistics found therein.

4 **D'un pays à l'autre: mille et un faits divers au Québec: 1600-1900.**
(From one country to another: 1,001 facts on Québec: 1600-1900.)
Edited by Guy Giguère. Sainte-Foy, Québec: A. Sigier, 1994. 215p.

The author presents Québec's history in the form of vignettes based on primary sources and accompanied by illustrations by famous painters and illustrators. The book's emphasis is on the daily lives of the French colonists and their descendants. It is not meant for the specialist.

5 **L'hiver dans la culture québécoise, XVIIe-XIXe siècles.** (Winter in Québec culture: 17th to 19th century.)
Sophie-Laurence Lamontagne. Québec: Institut québécois de Recherche sur la Culture, 1983. 197p.

Provides a cultural history of Québec winters from an ethnological perspective, focusing solely on the original colonists and their descendants: immigrants and aboriginals are not dealt with in this study. Daily life is examined as a function of winter, illustrating the impact of the season on domestic, economic and social life. Lamontagne describes three phases which characterize the transformation of colonists' European culture into a distinct Québec culture: a period of apprehension marked by fear and disarray; a second phase distinguished by the inhabitants' desire to adapt and understand the physical phenomena surrounding them; and, finally, a phase of domestication where man sought a balance between nature and his needs. Other works on this theme are Pierre-Phillipe Brunet and Marie-Josée Thériault's *Le Québec des quatre saisons* (Québec of the four seasons, 1600-1900) (Montréal: Éditions Hurtubise HMH, 1994) and Jean Provencher's *C'était l'hiver* (It was winter) (Montréal: Boréal Express, 1986).

6 **Le Québec en question: une centaine de sondages reflétant le profil des Québécois et Québécoises d'aujourd'hui.** (Québec in question: a hundred surveys reflecting today's Quebecers.)
Jean-Marc Léger, Marcel Léger. Montréal: Éditions Quebecor, 1990. 276p.

An attempt to popularize Québec's distinctiveness by revealing the opinions and values of Quebecers based on surveys and polls taken between 1988 and 1990. Each of the nine chapters is introduced with an analysis of general trends and illustrated with statistics and graphs. Produced by one of the leading, and among the most respected, polling companies in Québec and Canada, this book provides the reader with a quick and insightful glimpse into the psyche of Quebecers.

7 **Montréal au XXe siècle: regards de photographes.** (Montréal in the 20th century through photographs.)
Edited by Michel Lessard, Serge Allaire, Martin Brault, Lise Gagnon, Jean Lauzon. Montréal: Éditions de l'Homme, 1995. 335p.

Photographers from the 20th century explore and illustrate by means of provocative, dramatic photographs, four periods in the life of Montréal. These periods are divided into subsections: the animated city (1910-50); the international city (1950-70); the claimed city (1970-80); and the plural city (1980-90). Demonstrating Montréal's rapid development, this book also marks the multiple trends in photography in the 20th century.

8 **Montréal.**
   Mia and Klaus.   Montréal: Éditions Libre Expression, 1983. 186p.
   A collection of photographs of the City of Montréal. While the majority of them depict the city's architecture, the book also includes pictures of the people and of the city's green space. Many more of Québec's most well-known regions are captured by Mia and Klaus' photography: see *Québec* (Montréal: Éditions Libre Expression, 1981); *Charlevoix* (Montréal: Éditions de l'Homme, 1994); *Îles-de-la-Madeleine* (Montréal: Éditions de l'Homme, 1994); and *Le St-Laurent* (Montréal: Éditions Libre Expression, 1984), which focuses not only on the Saint-Lawrence River, but also on the cities, villages and inhabitants along its shores.

9 **Profil statistique des régions du Québec.** (Statistical profile of Québec's regions.)
   Michel Thérrien.   Québec: Ministère du Conseil exécutif, 1991. 171p. (Collection Dossiers de Développement Régional).
   A very useful work on the statistical characteristics of Québec's regions. Population, the labour market and industrial structure constitute the principal variables examined. The study also makes predictions regarding demographic changes in Québec's regions.

Geography

General

10 **L'organisation territoriale au Québec: dislocation ou restructuration.** (Territorial organization in Québec: dislocation or restructuring?)
Pierre Bérubé.   Québec: Les Publications du Québec, 1993. 172p.

In response to the problems of exodus and economic decline in Québec's regions, the author presents a new model of regional planning. Bérubé argues that collective action has proven itself as the best way to ensure the survival of communities. Consequently, he urges the creation of more autonomous regional units within Québec which would facilitate the mobilization of communities to deal with the challenges of demographic and economic problems.

11 **Cahiers de Géographie du Québec.** (Québec Geography Journal.)
Sainte-Foy, Québec: Département de Géographie, Université Laval, 1956- . 3 issues per year.

A bilingual scholarly journal focusing on, but not limited to, issues relating to Québec and North America, other northern regions and the problem of regional development. Each issue typically contains scholarly essays, research notes, bibliographical studies, and book reviews on the following topics: human geography, land management and planning, and the environment.

12 **Espace et culture = Space and culture.**
Edited by Serge Courville, Normand Séguin.   Sainte-Foy, Québec: Presses de l'Université Laval, 1995. 404p.

Comprises the proceedings of a conference organized within the scope of the activities of an inter-university research group on Québec studies. This conference focused on the growth of historical geography in Québec and its role as a mediator between the various social sciences. Historical geography's focus on space-time encourages an interdisciplinary approach to understanding Québec by reuniting a great number of specialists researching different aspects of Québec.

13 **Introduction à la géographie historique.** (Introduction to historical geography.)
Serge Courville. Sainte-Foy, Québec: Presses de l'Université Laval, 1995. 225p. maps. bibliog.

Provides an introduction to historical geography. This manual traces the origins of the discipline and describes how it is practised from the perspective of the Québec scientists. Courville provides a comprehensive bibliography for those willing to broaden and deepen their understanding of the subject. More importantly, however, this volume provides an important French reference work within an area dominated by English-language literature.

14 **Le pays laurentien au XIXe siècle: les morphologies de base.**
(The Laurentian region during the 19th century: basic morphology.)
Serge Courville, Jean-Claude Robert, Normand Séguin. Sainte-Foy, Québec: Presses de l'Université Laval, 1995. 171p. maps.

The historical geography of Québec's socio-economic profile during the 19th century. This study proposes an approach based on the centrality of the Laurentian region around which the rest of the Québec territory organized itself. The authors use data from three years (1831, 1851 and 1871) to analyse the changes in population, agriculture, industry, commerce, and the communication infrastructure.

15 **Les noms de lieux et le contact des langues = Place names and language contact.**
Edited by Henri Dorion, Christian Morissonneau. Sainte-Foy, Québec: Presses de l'Université Laval, 1972. 373p. maps.

Starting from the premise that place-names are the fossils of human geography, this collection of essays examines the toponymy of various multiethnic and multilingual societies including Québec. In this work, authors analyse patterns of language policy from the practice of place-naming in the regions being studied; i.e., Russia, Belgium, Bohemia, South Africa, Poland, Québec, and Canada. This work is meant for the professional and contains a significant amount of methodology and theory.

16 **Géographie Physique et Quaternaire.** (Physical and Quaternary Geography.)
Montréal: Presses de l'Université de Montréal, 1977- . semi-annual.

Publishes both French and English essays and research notes on the Quaternary period and Québec's physical geography. The journal's main focus is on past and present glacial and preglacial environments. Abstracts are typically written in French, English and usually German.

17 **Nordicité canadienne.** (The Canadian North.)
Louis-Edmond Hamelin. Montréal: Éditions Hurtubise HMH, 1980.
438p. maps. (Cahiers du Québec, no. 18).

This book marks an important contribution to the study of human and political geography. Problems such as centre-periphery struggles, cultural and economic underdevelopment, infrequently considered in the Northern context, are examined and analysed in this work. Readers should not expect a description of the climate, relief and other traditional geographical concepts. Instead, Hamelin's model is useful in examining the Canadian North, and particularly northern Québec and the Northwest Territories, as an entity with its own intra-nordic structures. Hamelin raises questions that fundamentally influence constitutional issues, and matters of political organization and territorial management.

18 **Le rang d'habitat: le réel et l'imaginaire.** (The line village: real and imaginary.)
Louis-Edmond Hamelin. Montréal: Éditions Hurtubise HMH, 1993.
322p. (Les Cahiers du Québec, Collection Géographie, no. 107).

A fascinating study of the structural organization of agriculture in Québec. 'Le rang', a long and narrow division of land, was the principal arrangement of Québec farms. Hamelin examines the etymological, toponymical and historical roots of this arrangement, along with its depiction in French literature.

19 **The seigneurial system in early Canada: a geographical study.**
Richard Colebrook Harris. Montréal; Kingston, Ontario:
McGill-Queen's University Press, 1984. 247p.

This work challenges the argument that the seigneurial system was the fulcrum of rural French Canada. Opposing Marxist interpretations which hold that the seigneurial system mediated resources and people, Harris argues that feudal institutions were not especially relevant to the patterns of colonization, settlement and economy in rural Canada. This study puts the seigneurial system into context with its French heritage, highlighting how the geographical differences between New France and France, rather than the seigneurial system itself, were responsible for social and economic relationships in Canada.

20 **Le Saint-Laurent, grande porte de l'Amérique.** (The Saint-Lawrence, gateway to America.)
Jean-Claude Lasserre. Québec: Éditions Hurtubise HMH, 1980. 753p.

Provides an analysis of the Saint-Lawrence Seaway based on two central functions of the Saint-Lawrence River: the part it played in populating the continent; and its role as a continental gateway by virtue of the Seaway, which opened on 26 June 1959. Following a description of the hydrographic characteristics of the Saint-Lawrence basin, Lasserre examines the population of its shores, its development, and its evolution. The author then discusses the economic role of the Saint-Lawrence from its origins to the construction of the Seaway. Finally, the Saint-Lawrence as a maritime highway is examined.

Maps, atlases and travel guides

21   **Clés pour l'histoire de Montréal.** (Keys to the history of Montréal.)
Céline Bouchard, Rémi Bourdeau, Michèle Dagenais, Lucy Sicard.
Montréal: Éditions du Boréal, 1992. 247p.
A bibliography of 3,900 items divided into 4 chronological sections and classified according to various themes. Only published works are covered; primary sources have deliberately been excluded.

22   **Les villes du Saguenay: étude géographique.** (The cities of the
Saguenay region: a geographical study.)
Louis-Marie Bouchard.   Montréal: Leméac, 1973. 212p.
The geographical proximity of the larger cities in the Saguenay region – Chicoutimi, Jonquière, Arvida, Kénogami, Bagotville, and Port-Alfred are all within twenty miles of each other – often obscures the degree to which their interdependence has defined their development. Although this study does not extend beyond 1970, it provides a clear lens through which one can analyse the region. Bouchard suggests that these communities constitute an interdependent and continuous network of urban centres. The section on the evolution of these urban complexes is especially valuable in explaining the different functions each community fulfils for the region at large.

23   **Les Cantons de l'Est: aspects géographiques, politiques,
socio-économiques et culturels.** (The Eastern Townships:
geographical, political, socio-economic and cultural aspects.)
Edited by Jean-Marie M. Dubois.   Sherbrooke, Québec: Éditions de
l'Université de Sherbrooke, 1989. 294p. maps.
Twenty-seven essays from a variety of disciplines combine to provide a comprehensive portrait of the Eastern Townships; a region located to the southeast of Montréal and bordering the United States. The collection is divided into four sections covering the physical, geographical, political, socio-economic, and cultural aspects of the region.

24   **Un pays de distance et de dispersion.** (A country of distance and
dispersal.)
Clermont Dugas.   Québec: Presses de l'Université du Québec, 1981.
221p.
Eastern Québec is a region that suffers from significant economic dislocation resulting from the marginalization of its economy in the North American market. Nonetheless, the people of this region have frequently found solutions to their problems. The author argues that future collective initiatives should be prepared to recognize the sprawling character of the region. In this book, Dugas examines the impact of demographics and geography on the region's political, economic and social character. This study reveals the heterogeneous character of the region.

25 **Baie James: le guide touristique.** (James Bay: tourist guide.)
Roxane Fraser. Outremont, Québec: VLB Éditeur, 1995. 404p. maps.

An original tourist guide that suggests a tour of the James Bay region. The author focuses both on the large industrial infrastructure of the region and on the Cree villages as interesting sites to visit. The book includes photographs of the region in addition to detailed maps.

26 **Québec.**
Guide Gallimard. Paris: Éditions Nouveaux-Loisirs, 1995. 408p.

Rather than a typical travel guide, this book is a wonderful introduction to Québec society. It describes, in a historical context, a plethora of important sites in the different regions of Québec. The guide is particularly useful for travellers or curious people who want to know about the customs, the traditions, and the particularities of Québec's regions. The book also includes many pictures and a very good section on the images of Québec and Québec society in the writing of various authors.

27 **Discover Montreal.**
Cécile Grenier, Joshua Wolfe. Montréal: Éditions Libre Expression, 1990. 331p.

A very detailed and useful tourist guide to Montréal. The authors provide invaluable tips on the use of transportation in Montréal. The section on Montréal's colourful neighbourhoods is particularly well done: it presents a short history of each district and outlines a series of tours for the reader to follow. This guide is ideal not only for tourists, but also for Quebecers.

28 **L'avenir du Nord québécois.** (The future of the Québec North.)
Edited by Louis-Edmond Hamelin, Micheline Potvin. Sillery, Québec: Presses de l'Université du Québec, 1989. 275p. maps.

This work comprises the proceedings of a conference, held in 1987, on northern Québec. The essays contained in this volume deal mainly with the socio-economic aspects of economic development in this vast area, notably the development of a large hydro-electric superstructure. The book's strengths are in its inclusion of comparative case-studies with Russia and Norway's socio-economic development, and the incorporation of aboriginal points of view in the evaluation and analysis of territorial development.

29 **Québec.**
Michelin Touring Guide. Dorval, Québec: Michelin Tires (Canada), 1996. 276p. maps.

A very useful guide for those who intend to travel far and wide by car while holidaying in Québec. It contains a lot of maps and provides a comprehensive list and description of most of the main attractions in Québec; these attractions are assigned ratings based on their tourist value. The book includes an index and information on important dates in Québec's tourist season, on various means of transportation, and on important contacts.

30 **Québec.**
Edited by François Rémillard. Québec: Ulysses Travel Publications,
1996. 2nd ed. 656p.
A very detailed tourist guide that provides a large amount of information on places to
visit in Québec such as bars, restaurants, hotels, and tourist attractions. The guide also
suggests some itineraries that are relatively well explained. The descriptions of places
to visit are well presented. Ulysses also publishes excellent guides to Québec's
regions: Gabriel Audet's *Gaspésie, Bas-St-Laurent, Îles-de-la-Madeleine* (Montréal:
Ulysses Travel Publications, 1997. 3rd ed.); François Rémillard and Benoit Prieur's
Montréal (Montréal: Ulysses Travel Publications, 1997. 4th ed.); Yves Ouellet's *Côte-
Nord, Manicouagan, Duplessis* (Montréal: Ulysses Travel Publications, 1997) and his
Charlevoix, Saguenay, Lac-Saint-Jean (Montréal: Ulysses Travel Publications, 1994).
All of the latter are illustrated and contain maps. Ulysses also publishes a listing of
Québec's bed and breakfasts, entitled *Gîtes du passant au Québec: bed and break-
fasts, maisons de campagne, gîtes à la ferme* (The traveller's shelter in Québec: bed
and breakfasts, country cottages and farm lodgings) (Montréal: Ulysses Travel
Publications, 1996).

31 **Atlas historique de Montréal.** (A historical atlas of Montréal.)
Jean-Claude Robert. Montréal: Art Global, 1994. 167p. maps.
An excellent atlas illustrating the urban transformation that made Montréal the city we
know today. Following a chronological order, the author explains the transformation
of Montréal through geography, sociology and demography. The text is well supported
with maps and photographs that show the city's evolution through important historical
events like the Conquest of 1759, the transport revolution, and immigration.

32 **Peuplement et dynamique migratoire au Saguenay, 1840-1960.**
(The populating and migratory dynamic in the Saguenay, 1840-1960.)
Marc St-Hillaire. Sainte-Foy, Québec: Presses de l'Université Laval,
1996. 285p. bibliog.
On the premise that demographic dynamics, such as migration, can help explain the
sociocultural character of a given population, this book examines the formation of a
Québec society in the Saguenay region from the first European arrivals to the 1990s.
While economic factors are often cited as the principal causes of migration, St-Hillaire
posits that migratory decisions are equally influenced by social and cultural factors.

33 **Atlas historique du Canada français: des origines à 1867.**
(A historical atlas of French Canada: from its origins to 1867.)
Marcel Trudel. Québec: Presses de l'Université Laval, 1961. 92p.
maps.
A collection of maps of French Canada, originally drawn between the 15th century
and 1867. Each map is accompanied by a brief description of its source and content.
This collection also contains maps detailing population in certain regions. Several
maps of various seigneuries are also included.

Flora and Fauna

General

34 **Plantes vasculaires susceptibles d'être désignées menacées ou vulnérables au Québec.** (Vascular plants in Québec in danger of becoming threatened or vulnerable.)
Gildo Lavoie. Québec: Ministère de l'Environnement, 1992. 180p.

Provides a list of vascular plants likely to become endangered or vulnerable in Québec. The author stresses the importance of knowing the species in order to protect them, and he cites the rights and obligations of the Ministry of the Environment towards the protection of these plants. He presents the different classification criteria on which this study is based, as well as a list of these species. See also *Les espèces animales en situation précaire du Québec et leur protection* (Animals in precarious situations and their protection) by Jean-Marc Evenat and Marie-Claude Martineau (Montréal: Université du Québec à Montréal, 1988) for a description of endangered fauna.

35 **Promenades dans les jardins anciens du Québec.** (Walking tours of old Québec gardens.)
Paul-Louis Martin, Pierre Morisset, Janouk Murdoch. Outremont, Québec: VLB Éditeur, 1996. 177p. bibliog.

Examines the gardens of Québec as a symbol of human investment. Three views of the gardens are presented and contrasted: the photographer's, the biologist's, and the historian's. The first section offers a photographer's perspective of gardens, while the second presents Québec gardens from historical and biological points of view. The book is beautifully illustrated.

36 **L'oeil américain: histoires naturelles du Nouveau Monde.**
(The American eye: natural histories of the New World.)
Pierre Morency. Montréal: Éditions du Boréal, 1989. 364p.
A collection of texts which present the author's encounters with birds, plants, trees and insects; encounters that most people do not usually notice. The 'American eye' is a European expression used to describe someone who is very sensitive to his environment. It was first used as the title of a radio programme broadcast in the aim of heightening public awareness of the importance of the environment.

37 **Québec sauvage: du Saint-Laurent à l'Arctique.** (Wild Québec: from the Saint-Laurence to the Arctic.)
Catherine Raoult, Marc Poirel. Xonrupt-Longemer, France: Anako, 1990. 128p.
A personal presentation of Québec and its wild territories. The authors propose a different view of Québec, focusing on the fauna, flora, natives, the forgotten northern territory, and the effect of humans on the region's health. This illustrated book constitutes an excellent introduction to the largest, yet paradoxically, the most unknown, part of Québec.

Fauna

Mammals

38 **Guide des mammifères terrestres du Québec, de l'Ontario et des Maritimes.** (Guide to land mammals in Québec, Ontario and the Maritimes.)
Louise Beaudin. Québec: Éditions du Nomade, 1983. 301p.
The author provides information for beginners and specialists, in the belief that a better knowledge of the surrounding fauna will accentuate interest, curiosity, and respect for animals. Animals are classified according to taxonomy. The book presents their distinctive characteristics, their feeding and social habits, their reproductive habits, and their relationship with predators, including man. See also *Les animaux du Grand Nord* (Animals of the Great North) by Angèle Delaunois (Montréal: Éditions Héritage, 1993).

39 **Mammalogie: mammifères du Québec.** (Mammalogy: mammals of Québec.)
Jean Pierard Laprairie. Québec: Éditions M. Broquet, 1983. 255p.
Targeted towards students, this book is organized around three fundamental topics: homoeothermy, morphology and the relationship between mammals and man. It presents elements of classification, transformation of species, dietary needs and use of the territory. The work focuses on the characteristics of mammals, and the reproductive and adaptive successes of species. Identification keys are provided.

40 **Mammifères du Québec et de l'Est du Canada.** (Mammals in Québec and Eastern Canada.)
Jacques Prescott. Montréal: France-Amérique, 1982. 2 vols.

This two-volume work presents the classification, nomenclature, distribution and characteristics of ninety-one of the most common mammals in Québec and Eastern Canada. The distinctive characteristics, habitat, reproduction, longevity, and feeding habits of every species are described. Photographs and illustrations are provided.

Birds

41 **Les oiseaux du Québec.** (Birds of Québec.)
Carole Bérubé. Outremont, Québec: Éditions Quebecor, 1994. 140p.

The author is a nature painter. In this book, Bérubé presents Québec's birds through her painting, along with a short description of the species.

42 **Atlas saisonnier des oiseaux du Québec.** (Seasonal atlas of birds in Québec.)
André Cyr. Sherbrooke, Québec: Presses de l'Université de Sherbrooke, 1995. 711p. maps. bibliog.

This work describes the seasonal and spacio-temporal distribution of birds in southern Québec between 1969 and 1989. It first presents the important characteristics of the territory, as well as the methods that have been used throughout the study. General tendencies in birds' spacio-temporal distribution, abundance, and biodiversity are presented. A complete description of every species is presented, as well as illustrations and seasonal maps of their distribution.

43 **Atlas des oiseaux nicheurs du Québec méridional.** (Atlas of nesting birds in southern Québec.)
Jean Gauthier. Montréal: L'Association québécoise des Groupes d'Ornithologues, 1995. 1,295p. maps. bibliog.

A work presenting the distribution of nesting birds native to Québec between 1984 and 1989. The history of ornithology is summarized; the territory, its environment and the influence of man, as well as natural perturbations, are also described. Information on taxonomy, habitat, behaviour, and species' characteristics are provided. In addition, the distribution, history and tendencies of each species are presented. The reader will also appreciate the many illustrations and maps of the various birds' nesting areas.

44 **Percé et les oiseaux de l'Île Bonaventure.** (Percé and the birds of Bonaventure Island.)
Claude Melançon. Montréal: Éditions du Jour, 1963. 94p.

Describes the Percé region and its attractions. This book contains two sections: the first one describes the town of Percé, its history and its surroundings, as well as some regional legends; and the second part of the book describes Bonaventure Island, its geography and history, and focuses particularly on a description of its birds, their behaviour and dietary habits. Bonaventure is a very important bird sanctuary, containing numerous colonies of many bird species.

45 **Oiseaux chanteurs du Québec et de l'Amérique du Nord: comment les attirer et les identifier par leur chant.** (Song birds in Québec and North America: how to attract and identify them by their songs.) Noble Proctor. Montréal: Éditions Quebecor, 1991. 160p.
Deals with the various song birds of Québec and Eastern Canada. The songs' meanings are presented, as well as observation strategies for the bird enthusiast. An identification guide lists the characteristics and nomenclature of each bird.

46 **Les oiseaux menacés du Québec.** (Endangered birds in Québec.) Michel Robert. Montréal: L'Association québécoise des Groupes d'Ornithologues, 1989. 109p. bibliog.
An assessment of Québec's endangered bird species, co-published by the Canadian Fauna Service. The book includes descriptions of the different endangered species categories and their definitions, the methodology and references consulted, and the species themselves, classified according to their endangered status.

47 **Les oiseaux aquatiques du Québec, de l'Ontario et des Maritimes.** (Aquatic birds of Québec, Ontario and the Maritimes.) Marc Surprenant. Québec: Éditions M. Quinlin, 1993. 285p. maps.
Provides a field guide for beginners and the general public. The author chose to classify the birds according to their size and colour instead of according to the classic nomenclature, which often seems quite daunting to the budding enthusiast. This book presents: the various names of the species; descriptions, including the characteristics that facilitate identification; their habitats; and their nesting and nutritional habits. Pictures and range maps are provided for each species. The presentation is meticulous, which makes this work a good field guide, especially for the general public who do not need to learn the scientific terms and nomenclature in order to be interested in birds. Nevertheless, the official nomenclature is included in each of the species' summary.

Fish

48 **Guide des poissons d'eau douce du Québec, et leur distribution dans l'Est du Canada.** (Guide to freshwater fish in Québec and their distribution across Eastern Canada.) Louis Bernatchez, Marie Giroux. La Prairie, Québec: Éditions M. Broquet, 1991. 304p. maps. bibliog.
This field guide to freshwater fish in Québec provides outlines of the identification characteristics, habitat and biology of each species, in addition to comments regarding similar species. It also presents elements of taxonomy. Photographs, illustrations, and distribution maps are included alongside the descriptions.

49 **La biomasse aquatique.** (The aquatic biomass.)
Paquet, Dutil et Associés.   Sainte-Foy, Québec: Centre québécois de
Valorisation de la Biomasse, 1987. 3 vols. bibliog.

Written especially for managers and other fisheries professionals, this is a study of the
biological, economic and technical potential of the aquatic biomass in Québec. The
book presents an inventory of the species of fish, focusing on non-commercial or
under-exploited species, and discusses the actual process of aquaculture.

50 **Poissons d'eau douce du Canada.** (Freshwater fish in Canada.)
W. B. Scott, E. J. Crossman.   Ottawa: Office de la Recherche sur les
Pêcheries du Canada, 1974. 1,026p. maps.

One of the most consulted works on fish commonly found in Canada, including
Québec. Covering the identification, distribution and biology of fish, this work also
presents the economic importance of Canadian freshwater species. It contains
identification keys, illustrations and distribution maps, and briefly reviews the nomenclature and vernacular names of the species.

Miscellaneous

51 **Les amphibiens du Québec: biologie des espèces et problématique
de conservation des habitats.** (Amphibians of Québec: biology of the
species and problems associated with habitat conservation.)
Raymond Leclair.   Québec: Ministère du Loisir, de la Chasse et de la
Pêche, 1985. 121p. maps. bibliog.

This work describes the biological characteristics of Québec's amphibians, their status
and exploitation, as well as the legal protection they benefit from. The book also puts
forward several recommendations to ensure their survival.

52 **Entomofaune du Québec. Diversité et classification des insectes et
autres hexapodes.** (Diversity and classification of insects and other
hexapods.)
Robert Loiselle, A. Francoeur.   Chicoutimi, Québec: Université du
Québec à Chicoutimi, Laboratoire de Biosystématique, 1992. 70p.
bibliog.

Published by the University of Québec at Chicoutimi, this classification work attempts
to list the different families of invertebrates and other hexapods of Québec. Some text
and several tables are presented for each taxon.

53 **Insects harmful to trees.**
René Martineau.   Montréal: Multiscience Publications, 1984. 261p.

Written for the general public, this book describes insects harmful to trees in Eastern
Canada. The chapters are divided according to species; for each insect, there is a
historical summary of the insects' invasions and a description. The book's many
illustrations help the reader to identify various species. Natural and artificial means of
insect control are discussed.

54 **Abrégé d'entomologie.** (Abridged entomology.)
    Jean-Marie Perron. Sillery, Québec: Association des Entomologistes
    amateurs du Québec, 1985. 2nd ed. 125p.
    A compilation of ideas from specialized works on insect taxonomy. This book was
    designed to help amateurs interested in entomology. It contains brief descriptions of
    the various taxa found in Québec, as well as identification keys to the major taxa.

Flora

55 **Guide de la forêt québécoise saison par saison.** (A guide to Québec
    forests, season by season.)
    André Croteau, Michel Sokolyk. Montréal: Éditions de l'Homme,
    1996. 315p.
    An illustrated book of Québec forests throughout the seasons. Divided into four
    sections, one for every season, the book presents different elements and characteristics
    of the forest during each season, as well as the impact of man on the forest. The
    anatomy of the various trees is discussed, and a description of how to gain access to
    Québec's forests is provided.

56 **Trees in Canada = Les arbres du Canada.**
    John Laird Farrar. Markham, Ontario: Fitzhenry & Whiteside, 1995.
    502p. maps.
    This book presents 300 species of both native and introduced trees that are now found
    in Canada. It contains summer and winter dichotomous keys to the genera and it
    details the English, French and Latin names of the species, and their habitats, sizes,
    and shapes. To help the reader with the identification of tree species, the book is
    divided into twelve groups, classified according to leaf form and arrangement, buds,
    twigs, seeds, bark, size and shape. Drawings, photographs and range maps are also
    presented. The organization of the book renders it ideal for students, specialists and
    amateurs alike.

57 **Arbres, arbustes et plantes herbacées du Québec et de l'Est du
    Canada.** (Trees, shrubs, and herbaceous plants in Québec and Eastern
    Canada.)
    Daniel Fortin, Michel Famelart. Saint-Laurent, Québec: Éditions du
    Trécarré, 1989. 2 vols.
    This two-volume work provides an illustrated introduction to Québec's vegetation
    heritage. The biogeography of the Canadian territory is introduced along with a
    description of the different communities and the common species that can be found.
    The first volume presents the species found in forests; the second volume presents
    species in other environments such as marshes. See also Fortin's *Plantes vivances
    pour le Québec* (Hardy perennials for Québec) (Saint-Laurent, Québec: Éditions du
    Trécarré, 1993).

58   **La végétation forestière du Québec méridional.** (Forest vegetation in
      southern Québec.)
      Miroslav Marian Grandtner.   Sainte-Foy, Québec: Presses de
      l'Université Laval, 1980. 2nd ed. 216p.

In order to encourage better management of forests through the integration of the
environmental variables, this book describes the physical elements of Québec's southern
forests and initiates the reader to their flora and vegetation.

59   **L'herbier québécois.** (The Québec herbarium.)
      Estelle Lacoursière.   Sillery, Québec: Québec Science, 1982. 99p.

A scrapbook presenting Québec's flora, with space for live specimens. See also Daniel
Fortin's *L'herbier médicinal* (Medicinal herbarium) (Sillery, Québec: Québec Science,
1983. 118p.) and Lacoursière's *L'arbrier québécois* (The Québec tree and shrub
identification guide) (Sillery, Québec: Québec Science, 1981. 64p.).

60   **La forêt derrière les arbres: initiation au milieu forestier québécois.**
      (The forest behind the trees: introduction to the Québec forest milieu.)
      Monique Laforge.   La Prairie, Québec: Éditions M. Broquet, 1985.
      235p. maps.

Written for a broad readership, this book initiates people to the fauna, flora, and ecology
of Québec's forest regions. It is not meant to serve as an identification manual, but
rather as an information guide. First, it presents a global, ecological portrait of the
forest and the relationships between its denizens. The second part consists of an
introduction to trees, fungi, mammals, birds, insects, and other forest dwellers. The
last part discusses forest management as a collective resource. The authors present a
list of sites that can be visited.

61   **Plantes sauvages des lacs, rivières et tourbières.** (Wild plants of
      lakes, rivers and peat bogs.)
      Edited by Gisèle Lamoureux.   Saint-Augustin, Québec: Groupe
      Fleurbec, 1987. 399p.

This field guide, intended for the general public, presents the most common plants
found in lakes, rivers and peat bogs in Québec. It first describes the various vegetation
communities of North America. For each species, the nomenclature, origin, geographic distribution and habitat are presented and descriptions of both the plants
and similar species are given. Elements of folklore, horticulture, agricultural interest,
edibility, toxicity and medical use are examined as well.

62   **Plantes sauvages des villes, des champs et en bordure des chemins.**
      (Wild plants in cities, fields and road ditches.)
      Edited by Gisèle Lamoureux.   Saint-Augustin, Québec: Groupe
      Fleurbec, 1983. 208p.

An updated version of *Plantes sauvages des villes et des champs* (Québec: Éditeur
officiel du Québec, 1978. 273p.), this work presents the most abundant plants found in
Québec's fields and ditches. Each description of the sixty-seven species listed in this
book is accompanied by a picture of the plant. Descriptions include information on
the plant's habitat, nomenclature, ideal living conditions, distribution, utilization in

agriculture, culinary use and differences from other species. It is a good field guide for a general readership.

63 **Plantes sauvages du bord de la mer.** (Wild plants by the sea.)
Edited by Gisèle Lamoureux. Saint-Augustin, Québec: Groupe Fleurbec, 1985. 286p.

Targeted towards coastal residents or visitors, this field-book introduces the inquisitive reader to Québec's coastal vegetation: shrubs, herbs and algae. Nomenclature, distribution, culinary possibilities and primary uses are identified in each plant's description.

64 **Les plantes sauvages printanières.** (Wild, spring plants.)
Edited by Gisèle Lamoureux. Québec: La Documentation québécoise, 1975. 247p.

Introduces the general public to seventy-five of the most common species of spring wild plants found in Québec. It presents the taxonomy and ecology of each species, folklore and culinary information. Illustrations are provided and plants are categorized according to the colour of their flowers. This accelerates the plants' identification and renders this book accessible to a large audience.

65 **Flore de l'Anticosti-Minganie.** (Flora of Anticosti-Minganie.)
Frère Marie-Victorin. Montréal: Presses de l'Université de Montréal, 1969. 527p.

Written by the father of Québec botany, this book presents the flora of the island region of the Saint-Lawrence Gulf, called Anticosti-Minganie. Divided into four sections, the first part describes the history and geography of the territory. The second section consists of a journal of Victorin's fieldwork between the summers of 1917 and 1928, while the third part contains a list of the vascular plants of the region. The fourth part discusses the research done on allogeneous flora whose origin lies beyond the simple factors of the fundamental flora, and which is not found elsewhere near the region. More than a simple field guide, this work relates the history of the initial research performed in that region of Québec around Anticosti Island.

66 **Flore laurentienne.** (Laurentian flora.)
Frère Marie-Victorin. Montréal: Presses de l'Université de Montréal, 1995. 3rd ed. 1,083p.

This is the third edition of a work first published in 1935, written by Frère Marie-Victorin, Québec's most famous botanist and natural scientist. Through his work, Marie-Victorin aimed to show that a knowledge of natural sciences is necessary in order to have control over one's economic and cultural destiny. However, he first wanted his fellow citizens to understand and appreciate the natural world that surrounded them. After sixty years, this book is still one of the most complete works of botany, rich in nomenclature and updates of new species. The various section introductions and preface consist of a thorough explanation of the issues and topics discussed in the book. Moreover, they also tackle the scientific debate which opposes genetics and taxonomy. The first part is an introductory and general description of the flora of the Laurentian valley. The second part contains an identification key to the various species. Photographs have been added to provide more information for the modern reader.

67   **Le couvert végétal au Québec-Labrador et son histoire postglaciaire.** (Vegetation cover in Québec and Labrador and its post-glacial history.)
Pierre J. H. Richard.   Montréal: Université de Montréal, 1987. 74p.

The present-day flora of Québec and Labrador is described in this work which focuses on the physiography and physiognomy of the vegetation, its richness gradients, and the most abundant vegetal populations. The post-glacial stages are summarized, providing a temporal perspective of the spatial differentiation of vegetation in Québec and Labrador.

68   **Petite flore forestière du Québec.** (A pocket guide to forest flora in Québec.)
Raymond Rouleau.   Québec: Ministère de l'Énergie et des Ressources, 1990. 2nd ed. 249p.

A field guide to Québec's trees and forest plants, developed for specialists and amateurs. Divided into seven sections, the first describes the principal vegetation zones of Québec, while the other sections tackle commercial and non-commercial species. A complete description of every species, their distribution and use is provided, as well as illustrations to aid identification.

69   **250 champignons du Québec et de l'Est du Canada.** (250 mushrooms from Québec and Eastern Canada.)
Maurice Thibault.   Montréal: Éditions du Trécarré, 1989. 312p.

A field identification guide for mushrooms, targeted towards a public interested in picking and eating mushrooms. A description of each species is presented, and photographs are included to aid identification. Symbols give information on their habitat and ideal harvest time, and colour codes indicate the edibility.

History

Reference

70 **Bibliographie de l'histoire du Québec et du Canada, 1981-1985.**
(A bibliography on the history of Québec and Canada, 1981-85.)
Paul Aubin, Louis-Marie Coté.   Québec: Institut québécois de
Recherche sur la Culture, 1990. 2 vols.

An inventory of 29,000 titles relating to the history of Canada and Québec published
between 1981 and 1985. This work, together with the three tomes preceding it (see
item nos. 71-73), is the most complete guide to both English- and French-language
published works on Québec and Canada.

71 **Bibliographie de l'histoire du Québec et du Canada, 1946-1965.**
(A bibliography on the history of Québec and Canada, 1946-65.)
Paul Aubin.   Québec: Institut québécois de Recherche sur la Culture,
1987. 2 vols.

An inventory of historical works published between 1946 and 1965, relating to
Québec and Canadian history. This book is an essential tool for any historian of
Canadian and Québec history. See also item nos. 70 and 72-73.

72 **Bibliographie de l'histoire du Québec et du Canada, 1976-1980.**
(A bibliography on the history of Québec and Canada, 1976-80.)
Paul Aubin.   Québec: Institut québécois de Recherche sur la Culture,
1985. 2 vols.

An inventory of titles relating to Canadian and Québec history published between
1976 and 1980. This tome continues the daunting project which began with the first
two volumes on works published between 1966 and 1975 (see item no. 73, and also
item nos. 70-71).

73 **Bibliographie de l'histoire du Québec et du Canada, 1966-1975.**
(A bibliography on the history of Québec and Canada, 1966-75.)
Paul Aubin.   Québec: Institut québécois de Recherche sur la Culture,
1981. 2 vols.

This work comprises an inventory of publications (books, journal articles, periodicals) relating to the history of Québec and Canada published between 1966 and 1975. By the author's own admission, no judicial selection was made regarding the inclusion of titles. Consequently, this reference tool is invaluable for its thoroughness if slightly unmanageable due to its size. The bibliography is divided into six thematic sections: general history, prehistory, ethnohistory, explorations, Euro-Canadian occupation and demographic and genealogical repertories. Listing over 400 journals and containing close to 18,000 entries, this is certainly one of the most thorough historical reference books available. See also item nos. 70-72.

74 **Bulletin d'Histoire Politique.** (Bulletin of Political History.)
Montréal: Association québécoise d'Histoire politique; Sillery, Québec: Éditions du Septentrion, 1994- . quarterly.

A unique academic journal by virtue of its flexible structure. This journal makes a point of publishing commentaries, short research reports, and debates which together comprise the core of the *Bulletin*. While each issue typically focuses on one topic, for example, francophone involvement in the Second World War, there are a number of non-thematic articles published as well. The *Bulletin* frequently contains assessments of major political events such as referenda and general elections.

75 **The history of Quebec: a bibliography of works in English.**
Edited by Claudette Cardinal, Graeme Decarie, Ronald Rudin.
Montréal: Concordia University, Centre for the Study of Anglophone Québec, 1981. 202p.

Although the study of Québec history is impossible without an adequate knowledge of French, there does exist a significant corpus of literature written in English. This bibliography classifies approximately 3,500 titles, published before 1976, on themes such as Québec's polity, politics, education, religion and ideology.

76 **Bibliographie d'histoire des Cantons de l'Est = History of the Eastern Township: a bibliography.**
Guy Laperrière.   Sherbrooke, Québec: Université de Sherbrooke, 1986. 2nd ed. 210p. maps.

A bilingual and exhaustive bibliography of 1,762 titles on the history of the 12 counties which constitute the Eastern Townships. Newspaper articles, government publications and essays under five pages have been omitted. This work achieves an important feat in providing a reference tool to both French and English historical titles.

77 **Revue d'Histoire de l'Amérique Française.** (Journal of the History of French America.)
Montréal: Institut d'Histoire de l'Amérique française, 1947- . quarterly.

An essential journal for anyone interested in French American history. Research-length articles are published alongside historical assessments and research reports.

The substantial number of book reviews contained in each issue contributes further to the periodical's utility for students and researchers in history, political science, anthropology and sociology. Another useful source is *Social History = Histoire Sociale* (Ottawa: University of Ottawa Press, 1968- . 2 issues per year).

78 **Guide d'histoire du Québec du régime français à nos jours: bibliographie commentée.** (A historical guide to Québec from the French regime to the present: an annotated bibliography.)
Edited by Jacques Rouillard. Montréal: Éditions du Méridien, 1991. 2nd ed. 367p.

One of the most useful and well-written guides to published works on Québec history. Three large sections are further subdivided into thematic sections, making it easy for the reader to find information on the topic desired. Each chapter describes relevant and important works published and provides brief criticisms of most works, the relative importance of some works compared to others, and a summary of the important milestones reached in the writing of Québec's history. An author index is provided.

General

79 **Les grands débats parlementaires 1792-1992.** (The great parliamentary debates, 1792-1992.)
Edited by Réal Bélanger, Richard Jones, Marc Vallières. Sainte-Foy, Québec: Presses de l'Université Laval, 1994. 487p.

The 147 excerpts from among the most important parliamentary debates in Québec compiled in this work challenge the contemporary view that Parliament has lost power to other branches of government. Classified into six sections (constitution, institutions, the economy, education, society, and culture and language), these excerpts will undoubtedly provide invaluable context to current issues.

80 **Histoire politico-militaire des Canadiens français, 1763-1945.** (French Canadian political and military history from 1763-1945.)
Charles-Marie Boissonnault. Trois-Rivières, Québec: Éditions du Bien Public, 1967. 310p.

A history of the involvement of French Canadians in various battles and wars between 1763 and 1945: namely the British battle against Pontiac, Illinois in 1763; the American invasion of 1775; the War of 1812; the Rebellions against the British of 1837-38; the Boer Wars; and the First and Second World Wars.

81 **Debts to pay. English Canada and Quebec from the Conquest to the Referendum.**
John F. Conway.   Toronto: James Lorimer & Co., 1992. 240p.

Against an analysis of historical power relations between English-speaking Canada and Québec, Conway places Québec's contemporary grievances directed at the rest of Canada. He suggests that secession is inevitable unless English-speaking Canada sees fit to offer a sincere and meaningful accommodation to Québec nationalists. Conway pays particular attention to the Conquest of 1760, the Quiet Revolution of 1960-66, the 1980 referendum as well as the 'patriation' of the Canadian Constitution (transfer of the Constitution to Canada) in 1982, the Meech Lake Accord of 1990, and the 1992 Charlottetown Accord in arguing for the legitimacy of a number of Québec's grievances and, by extension, separation.

82 **A short history of Québec.**
John A. Dickinson, Brian J. Young.   Toronto: Copp Clark, 1993.
2nd ed. 400p.

Provides a complete and concise history of Québec from prehistoric times to the present day. In part because it includes historical perspectives traditionally neglected by other English-language histories, this text has been praised as one of the best histories of Québec written in English. The authors interpret Québec's history using a socio-economic framework, resulting in a periodization that focuses on Québec's class, ethnic, and regional, diversity. Consequently, this history is not dominated by the Conquest, Confederation, or similar political events. Rather, the periodization followed in this book mirrors Québec's economic and social evolution. This is a readable and highly recommended text for the non-specialist as well as the student of Québec.

83 **Quebec and its historians, 1840-1920.**
Serge Gagnon, translated by Yves Brunelle.   Montréal: Harvest House, 1982. 161p.

One of the best books on the historiography of Québec, this analyses the work of historians from François-Xavier Garneau, Québec's first historian, to Lionel Groulx, remembered for his conservative nationalism. Concomitant with the rise of French Canadian nationalism, most historians of this period were reasonably ideologically and politically motivated. Gagnon goes over their work with a fine tooth-comb and reveals the fundamental aspects of their arguments and methodology.

84 **Quebec and its historians: the twentieth century.**
Serge Gagnon, translated by Jane Brierley.   Montréal: Harvest House, 1985. 205p.

Explores the relationship between society and ideology as illustrated by the writing of Québec history. This book complements Gagnon's other major work, *Quebec and its historians, 1840-1920* (see item no. 83), and examines the major scholarly trends of the 20th century, beginning with the emergence of professional historians in post-war Québec. Gagnon traces the shift in historical writing from methodological analyses to ideological analyses and the emergence of a prevailing emphasis on economics. The work of historians such as Marcel Trudel, Jean Hamelin, Louise Dechêne, and Fernand Ouellet is discussed.

85   **Brève histoire du Québec.** (A brief history of Québec.)
Jean Hamelin, Jean Provencher.   Montréal: Éditions du Boréal, 1987.
3rd ed. 126p.

By far the briefest and most accessible history of Québec written in French. Designed as a memory aid for the student or non-specialist, this book relates only the broad trends in the political, economic and social evolution of Québec. Provencher has also written a chronology of Québec history entitled *Chronologie du Québec, 1534-1995* (A chronology of Québec, 1534-1995) (Montréal: Bibliothèque québécoise, 1997. rev. ed. 365p.).

86   **Québec. A history 1867-1929 & Québec since 1930.**
Paul-André Linteau, René Durocher, Jean-Claude Robert, François Ricard, translated by Robert Chodos, Ellen Germaine.   Toronto: James Lorimer & Co., 1991. 2 vols.

A solid and popular academic history of Québec society. This two-volume study relates Québec's history by theme rather than in a strict chronological manner. Rejecting the idea that Québec's modernization was a rapid phenomenon whose occurrence only followed the end of the Second World War, the authors portray Québec's history as a gradual evolution similar to that of other North American societies. The reader will appreciate this thorough study which relates Québec's complex and diversified history in an accessible and engaging style.

87   **Bleeding hearts – bleeding country. Canada and the Quebec crisis.**
Denis Smith.   Edmonton, Alberta: Hurtig, 1971. 177p.

Critical of the way the Federal Government dealt with the October Crisis in 1970, Smith analyses the morality of the decisions made and actions taken during what he calls the 'largest shock to Canadian society since 1867'. The October Crisis was precipitated by the kidnapping of James Cross, British Trade Commissioner, and the kidnapping and ultimate murder of Pierre Laporte, Provincial Cabinet minister, by the marginal FLQ (Front de libération du Québec). Taking a philosophical approach, Smith reveals the way that the October Crisis fits into the wider context of ideological battles.

88   **The dream of a nation. A social and intellectual history of Québec.**
Susan Mann Trofimenkoff.   Toronto: Gage Publishing, 1982.
334p. 455p. bibliog.

Among the first syntheses of Québec history written in English, this superb book traces Québec's development from the French regime in the 1600s to the referendum on 'sovereignty-association' in 1980. Emphasis is placed on social change, economic reform and nationalism.

89   **The French-Canadian outlook. A brief account of the unknown North Americans.**
Mason Wade.   Toronto: McClelland and Stewart, 1964. 94p.
(Carleton Library, no. 14).

Originally published in 1945, this work was written in the hope of dispelling some of the tensions between English and French Canadians during the conscription crisis of the Second World War. Wade, an American, provides an account of the French Fact (a term used to refer to the demographic majority of French-speaking people in Québec) in North America between 1534 and 1945, assessing why the French have always possessed a different outlook from that of English speakers on the continent.

90　The French-Canadians, 1760-1967.
　　Mason Wade.　Toronto: Macmillan, 1968. 2 vols. 1,136p.

In one of the most widely known English-language histories of French-speaking Canada, Wade attempts to explain the differences between French Canadians and English North Americans. Originally written in 1954, Wade's conception of nationalism – a mingling of religious and ethnic factors – lacks the nuance current historians now accord the various expressions of Québec nationalism. Nevertheless, this work constitutes an important intellectual and cultural history of the French Canadian people from Cartier's first voyage to the New World in 1534 to the years of the Quiet Revolution in the 1960s. It should be noted that Wade was critical of what he called the partisan writing of Canadian history and he had a certain desire to unite the 'two solitudes'.

Pre-colonial

91　Images de la préhistoire du Québec. (Images of prehistoric Québec.)
　　Edited by Claude Chapdelaine.　Montréal: Société des Recherches
　　amérindiennes du Québec, 1978. 141p. maps. bibliog.

Reveals aboriginal history in Québec through an investigation of archaeology. Each chapter covers a different region of the province. This book is intended for the non-specialist.

92　Western subarctic prehistory.
　　Donald W. Clark.　Hull, Québec: Archaeological Commission of
　　Canada, 1993. 151p.

Richly illustrated and intended for the non-specialist, this work provides insight into the population and repopulation of the subarctic at the end of the last Ice Age. With the help of archaeology, Clark describes the people who stayed in the north as opposed to those who continued to migrate south. Information regarding the ancestors of present-day aboriginals and their lifestyles is the focus of this book.

93　L'occupation historique et préhistorique de la Place-Royale.
　　(Historic and prehistoric settlement of the Place-Royale.)
　　Normand Clermont, Claude Chapdelaine, Jacques Guimont.　Québec:
　　Ministère des Affaires culturelles, 1992. 426p. maps.

An analysis of archaeological digs performed at the Place-Royale, the earliest French settlement in North America. The work is divided into two sections: the first contains an analysis of aboriginal vestiges dating from prehistoric times while the second examines the relevant findings from the period between Champlain's arrival and the 19th century.

94 **L'archéologie et la rencontre des deux mondes: présence européenne sur des sites amérindiens.** (Archaeology and the meeting of two worlds: European presence on Indian land.)
Edited by Michel Fortin. Québec: Musée de la Civilisation, 1992. 206p.

Five scholars discuss their research on the period during which Europeans and aboriginals first came into contact with one another. These five essays focus on the material culture of both Europeans and aboriginal peoples in order to illustrate the nature and development of this first contact. Debunking a few Eurocentric myths regarding the 'discovery' of North America, these essays present solid archaeological evidence of European-aboriginal interaction in the Saguenay region, for example, fifty years before the first written records of European settlements.

95 **Québec prehistory.**
J. V. Wright. Toronto: Van Nostrand Reinhold, 1979. 128p. maps. bibliog. (Canadian Prehistory Series).

Part of a series of archaeological studies published alongside visual aids produced by the National Museum of Canada, Ottawa, this work presents an outline of 11,000 years of aboriginal life in the province. The study is divided into four categories: the Palaeo-Indian period, the Archaic period, the Woodland period, and the Palaeo-Eskimo and Thule cultures. Through the use of time charts, maps, graphs, and photographs, the author gives a sense of aboriginal life before Jacques Cartier. This book is written for the non-specialist.

Colonial (1534-1866)

96 **Les rébellions de 1837-1838. Les patriotes du Bas-Canada dans la mémoire collective et chez les historiens.** (The rebellions of 1837-38. The Patriots of Lower Canada in the collective memory and according to historians.)
Edited by Jean-Paul Bernard. Montréal: Éditions du Boréal, 1983. 349p. bibliog.

Historians continue to debate the cause and meaning of the rebellions of 1837-38 in Lower Canada (present-day Québec). Did they represent a progressive nationalist movement or were they motivated by conservative reaction? This work brings together the most prominent of diverging viewpoints, including articles by Donald Creighton, W. H. Parker, Maurice Séguin, Fernand Ouellet and Stanley Ryerson. The editor also includes a useful chronology of the conflict and a list of the names and professions of 2,100 Patriots. This is an excellent introduction to the historiography of this pivotal moment in Québec history. For a more regionally focused study of the rebellions that also contains a biography of the insurgents, see Réal Fortin's *La guerre des Patriotes: le long du Richelieu* (The Patriots' war along the Richelieu River) (Saint-Jean-sur-Richelieu, Québec: Éditions Milles Roches, 1988. 35p.). Bernard completed an interesting study on the ideology of the political party that grew out of the Patriot Party, entitled *Les Rouges: libéralisme, nationalisme et anticléricalisme au milieu du XIXe siècle* (The Reds: liberalism, nationalism, and anticlericalism during the mid-19th century) (Montréal: Presses de l'Université du Québec, 1971. 394p.).

97   **The shaping of Québec politics and society.**
Gérald Bernier, Daniel Salée.   Washington, DC: Crane Russak, 1992. 170p.
A resolutely revisionist interpretation of Québec history between the Conquest (1760) and the Act of Union (1840). Adopting a class-based approach, Salée and Bernier argue that economic relations among individuals during this period were of a pre-capitalist or even feudal nature. Moreover, the thorough analysis of class in explaining political and social history provides a counterbalance to the arguments put forward by those historians who claim this period of Québec history was dominated by the national question. Throughout this work, the authors suggest that class transcended ethnicity, thereby providing a modified interpretation of Québec's political culture and of French-English relations.

98   **Rural life in nineteenth-century Québec.**
Serge Courville, Normand Séguin, translated by Sinclair Robinson. Ottawa: Canadian Historical Association, 1989. 30p. (Historical Booklet, Canadian Historical Association, no. 47).
A brief survey of the major milestones in the evolution and transformation of Québec rural society during the 19th century. The authors emphasize industrialization, urbanization and increasing market pressures as contributing factors in the decline of rural life and the increasing urban influence in the countryside. Another study of rural society is worth mentioning: Joseph Goy and Jean-Pierre Wallot's *Évolution et éclatement du monde rural* (The evolution and break-up of rural society) (Montréal: Presses de l'Université de Montréal, 1986. 519p.) which compares rural society in both France and Québec between the 17th and 20th centuries.

99   **Lord Durham's Report. An abridgement of the Report on the Affairs of British North America by Lord Durham.**
Edited by Gerald M. Craig.   Toronto: McClelland and Stewart, 1963. 179p. (Carleton Library, no. 1).
Upon examining the state of political disarray in Upper and Lower Canada following the rebellions of 1837 and 1838, Lord Durham wrote that he found 'two nations warring in the bosom of a single state'. Lord Durham's telling phrase has since been quoted in virtually every textbook of Québec and Canadian history. Over half of the report, first published in 1839, scrutinizes the affairs of Lower Canada (Québec). The report remains noteworthy and notorious for its low estimation of French civilization and its call for the establishment of limited responsible government in the colony. Craig provides an excellent introduction to this historic and controversial document. On Durham's philosophy, see Janet Ajzenstat's *The political thought of Lord Durham* (Montréal; Kingston, Ontario: McGill-Queen's University Press, 1988. 137p.).

100 **Habitants and merchants in seventeenth century Montreal.**
Louise Dechêne, translated by Liana Vardi. Montréal; Kingston,
Ontario: McGill-Queen's University Press, 1992. 428p.

One of the most important studies of settlement in Québec. Dechêne looks at colonial
society on the island of Montréal in the 17th century, focusing on immigration, trade
and agriculture, social hierarchies, religion and family life. The French edition of this
text, published in 1974, *Habitants et marchands de Montréal au XVIIe siècle* (Paris:
Plon, 1974. 588p.) was among the very first works on colonial Québec that gave voice
to the peasants as opposed to the politicians. Like fellow historian Allan Greer (see
entry 109), Dechêne emphasizes the continuity of rural life during this period.
Dechêne examines the regulation of subsistence goods in *Le partage des subsistances
au Canada sous le Régime français* (The distribution of subsistence goods in Canada
under the French regime) (Montréal: Éditions du Boréal, 1994. 283p.).

101 **Contributions à l'étude du régime seigneurial canadien.**
(Contributions to the study of the Canadian seigneurial land tenure
system.)
Sylvie Dépatie, Mario Lalancette, Christian Dessureault. LaSalle,
Québec: Éditions Hurtubise HMH, 1987. 290p. maps. (Les Cahiers du
Québec, Collection Histoire, no. 88).

Comprises three case-studies on the seigneuries of Île-Jésus, Île-aux-Coudres and
Lac-des-Deux-Montagnes. Sensitive to the socio-economic contexts of their three
cases, the authors suggest that the Canadian seigneurial regime typifies a feudal
system which, by virtue of judicial and economic rights, assured the privileges of the
seigneurial class over those of the censitaires (those who had to pay a tax for the
'privilege' of working the land). The detailed attention given to each case-study sets
this work apart from other global studies of the seigneurial system. For other works on
the seigneurial system, see Claude Baribeau's *La seigneurie de la Petite-Nation, 1801-
1854: le rôle économique et social du seigneur* (The seigneury of Petite-Nation,
1801-54: the seigneur's economic and social role) (Hull, Québec: Asticou, 1983.
166p.). Also of interest is Françoise Noël's analysis of estate management within the
seigneurial system, entitled *The Christie Seigneuries: estate management and settlement in the Upper Richelieu Valley, 1760-1854* (Montréal; Kingston, Ontario:
McGill-Queen's University Press, 1992. 221p.). Noël concludes that economic
development under the seigneurial system during this period was not so different to
development under other systems of land tenure.

102 **Québec en Amérique au XIXe siècle: essai sur les caractères
économiques de la Laurentie.** (Québec in America during the
19th century. An essay on the economic character of Laurentia.)
Albert Faucher. Montréal: Fides, 1973. 247p. (Histoire Économique
et Sociale du Canada Français).

In an effort to understand the lag in development between Québec and North America,
Faucher presents a study of the dominant economic phases in Québec's history in
relation to those of the United States and Ontario. This study represents the crossing
of two schools of thought which at once reject purely cultural/anthropological
explanations for Québec's lag, yet criticize the lack of entrepreneurial qualities in
Québec due to its historical evolution. It is important to note that Québec, as opposed

to French-speaking Canada, is the object of this study, representing a shift in the mentality of the social sciences towards the study of Québec.

103 **Un nouvel ordre des choses: la pauvreté, le crime, l'État au Québec, de la fin du XVIIIe siècle à 1840.** (A new development: poverty, crime and the Québec state from the end of the 18th century to 1840.)
Jean-Marie Fecteau.   Outremont, Québec: VLB Éditeur, 1989. 287p. bibliog. (Collection Études Québécoises, no. 10).

A social history of how society managed its social problems, notably poverty and crime, from the end of the 18th century to 1840. Fecteau examines the history of social regulation at a time when capitalist development was ascendant in the West. This book notes the change from a feudal model of social regulation based on charity to a more active form of regulation by the state based on repression. For other titles on crime and criminality in Québec, see André Lachance's *Crime et criminels en Nouvelle-France* (Crime and criminals in New France) (Montréal: Éditions du Boréal Express, 1984. 184p.).

104 **Histoire des patriotes.** (A history of the Patriots.)
Gérard Filteau.   Montréal: L'Aurore/Univers, 1980. 492p.

Originally published on the centenary of the rebellions of 1838, this book followed closely the rehabilitation into Québec and Canadian history of the Patriots episode by Lionel Groulx. This rehabilitation followed, in turn, a century of the Patriots' exclusion from official history due to their anticlerical position. Filteau justifies the rebellion on the basis that those involved were fighting a bureaucratic conspiracy against the French Canadian nation. This book influenced a generation of nationalists.

105 **Par la bouche de mes canons! La ville de Québec face à l'ennemi.** (From the mouth of my canons! Québec City against the enemy.)
Gérard Filteau.   Sillery, Québec: Éditions du Septentrion, 1990. 271p. maps.

A military history of Québec City. The author examines five attacks on the city, four by the British (1628-29, 1690, 1711 and 1759) and the last by the Americans (1775-76).

106 **Partners in fur.**
Daniel Francis, Toby Morantz.   Montréal; Kingston, Ontario: McGill-Queen's University Press, 1983. 203p.

The significant interest historians have paid to the economic relations between French fur traders and aboriginals has provided a better understanding of the people living in northern Québec. Combining historical and ethnohistorical methods, this work provides a comprehensive introduction to the impact of the fur trade on Cree society and their subsistence way of life. On the impact of the fur trade, Francis and Morantz dispel the traditional interpretation of the Crees as the passive and defenceless victims of European traders. Moreover, their research leads them to conclude that aboriginals were 'crucial to all aspects of the fur trade and were responsible to a considerable degree for establishing its procedures'. At the same time, this book serves as a general history of the eastern James Bay region.

107 **La civilisation de la Nouvelle-France, 1713-1744.** (The civilization of New France, 1713-44.)
Guy Frégault. Montréal: Bibliothèque québécoise, 1990. 318p. bibliog.

Between the signing of the Treaty of Utrecht in 1713 and the War of Austrian Succession in 1744, New France found itself free from the entanglements of international conflict. The author argues that this represents a period of early national formation signalled by the emergence of a distinct French Canadian moral and national consciousness. This influential and thought-provoking work was originally published in 1944. For a longer history of New France (from the first settlements to 1760), the most recent study is Jacques Mathieu's *La Nouvelle-France. Les Français en Amérique du Nord, XVIe-XVIIIe siècle* (New France. The French in North America, 16th-18th century) (Paris: Belin; Sainte-Foy, Québec: Presses de l'Université Laval, 1991. 254p.). The other seminal work on New France is by renowned historian Marcel Trudel in his *Introduction to New France* (Toronto: Holt, Rinehart & Winston of Canada, 1968. 300p.).

108 **Les délices de nos coeurs. Marie de l'Incarnation et ses pensionnaires amérindiennes, 1639-1672.** (Our heart's delight. Mary the Incarnate and her Amerindian charges.)
Claire Gourdeau. Sillery, Québec: Éditions du Septentrion, 1994. 128p.

The arrival of French Ursulines in 1639 marked the beginning of female education in North America. Headed by Mary the Incarnate, this religious order was charged with the education and conversion of female Amerindians. This book looks at the cultural exchanges between both groups of women and examines how these exchanges were interpreted by each group. Gourdeau takes an interesting and novel approach towards understanding what was one of the first contacts between Europeans and aboriginal peoples.

109 **The Patriots and the people. The rebellion of 1837 in rural Lower Canada.**
Allan Greer. Toronto: University of Toronto Press, 1993. 385p. maps.

An important reinterpretation of the 1837 rebellion. Though this episode has usually been explained as a response to economic distress or racial conflict, Greer emphasizes the Patriots' demand for popular sovereignty. Rather than being passively manipulated by middle-class politicians, the Patriots actively responded to democratic appeals. The author maintains that the rhetoric of republicanism corresponded to the experiences and wishes of these revolutionaries.

110 **Peasant, lord and merchant: rural society in three Quebec parishes, 1740-1840.**
Allan Greer. Toronto: University of Toronto Press, 1985. 304p.

A social history of three rural parishes in the Lower Richelieu valley (i.e., Sorel, St. Ours, and St. Denis). Greer examines the workings of the family-based economy in pre-industrial Québec, emphasizing the feudal obligations to the Church and the seigneur. He argues that, although the growing commercial activity created new lines of dependency, the basic structure of rural life in Québec remained largely unchanged between 1740 and 1840. This is one of the best and most thoroughly researched studies of this genre.

111   **Économie et société en Nouvelle-France.** (Economy and society in New France.)
Jean Hamelin.   Sainte-Foy, Québec: Presses de l'Université Laval, 1970. 3rd ed. 137p. maps. bibliog.

An examination of the economy between 1672 and 1763 which emphasizes the fur and wheat trades, the monetary system, and immigration. Hamelin argues that the absence of a well-developed bourgeoisie in New France led to deficiencies in the colony's economic development. The colony did not develop a middle class that could adequately exploit the natural resources of the colony.

112   **Nationalismes et conflits de droits: le débat du droit privé au Québec 1760-1840.** (Nationalism and rights conflicts: the private law debate in Québec between 1760 and 1840.)
Evelyn Kolish.   LaSalle, Québec: Éditions Hurtubise HMH, 1994. 325p. bibliog. (Les Cahiers du Québec, Collection Histoire, no. 108).

Examines the conflict between Lower Canada's House of Assembly, dominated by elected representatives, and the Legislative Council, largely dominated by the British elite, as it manifested itself in debates over which legal system should prevail in the colony. During this period (between the Conquest, 1760, and the Act of Union, 1840), the French and English legal systems became the principal vehicles of the English and French elites' respective national aspirations, revealing their divergent visions of the colony's future. Moreover, Kolish concludes that the opinions of these elites on law and the administration of justice were largely inspired by national aspirations. Kolish's research and arguments are structured in two sections. The first examines the evolution of attitudes towards jurisprudence and legislation in a chronological framework, clearly revealing the importance of law in the elites' struggle for control of the government and the colony. The second section explores the more controversial debates on private law, i.e., land tenure, bankruptcy and registration offices, highlighting the role played by socio-economic interests, judicial traditions and national aspirations.

113   **La Prairie en Nouvelle-France, 1647-1760: étude d'histoire sociale.** (La Prairie in New France, 1647-1760: a study of social history.)
Louis Lavallée.   Montréal; Kingston, Ontario: McGill-Queen's University Press, 1992. 301p. maps. bibliog.

A detailed study of a small seigneury and Jesuit parish, Village de La Prairie-de-la-Madeleine. By examining social stratification and rules of inheritance, the author determines how obligations to the Church and the seigneur framed the life of the peasant. An extensive bibliography is included.

114 **Nationalism, capitalism, and colonization in nineteenth-century Quebec: the Upper St. Francis District.**
John Irvine Little. Montréal; Kingston, Ontario: McGill-Queen's University Press, 1989. 306p. bibliog.

A detailed social history examining the response to industrialization in a small district in Québec during the mid-19th century. Beginning in 1848, many of French-speaking Canada's elite, most notably the Roman Catholic Church, encouraged the province's surplus rural population to migrate to marginal rural land. According to the author, this constituted a carefully orchestrated campaign to prevent emigration to the United States rather than a conservative reaction against the rise of industrial capitalism.

115 **Le commerce entre la Nouvelle-France et les Antilles au XVIIIe siècle.** (Commercial relations between New France and the West Indies during the 18th century.)
Jacques Mathieu. Québec: Fides, 1981. 276p. maps. bibliog. (Collection Fleur de Lys).

Based on numerous detailed colonial reports on trade between New France and the West Indies, the author attempts to gauge the importance of this commercial relationship in the 18th century, reconstruct the nature and conditions of these relations, and finally assess their influence on Canadian society.

116 **The last cannon shot: a study of French-Canadian nationalism, 1837-1850.**
Jacques Monet. Toronto: University of Toronto Press, 1969. 422p.

The author examines the development of French nationalist opinion during this period. The perceptions of, and responses to, three important events are assessed. These include the debate surrounding the Union between Lower and Upper Canada (1837-42), the campaign for responsible government (1843-48) and the agitation for repeal of the Union and annexation to the United States (1848-50).

117 **Lower Canada 1791-1840: social change and nationalism.**
Fernand Ouellet, translated by Patricia Claxton. Toronto: McClelland and Stewart, 1980. 427p. map.

Ouellet is generally regarded as the representative of a school of Québec historians who, in breaking continuity with traditional historiography, attempted to evacuate the national question from the study of history. The main thrust behind Ouellet's argument is that the principal challenge in Lower Canadian society resided in a 'resistance of mentalities' deeply rooted within the socio-economic heritage of the *ancien régime*. This work focuses on an analysis of the emergence of a crisis that paralysed the functioning of the parliamentary system and consequently degenerated into the insurrections of 1837-38. Directly confronted by the national question, Ouellet attempts to demonstrate that crises of capital were the cause of the rebellions. The interpretative approach adopted in this book stands in opposition to the revisionist school of history best represented in the works of Jean-Pierre Wallot and Gilles Paquet (see item nos. 119-20).

118 **Histoire de l'insurrection du Canada, et réfutation de l'écrit de Louis-Joseph Papineau par Hubert Aquin.** (A history of the insurrection in Canada and a refutation of Louis-Joseph Papineau's essay by Hubert Aquin.)
Louis-Joseph Papineau.   Montréal: Leméac, 1968. 104p.

Written by Louis-Joseph Papineau, the principal leader of the 1837-38 rebellions in Lower Canada, this essay is a refutation of Lord Durham's report which proposed the union of Upper and Lower Canada. This edition is prefaced by an essay written by Hubert Aquin, a well-known novelist. For an abridged version of the report see Gerald M. Craig's *Lord Durham's Report. An abridgement of the Report on the Affairs of British North America by Lord Durham* (see item no. 99).

119 **Lower Canada at the turn of the nineteenth century: restructuring and modernization.**
Gilles Paquet, Jean-Pierre Wallot.   Ottawa: Canadian Historical Association, 1988. 25p. (Canadian Historical Association Historical Booklet, no. 45).

The work of these authors stands in contrast to that of Fernand Ouellet – see *Lower Canada 1791-1840: social change and nationalism* (see item no. 117) – in interpreting pre-Confederation Lower Canadian society. Rather than reject the central focus of the national question in traditional Québec historiography, this book studies its manifestation in the socio-economic aspirations of French Canadian entrepreneurs. Wallot and Paquet present a more dynamic vision of a society in full transformation under the economic and social forces that were sweeping all of Atlantic North America. This societal transformation is characterized by the rise of new institutions, the consolidation of power among new social groups and the polarization of power among concurrent elites solidly based within distinct socio-ethnic networks. Wallot and Paquet suggest that the first sparks of nationalism are found in the efforts of the French Canadian elite to consolidate its power in the face of discriminatory barriers. As a summary of Wallot and Paquet's work over twenty years, this essay best represents the difference between the conventional and the revisionist schools.

120 **Patronage et pouvoir dans le Bas-Canada, 1794-1812: un essai d'économie historique.** (Patronage and power in Lower Canada, 1794-1812: an essay on economic history.)
Gilles Paquet, Jean-Pierre Wallot.   Montréal: Presses de l'Université du Québec, 1973. 182p.

An analysis of the Civil list in Lower Canada and its importance in the power and patronage relations of the times. This work focuses on competing elite groups and their attempts to consolidate power. The Civil list is interpreted as a political institution whose rise, evolution and decline need to be understood not as a pathology of Lower Canada's evolution, but rather as part of a theory of institutional transformation in the colony. The authors suggest that the Civil list reveals several characteristics of the society writ large: e.g., colonial bias, collective action, and conflict in Lower Canada. Related works include *Lower Canada at the turn of the nineteenth century: restructuring and modernization* (see item no. 119).

121 **The long journey to the country of the Hurons.**
Gabriel Sagard, with an introduction and notes by G. M. Wrong.
New York: Greenwood Press, 1968. 411p.
The first English translation of the book written by Gabriel Sagard of his voyages in
Canada in 1623 and 1624. This book provides the reader with the first written record
of the Hurons, before their dispersion, from the perspective of a French Catholic
missionary working in Canada at the time. A Recollet missionary, Sagard reveals his
admiration of the Hurons in comparison to other tribes; an admiration which led future
missionaries to consider the Hurons as the most promising prospects for religious
conversion. This book enables the reader to experience the world view of the French
missionaries, their goals and their aspirations, and also provides an important record
of Huron customs and culture before European settlement destroyed much of their
way of life.

122 **Les modes de vie des habitants et des commerçants de
Place-Royale 1660-1760.** (The lifestyles of dwellers and traders of
the Place-Royale 1660-1760.)
Serge Saint-Pierre. Québec: Ministère des Affaires culturelles, 1993.
2 vols.
A synthesis of the archaeological finds at the Place-Royale, the oldest part of Québec
City where Samuel de Champlain built the first permanent French residence. This
book focuses on what archaeology tells us about the lifestyles of those first inhabitants,
from how they ate to how they entertained themselves. This work is accessible to the
non-specialist.

123 **Redcoats and Patriots: the rebellions in Lower Canada, 1837-1838.**
Elinor Kyte Senior. Stittsville, Ontario: Canada's Wings, in
collaboration with the Canadian War Museum, National Museum of
Man, National Museums of Canada, Ottawa, 1985. 218p. maps.
Jointly published by the Canadian War Museum, this work focuses on the military
operations during the rebellions of 1837-38. With extensive use of maps and illustrations, it examines the build-up of armed factions in the city of Montréal, the relations
between militant reformers in Upper and Lower Canada, and the breakdown of militia
organizations. This work remains one of the rare studies on the military aspects of the
Lower Canadian rebellions.

124 **The politics of codification: the Lower Canadian Civil Code of
1866.**
Brian Young. Montréal; Kingston, Ontario: McGill-Queen's
University Press, 1994. 264p.
Analyses the institution of the Québec Civil Code in the broader context of political
issues of the time. Young demonstrates the links between legal history and class
history in situating the implementation of the Civil Code of 1866 against the backdrop
of the failed Lower Canadian rebellions, the advent of responsible government,
Confederation and the end of seigneurial tenure. Young suggests that the Civil Code
was essential to the transformation of Québec from a society based on feudal privileges to one based on central government, individual rights, and universal institutions.
Aware of the motivations and roles of both the anglophone and francophone

bourgeoisies, Young illustrates the political impact of the Civil Code in state formation. The work is particularly useful for providing the background to recent changes made to the Civil Code in 1994.

1867-1960

125 **Dossier sur le pacte fédératif de 1867. La Confédération: pacte ou loi?** (Notes on the federal pact of 1867. The Confederation: compact or law?)

Richard Arès.   Montréal: Éditions Bellarmin, 1967. 2nd ed. 264p.

Examines the tension between the moral and legal interpretations of the Canadian Constitution. Updated in 1967, this book raises fundamental questions that dominated the debate on 'patriation' in 1982 regarding the founding nature of the country. Arès examines both arguments through the lens of those who defended the two theses: i.e., provincialist versus centralist. While there is no shortage of recently published books on the subject, this work illustrates the established French Canadian interpretation of the Constitution and its founding principles.

126 **The crisis of Quebec, 1914-1918.**

Elizabeth Armstrong.   Toronto: McClelland and Stewart, 1974. 275p. bibliog. (Carleton Library, no. 74).

Originally published in 1937, this work remains one of the most vivid descriptions of the conscription crisis during the First World War. It provides an analysis of the roots of French Canadian nationalism and its manifestation between 1914 and 1918. The roles and ideas of the prominent figures in this crisis are discussed – most notably Robert Borden, Henri Bourassa and Wilfrid Laurier. See also Jean Provencher, *Québec sous la loi des mesures du guerre: 1918* (Québec under war-time legislation: 1918) (Montréal: Éditions du Boréal, 1971. 146p.) which focuses on the conscription protests in Québec between March and April 1918. Réal Bélanger has written two books specifically on the federal politicians involved in the debates, the first entitled *L'impossible défi. Albert Sévigny et les conservateurs fédéraux 1902-1918* (The impossible challenge. Albert Sévigny and the federal Conservatives 1902-18) (Québec: Presses de l'Université Laval, 1983. 368p.) and *Wilfrid Laurier. Quand la politique devient passion* (Wilfrid Laurier. When politics becomes a passion) (Québec: Presses de l'Université Laval, 1986. 484p.).

127 **Le Québec et la confédération, un choix libre? Le clergé et la constitution de 1867.** (Québec and Confederation, a free choice? The Church and the Constitution of 1867.)

Marcel Bellavance.   Sillery, Québec: Éditions du Septentrion, 1992. 214p. maps. bibliog.

Bellavance argues that the Catholic clergy in the province unduly influenced Quebecers to accept Confederation. Given this alleged coercion of the Church and evidence of electoral fraud, the author raises questions about the legitimacy of the 1867 federal election. The volume includes a comprehensive bibliography.

128 **Le Duplessisme: politique économique et rapports de force.**
(Duplessisism: political economy and power relations.)
Gérard Boismenu. Montréal: Presses de l'Université de Montréal,
1981. 432p.

From a political-economic perspective, Boismenu explains the paradox between the
static political programme of the Union nationale (the conservative political party in
power under Duplessis during the years indicated below, under Daniel Johnson from
1966-68, and under Jean-Jacques Bertrand from 1968-70) and the rapidly changing
social reality of Québec society. Focusing primarily on the economic policy of the
Duplessis Government (1936-39 and 1944-59), Boismenu at once dispels the notion of
a closed society by demonstrating the growing relationship between the state, certain
traditional industries of the private sector, and foreign capital.

129 **Working families. Age, gender, and daily survival in
industrializing Montréal.**
Bettina Bradbury. Toronto: McClelland and Stewart, 1993. 310p.
(Canadian Social History Series).

A detailed portrait of the way working-class families responded to industrialization in
Montréal. Bradbury takes the reader into the homes of these families to witness how
wage labour transformed the household. This book examines continuity and change in
the way families adapted to new problems such as unemployment and child wage
labour. Further to a socio-economic investigation of working-class life, Bradbury
relates the experience of women and describes the crucial role they played in ensuring
the survival of the family. Another social history of Montréal is Lucia Ferretti's *Entre
voisins. La société paroissiale en milieu urbain: Saint-Pierre-Apôtre de Montréal,
1848-1930* (Between neighbours. Parish society in an urban milieu: Saint Peter the
Apostle of Montréal, 1848-1930) (Montréal: Éditions du Boréal Express, 1992.
264p.).

130 **La démocratie en veilleuse.** (Democracy hidden from view.)
Paul-André Comeau, Claude Beauregard, Edwidge Munn. Montréal:
Éditions Québec Amérique, 1995. 300p.

Following the onset of the Second World War, Parliament passed a law according the
Canadian federal government the power to examine all forms of domestic communication.
A final report was commissioned at the end of the war in the aim of discovering how
government censors might improve their efficiency in the event of future national
emergencies. Released in 1984, this report reveals the 'fragility' of a democracy
submitted to internal censoring in the name of supranational interests'.

131 **Le droit de se taire. Histoire des communistes au Québec, de la
Première guerre mondiale à la Révolution tranquille.** (The right to
be silent. A history of the communists in Québec from the First World
War to the Quiet Revolution.)
Robert Comeau, Bernard Dionne. Outremont, Québec: VLB Éditeur,
1989. 542p. (Collection Études Québécoises).

A collection of essays written by some of the most important historians in Québec
testifies that while the Communist Party may not have enjoyed significant electoral
success, its intellectual and ideological influence remains significant. Organized into

three sections, this book analyses the relationships between the Communist Party and Québec society, between the party and its leaders, and between the party and the labour movement. On the same subject see Andrée Lévesque's *Virage à gauche interdit: les communistes, les socialistes et leurs ennemis au Québec, 1929-1939* (Left turn forbidden: communists, socialists and their enemies in Québec, 1929-39) (Montréal: Éditions du Boréal Express, 1984. 186p.).

132 **Québec 1945-2000: les intellectuels et le temps de Duplessis.**
(Québec 1945-2000: intellectuals and the Duplessis era.)
Léon Dion. Sainte-Foy, Québec: Presses de l'Université Laval, 1993. 2 vols. 452p. bibliog.

Many of the intellectuals during this period shared a common ideological outlook, fuelled by what they saw as the undemocratic practices of Premier Maurice Duplessis. Dion examines Maurice Lamontagne, Jean Marchand, Paul-Émile Borduas, Jean-Paul Desbiens, and Georges-Henri Lévesque. The author examines their influence on trade unions, the provincial Liberal Party (PLQ), the Faculty of Social Sciences at Laval University and the publication *Cité Libre*.

133 **The bitter thirties in Québec.**
Évelyne Dumas, translated by Évelyne Dumas. Montréal; New York: Black Rose Books, 1975. 151p.

Relying largely upon oral histories, this book argues that the origins of Québec labour's militancy may be traced back to the 1930s rather than to the post-Second World War era as is commonly believed. The author highlights changes in labour organization and legislation as well as the role of immigrant organizers during the period.

134 **Communisme et anticommunisme au Québec: 1920-1950.**
(Communism and anti-communism in Québec: 1920-50.)
Marcel Fournier. Montréal: Éditions coopératives Albert Saint-Martin, 1979. 165p.

Structured as a sociological history of the Canadian Communist Party in Québec, this book analyses why the Communist Party did not enjoy any electoral success in Québec. Fournier suggests that the party's inability to achieve electoral success can be blamed on the lack of congruence among economic, ideological and political factors, rather than on the shortcomings of its leaders and volunteers.

135 **French Canadian thinkers of the nineteenth and twentieth century.**
Edited by Laurier LaPierre. Montréal: McGill University Press, 1966. 117p.

A series of scholarly essays on a number of French Canadian intellectuals and politicians – Louis-Joseph Papineau (1786-1871), François-Xavier Garneau (1809-66), Sir George-Étienne Cartier (1814-73), Ignace Bourget (1799-1885), Sir Wilfrid Laurier (1841-1919), Henri Bourassa (1868-1952), Léon Gérin (1863-1951), Édouard Montpetit (1881-1954) and Lionel Groulx (1878-1967). This is a valuable introduction to Québec's early intellectual pioneers.

136   The Bernonville Affair. A French war criminal in post-WWII
      Québec.
      Yves Lavertu, translated by George Tombs.   Montréal: Robert
      Davies Publishing, 1995. 154p.

Lavertu attempts to broach the issue of the relationship between the Vichy regime and
Québec through a well-researched investigation of one case-study – the deportation
of Jacques Dugé de Bernonville, a war criminal who later fled to Brazil and was
assassinated there in 1974. Lavertu's focus on the facts and events surrounding the
Bernonville deportation trial denies this book the mantle of being an authoritative
history on the Québec-Pétain relationship. Nevertheless, it does present an objective
view of the circumstances surrounding this one event.

137   Québec in the Duplessis era, 1935-1959: dictatorship or
      democracy?
      Cameron Nish.   Toronto: Copp Clark, 1970. 164p.

A collection of articles from contemporary newspapers and periodicals about the life,
character, politics and legacy of Maurice Duplessis. It focuses on Duplessis's view of
the state and provincial autonomy along with his relationship with labour and the
Church.

138   Years of impatience, 1950-1960.
      Gérard Pelletier, translated by Alan Brown.   Toronto: Methuen, 1983.
      240p.

Though generally regarded as an autobiography, this work could be classified as a
series of recollections of one of Québec's three so-called 'wise men' who entered
federal politics in 1965 (along with Pierre Trudeau and Jean Marchand). Before his
entry into politics, Pelletier was editor of La Presse and an outspoken critic of French
Canadian nationalism. Pelletier provides an insiders' perspective on the founding of
Cité Libre, the periodical he started up with Pierre Trudeau and other liberals and
social democrats during the 1950s as a vehicle for expressing dissatisfaction with
Duplessis and the conservative institutions which they believed to stand in the way of
the establishment of a modern, francophone society. For more about Cité Libre, see
Cité Libre: une anthologie (item no. 521). Pelletier also provides commentary on
many of Québec's most notable figures during this period, including René Lévesque,
Pierre Trudeau, Jean Marchand, Maurice Duplessis, André Laurendeau, Claude Ryan,
Paul-Émile Léger, Jean Drapeau and Réal Caouette.

139   Progrès, harmonie, liberté: le libéralisme des milieux d'affaires
      francophones de Montréal au tournant du siècle. (Progress,
      harmony, liberty: liberalism of the French business class in Montréal
      at the turn of the century.)
      Fernande Roy.   Montréal: Éditions du Boréal, 1988. 301p.

This work is a major contribution to the growing revisionist literature on ideological
diversity in Québec during the 19th and early 20th centuries. Departing from the traditional premise that liberalism was absent from the Québec ideological spectrum, Roy
suggests that liberalism did indeed exist and was present throughout Québec society
(e.g., on political, economic, social and ethical fronts). The existence of liberalism
within the francophone business elite between 1881 and 1914 questions not only the

hegemony of traditional clerical-nationalism, but also the issue of dominant social groups and their place within the power networks of the time. For an account of liberalism in a different social group see Yvan Lamonde's *Louis-Antoine Dessaules, 1818-1895: un seigneur libéral et anti-clérical* (Louis-Antoine Dessaules, 1818-95: a liberal and anticlerical seigneur) (Saint-Laurent, Québec: Fides, 1994. 369p.).

140   **The French-Canadian idea of Confederation, 1864-1900.**
Arthur Silver.   Toronto: University of Toronto Press, 1982. 257p. bibliog.

The author examines some of the most divisive events and widely interpreted concepts during this period: the compact theory of Confederation; the Riel affair; the Manitoba schools issues; and bilingualism. Riel led two rebellions (one in 1869-70 and one later in 1885) resisting the incorporation of the Prairies into the Confederation. He was hanged as a 'traitor' by 'English Canadian' authorities in Regina, Saskatchewan in 1885 but revered by the French-speaking Catholic Métis as a leader who defended their linguistic, educational and religious rights (many English-speaking settlers also bore arms under Riel, incidentally). At the heart of the polarized debate over Riel's rebellion (i.e., traitor and murdered, or martyr and patriot) is a more fundamental difference over the character of Confederation. The Manitoba schools issue refers to the unconstitutional abolition of French in Manitoba's schools by the province's legislature. Its significance is as part of a larger series of events which signalled that Québec was to have no influence in the westward expansion of the country. Silver argues that French Canadians have long been accustomed to seeing themselves as a nation. According to Silver, this meant that at the time of Confederation in 1867, they had little concern for French-speaking groups outside of Québec. Witnessing the struggle of Acadians, Franco-Ontarians and western Métis after 1867, however, French Canadians converted to the cause of protecting minority rights throughout Canada by 1900. This is a scholarly and well-researched work. For a good account of the motivation of the francophone fathers of the Confederation see Stéphane Kelly's *La petite loterie* (The little lottery) (Montréal: Éditions du Boréal, 1997. 283p.).

1960 to the present

141   **René Lévesque: l'homme, la nation, la démocratie.** (René Lévesque: the man, the nation and democracy.)
Edited by Yves Bélanger, Michel Lévesque.   Sillery, Québec: Presses de l'Université du Québec, 1992. 495p. (Les Leaders Politiques du Québec Contemporain, no. 5).

Organized into a series of over sixty essays and classified into eight subjects, this book highlights René Lévesque's immense impact on contemporary Québec as one of the founders of the Parti québécois in 1968 and Québec Premier from 1976-85. Prominent academics, journalists, politicians and union leaders demonstrate how Lévesque incarnated the convergence of modernity and democracy in Québec politics. Published following Lévesque's death, this book is a must for anyone who wants to discover the evolution of Québec society over the past few decades.

142   **Canada and Quebec: one country, two histories.**
Robert Bothwell.   Victoria, British Columbia: University of British
Columbia Press, 1995. 288p.

Structured as a series of conversations with prominent Canadian politicians, journalists and academics, this book highlights the discordant relationship between Québec and the rest of Canada. As one of Canada's most prominent historians, Bothwell brings a sweeping historical perspective to this work, starting with the British Conquest of New France in 1763 and ending with the post-Meech Lake Accord (1990) era. Though somewhat disjointed, the work benefits from the expertise and insight of the nearly 100 contributors.

143   **Thérèse Casgrain: une femme tenace et engagée.** (Thérèse Casgrain:
a tenacious and committed woman.)
Edited by Anita Caron, Lorraine Archambault.   Sainte-Foy, Québec:
Presses de l'Université du Québec, 1993. 393p. (Les Leaders
Politiques du Québec Contemporain, no. 6).

Though never elected to office, Thérèse Casgrain (1896-1981) fought for a myriad of political causes: women's suffrage in Québec, equal rights, consumers' rights, social justice, and nuclear arms reduction. As an advocate of these causes and as an ardent social democrat, Casgrain's public influence spanned an entire half century. The contributors to this volume assess her character and legacy.

144   **Daniel Johnson: rêve d'égalité et projet d'indépendance.** (Daniel
Johnson: dream of equality and project of independence.)
Edited by Robert Comeau, Michel Lévesque, Yves Bélanger.
Montréal: Presses de l'Université du Québec, 1991. 449p. bibliog.
(Les Leaders Politiques du Québec Contemporain, no. 4).

This volume stems from a major conference on the life and legacy of Daniel Johnson, leader of the Union Nationale and Premier of Québec between 1966 and 1968. Essays from several scholars, journalists and politicians examine the period of his leadership, focusing on political parties and elections, federal-provincial and international relations, as well as the growth of the independence movement and nationalism. The authors assess the relevance of his message for today. Daniel Johnson's perspective on Québec's place in Canada is best represented in his *Égalité ou indépendance* (Equality or independence) (see item no. 549).

145   **Jean Lesage et l'éveil d'une nation: les débuts de la Révolution
tranquille.** (Jean Lesage and the awakening of a nation: the beginnings
of the Quiet Revolution.)
Edited by Robert Comeau.   Sillery, Québec: Presses de l'Université
du Québec, 1989. 367p. (Series: Les Leaders Politiques du Québec
Contemporain, no. 2).

A series of essays on Jean Lesage, federal Member of Parliament from 1945 to 1958 and Premier of Québec between 1960 and 1966. The numerous contributors examine his personality and political legacy, focusing on the most salient issues of the period: federal-provincial relations; health and educational reforms; labour; the nationalization of electricity; and nationalism.

146 **Georges-Émile Lapalme.**
Edited by Jean-François Léonard. Sainte-Foy, Québec: Presses de
l'Université du Québec, 1988. 297p. (Series: Les Leaders Politiques
du Québec Contemporain, no. 1).
This book presents a collection of essays by leading academics on Lapalme's role as
'the father of the Quiet Revolution'. Leader of the Québec Liberal Party from 1950-58
and then the first minister of Cultural Affairs in Québec, Lapalme had an important
impact on the formulation of the Liberal Party's 1960 programme. Together, these
essays discuss Lapalme's influence and activity in the context of economic development during the 1950s, nationalism before and after the Quiet Revolution (1960-66),
the increasing importance of government intervention in culture, and the political
ideologies of the time.

147 **The trickster: Robert Bourassa and Quebecers, 1990-1992.**
Jean-Francois Lisée, abridged and translated by Robert Chodos,
Simon Horn, Wanda Taylor. Toronto: James Lorimer & Co., 1994.
385p. bibliog.
Discusses the role of Robert Bourassa, Premier of Québec from 1970 to 1976 and
1985 to 1992, and provides an insider's account of political events during the two
years that followed the defeat of the Meech Lake Accord (1990), an ill-fated attempt
to gain Québec's assent to the federal constitution. This was a period when support for
sovereignty reached record proportions in the province. Lisée, a noted Québec journalist
and current advisor to the Québec government, argues that Bourassa misled Quebecers
into believing that he was moving towards sovereignty while privately assuring prominent
English-speaking Canadians that he was loyal to federalism. For Robert Bourassa's
personal account of his years in office see his *Gouverner le Québec* (Governing
Québec) (Saint-Laurent, Québec: Fides, 1995. 305p.).

148 **La crise d'octobre.** (The October Crisis.)
Gérard Pelletier. Montréal: Éditions du Jour, 1971. 265p.
Silent during the actual crisis and member of the Federal Cabinet at the time the War
Measures Act was passed in 1970, Gérard Pelletier published his own analysis. Aside
from the insight of one of Québec's most respected journalists and politicians, this
book provides an insight into the crisis from a government official's perspective.

149 **Quebec states her case: speeches and articles from Quebec in the
years of unrest.**
Edited by Frank Scott, Michael Oliver. Toronto: Macmillan, 1964.
165p.
Published during the Quiet Revolution (1960-66), this book epitomizes the curiosity
that English-speaking Canada felt towards the massive changes transpiring in Québec.
The tumultuous social and institutional changes occasioned a debate within the
province over the nature of the Confederation deal itself. This work presents selection:
from political debates, speeches, newspapers, editorials, interviews and pamphlets tha
reflect varying shades of opinion in Québec. Authors include Jean Lesage, Andr
Laurendeau, Gérard Pelletier, Pierre Trudeau, Léon Dion, René Lévesque and Jea
Marchand.

150   **Jean Lesage & the Quiet Revolution.**
      Dale C. Thomson.   Toronto: Macmillan, 1984. 500p.

One of the best histories in English of the Quiet Revolution, 1960-66, in Québec. The work is divided into three sections: the first comprises a biography of Lesage, Liberal Party leader and Premier of the province between 1960 and 1966, and presents an overview of his administration; the second part examines the modernization of Québec, focusing on economic and institutional reform; and the third section looks at the new initiatives taken in federal-provincial and international affairs.

Regional

151   **La colonisation de l'Abitibi: 'un projet géopolitique'.**
      (The colonization of the Abitibi region: 'a geopolitical project'.)
      Maurice Asselin.   Rouyn, Québec: Collège de l'Abitibi-
      Témiscamingue, 1982. 171p. map. bibliog.

A revisionist history of the Abitibi colonization project. Against the backdrop of the 'Grande noirceur' (Great Darkness) in Québec, and the popular view that the colonists were merely victims of forestry magnates, Asselin brings to light the entrepreneurial and innovative spirit of the colonists. The 'Grande noirceur' refers loosely to the decades preceding the Quiet Revolution. It is meant to serve as a contrast to the modernization and liberalization of Québec society that occurred after 1960 and is supposed to evoke the conservatism and ideological backwardness of the province prior to 1960.

152   **Histoire de la Gaspésie.** (A history of the Gaspé.)
      Jules Bélanger, Marc Desjardins, Jean-Yves Frenette, Pierre
      Dansereau.   Montréal: Éditions du Boréal Express, 1981. 797p.

A wide-ranging history of the Gaspé which synthesizes its geographic, demographic, economic, political and cultural aspects into one volume. It is divided into six sections representing the different phases of economic development in the region. Without sacrificing academic rigour, this book remains accessible to the public at large in presenting a balanced and thematic history of the Gaspé.

153   **Quelques arpents d'Amérique. Population, économie, famille au
      Saguenay, 1838-1971.** (A few acres in America. Population, economy
      and family in the Saguenay, 1838-1971.)
      Gérard Bouchard.   Montréal: Éditions du Boréal Express, 1996. 640p.

The result of more then twenty years of work, this major volume demonstrates that the process of colonization in the Saguenay region between 1838 and 1971 followed similar patterns to those that occurred in the rest of North America. In illustrating the egalitarian nature of the Saguenay region of the 19th century, Bouchard brilliantly highlights the American characteristics of Québec society. The book includes major statistical data on the demographic evolution of the region.

154 **Histoire de Chicoutimi.** (A history of Chicoutimi.)
   Russel Bouchard.   Chicoutimi-Nord, Québec: R. Bouchard, 1992.
   241p. maps.

Chicoutimi, the regional capital of the Saguenay region, was the 19th century wonder-city that never materialized. This book deals with the period from Chicoutimi's first settlers to its incorporation in 1893 (the year when it was granted its Charter from the provincial government). The author focuses mainly on the economic and spatial developments in Chicoutimi. If the book neglects the external elements that limited the development of Chicoutimi, the author nonetheless shows how the different elites of the city managed to collectively control the population in their own interests. The book includes maps and pictures that illustrate the rapid development of the city. See also the same author's *Histoire de Chicoutimi-Nord* (A history of Chicoutimi-Nord), which focuses on the 20th century.

155 **Les origines de Montréal.** (The origins of Montréal.)
   Edited by Jean-Rémi Brault.   Montréal: Leméac, 1993. 282p.

Comprises the proceedings of a symposium held by the Montréal Historical Society on the early history of the city. The majority of the texts focus on various aspects of the city's early religious history, leaders and institutions.

156 **Sources de l'histoire du Saguenay-Lac-Saint-Jean: inventaire des archives paroissiales.** (Historical sources of the
   Saguenay-Lac-Saint-Jean region: inventory of parish archives.)
   André Côté.   Québec: Ministère des Affaires culturelles, 1977. vol. 1.
   329p.

An inventory of the religious and civil records of the parishes in the diocese of Chicoutimi. In addition to its intrinsic value, the inventory also enables the reader to examine the evolution of religious, state and judicial institutions which have existed since the middle of the 17th century in this region. Introductory essays on the nature of religious law and the nature of Catholic registers provide the necessary historical context within which early records were kept.

157 **Montréal, 1642-1992.** (Montréal, 1642-1992.)
   Edited by Jean-Pierre Duquette.   Montréal: Éditions Hurtubise HMH,
   1992. 162p. (Les Cahiers du Québec, Collection Album, no. 104).

Written on the occasion of Montréal's 350th anniversary, this collection of essays focuses on the cultural history of the city. The different contributors study both the situation and place of various art forms in Montréal. The artistic domains studied are cinema, music, literature, theatre and visual art.

158 **Histoire du Bas-Saint-Laurent.** (A history of the Lower
   Saint-Lawrence.)
   Jean-Charles Fortin, Antonio Lechasseur.   Québec: Institut québécois
   de Recherche sur la Culture, 1993. 860p.

A historical synthesis of the Lower Saint-Laurence, a region located between Côte-du-Sud and the Gaspé. This book explains the economic and demographic forces which have given rise to the present-day character of the region. See also *Revue d'Histoire du Bas Saint-Laurent* (Journal of the History of the Lower Saint-Lawrence) (Rimouski, Québec: Société d'Histoire du Bas-Saint-Laurent, 1973- . quarterly) for research on this region.

159 **Histoire de l'Outaouais.** (A history of the Outaouais.)
Edited by Chad Gaffield. Québec: Institut québécois de Recherche sur la Culture, 1994. 876p. (Les Régions du Québec, no. 6).

Part of the regional history series published by the IQRC. The Outaouais region is presented as being 'caught between two worlds' in an attempt to reveal the complex evolution of the region beyond its import to the fur trade or the lumber industry. Divided into four chronological sections, this book reveals a pattern of development which is neither monolithic or simple, thanks in part to balanced research. Instead of focusing solely on those elites and external forces which have traditionally been held responsible for the shape of the Outaouais, this work places equal emphasis on those groups often forgotten by previous histories: the working class, women, native peoples, and ethnic groups.

160 **Histoire du Saguenay Lac-Saint-Jean.** (A history of the Saguenay Lac-Saint-Jean region.)
Camil Girard, Normand Perron. Québec: Institut québécois de Recherche sur la Culture, 1989. 665p. bibliog.

Tracing the development of demographic and economic trends, the authors explain not only the history of the region, but also what forces created the region. The authors emphasize the role of industry and economic development in writing this history and its impact on the institutions and culture of the region. An impressive bibliography and the completeness of this history make this work invaluable as an introduction to the region.

161 **Histoire de la ville de Québec 1608-1871.** (A history of Québec City – 1608-1871.)
John Hare, Marc Lafrance, David-Thiery Ruddel. Montréal: Éditions du Boréal, 1987. 400p.

Provides a socio-economic history of Québec City from its origins in the 1600s to its decline as a major Canadian and North American city in the late 1800s. The book provides an urban biography of the city, examining economic and demographic trends in an attempt to explain the development of the countryside, the community and the city's institutions. See also Danielle Gauvreau's *Québec. Une ville et sa population au temps de la Nouvelle-France* (Québec. A city and its population during the French colonial period) (Sillery, Québec: Presses de l'Université du Québec, 1991. 232p.), which provides a well-researched demographic study of the city.

162 **The history of James Bay: 1610-1686.**
Walter Andrew Kenyon. Toronto: Royal Ontario Museum, 1986. 153p.

Richly illustrated, this book presents an impressive archaeological inventory of the European discovery and exploration of James Bay, 1610-86. The major sites examined are Charleston Island and Fort Albany.

163 **Histoire de la Côte-du-Sud.** (A history of the South Shore.)
Edited by Alain Laberge. Québec: Institut québécois de Recherche
sur la Culture, 1993. 644p. (Les Régions du Québec, no. 4).
Settled in the last quarter of the 17th century, the Côte-du-Sud occupies the southern
shore of the Saint-Lawrence River to the east of Québec City. This book resuscitates
the distinctiveness of an often forgotten, but historically important, region by
examining the economic and social forces which exerted assimilatory pressures on the
Côte-du-Sud. The book is divided into three sections corresponding to the different
phases of economic and social development of the Côte-du-Sud. A history of the
North Shore is contained in Pierre Frenette's *Histoire de la Côte-Nord* (A history of
the North Shore) (Québec: Institut québécois de Recherche sur la Culture, 1996. 667p.
Les Régions du Québec, no. 9).

164 **Baie James: une épopée.** (James Bay: an epic.)
Roger Lacasse. Montréal: Éditions Libre Expression, 1983. 655p.
bibliog.
A narrative history of the James Bay La Grande hydro-electric development project
(1971-84). Written by a former journalist, this work goes beyond a political history to
describe the experiences of the 100,000 Quebecers who moved to the construction
sites. Lacasse also describes the major problems that faced the project, including the temporary halt to construction following a court case over aboriginal rights in the area.
Spanning over a decade, the La Grande project was one of the largest in the world at
the time and constitutes an important chapter in Québec's history and psyche.

165 **La vie quotidienne des premiers colons en Abitibi-Témiscamingue.**
(Daily life of the colonists in Abitibi-Témiscamingue.)
Normand Lafleur, Donat Martineau, Alice Descoteaux. Montréal:
Leméac, 1976. 197p.
Provides a history of the region from the perspective of those who colonized it and
lived there. Based on personal interviews, the authors have recreated the history of the
first colonists who settled in the Abitibi-Témiscamingue. While the reliance on memory might taint the objectivity of this history, the book is an invaluable resource for
understanding daily life based on first-hand knowledge.

166 **Histoire des Laurentides.** (A history of the Laurentians.)
Serge Laurin. Québec: Institut québécois de Recherche sur la
Culture, 1989. 892p. bibliog. (Les Régions du Québec, no. 3).
A wide-ranging synthesis of the region's history. Comprehensive and well researched,
this work is ideal for the reader interested in the history of the Laurentians, a region to
the north of Montréal. A solid bibliography will direct readers to additional sources.

167 **Histoire de Montréal depuis la Confédération.** (A history of
Montréal since Confederation.)
Paul-André Linteau. Montréal: Éditions du Boréal Express, 1992.
613p. maps.
The most recent and most complete synthesis of the city's economic, political, cultural
and social history since 1867. Linteau, a renowned historian, focuses on the role of

44

Montréal as a crossroads, its industrial structure and metropolitan functions, as well as inter-ethnic relations in the city. Change and continuity between the subjects of each of the book's sections is emphasized.

168　**Maisonneuve: comment les promoteurs fabriquent une ville, 1883-1918.** (Maisonneuve: how promoters build a city, 1883-1918.)
Paul-André Linteau.　Montréal: Éditions du Boréal Express, 1981.
280p. bibliog.

Examines the development of Maisonneuve from a peaceful rural village into a premier industrial centre in Canada. Using Maisonneuve as an example, Linteau reveals the existence of a developed francophone land-owning bourgeoisie with its own distinctive capitalist strategies. Concomitant with the city's economic growth came many embellishments: imposing public buildings; spacious boulevards; and vast recreational parks. The author examines Maisonneuve's promoters and institutional structures, ending his study with the city's annexation to Montréal in 1918. This is a detailed work of urban history containing excellent illustrations.

169　**State and society in transition. The politics of institutional reform in the Eastern Townships, 1838-1852.**
John Irvine Little.　Montréal; Kingston, Ontario: McGill-Queen's University Press, 1997. 320p.

Demonstrates the existence of a dialectical relationship between state and society in the development of educational, legal, social and municipal institutions in the Eastern Townships following the end of the 1837-38 rebellions. Using a variety of primary sources such as petitions and letters, Little examines the actions of local communities and suggests that they had an important impact on the way institutional development occurred in the region. In contrast to the centralizing effects of responsible government, this book relates how the government was forced to decentralize many services and institutions to the local level, demonstrating the power exercised by the local population. This is an impressive study of centre-periphery relations which reveals a piece of Québec's history from a local perspective. For a broader examination of state formation in Upper and Lower Canada during the 19th century, see Allan Greer and Ian Radforth's *Colonial Leviathan: state formation in mid-nineteenth century Canada* (Toronto: University of Toronto Press, 1992. 328p.).

170　**Les Abitibis.** (The Abitibis.)
Roger Marois, Pierre Gauthier.　Hull, Québec: Musée canadien des Civilisations, 1989. 253p. maps.

An examination and analysis of material collected at Lake Abitibi between 1970 and 1976. This book suggests that primitive Laurentian people were the first to discover this land which still bears their name. Based on consistent changes in their dwellings and the gradual change in their use of tools, this study also suggests that there existed a distinct Abitibian tradition. This book is an exercise in archaeological methodology as it seeks scientific means to classify and distinguish various objects.

171 **Histoire de l'Abitibi-Témiscamingue.** (A history of
Abitibi-Témiscamingue.)
Normand Paquin. Rouyn, Québec: Collège du Nord-Ouest, 1981.
172p.

A general and accessibly written history of the Abitibi-Témiscamingue region. This
work begins by examining the region's history as a fur-trading zone, and then charts
its evolution through various stages of industrial development: from rural development in the 1880s to the creation of the mining industry after the turn of the century.

172 **Montréal: a history.**
Robert Prévost, translated by Elizabeth Mueller, Robert Chabos.
Toronto: McClelland & Stewart, 1993. 416p.

A popular and readable account – with excellent illustrations – of the city's history
from the founding of Ville-Marie (Montréal's predecessor) by de Maisonneuve in
1642 to the early 1990s. Other relevant studies are: John Irwin Cooper's *Montréal: a
brief history* (Montréal; Kingston, Ontario: McGill-Queen's University Press, 1969.
217p.); and Marcelle Brisson and Suzanne Côté-Gauthier's *Montréal de vive mémoire*
(Montréal in living memory) (Montréal: Éditions Triptyque, 1994. 340p.), which
records the oral history of Montréal and its neighbourhoods between 1900 and 1939.

173 **Histoire de Montréal.** (A history of Montréal.)
Robert Rumilly. Montréal: Fides, 1970-74. 2 vols.

Written by one of Québec's most well-known historians, this book begins Montréal's
history with Jacques Cartier, who was the first visitor to the site of Montréal in 1535.
Rumilly focuses mostly on the leaders and popular figures of Montréal.

174 **Saguenayensia.**
Chicoutimi, Québec: Société historique du Saguenay, 1959- . 3 issues
per year.

A regional publication focusing on issues of relevance to the Saguenay, its people,
geography, industry and economy. It is published by the Historical Society of the
Saguenay.

175 **L'Outaouais québécois: guide de recherche bibliographique.**
(The Outaouais: a bibliographical research guide.)
Jean-Pierre F. St-Amour. Hull, Québec: Université du Québec,
Centre d'Études universitaires dans l'Ouest québécois, 1978. 178p.

This work classifies 1,315 titles into 5 general thematic chapters covering: general
aspects; physical characteristics; the economy; the management of the region; and the
human world. An introductory chapter provides interesting information on the region.
Also provided is a short bibliographical guide to the region of Outaouais, which is
located on the border of Québec and Ontario. The main part of the work lists a series
of books or publications that cover five main themes: the history of the region; the
physical environment; the human environment the economy of the region; and the
management of the environment. An index is also included.

176   **Histoire de Lévis-Lotbinière.** (A history of Lévis-Lotbinière.)
       Edited by Roch Samson.   Québec: Institut québécois de Recherche
       sur la Culture, 1996. 816p. maps. (Les Régions du Québec, no. 8).
Located on the southern shore of the Saint-Lawrence River near Québec City, the
region of Lévis-Lotbinière has often been neglected by historians. This major work
attempts to correct this error by presenting a detailed history of the region. In examining the evolution of Lévis-Lotbinière, the authors focus on the economic and social
impact of neighbouring regions, distinguishing their work from other regional studies
which focus exclusively on the region in question. The book also discusses the
emergence and development of a distinct regional identity. Maps and pictures are
included.

177   **Histoire de l'Abitibi-Témiscamingue.** (A history of the
       Abitibi-Témiscamingue.)
       Edited by Odette Vincent.   Québec: Institut québécois de Recherche
       sur la Culture, 1996. 763p. (Les Régions du Québec, no. 7).
One of the most recently colonized regions of Québec, the Abitibi-Témiscamingue is
well known for its abundance of precious metals and the tenacity of its population.
The authors demonstrate the importance natural resources had on the demographic and
economic development of the region. The book also provides a good analysis of how
the region gradually became part of the Québec collective imagination.

Biography

Reference

178 **Biographies canadiennes-françaises.** (French Canadian biographies.)
Montréal: Éditions biographiques canadiennes-françaises, 1920-85.
annual.

Similar to the Canadian 'Who's who' guide, this publication lists prominent French
Canadians alongside brief biographies of directorships and achievements. This annual
work ceased publication in 1985.

179 **Dictionary of Canadian biography.**
Toronto: University of Toronto Press, 1966- . bibliog.

An ongoing project of scholarship whose purpose is to provide brief biographical
articles on Canadians up to and including the 19th century. Articles vary in length but
provide basic contextual information as well as useful cross-references to other entries
in other volumes. Overall, these volumes will be of use to anyone interested in Québec
history by providing concise biographical information.

General

180 **J.-Louis Lévesque. La montée d'un Gaspésien aux sommets des
affaires.** (The rise of a Gaspésien to the summit of the business world.)
Jules Bélanger.   Montréal: Éditions Fides, 1996. 310p.

Born in 1911, J.-L. Lévesque was one of the first francophones to reach the pinnacle
of the Canadian business world which was, at the time, the exclusive domain of

English-speaking Canadians. Born into moderate means in the Gaspé, Lévesque moved to Montréal and built a financial empire which is still expanding today. He founded one of Québec's largest brokerage houses, Lévesque Beaubien (now Lévesque Beaubien Geoffrion). This biography tells his story from his birth in Nouvelle to his death in Montréal in 1994. Aside from his financial exploits, this book also reveals Lévesque's pastimes and his philanthropic activities.

181 **Lire Étienne Parent, 1802-1874: notre premier intellectuel.**
     (A reading of Étienne Parent, 1802-74: our foremost intellectual.)
     Gérard Bergeron.   Sainte-Foy, Québec: Presses de l'Université Laval,
     1994. 300p.

The author describes Étienne Parent as the most important French Canadian thinker of the 19th century. Born in Beauport, Québec, Parent worked as a journalist for *Le Canadien* between 1822 and 1842. This book focuses on Parent's economic, social, and religious ideas. His works can be sampled in *Étienne Parent, 1802-1874: textes choisis et présentés* (Étienne Parent, 1802-74: selected texts) (Montréal: Fides, 1964. 344p.).

182 **Lire François-Xavier Garneau, 1809-1866: historien national.**
     (A reading of François-Xavier Garneau, 1809-66: national historian.)
     Gérard Bergeron.   Québec: Institut québécois de Recherche sur la
     Culture, 1994. 237p.

As one of French-speaking Canada's first poets and historians, Garneau was instrumental in giving voice to a new form of literature in Canada. His writing is marked by anticlericalism and strong support of French Canadian nationalism. This is a biography of his life and an analysis of his work. Readers can sample Garneau in *Histoire du Canada depuis sa découverte jusqu'a 1840* (A history of Canada from its discovery until 1840) (Montréal: Bibliothèque québécoise, 1995. 244p.).

183 **Duplessis.**
     Conrad Black.   Toronto: McClelland and Stewart, 1977. 743p.
     bibliog.

An accessible and epic biography of Maurice Duplessis, Premier of Québec from 1936 to 1939 and 1944 to 1959. Duplessis has been described variously as a dictator, a conservative nationalist and a staunch protector of Québec interests. As Black writes, Duplessis was a paradoxical figure, 'gregarious and aloof, generous and cruel, all-forgiving and vindictive, a fanatical upholder of Parliament and the courts and the rule of law who did not hesitate to bend them to his own purposes'. For a more eulogistic biography of the former premier, see Robert Rumilly's *Maurice Duplessis et son temps* (Maurice Duplessis and his times) (Montréal: Fides, 1978. 2 vols.). For a balanced account see Alain-G. Gagnon and Michel Sarra-Bournet's *Duplessis: entre la grande noirceur et la société libérale* (Duplessis: between the darkness and a liberal society) (Montréal: Éditions Québec Amérique, 1997. 397p.).

184 **Stanley Bréhaut Ryerson, un intellectuel de combat.** (Stanley Bréhaut Ryerson, an engaged intellectual.) Edited by Robert Comeau, Robert Tremblay. Hull, Québec: Vents d'Ouest, 1996. 426p. bibliog. (Collection Asticou/Histoire des Idées Politiques).

Ryerson has been acclaimed as one of Canada's most important Marxist historians and political activists. Moreover, his academic work testifies to an openness towards the national question in Québec. Since Ryerson's political activism cannot be separated from his intellectual pursuits, the first section of this collection comprises essays on Ryerson's personal life. The following sections discuss the important themes in Ryerson's many publications: the national question; class and democracy; and Confederation. The final section reveals Ryerson's prominent place in Québec and Canada's historiography. A comprehensive bibliography of Ryerson's articles and books is included.

185 **Jeanne Mance: de Langres à Montréal, la passion de soigner.** (Jeanne Mance: from Langres to Montréal, a passion for healing.) Françoise Deroy-Pineau. Saint-Laurent, Québec: Bellarmin, 1995. 167p. bibliog.

A concise and accessible biography of Jeanne Mance (1606-73), founder of the Hôtel-Dieu Hospital of Montréal in 1659, the oldest hospital in the city. Jeanne Mance was one of the co-founders, with de Maisonneuve, of Ville-Marie (the predecessor of Montréal) in 1642.

186 **The politics of imagination. A life of F. R. Scott.** Sandra Djwa. Toronto: McClelland and Stewart, 1987. 528p.

An excellent authorized biography of one of Canada's most influential intellectuals. Djwa, chosen by Scott himself to write his biography, brings to life the man whose life 'in broad outline contains much of what we recognize as central to the Canadian experience'. Aside from Scott's contribution to the construction of a distinct 'Canadian nation', what is most remarkable about this poet, constitutional lawyer and political activist is that no other English-speaking Canadian has had such a profound impact on Québec. While this biography emphasizes Scott's diverse impact on Canadian and Québec society, Djwa focuses on his constant concern for the creation of a Canadian culture, a Canadian legal order, and a Canadian social order.

187 **James McGill of Montréal.** Stanley Brice Frost. Montréal; Kingston, Ontario: McGill-Queen's University Press, 1995. 186p.

This recent and accessible biography of James McGill (1744-1813) focuses on the contributions he made to the development of Canada, Québec and Montréal. Frost traces his roots as a young adventurer to the famous bequest that facilitated the creation of McGill University. James McGill was an important trader and business figure in Montréal.

188 **Honoré Mercier. La politique et la culture.** (Honoré Mercier.
Politics and culture.)
Gilles Gallichan. Sillery, Québec: Éditions du Septentrion, 1994.
212p.

Focuses on the political career of Honoré Mercier (1840-94) and the legislative action
he undertook as Liberal Premier of Québec (1887-91) in the jurisdictions of education
and culture. A fervent defender of provincial rights, Mercier considered these two
areas of public policy of paramount importance to democracy and the key to social
progress. Gallichan also examines the relationship between the state and the publishing
industry. This book demonstrates the direct and fervent activity of the government in
cultural, educational and publishing affairs and identifies one of the first attempts of
the Québec government to define a cultural policy.

189 **Daniel Johnson.**
Pierre Godin. Montréal: Éditions de l'Homme, 1980. 2 vols.

A comprehensive two-volume history of Daniel Johnson, Premier of Québec between
1966 and 1968, with a focus on his years in politics. The first volume, subtitled 'La
passion du pouvoir' (The passion of power), covers the years 1946 to 1964. The
second volume, called 'La difficile recherche de l'égalité' (The difficult search for
equality), examines his political leadership from 1964 to 1968. Daniel Johnson coined
the popular political slogan, 'Egalité ou indépendance' (Equality or independence),
which symbolized the frustration of many Quebecers with Ottawa and which signalled
the ascendance of national spirit in Québec.

190 **Les frères divorcés.** (The divorced brothers.)
Pierre Godin. Montréal: Éditions de l'Homme, 1986. 360p.

In a quick-paced and engaging narrative, Godin describes the crumbling of the Quiet
Revolution consensus of the 1960s and the genesis of the sovereignty-association
movement as symbolized by the ideological conflict between René Lévesque and
Robert Bourassa, two politicians who would be instrumental in Québec's development
during the 1970s and 1980s. Lévesque, one of the architects of the Quiet Revolution
with Jean Lesage's PLQ (Parti libéral du Québec), quit the party in 1967 and formed the
Mouvement souveraineté-association (Sovereignty-association Movement). Moreover,
this rupture signalled the beginning of an important realignment in Québec's party
system. Godin describes Lévesque's departure and Bourassa's ascendance in the PLQ
in a detailed account of the power relations within the party, all of which reveal the
more fundamental social and economic changes that were sweeping through Québec.
The book is written in captivating and accessible prose.

191 **René Lévesque.**
Pierre Godin. Montréal: Éditions du Boréal, 1994- . 3 vols.

The first exhaustive and complete biography of former Québec premier (1976-85) and
Parti québécois leader, René Lévesque, from his childhood until the end of his political
career. Examining both the private and the public aspects of his life, Godin reveals the
myth behind the cult of a political hero. Godin's research into his private life reveals
the man few people knew, the formation of his humanist and democratic ideology, and
the political life of a man whose impact on Québec is hardly measured by the nine
years he was premier. This is an excellent work for anyone who wants to gain an
understanding of one of Québec's most important politicians.

192 **Morgentaler, l'obstiné.** (Morgentaler, the stubborn one.)
Sylvie Halpern. Montréal: Éditions du Boréal, 1992. 203p. bibliog.

Canada is the only Western country without a law on abortion. This can be partly attributed to Henry Morgentaler, a Montréal doctor who started and continues the battle for abortion rights. This is a personal biography of Henry Morgentaler which is sensitive to Morgentaler's place in Québec. Halpern claims that it was post-Quiet-Revolution Québec which provided the necessary freedom for Morgentaler's initial crusade to legalize abortion in Canada.

193 **André Laurendeau. French-Canadian nationalist 1912-1968.**
Donald J. Horton. Toronto: Oxford University Press, 1992. 261p.

Known in Québec as a political journalist for *Le Devoir*, English-speaking Canadians really became aware of André Laurendeau (1912-68) when he assumed the position of co-chair of the Royal Commission on Bilingualism and Biculturalism. In this first English-language biography of Laurendeau, Horton delves into his political activity prior to his involvement with the Royal Commission. Horton examines: Laurendeau's nationalist tradition; the impact of personalism on his thought; his involvement with the periodical – and political movement – *Action Nationale*; his role in the conscription crisis of 1942 and founding of the political party, Bloc populaire, that same year; and his intellectual battle against Duplessis and French Canadian conservatism. This book is a solid presentation of the formative events in the making of a man English-speaking Canadians only knew at the end of his career.

194 **Souvenances.** (Memories.)
Georges-Henri Lévesque. Montréal: Éditions La Presse, 1983. 3 vols.

Ordained into the priesthood in 1928, Lévesque founded the Faculty of Social Sciences at Laval University in 1943. This institution was one of the key actors in the post-war ideological contestation of clerical hegemony. Structured as a series of interviews, these three volumes relate this period of contestation in a narrative manner, but nonetheless capture the essence of the changes well. One of Lévesque's former students, Robert Parise, wrote a brief biography of Lévesque entitled *Georges-Henri Lévesque, père de la renaissance québécoise* (Georges-Henri Lévesque, father of the Québec renaissance) (Montréal: Éditions internationales Alain Stanké, 1976. unpaginated). André-J. Bélanger's *Ruptures et constantes: quatre idéologies du Québec en éclatement: la Relève, La JEC, Cité libre, Parti pris* (see item no. 517), is an excellent description of the post-war ideological movements.

195 **René Lévesque. Memoirs.**
René Lévesque, translated by Philip Stratford. Toronto: McClelland and Stewart, 1986. 377p.

The engaging recollections of one of Québec's foremost political figures of the post-Second World War era. As leader of the Parti québécois and Premier of Québec between 1976 and 1985, Lévesque brought legitimacy and vigour to the independence movement. These memoirs, published shortly before Lévesque's death in 1987, provide a vivid image of his personality and ideas.

196   **Henri Bourassa and the golden calf: the social program of the nationalists of Quebec, 1900-1914.**
Joseph Levitt.   Ottawa: Presses de l'Université d'Ottawa, 1972. 2nd ed. 178p. bibliog.

Henri Bourassa (1868-1952), journalist and statesman, was one of the foremost defenders of both French Canadian nationalism and Canadian independence from Great Britain. This work examines Bourassa's view of industrialization in an effort to demystify traditional interpretations of Bourassa as a social conservative. Levitt believes that Bourassa accepted large-scale industrialism while making serious efforts to reform it. A classic work that examines Bourassa's life and thought more broadly is Robert Rumilly's *Henri Bourassa: la vie publique d'un grand Canadien* (Henri Bourassa: the public life of a great Canadian) (Montréal: Éditions Chantecler, 1953. 791p.). See also *Henri Bourassa* by André Bergevin (Montréal: Éditions de l'ACF, 1966. 150p.).

197   **Marie Gérin-Lajoie: de mère en fille, la cause des femmes.**
(Marie Gérin-Lajoie: from mother to daughter, the feminist cause.)
Hélène Pelletier-Baillargeon.   Montréal: Éditions du Boréal Express, 1985. 382p.

The daughter of an enlightened liberal Catholic family, Marie Gérin-Lajoie was the first French Canadian woman to receive a university degree. She was subsequently involved in the promotion of women's education. She also founded the Institut Notre-Dame du Bon-Conseil (Notre-Dame Institute of Good Advice), a religious group dedicated to social action. This book is the first major biography of this incredible woman and constitutes an important addition to the historical work on the relationship between the feminist movement and Catholicism during the late 19th and early 20th centuries.

198   **Olivar Asselin.**
Hélène Pelletier-Baillargeon.   Montréal: Fides, 1996- . 2 vols.

Olivar Asselin (1874-1937) was one of the most important journalists of his generation. In contrast to Henri Bourassa, one of Asselin's contemporaries, he was a progressive nationalist who was extremely concerned with social issues. The first volume deals with the period ending with Asselin's enrolment in the Canadian army, a gesture that represents well the ambiguous nature of the man who had earlier fought against conscription. The book presents the life of an important progressive nationalist visionary, and provides a good overview of the tensions that rocked the conscience of many nationalists who were divided between their attachment to Canada, the Church and the mother nation, France. For more on Asselin's thought, see his *Liberté de pensée. Choix de textes politiques et littéraires* (Freedom of thought. Selected political and literary texts) (Montréal: Éditions Typo, 1997. 150p.).

199   **Honoré Mercier et son temps.** (Honoré Mercier and his times.)
Robert Rumilly.   Montréal: Fides, 1975. 2 vols.

The most thorough examination of the life and career of Honoré Mercier (1840-94), Québec's Liberal Premier between 1887 and 1891 and staunch defender of provincial rights. The first volume encompasses the years between 1840 and 1888; the second volume those between 1888 and 1894. For an analysis of Mercier's policies in the fields of education and culture, see Gilles Gallichan's *Honoré Mercier. La politique et la culture* (see item no. 188). For a broader assessment of Mercier's political ideology, see Pierre Charbonneau's *Le projet québécois d'Honoré Mercier* (Honoré Mercier's Québec project) (Saint-Jean-Sur-Richelieu, Québec: Éditions Milles Roches, 1980. 254p.).

200 **Gratien Gélinas. La ferveur et le doute.** (Gratien Gélinas. The ardour and the doubt.)
Anne-Marie Sicotte. Montréal: Éditions Québec Amérique, 1995. 2 vols.

The writer and actor Gratien Gélinas is considered to be the father of Québec theatre. The immensely popular characters he created on stage such as Fridolin, a rebellious youth from an average Montréal neighbourhood, and Tit-Coq, an illegitimate child in search of an identity, are among the first landmarks of a distinctly Québec theatre scene. Based in part on interviews with family members, this biography not only charts the emergence of Québec theatre, but also presents a very personal history of Gélinas himself. A book reproducing a series of interviews with Gratien Gélinas originally broadcast on national radio and entitled *Gratien, Tit-Coq, Fridolin, Bousille et les justes* (Gratien, Tit-Coq, Fridolin, Bousille and the righteous ones) (Montréal: Stanké, 1993. 190p.), is also of interest.

201 **The diary of André Laurendeau written during the Royal Commission on Bilingualism and Biculturalism, 1964-1967.**
Edited by Patricia Smart, Dorothy Howard. Toronto: James Lorimer & Co., 1991. 171p.

André Laurendeau (1912-68) remains one of Québec and Canada's most influential intellectuals. A determined neo-nationalist of the 1950s, Laurendeau nevertheless fought for Canadian federalism, albeit in a modified form. He is best known as the co-chair of the Royal Commission on Bilingualism and Biculturalism. His diary is an informal collection of thoughts on the people and events he met and experienced while travelling throughout Canada. Together, these memoirs reveal the way French-speaking Canada felt towards English-speaking Canada in the 1960s and vice versa.

202 **André Laurendeau: witness for Quebec.**
Edited and translated by Philip Stratford. Toronto: Macmillan Canada, 1973. 280p.

As publicist, politician, novelist, journalist and royal commissioner, André Laurendeau (1912-68) argued continuously for social reform, provincial autonomy for Québec and genuine federalism within Canada. This work includes a translation of his book on the conscription crisis of the Second World War, entitled *La crise de la conscription, 1942* (The conscription crisis, 1942) (Montréal: Éditions du Jour, 1962. 158p.). It also includes articles published in *Le Magazine Maclean* (Maclean Magazine), and in *Le Devoir*, of which he was editor during the post-war years. See also *The essential Laurendeau*, edited by Ramsay Cook and Michael Behiels (Toronto: Copp Clark Publishing, 1976. 256p.) which includes a collection of writings that span his entire life, from his membership in the *Action Nationale* in 1933 to his co-chairmanship of the influential Bilingualism and Biculturalism Commission during the 1960s.

203 **Quebec before Duplessis: the political career of Louis-Alexandre Taschereau.**
Bernard L. Vigod. Montréal; Kingston, Ontario: McGill-Queen's University Press, 1986. 312p. bibliog.
A study of Louis-Alexandre Taschereau, Premier of Québec between 1920 and 1936. The author describes Taschereau's coherent vision of French Canadian society; one which encompassed material progress and rejected the isolationism and conservatism of the traditional nationalist and ultramontane intellectuals. Indeed, Taschereau emerged as the pre-eminent champion of industrial development in early 20th-century Québec through his encouragement of private, typically non-French Canadian entrepreneurs. Overall, this work constitutes a sympathetic analysis of Taschereau, concentrating mostly on his years in office. Another work which focuses on issues involving the Church is Antonin Dupont's *Taschereau* (Montréal: Guérin Éditeur, 1997. 366p.).

204 **George-Étienne Cartier: Montreal bourgeois.**
Brian Young. Montréal; Kingston, Ontario: McGill-Queen's University Press, 1981. 181p. maps.
The author eschews traditional accounts of George-Étienne Cartier (1814-73), which focus on Cartier's role as national leader and a father of the Canadian Confederation, in favour of a socio-economic and social analysis of this figure. Young focuses on Cartier's role as spokesman for the Montréal bourgeoisie and how he influenced Québec's landholding, legal, business and educational institutions. This book emphasizes Cartier's activities as a corporate lawyer, company director, landlord and railway promoter more than his position as French-speaking Canada's most prominent politician. The study of Québec's petit bourgeoisie is further articulated in George Bervin's *Québec au XIXe siècle. L'activité économique des grands marchands* (Québec during the 19th century. The economic activity of powerful merchants) (Sillery, Québec: Éditions du Septentrion, 1991. 290p.).

Religion

205 **The Church in Quebec.**
Gregory Baum. Montréal: Novalis, 1991. 184p.
The author begins by tracing the secularization of Québec society during the 1960s.
Though little attention is paid to the Church in Québec before this time, a considerable
amount of space is devoted to the Christian socialists of the 1970s, namely Jacques
Grand'Maison and Douglas Hall. The final two chapters examine the ethical
dimensions of both the language debate and the separatist movement in Québec. For
histories of various religious communities which cover the period prior to 1960, see
the following: Huguette Lapointe-Roy's *Charité bien ordonnée* (Orderly charity)
(Montréal: Éditions du Boréal, 1987. 330p.) which discusses the Grey Sisters, the
Sulpicians and the Sisters of Providence; Giselle Huot's *Une femme au séminaire:
Marie de la Charité, 1852-1920, fondatrice de la première communauté dominicaine
du Canada* (A women in the seminary: Mary of the Charity, 1852-1920, foundress of
the first Dominican community in Canada) (Montréal: Bellarmin, 1987. 525p.); and
Jean Hamelin's *Les Franciscains au Canada, 1890-1990* (The Franciscans in Canada,
1890-1990) (Sillery, Québec: Éditions du Septentrion, 1990. 438p.).

206 **Taking the veil: an alternative to marriage, motherhood, and
spinsterhood in Québec, 1840-1920.**
Marta Danylewycz. Toronto: McClelland and Stewart, 1987. 203p.
(Canadian Social History Series).
A fascinating study of the relationship between the women who joined religious
orders and the rise of feminism at the turn of the 20th century. This book reveals the
strength of the women's faith and resolve in addition to 'the uniqueness of the Québec
nuns' experience'. It focuses on two religious communities based in Montréal: the
Sisters of the Congregation of Notre-Dame and the Misericordia Sisters. In the first
two chapters, the author discusses the social, economic and religious factors that led to
a dramatic increase in the membership of these religious communities. The structural
changes that took place are linked to the changes and transformations of society at
large. The following two chapters look at changes within the convents and, finally, the

last chapter examines the increasing interest lay women manifested towards improving their situation and playing a more active role in society.

207 **Histoire du catholicisme québécois: le XXe siècle.** (A history of Québec Catholicism: the 20th century.)
Jean Hamelin, Nicole Gagnon. Montréal: Éditions du Boréal Express, 1984. 2 vols.

A two-volume study of Catholicism from 1898 to the 1980s. The study begins with Pope Leo XIII's new Christian project which emphasized the social role of the Church. This study is limited exclusively to Catholicism and is, by far, one of the best institutional studies of the Church's development.

208 **Religion populaire au Québec. Typologie des sources, bibliographie sélective, 1900-1980.** (Popular religion in Québec. Typology of selective bibliographical sources, 1900-80.)
Benoît Lacroix, Madeleine Grammond. Québec: Institut québécois de Recherche sur la Culture, 1985. 175p. (Instruments de Travail, no. 10).

A selective bibliography of over 900 items relating to popular religion in Québec between 1900 and 1980. The titles listed focus exclusively on the French Canadian population thereby informing the reader about Québec's particular Catholic heritage. The authors have tried to include works which discuss the visual characteristics of Catholicism, such as religious attire and garments, statues, and religious art. Three other categories of sources are included: documents detailing song lyrics and dances; manuscripts; and religious books. Two indexes are included (by author and by subject) which aid in locating works on specific topics.

209 **Les congrégations religieuses de la France au Québec, 1880-1900.** (Religious congregations from France to Québec, 1880-1900.)
Guy Laperrière. Sainte-Foy, Québec: Presses de l'Université Laval, 1995. 228p.

This is the first volume of a study that examines the impact of French secular society on Catholic Québec during the late 19th century. It discusses the impact on Québec society of the 1880 expulsions, the military law of 1889, and school reform, among other events. Of the fifty religious orders in Québec, the majority came from France between 1880 and 1914. Given the predominance of the Church during this period of Québec's history, this book explains the sudden influx of religious orders in addition to discussing the circumstances in which they found themselves once they arrived and how they adapted. Another relevant study is René Hardy's *Les Zouaves: une stratégie du clergé québécois au XIXe siècle* (The Zouaves: a strategy of the Québec clergy during the 19th century) (Montréal: Éditions du Boréal Express, 1980. 312p.). The latter analyses the *Zouaves* movement as a religious strategy whose goal was to implement its particular societal project.

210 **L'établissement de la première province ecclésiastique au Canada.**
(The establishment of the first ecclesiastic province in Canada.)
Lucien Lemieux.   Montréal: Fides, 1968. 559p.

An institutional and political history of the struggle to consolidate the Catholic Church in Québec and British North America. Following multiple battles with the state and other Churches, and racked by internal division arising from ethnic tensions, the establishment and the growth of a Catholic administrative hierarchy was consolidated following the Act of Union in 1840. Lemieux describes this transformation, the actors involved and the factors behind this consolidation.

211 **Histoire du catholicisme québécois: les XVIIIe et XIXe siècles.**
(A history of Québec Catholicism: the 18th and 19th centuries.)
Lucien Lemieux.   Montréal: Éditions du Boréal, 1984. 2 vols.

The author describes Roman Catholicism as the second 'empire' which dominated Québec, in tandem with the British Empire, during the 18th and 19th centuries. Highlighting the political and social power of the Church, this book chronicles the ascendance of the conservative ultramontane ideology. The author suggests that Catholicism was the central reference point for French Canadian society, defining and organizing the way of life in Québec by virtue of its dominance over parish life, educational institutions and the provision of social services. Further information on ultramontanism is readily available in Nive Voisine and Jean Hamelin's *Les ultramontains canadiens-français* (The French Canadian ultramontanes) (Montréal: Éditions du Boréal, 1985. 347p.). Also of interest are: Pierre Savard's *Aspects du catholicisme canadien-français au XIXe siècle* (Aspects of French Canadian Catholicism during the 19th century) (Montréal: Fides, 1980. 196p.); and Nadia Fahmy-Eid's *Le clergé et le pouvoir politique au Québec* (The clergy and political power in Québec) (LaSalle, Québec: Éditions Hurtubise HMH, 1978. 318p.).

212 **Mystic in the New World. Marie de l'Incarnation, 1599-1672.**
Anya Mali.   New York: E. J. Brill, 1996. 190p.

Demonstrates the impact of the New World on the thinking of early missionaries to New France. Confronted by a completely new environment, missionaries were required to pursue 'rational experimentation', combining a respect for their traditions while being 'flexible in their pursuit of knowledge'. According to the author, this yielded new expressions of spirituality in contrast to the prevailing trends in Europe. Based on the writings of the Ursuline missionary Marie de l'Incarnation, Mali describes the 'impact of this cultural encounter on the formation of spiritual identity in the colony'. Moreover, Mali illustrates Marie's distinct spiritual relationship which was uncharacteristic of typical French mysticism. John Webster Grant's work, entitled *Moon of wintertime: missionaries and the Indians of Canada in encounter since 1534* (Toronto: University of Toronto Press, 1984. 315p.) is a broader examination of the activities of missionaries and aboriginals' reactions in Canada.

213 **La paroisse lépreuse ou l'affaire Saint-Étienne.** (The leprous parish or the Saint-Étienne affair.)
Pierre Michaud.   Montréal: Presses d'Amérique, 1994. 175p.

The Church in Québec has often been plagued by scandals. This book relates the story of the Saint-Étienne affair, a financial scandal in which a Montréal parish priest used parishioners' money for his own purposes. This work focuses on the cover-up orchestrated at the hands of the Church. Highlighting the parishioners' struggle for justice, the author illustrates the corruption that too frequently prevailed in Québec during the first half of the 20th century.

214   **Le Cardinal Léger: l'évolution de sa pensée, 1950-1967.** (The evolution of Cardinal Léger's thought, 1950-67.)
Denise Robillard.   LaSalle, Québec: Éditions Hurtubise HMH, 1993. 292p.

Bishop of Montréal from 1950 to 1967, Paul-Émile Léger represented a society divided between its attachment to the past and its new, modernized political and social institutions. Based on the Bishop's official statements, the author demonstrates the evolution of his thought from 1950 to his resignation in 1967. She argues that Bishop Léger's incapacity to adapt to new changes in the Church was partly responsible for his resignation. A related work is Micheline Lachance's *Le prince de l'église: le cardinal Léger* (The Church's prince: Cardinal Léger) (Montréal: Éditions de l'Homme, 1982. 427p.).

215   **La paroisse en éclats.** (The parish in fragments.)
Edited by Gilles Routhier.   Outremont, Québec: Novalis, 1995. 275p.

The persistence of parish life, despite predictions to the contrary, comprises the subject of this collection of essays based on the proceedings of the 1994 conference of the Research Group on Pastoral Studies (GREP). These essays testify to the significant changes experienced by the parish institution regarding its membership, how this membership defines itself, and the social role played by this institution in community life. Together these essays reveal a diversity of experiences within what is traditionally regarded as a static religious institution. Moreover, the authors of this collection provide an important launching pad for further research into the changing nature and role of parishes in contemporary, late 20th-century Québec. See also the collection edited by Maurice Comeau, *Prêtre au Québec aujourd'hui* (Priests in contemporary Québec) (Montréal: Fides, 1992. 137p.). Of related interest is Richard Chabot's *Le curé de campagne et la contestation locale au Québec* (The country priest and local contestation in Québec) (LaSalle, Québec: Éditions Hurtubise HMH, 1975. 242p.).

216   **Les religieuses au Québec.** (Nuns in Québec.)
Lucie Rozon, Diane Bélanger.   Montréal: Éditions Libre Expression, 1982. 339p. bibliog.

This book recalls the major events in the establishment of various women's religious communities in Québec between the 17th century and the mid-20th century. Written in engaging prose, the book provides important information on the daily routine of religious women and on the evolution of their role in Québec. The book accords tremendous importance to the mythic portrayal of religious life in Québec. This work is rich with photographs and pictures of sisters and the different installations they helped build. See also Nicole Laurin, Danielle Juteau and Lorraine Duchesne's *À la recherche d'un monde oublié: les communautés religieuses de femmes au Québec de 1900 à 1970* (In search of a forgotten world: women's religious communities in Québec between 1900 and 1970) (Montréal: Éditions le Jour, 1991. 424p.).

217 **Clergy and economic growth in Quebec, 1896-1914.**
William Ryan.   Québec: Presses de l'Université Laval, 1966. 348p.

Ryan focuses on the clergy's role in Québec's economic development, using the Mauricie and the Saguenay-Lac-Saint-Jean regions as his two case-studies. The author presents an excellent overview of economic development during the 19th century illustrated by an original set of indicators. This study is important for its break with the traditional religious historiography which consistently interpreted the Church as a source of ideological reaction. Ryan suggests that several members of the Church were progressive, as demonstrated by their proactive role in local and regional economic development.

218 **L'affaire Roncarelli. Duplessis contre les Témoins de Jéhovah.**
(The Roncarelli Affair. Duplessis versus the Jehovah's Witnesses.)
Michel Sarra-Bournet.   Québec: Institut québécois de Recherche sur la Culture, 1986. 196p.

Roncarelli's thirteen-year-long legal battle against Maurice Duplessis and the Québec Government, culminating with the Supreme Court decision in 1959, remains one of the pivotal struggles in the defence of civil liberties within the province. A member of the Jehovah's Witnesses, Roncarelli – with the help of legal scholar Frank R. Scott – successfully defended the right to practise his religion without interference from the state. This is a well-researched history of the episode.

Population

Reference

219 **La population du Québec: études rétrospectives.** (The population of Québec: retrospective studies.)
Edited by Hubert Charbonneau. Montréal: Éditions du Boréal Express, 1973. 111p.
Comprises the pioneer studies in Québec demography. The introductory essay, by Charbonneau, serves as a useful bibliographic guide to works written before 1973. This book contains many of the first works on such issues as the demographic-linguistic challenges in Montréal, rural exodus, and the demographic changes in Québec society, all of which provide a solid background for contemporary debates. See also Charbonneau's important study of French colonists during the 17th century, entitled *Naissance d'une population. Les français établis au Canada au XVIIe siècle* (Birth of a population. French settlers in Canada during the 17th century) (Montréal: Presses de l'Université de Montréal, 1987. 232p.). Another relevant study is Yves Landry's *Les filles du roi en Nouvelle-France: étude démographique* (Daughters of the King in New France: a demographic study) (Montréal: Leméac, 1992. 434p.). On the important relationship between demography and women, the reader should consult the following two works: 'Démographie et femmes', a themed issue of the *Cahiers Québécois de Démographie* (vol. 18, no. 1 (1989). 69p.); and Esther Létourneau's *Regards sur l'analyse de la situation démographique québécoise en rapport avec la condition féminine* (Perspectives on the analysis of the demographic situation and its relationship with the female condition) (Québec: Le Conseil du Statut de la Femme, 1989).

220 **Cahiers Québécois de Démographie.** (Québec Journal of Demography.)
Montréal: Association des Démographes du Québec, 1975- . quarterly.
Formerly the *Bulletin de l'Association des Démographes du Québec* (Bulletin of the Québec Association of Demographers), this periodical is the official scholarly publication of the Québec Demographers' Association.

221 **La Situation Démographique au Québec.** (The Demographic
Situation in Québec.)
Québec: Bureau de la Statistique du Québec, 1985- . annual.

Comprises general statistics relating to the demographic behaviour of the population.
In addition to birth, death and marriage statistics, this book provides revealing statistics
on divorce rates, abortions and sterilizations. Some chapters go back ten years and
some statistics are also printed according to municipality or administrative region.
Migration and sociocultural statistics (language, for example) are also included. This
annual work updates a major government publication entitled *Démographie québécoise:
passé, présent, perspectives* (Québec demography: past, present, future) (Québec:
Bureau de la Statistique du Québec, 1983. 457p.). The Canadian government also
releases an annual publication on Canadian and provincial demographic statistics,
entitled *Rapport sur l'État de la Population du Canada* (Report on the State of the
Canadian Population) (Ottawa: Statistics Canada, 1990- . annual).

General

222 **Les déterminants de l'évolution récente de la fécondité au Québec.**
(Factors affecting the recent developments in Québec's fertility rate.)
Gary Caldwell, Guy Fréchet, Normand Thibault.   Québec: Institut
québécois de Recherche sur la Culture, 1992. 72p.

Examines fertility rates and their tendencies between 1960 and 1990 in an attempt to
discern the causes of these tendencies as well as to predict trends for the future.

223 **Les antécédents et les conséquents de la baisse de fécondité au
Québec, 1960-1990. Une analyse des interdépendances.**
(Antecedents and consequences of the decreasing fertility rate in
Québec, 1960-90. An analysis of interdependencies.)
Madeleine Gauthier, Johanne Bujold.   Québec: Institut québécois de
Recherche sur la Culture, 1993. 56p.

An examination of the significant decrease in Québec's fertility rate between 1972 and
1982, and the slower but discernible decrease that followed 1982. This work attempts
to establish empirical links between a series of interdependent events which have
contributed to lowering the birth rate.

224 **Genealogy and local history to 1900 = Généalogie et histoire locale
d'avant 1900.**
Compiled by J. Brian Gilchrist, Clifford Duxbury Colier.   Ottawa:
Canadian Institute for Historical Microreproductions, 1995. 514p.

Lists over 6,000 titles selected from the seventh edition (1988) of *Canada The Printed
Record* (Ottawa: The Institute = L'Institut, 1983- . annual. microform). While this
covers Canada proper, researchers interested in local and family history in Québec
will undoubtedly find this guide useful because of its recent publication and its
user-friendly presentation.

225 **Les enfants qu'on n'a plus au Québec.** (The children we no longer have in Québec.)
Jacques Henripin. Montréal: Presses de l'Université de Montréal, 1981. 410p. bibliog.

An analysis of the declining birth rate in Québec. Based on surveys conducted in 1971 and 1976, the authors examine the transformation of attitudes among couples towards family planning, the number of children wanted, unplanned versus planned pregnancies, the uses of contraception and other related issues. This study is a follow-up to Henripin's *La fin de la revanche des berceaux: qu'en pensent les québécoises?* (The end of the revenge of the cradle: what do Québec women think?) (Montréal: Presses de l'Université de Montréal, 1974. 164p.). Citing an end to the extraordinarily high birth rate in Québec, Henripin and his colleagues manifest a clear pessimism regarding the impact of the declining birth rate which can no longer ensure positive growth. Following this discovery, several studies were written on the impact of declining birth rates on the family structure. Readers interested in this subject should also consult *Couples et parents des années quatre-vingt: un aperçu des nouvelles tendances familiales* (Couples and parents in the 1980s: a study of new family trends) (Québec: Institut québécois de Recherche sur la Culture, 1987. 284p.), edited by Renée Dandurand.

226 **Naître ou ne pas être.** (To be born or not to be.)
Jacques Henripin. Québec: Institut québécois de Recherche sur la Culture, 1989. 140p.

An analysis of the major demographic shifts and their likely impact on the maintenance of a French-speaking society in Québec. In this historical demographic analysis, Henripin places Québec's declining birth rate in the context of changing social conditions and attitudes affecting a majority of modern industrial societies. This is an important book which explains how social transformations riding the wave of modern industrialization affected the particular context of Québec. Henripin's opinions regarding the need to increase the birth rate in order to safeguard economic growth and the survival of Québec society are also expressed in this work.

227 **La population du Québec d'hier à demain.** (Québec's population from yesterday to today.)
Edited by Jacques Henripin, Yves Martin. Montréal: Presses de l'Université de Montréal, 1991. 216p.

Sixteen authors from varied backgrounds focus on the causes and consequences of various demographic challenges facing Québec, namely: an ageing population; a fragile linguistic equilibrium; increasing immigration; and a declining birth rate. Although this book intends to introduce the general public to the significant evolution of Québec's population, the non-specialist will require some effort in reading through some of the more technical essays. A study of Québec's regions will provide the reader with a more nuanced portrait of Québec. Among the better studies are: *Deux Québec dans un: rapport sur le développement social et démographique* (see item no. 373); and *Les Saguenayens. Introduction à l'histoire des populations du Saguenay, XVIe- XXe siècle* (The Saguenesians. An introduction to the demographic history of the Saguenay between the 16th and 20th centuries) (Sillery, Québec: Presses de l'Université du Québec, 1983. 386p.), by Christian Pouyez and Yolande Lavoie.

228   **Dictionnaire généalogique des familles du Québec. Des origines à
1730.** (Genealogical dictionary of families in Québec. From earliest
times to 1730.)
René Jetté.   Montréal: Presses de l'Université de Montréal, 1983.
1,177p.

Provides a classification of families established in Québec between the time of the
arrival of the first French settlers and 1730. Where possible, the author has attempted
to include those individuals that remained single during the time period.

229   **Le choc démographique: le déclin du Québec est-il inévitable?**
(Demographic shock: is the decline of Québec inevitable?)
Georges Mathews.   Montréal: Éditions du Boréal Express, 1984.
204p.

Examines the various interpretations and conclusions drawn from the declining birth
rate in industrialized countries and how Québec's experience fits well into this world
trend. Mathews examines the issues surrounding declining birth rates, the causes of
the current decline, the difference between this decline and previous downward cycles,
and possible policy options. The author concludes that governments should encourage
social conditions that allow society to realize its desire to procreate. This book is
coloured by a certain polemicism in favour of a natalist public policy. The reader
should be aware that several of Mathews' critics have, however, pointed to the
absence of any consideration of Malthusian counter-arguments to his thesis.

230   **L'avenir démolinguistique du Québec et de ses régions.**
(The 'demolinguistic' future of Québec and its regions.)
Marc Termotte, Jacques Ledent.   Québec: Conseil de la Langue
française, 1994. 266p. bibliog. (Dossier CLF).

Analyses the demographic evolution of the various linguistic groups in Québec's
regions during the last decade. In addition, this study uses immigration, emigration
and birth rate statistics to project future demographic patterns of the francophone,
anglophone and allophone (those whose mother tongues are neither French nor
English) linguistic groups. The author suggests in his conclusion that many regions
may face a decline in population during the next decade. A good bibliography is
included.

Aboriginal Inhabitants

Reference

231 **Cultures et sociétés autochtones du Québec: bibliographie critique.** (Autochthonous cultures and societies of Québec: a critical bibliography.)
Richard Dominique, Jean-Guy Deschênes.   Québec: Institut québécois de Recherche sur la Culture, 1985. 221p. maps.

An annotated bibliography of works published on Québec aboriginal peoples. It distinguishes itself from other reference works through its use of critical text to contextualize each work in relation to others. Consequently, in addition to imparting the relative importance of each title, this reference tool permits the reader to reflect on the way academic research has analysed and described aboriginal culture. Moreover, each chapter also serves as a useful tool for the elaboration of potential research projects.

232 **Bibliographical directory of Amerindian authors in Québec.**
Charlotte Gilbert.   Saint-Luc, Québec: Centre de Recherche sur la Littérature et les Arts autochtones du Québec, 1993. 46p.

Designed for researchers, students and professionals with an interest in Amerindian literature, this directory contains a select number of titles classified according to the author's nation (Iroquois, Algonquin, etc.). Also included are contact numbers for Amerindian media and publishing houses.

233 **Les langues autochtones du Québec.** (Autochthonous languages of Québec.)
Edited by Jacques Maurais.   Québec: Conseil de la Langue française, 1992. 455p. maps.

One of the first academic assessments of the state of Québec aboriginal languages. The research in this book is divided into several thematic chapters, namely: historical evolution; linguistic structure; federal and provincial policies towards aboriginal languages; usage; and prospects for ensuring the survival of these languages as presented by aboriginal people themselves. See also *Inuktitut et langues amérindiennes du Québec* (Inuktitut and Amerindian languages of Québec) (Sainte-Foy, Québec: Presses de l'Université du Québec, 1980. 228p.) by Louis-Jacques Dorais. Related works include Louis-Jacques Dorais' study of ethnic identity and social conditions of the Quaqtaq Inuit in his work entitled *Quaqtaq: modernity and identity in an Inuit community* (Toronto: University of Toronto Press, 1997. 132p.).

234 **Recherches Amérindiennes au Québec.** (Amerindian Research in Québec.)
Montréal: La Société de Recherches amérindiennes au Québec, 1971- . quarterly.

A scholarly journal which provides an excellent source for material on current events and their impact and relevance to Québec aboriginal society.

General

235 **Heeding the voices of our ancestors: Kahnawake Mohawk politics and the rise of native nationalism.**
Gerald R. Alfred.   Toronto; Oxford: Oxford University Press, 1995. 220p.

Constitutes one of the few scholarly works on aboriginal political activism from an aboriginal point of view. In explaining the militancy and passion of Kahnawake Mohawk political culture and nationalism, Alfred focuses on the 'process of goal formation in the context of North American community politics'. Accordingly, the persistence of an aboriginal identity and the existence of aboriginal alternative institutions, combined with antagonistic relations with the state are cited as the main variables contributing to the militancy of aboriginal nationalism in Kahnawake. Of related interest is a survey of Inuit nationalism by Marybelle Mitchell, entitled *From talking chiefs to a native corporate élite: the birth of class and nationalism among Canadian Inuit* (Montréal; Kingston, Ontario: McGill-Queen's University Press, 1996. 533p.).

236 **Mythologie huronne et wyandotte.** (Huron and Wyandot mythology.)
Marius Barbeau, edited by Pierre Beaucage. Montréal: Presses de
l'Université de Montréal, 1994. 439p.

The work of Québec's first aboriginal ethnologist, Marius Barbeau (1883-1969), is
presented here in the only edition published since 1915. Barbeau was able to record,
first hand, many of the oral traditions and histories of the Huron (Wyandot) nation.
This work also has an invaluable appendix of historical documents containing the
myths and stories of the Wyandots in addition to historians' interpretations of
Wyandot mythology.

237 **Les Montagnais et la réserve de Betsiamites, 1850-1900.**
(The Montagnais and the Betsiamites reserve, 1850-1900.)
Hélène Bédard. Québec: Institut québécois de Recherche sur la
Culture, 1988. 149p.

Describes the consequences of the gradual settling process of the Montagnais nation
during the second half of the 19th century. Among the topics examined are: the economy,
health, and dependence relations following the arrival of non-aboriginals. The book
also contains an excellent chapter on the motivations behind the creation of the
Betsiamites reserve. Moreover, this book investigates the role of the Catholic authorities
who ran the reserve. Bédard's research refines our conception of this role by looking
into the paradoxical actions of the missionaries who, as mediators between the state
and the Montagnais, defended aboriginal rights while simultaneously eroding their
traditions through the imposition of Western value systems. See also Rémi Savard's
Le rire pré-colombien dans le Québec d'aujourd'hui (The pre-Columbian laugh in
today's Québec) (Montréal: Éditions de l'Hexagone, 1977. 157p.) which provides a
portrait of 19th-century Montagnais history. Moreover, the latter publication examines
the Montagnais' own self-perception. Another work of interest is Marie Wadden's
Nitassinan: the Innu struggle to reclaim their homeland (Vancouver: Douglas &
McIntyre, 1996. 218p.).

238 **Histoire de la littérature amérindienne au Québec: oralité et
écriture.** (A history of Amerindian literature in Québec: oral and
written.)
Diane Boudreau. Montréal: Éditions de l'Hexagone, 1993. 201p.
bibliog.

Traces the emergence of Québec Amerindian literature from its oral roots to its
contemporary written form. This work paints a profile of Amerindian history and
informs the reader of Amerindian perspectives too frequently eclipsed by 'official'
Western interpretations. In discussing the history of the Amerindian literary tradition,
Boudreau also introduces the reader to the work of approximately twenty contemporary Québec Amerindian poets, essayists, writers and singers.

239 **L'Indien généreux: ce que le monde doit aux Amériques.**
(The generous Indian: what the world owes to the Americas.)
Louise Côté, Louis Tardivel, Denis Vaugeois. Montréal: Éditions du
Boréal, 1992. 287p.

In an interesting twist, this work attempts to demonstrate the incredible impact the
Americas have had on Western civilization instead of the traditional perspective which

examines the impact Europeans had on aboriginal peoples. An investigation of French reveals the extent to which Quebecers are unaware of the ways Amerindian culture has influenced Québec culture. Terms and words borrowed from Amerindian culture are arranged into a dictionary format. Words are accompanied by a brief explanation of their significance and origins. This book was written for the general public.

240 **Traces du passé, images du présent: anthropologie amérindienne du moyen-nord québécois.** (Hints from the past, images of the present: Amerindian anthropology of Québec's middle-north.) Edited by Marc Côté, Gaëtan L. Lessard. Rouyn-Noranda, Québec: Cégep de l'Abitibi-Témiscamingue, 1993. 213p. maps.

A collection of essays and research reports which examines the archaeological past of aboriginal peoples in the Ottawa valley and the Abitibi-Témiscamingue region. Aside from the decidedly archaeological nature of the majority of these essays, other topics include the early colonial history of Ottawa valley aboriginals, inter-aboriginal conflict and trading relations, and the current problems facing aboriginal peoples living in urban areas.

241 **A nation within a nation: dependency and the Cree.** Marie-Anik Gagné. Montréal; New York: Black Rose Books, 1994. 161p. bibliog.

The author uses a classic dependency perspective to analyse the peripheralization of the Cree in Québec. As a remedy for the 'oppressed' and 'underdeveloped' status of the First Nations in Québec, the author suggests a greater degree of self-determination be conferred onto aboriginal nations. Ideally, this would be achieved through the establishment of representative and responsible political institutions, territorial bases for aboriginal groups, self-government, and financial support for economic development. The work includes a useful bibliography relating to aboriginal communities in Canada and elsewhere.

242 **First among the Hurons.** Max Gros-Louis, Marcel Bellier, translated by Sheila Fischman. Montréal: Harvest House, 1973. 151p.

An autobiography of the Huron (Wyandot) Chief Max Gros-Louis (1931-) whose successful leadership was instrumental in the aboriginal campaign that temporarily halted the construction of the James Bay hydro-electric project until it had received consideration by aboriginal peoples. This book also outlines Gros-Louis' interpretation of Canadian history as well as his actions as 'First among the Hurons', the title given to the leader of the Huron nation. The terms 'Huron' and 'Wyandot' are used interchangeably and refer to the same group of people. 'Huron' is the label which was used by the French when they arrived, whereas 'Wyandot' was the name used by the aboriginals themselves.

243 **One nation under the gun.** Rick Hornung. Toronto: Stoddart, 1991. 294p. maps.

A journalistic account of the years and events presaging the Oka crisis. The Oka crisis occurred in the summer of 1990 and lasted for seventy-eight days. It involved an intensive stand-off between Provincial police and the Canadian Army, on one side, and the Kanesetake Mohawks on the other. The immediate cause of the dispute was the attempted expansion of a golf course onto land claimed by the Amerindians. This dispute finds its source in the early 1700s. Hornung's work focuses mainly on the Akwesasne reserve which spans an area crossing Québec, Ontario and New York state. Aside from relating the conflict between state and provincial governments, Hornung also describes the internal Mohawk conflicts.

244 **Les Indiens blancs. Français et Indiens en Amérique du Nord, XVe-XVIIIe siècles.** (White Indians. The French and the Indians in North America from the 15th to the 18th century.)
Philippe Jacquin. Montréal: Éditions Libre Expression, 1996. 284p. bibliog.

A fresh look at the coureurs-de-bois (trappers) and their lifestyle. Distinctly un-European, many colonists decided to live among the aboriginal people and adopt their ideology and lifestyle. This period of history, when aboriginal people were typically analysed as passive subjects of their environment, is examined by Jacquin with a critical eye to the conditions which prompted some Europeans to adopt such 'un-European' values and lifestyles. Overall, this book presents the history of the emergence and development of the coureurs-de-bois, their impact, and their achievements. Another book which examines aboriginal and non-aboriginal contact and conflict during colonial times is Richard White's *The middle ground, Indians, empires and republics in the Great Lakes region, 1650-1815* (Cambridge, England: Cambridge University Press, 1991).

245 **A homeland for the Cree: regional development in James Bay, 1971-1981.**
Richard F. Salisbury. Montréal; Kingston, Ontario: McGill-Queen's University Press, 1986. 172p.

The James Bay hydro-electric project (1971-84) not only united the Cree in a common battle, it also began the process of modernization within Cree society. In this major study, Richard F. Salisbury compares the Cree society of 1971 with that of 1981 with regard to education, economics, politics and identity. He concludes that the project was a positive experience for the Cree in contrast to the experiences of most other aboriginal groups in North America.

246 **Destins d'Amérique: les autochtones et nous.** (America's destinies: autochthonous peoples and us.)
Rémi Savard. Montréal: Éditions de l'Hexagone, 1979. 189p.

Written for 'euro-Quebecers', this book comprises a series of Rémi Savard's previously published essays and speeches in an effort to demonstrate the inadequacy of mainstream political discourse in dealing fairly with aboriginal peoples. The essays are presented chronologically according to publication or presentation, and discuss aboriginal art, political action, language, and oral literature.

247   **Les Wendats: une civilisation méconnue.** (The Wendats: a poorly known civilization.)
Georges Sioui.   Sainte-Foy, Québec: Presses de l'Université Laval, 1994. 372p.

An important study of the philosophy and social ideas of Wendat society since its first contact with Europeans. The originality of this work lies in its incorporation of the Wendats' self-perception as conveyed by their oral histories. Following a description of the Wendats' conception of their origins, literature, philosophy and morality, Sioui uses archaeology to demonstrate the complex economic and social structures of Amerindian society. Moreover, by focusing on population history, he explains why this society eventually became sedentary and agricultural in relation to other aboriginal nations. The last section of the book examines Wendat society during the 17th century from an aboriginal perspective.

248   **The James Bay and Northern Quebec Agreement.**
Société d'Énergie de la Baie James.   Québec: Éditeur officiel du Québec, 1976. 455p.

The complete text of a landmark agreement between the Québec Government, Hydro-Québec, the Canadian Government, the Grand Council of Crees and the Northern Québec Inuit Association regarding aboriginal rights and state obligations in the James Bay and Northern Québec areas. The James Bay and Northern Québec Agreement of 1975 is important because it represents Québec's formal recognition of its responsibilities towards aboriginal peoples in northern Québec. It states the rights of aboriginal people in addition to the future duties of the Québec state in providing necessary resources to the aboriginals in the form of public support and self-government.

249   **Les figures de l'Indien.** (The many faces of the Indian.)
Edited by Gilles Thérien.   Montréal: Éditions de l'Hexagone, 1988. 398p.

Two research teams from France and Québec analyse the way in which their respective societies have viewed aboriginal peoples throughout history. The essays in this book examine the mental evolution of settlers' conceptions of aboriginals through time in addition to the way in which aboriginal peoples themselves have been trapped into interpreting themselves through the settlers' eyes. The authors suggest that the settlers' ideological and constitutional positions are based on a profound misunderstanding of aboriginal reality.

250   **L'Indien imaginaire: matériaux pour une recherche.** (The imaginary Indian: material for research.)
Edited by Gilles Thérien.   Montréal: Université du Québec à Montréal, 1991. 211p.

A collection of reprints of important articles, both published and unpublished, regarding North American aboriginal peoples as they are represented in literature.

251 **The children of Aataentsic: a history of the Huron people to 1660.**
Bruce Trigger.   Montréal; Kingston, Ontario: McGill-Queen's
University Press, 1987. 2nd ed. 913p. maps.

This colossal ethnohistorical study of the Huron (Wyandot) nation demonstrates that 'it is possible to write a history of native people that was not focused exclusively on their relations with Europeans'. Combining archaeology, history, and ethnology, Trigger argues that almost every aspect of Huron life underwent change prior to contact with the first fur traders. This work covers Iroquois society from the first hunting and gathering societies to its contact and trading relations with the fur traders. See also Conrad Heidenreich's *Huronia: a history and geography of the Huron Indians 1600-1650* (Toronto: McClelland and Stewart, 1971. 339p.) and Elisabeth Tooker's *Ethnography of the Huron Indians 1615-1649* (Syracuse, New York: Syracuse University Press, 1991. 183p.).

252 **Natives and newcomers. Canada's 'Heroic Age' reconsidered.**
Bruce Trigger.   Montréal; Kingston, Ontario: McGill-Queen's
University Press, 1985. 430p.

Dealing with the period of French colonization, this book does not focus exclusively on Canada. According to 19th-century liberal wisdom, European societies were seen as progressive in the face of 'static' aboriginal societies. Trigger uses both history and archaeology to illustrate how the writing of history has assigned a marginal place to aboriginal peoples. For the student of Québec history, this work is indispensable for an understanding of the historiography of various French historians, the relations between the French and the Iroquois in the Lower Saint-Lawrence, and the important impact of the relations between early French traders and aboriginal peoples on the viability of the colony.

253 **Autochtones et Québécois: la rencontre des nationalismes.**
(Autochthonous peoples and Quebecers: a meeting of nationalisms.)
Edited by Pierre Trudel.   Montréal: Recherches amérindiennes au
Québec, 1995. 228p.

The proceedings of a symposium held before the 1995 referendum on the state and evolution of the relations between aboriginal peoples and Quebecers. The work is divided into three sections: the first examines international law with respect to aboriginal self-determination; the second compares federal and provincial aboriginal policy; and the last explores prospects for the future regarding the collective rights of both aboriginal peoples and Quebecers. In addition to bringing out the important conceptual differences between aboriginal and Québec national projects, this work distinguishes itself by including opinions and debate from both politicians and academics. Moreover, in the context of the then approaching referendum, these symposium proceedings reveal the political strategies and issues at stake as well as the motives behind politicians' and aboriginal leaders' actions.

254 **La fin des alliances franco-indiennes: enquête sur un sauf-conduit de 1760 devenu un traité en 1990.** (The end of French-Indian alliances: a study of a 1760 safe-passage agreement which became a treaty in 1990.)
Denis Vaugeois. Québec: Éditions du Boréal/Éditions du Septentrion, 1995. 290p.

In the context of the Constitution Act of 1982 which recognizes aboriginal rights and past treaties and the increasing litigation related to aboriginal land claims, the history of aboriginal-British treaties has become an important and growing field for scholarly research. This work examines the history behind two court judgements which granted 'treaty' status to aboriginal-British safe-passage agreements written in between the capture of Québec City and the capitulation of Montréal at the end of the Seven Years War. Vaugeois attempts to construct a complete history of these agreements in three different ways: the first focuses on a detailed account of the events that transpired between the capitulation of Québec and that of Montréal in an effort to understand the context of the agreements reached between the aboriginals who were formerly French allies, and the British forces. The second section studies the judicial activity which has arisen as a result of these agreements between the Huron (Wyandot) people and the British. The third looks at how historians have interpreted the same agreements.

255 **Baie James et nord québécois: dix ans après = James Bay and northern Quebec: ten years after.**
Edited by Sylvie Vincent, Garry Bowers. Montréal: Recherches amérindiennes au Québec, 1988. 303p. bibliog. maps.

The proceedings of a forum held by the Société de Recherches amérindiennes au Québec (Québec Society of Amerindian Research), 14-15 November 1985, to mark the first ten years of the James Bay and Northern Québec Agreement of 1975. The forum proceedings focus on the origins of the agreement, its implementation and a prognosis. For those readers unfamiliar with the agreement, background essays have been included in the volume, dealing with the socio-economic context of aboriginal nations before the agreement, a chronology of the agreement's first ten years, and an analysis of hydro-electricity's importance for Québec society. The editors have also included two bibliographies to aid those readers in discovering more information about the agreement, and the region and its wildlife.

256 **La nation huronne.** (The Huron nation.)
Marguertine Vincent Tehariolina, with the cooperation of Pierre H. Savignac. Sillery, Québec: Éditions du Septentrion, 1995. 507p.

Written by a Huron (Wyandot), this work provides a general history of the Huron nation, from its prehistoric origins to its present-day form. Drawing from a rich range of sources, including several oral histories, the author presents a complete history of the nation including its migrations, its ethnic relations with other aboriginal nations, its everyday living habits, and its legends, myths and culture.

57 People of the pines: the warriors and the legacy of Oka.
Geoffrey York, Loreen Pindera. Toronto: Little, Brown & Company,
1991. 438p. maps.

A journalist's account of the Oka crisis in 1990 which pitted the Canadian and Québec
tate against aboriginal peoples over land rights. This book provides a favourable
interpretation of the aboriginal claims made during the crisis in addition to bringing
out the many injustices that were obscured in the press coverage of the issue. An
mple number of primary sources in this book present a portrait of the Kahnawake
warrior society. On the Oka crisis, readers should also consult Robin Philpot's *Oka:*
ternier alibi du Canada anglais (Oka: last alibi of English-speaking Canada)
Outremont, Québec: VLB Éditeur, 1991. 167p.).

Ethnic Minorities

258 **A minority in a changing society. The Portuguese communities in Québec.**
J. Antonio Alpalhào, Victor M. P. da Rosa.   Ottawa: University of Ottawa Press, 1980. 319p.

An impressive ethnographical work on the Portuguese communities in Québec. This work focuses primarily on issues of immigration, social integration, adaptation and social change. From a humanistic perspective, this book also presents a theoretical model which can be used for analysing any minority facing the challenge of integration into a new society. For this reason, this book will be of interest to those researchers studying the sociology of minorities.

259 **Juifs et réalités juives au Québec.** (Jews and Jewish realities in Québec.)
Pierre Anctil, Gary Caldwell.   Québec: Institut québécois de Recherche sur la Culture, 1984. 371p.

Provides a broad, yet nuanced collection of essays dealing with the Québec Jewish community in Montréal. Moreover, the authors attempt to discover how the Québec Jewish community, in comparison with Jews elsewhere in North America, have dealt with the nationalist project in Québec. Demographic pressures are also examined as they mark the Jewish identity. Other themes include: Jewish literature; ideology; expressions of anti-Semitism; and the socio-economic profile of the community. Another excellent work on the relationship between Jews and francophones is Jacques Langlais and David Rome's *Juifs et Québécois français: 200 ans d'histoire commune* (Jews and French-speaking Quebecers: 200 years of common history) (Montréal: Fides, 1986. 286p.).

260 **Le rendez-vous manqué. Les Juifs de Montréal face au Québec de l'entre-deux-guerres.** (Missed opportunity. Montréal Jews and Québec during the inter-war period.)
Pierre Anctil. Québec: Institut québécois de Recherche sur la Culture, 1988. 366p.

The Montréal Jewish community was the first non-Christian community which attempted to integrate itself into Québec before the Quiet Revolution of the 1960s. Anctil examines Québec society in its role as a host society to the Jewish community, thereby making an important contribution to the study of Québec's identity. Anctil also analyses the Jewish community's integration strategies, demonstrating how their desire to integrate was viewed by some as an effort to break the unanimity of a francophone society. This book also looks at the tension between the Jewish community and the anglophone Canadian community in Québec and the efforts of particular community leaders to bridge the ethnic divide. Anctil has examined Quebecers' attitudes towards immigration during this same period in a work entitled *Le Devoir, les Juifs et l'immigration de Bourassa à Laurendeau* (*Le Devoir*, the Jews and immigration from Bourassa to Laurendeau) (Québec: Institut québécois de Recherche sur la Culture, 1988. 172p.).

261 **The English fact in Quebec.**
Sheila McLeod Arnopoulos, Dominique Clift. Montréal; Kingston, Ontario: McGill-Queen's University Press, 1984. 2nd ed. 247p.

An award-winning historical overview of the relations between the English-speaking, and the French-speaking, communities in Québec. The authors look at both communities' divergent opinions on the role of the economy, the language conflict, the clash between anglophone business and French nationalism, the mediation of the federal Liberal Party and the struggle between individual and collective rights. It also explains the rise of a new 'progressive' anglophone leadership during the late 1970s and early 1980s as well as the cultural crisis experienced by the English-speaking community during this decade. Also included are a useful chronology and demographic tables.

262 **Les minorités au Québec.** (The minorities of Québec.)
Julien Bauer. Montréal: Éditions du Boréal Express, 1994. 125p.

Examines federal and provincial public policy towards immigrants and cultural communities, thereby providing a glimpse of how minorities fit into Québec society. Issues such as multiculturalism, citizenship, immigration policy, education, and the impact of the Canadian and Québec charters of human rights are analysed. Bauer concludes that both Canadian and Québec policies towards minorities are unsuccessful in treating minorities as equal partners in society.

263 **Jew or Juif? Jews, French Canadians, and Anglo-Canadians, 1759-1914.**
Michael Brown. Philadelphia: The Jewish Publications Society, 1986. 356p. bibliog.

A historical examination of Jewish relations with both English-speaking and French-speaking Canadians in Montréal, the unofficial capital of Canadian Jewry for over two centuries. The author emphasizes the challenges and difficulties of integration into both the English-speaking and French-speaking communities.

264 **The English of Quebec from majority to minority status.**
Edited by Gary Caldwell, Eric Waddell. Québec: Institut québécois
de Recherche sur la Culture, 1982. 464p. bibliog.

A collection of essays by mainly anglophone scholars. The topics addressed include
the history of English-speaking Québec, ethnic identity, Jews in Québec, the working
class, the educational establishment, the media, and political institutions. On the topic
of anglophones, see also Gary Caldwell's work entitled *A demographic profile of the
English-speaking population of Québec, 1921-1971* (Sainte-Foy, Québec: CIRB,
Université Laval, 1974. 175p.) which discusses the different ethnic groups within the
anglophone community. For additional information on the migratory changes which
have modified the composition of the anglophone community, see Uli Locher's *Les
anglophones de Montréal: émigration et évolution des attitudes, 1978-1983* (Montréal
anglophones: emigration and attitudinal evolution) (Québec: Conseil de la Langue
française, 1988. 219p.).

265 **Les études ethniques au Québec: bilan et perspective.** (Ethnic
studies in Québec: assessment and perspective.)
Gary Caldwell. Québec: Institut québécois de Recherche sur la
Culture, 1983. 108p.

Addresses the academic state of ethnic studies in Québec by examining publications
on Québec immigration, emigration, demographics, and inter-ethnic relations between
1760 and 1981. While Caldwell concludes that there has been a lack, as of 1981, of an
intellectual tradition within the domain of ethnic studies in Québec, he is optimistic
that one is about to emerge. This work brings into focus the increasing interest in
cultural communities which surfaced in the 1960s and 1970s, in addition to the reasons
behind this interest and its historical antecedents.

266 **La question du Québec anglais.** (The question of anglophone
Québec.)
Gary Caldwell. Québec: Institut québécois de Recherche sur la
Culture, 1994. 122p.

Examines the anglophone community's adoption of a neo-liberal discourse as illustrated
by claims that the rights of its members were abrogated by the Québec government.
Caldwell's demographic and psychological analysis of the community reveals that
although its demographic situation is stabilizing, its future remains vulnerable due to its
self-perception as a victimized people in Québec. In addition, Caldwell analyses and
explains the factors behind the dominant anglophone discourse through a historical
examination of the community as well as discerning the various class interests within the
community.

267 **The Armenian community of Québec.**
Garo Chichekian. Montréal: Dawson College, 1989. 200p. bibliog.

An introduction to, and description of, the Armenian community in Québec, which is
mostly concentrated in Montréal. Following a cultural introduction to the Armenian
nation, the author examines the origins of the Québec Armenian population, and its
motivations for emigrating to Québec. A description of the community's local
institutions is also provided. Chichekian also pays attention to the community's
demographic evolution within Montréal, its socio-economic make-up and its integration
into Québec.

268 **The Haitians in Quebec: a sociological profile.**
Paul Dejean, translated by Max Dorsinville. Ottawa: The Tecumseh
Press, 1980. 158p.
An analysis of the origins of Haitian immigrants and immigration to Québec. The
author also examines their contribution to Québec society and the problems they face
in adapting to a new culture. This study makes use of extensive statistical data.

269 **Les convergences culturelles dans les sociétés pluriethniques.**
(Cultural convergence in multiethnic societies.)
Edited by Khadiyatoulah Fall, Ratiba Hadj-Moussa, Daniel Simeoni.
Québec: Presses de l'Université du Québec, 1996. 374p.
An interdisciplinary study of cultural convergence in multiethnic societies, focusing
especially on Québec, Canada and Western European countries. Twenty scholarly
essays discuss the impacts of different contexts, such as integration and multiculturalism, on the adjustment process of ethnic groups and individuals, their
acceptance into society, their exclusion and their relationships with other groups and
individuals. Gary Caldwell's work, entitled *Immigration incorporation in Montréal in
the seventies* (Québec: Institut québécois de Recherche sur la Culture, 1994. 190p.), is
an especially interesting study of integration in Montréal during the 1970s.

270 **Les Juifs progressistes au Québec.** (Progressive Jews in Québec.)
Allen Gottheil. Montréal: Éditions par ailleurs . . . , 1988. 372p.
The Jewish community has often been perceived in Québec as conservative and not
very open towards the Québec question. Allen Gottheil tries to break away from this
myth in presenting the stories of ten progressive members of the Jewish community.
Dr. Henry Morgentaler, a pro-choice activist, Stan Gray, a former leader of the
'McGill français' demonstration (which attempted to turn McGill University into a
francophone institution), and Nancy Neamtan, an important social worker and specialist
on social economics, are among those individuals interviewed for this book. They all
explain their personal development, their attachment to Québec society and their
relationship with the Jewish faith.

271 **The Irish in Quebec: an introduction to the historiography.**
Robert J. Grace. Québec: Institut québécois de Recherche sur la
Culture, 1993. 265p. bibliog.
The first part of this work provides a short history of the Irish in New France and
modern Québec, focusing on Irish immigration and settlement patterns as well as their
contribution to Québec politics and culture. The Irish first began settling in Québec in
the early 19th century, with immigration in especially great numbers in the 1840s,
during the Irish Potato Famine. Up until 1871, the Irish comprised half of Québec's
population of British origin. The second part of the book provides an annotated bibliography of 1,089 titles related to the Irish in Québec. This is an excellent study and
reference work. One of the only book-length studies of the Irish community during the
19th century is Kerby Miller's work, entitled *Emigrants and exiles* (Ottawa: Ottawa
University Press, 1985. 684p.).

272 **The French quarter: the epic struggle of a family and a nation divided.**
Ron Graham. Toronto: Macfarlane Walter & Ross, 1992. 324p. map.

As an anglophone growing up in Montréal, Graham provides colourful vignettes of Québec's political history, highlighting the tension between English and French speakers.

273 **Les Chinois à Montréal, 1877-1951.** (The Chinese in Montréal, 1877-1951.)
Denise Helly. Québec: Institut québécois de Recherche sur la Culture, 1987. 315p.

A significant number of Chinese immigrants adopted Québec as their home at the end of the 19th century. The author of this ethnohistorical reconstitution attempts to explain why so many decided to return to China while those that remained gradually found themselves isolated from the rest of Québec society. This work not only provides a good description of the cosmopolitan character of Montréal at the beginning of the 20th century, it also demonstrates the mechanisms that potentially contribute to the isolation of a community within a society.

274 **Le Québec face à la pluralité culturelle: un bilan documentaire des politiques.** (Facing cultural pluralism: an assessment of policy based on documents.)
Denise Helly. Sainte-Foy, Québec: Institut québécois de Recherche sur la Culture; Presses de l'Université Laval, 1996. 491p. bibliog.

Describes Québec's immigration policy since the adoption of Bill 101 on language policy in 1977. The authors study the methods used by different institutions to facilitate the integration of immigrants into their organizations. Among the institutions studied are the public service, the health sector, the police, and the education sector. The author concludes that, while the period from 1978 to 1987 is characterized by a recognition of the positive effects of cultural diversity, the Government did not take proactive measures to promote this diversity. This book is essential for those who want to know more about the place of immigrants in Québec society.

275 **La communauté grecque du Québec.** (The Greek community in Québec.)
Tina Ioannou. Québec: Institut québécois de Recherche sur la Culture, 1984. 337p.

Provides a sociological portrait of the Greek community, whose membership is mostly concentrated in Montréal. Ioannou emphasizes the importance of culture and language throughout the work which explains, perhaps, the Greek community's isolation from Québec and Canadian society relative to other cultural communities. The author predicts, however, that integration into the host society is proceeding thanks to the Greeks' increasing attendance at post-secondary educational institutions.

276 **Ethnicité et enjeux sociaux. Le Québec vu par les leaders des groupes ethnoculturels.** (Ethnicity and social issues. Québec as seen by the leaders of cultural communities.)
Micheline Labelle, Joseph J. Lévy. Montréal: Liber, 1995. 380p. bibliog.

A collection of interviews with eighty-four leaders from the Italian, Jewish, Lebanese and Haitian communities in Montréal on different themes such as economy, politics, racism, language and education. The book provides a good overview of the plurality of opinions which prevail in each of the different ethnic communities. A comprehensive bibliography is included.

277 **Ethnicité et nationalismes: nouveau regard.** (Ethnicity and nationalism: a new perspective.)
Edited by Micheline Labelle. Montréal: Presses de l'Université du Québec à Montréal, 1993. 253p. (Cahiers de Recherche Sociologique, no. 20).

A presentation of the theoretical and political issues which surround the social relations between ethnic minorities and nation states. In addition, the authors pay special attention to the integration ideologies which act to legitimize those social relations. This approach permits an interesting insight into how government policy, public discourse and intellectuals play on the sociological definition of nation and ethnicity.

278 **Le Québec de demain et les communautés culturelles.** (The Québec of the future and cultural communities.)
Edited by Jacques Langlais, Pierre Laplante, Joseph Lévy. Montréal: Éditions du Méridien, 1990. 257p.

In an original approach to the question of immigration and Québec's declining birth rate, this work concentrates on the self-perception of cultural communities within Québec society. As Québec's future is increasingly dependent on the integration of new Quebecers into a distinct society, the authors devote the first half of the book to interviews with new Quebecers in an effort to understand their experiences. The second half of the book comprises the proceedings of the Intercultural Conference on the Future of Québec which examines the socio-economic, demographic and cultural issues facing Québec as they relate to immigration.

279 **Racines.** (Roots.)
Gérard LeBlanc. Montréal: Éditions du Méridien, 1993. 287p.

A series of interviews with several Québec personalities of various ethnic origins. The book is divided according to the different origins: Italian, Chinese, Portuguese, Greek, Latino, Haitian, Vietnamese, Lebanese and Jewish. The author seeks to understand their sense of identity and their relationship with the francophone majority.

280 **Montréal au pluriel. Huit communautés ethno-culturelles de la région montréalaise.** (Montréal's diversity. Eight ethnocultural communities from the Greater Montréal region.)
Alberte Ledoyen.   Québec: Institut québécois de Recherche sur la Culture, 1992. 329p.

In contrast to the relative ease with which early European immigrants to Québec integrated into either of the two founding nations, more recent immigrants have experienced social and economic marginalization due to ethnic and racial exclusion. This work attempts to address the relative lack of empirical academic work to date on the causes leading to this exclusion. Socio-economic indicators are used to evaluate the relative failure or success of integration, access to socio-economic resources, and inherent systemic barriers. Researchers will appreciate the chapter dedicated to methodological problems traditionally confronted in the study of cultural integration.

281 **L'invention d'une minorité. Les Anglo-québécois.** (The invention of the Anglo-Quebecer minority.)
Josée Legault.   Montréal: Éditions du Boréal, 1992. 282p.

An analysis of the increasingly vocal and visible manifestation of anglophones on the political scene since the 1960s. Couched in terms of individual rights, the anglophone discourse that sets out to portray the community as a victim of the majority is viewed by Legault as simply a refusal to accept minority status. Legault suggests that the vilification of francophone nationalists has little to do with rights and everything to do with political games. Legault argues that because they were once politically and economically dominant, anglophones are unfamiliar with their minority status and consequently they seek political tools to preserve a vision of themselves that no longer exists. Legault has written extensively on the anglophone community and its political activity in her columns in *Le Devoir*. These columns are published in *Les nouveaux démons. Chroniques et analyses politiques* (The new demons. Political columns and analyses) (Outremont, Québec: VLB Éditeur, 1996. 236p.).

282 **Les institutions face au pluralisme ethnoculturel.** (Institutions and ethnocultural pluralism.)
Fernand Ouellette.   Québec: Institut québécois de la Recherche sur la Culture, 1995. 543p.

Québec's society is increasingly multicultural. This book's mission is to discover new ways of adapting Québec's institutions to reality, mainly through the educational system. Different authors reveal their bias for a curriculum that would be more open to cultural difference by favouring new forms of intercultural exchange between students. The last part of the book describes how other institutions, such as the police and the city, have adapted themselves to the challenges of ethnocultural pluralism.

283 **Les Italiens au Québec.** (The Italians in Québec.)
Claude Painchaud, Richard Poulin.   Hull, Québec: Éditions Asticou, 1988. 231p.

Provides a general sociological portrait of the Italian community in Québec in addition to using history as a means to understand the present-day community. Italians began to settle in Québec in the late 19th century, but significant immigration occurred at the very beginning of the 20th century. As well as describing the Italian reality in Québec, this book is original in its suggestion that ethnic communities in Québec enjoy a larger community space than elsewhere in Canada as a result of the anglophone-francophone conflict. This larger manoeuvring space allows these communities to maintain their culture more easily. For a more historical overview of Italians in Québec, the reader should consult Bruno Ramirez's *Les premiers Italiens de Montréal: l'origine de la Petite Italie du Québec* (The first Italians in Montréal: the origin of Québec's Little Italy) (Montréal: Éditions du Boréal Express, 1984. 136p.), and his *On the move: French-Canadian and Italian migrants in the North Atlantic economy, 1860-1914* (Toronto: McClelland and Stewart, 1991. 172p.).

284   **An everyday miracle. Yiddish culture in Montréal.**
      Edited by Ira Robinson, Pierre Anctil, Mervin Butovsky.   Montréal:
      Véhicule Press, 1990. 169p.
Examines the establishment of a Yiddish cultural community resulting from the tens of thousands of Yiddish-speaking immigrants who arrived in Montréal between 1880 and 1920. These seven scholarly articles reveal the way in which the Yiddish-speaking community established its own network of schools, newspapers, religious institutions, political groups, unions and social services whose purpose was to reinforce the strength and viability of the community.

285   **Renewing our days. Montréal Jews in the twentieth century.**
      Edited by Ira Robinson, Mervin Butovsky.   Montréal: Véhicule Press,
      1995. 184p.
Eight scholars from the Jewish community consider the Montréal Jewish community and its relationship with the modern state and with Québec society. In addition, several essays discuss the important heritage of Montréal Jewish writers such as Irving Layton (1912-), Mordecai Richler (1931-) and A. M. Klein (1909-72), and the plurality of voices and identities within the Jewish community. Historically, the Montréal Jewish community has been examined from a pan-Canadian perspective. This book constitutes one of the first efforts to single out and describe the distinct features of the Montréal Jewish community.

286   **Les Juifs du Québec bibliographie rétrospective annotée.** (The Jews
      of Québec: a retrospective annotated bibliography.)
      David Rome, Judith Nefsky, Paule Obermeir.   Québec: Institut
      québécois de Recherche sur la Culture, 1981. 319p.
A bibliography of over 1,600 items relating to both the Ashkenazy and Sephardic Jewish communities in Québec between 1759 and 1981. The book is divided into four chronological sections which approximate the different phases of the Jewish community's development. Each section is further subdivided into thematic chapters which reflect the nature of the community, its interests, concerns and its relations with Québec society during that particular period. The first section of the book contains books which cover several historical periods.

287 **The forgotten Quebecers: a history of English-speaking Quebec, 1759-1980.**
Ronald Rudin. Québec: Institut québécois de Recherche sur la Culture, 1985. 315p. bibliog.

One of the few book-length studies of this kind. Rudin stresses the diversity of the English-speaking population in Québec, which is divided by ethnicity, religion and class. As they share a common language with the rest of North America, however, anglophones face fewer obstacles in migrating to other parts of the continent when economic opportunity presents itself. According to the author, anglophone emigration should not be regarded as a recent phenomenon. Moreover, this work is an excellent source for historical data on the anglophone community since the Conquest. This work combines political and socio-economic history. It also includes a bibliographical appendix.

288 **A different vision: the English in Quebec in the 1990s.**
Reed Scowen. Don Mills, Ontario: Maxwell Macmillan Canada, 1991. 172p.

A work that urges reconciliation between the French-speaking majority and the English-speaking minority in Québec. Scowen, a former English-speaking member of the Québec Liberal Party, argues that the English must reassert themselves in order to 'become fully accepted partners in Québec life'. He writes that, in order to stem the exodus of this language group, fifteen per cent of whom left the province between 1975 and 1990, English speakers must be prepared to use – and defend the right to use – their language in public settings and institutions.

289 **Les Acadiens du Québec.** (The Acadians of Québec.)
Pierre Trépanier. Montréal: Éditions de L'Écho, 1994. 478p.

A landmark work in the history of the Acadians in Québec from their forcible deportation in 1755 to the time of publication. The Acadians were French colonists from what is now Nova Scotia and New Brunswick. Acadia was 'founded' in 1604 by De Monts and Champlain. In 1713, Acadia was ceded to Great Britain under the terms of the Treaty of Utrecht. In 1755, the British deported over 10,000 Acadians, seized their goods and destroyed their homes. Many Acadians ultimately fled to Louisiana, the Carolinas and Virginia. A century later, many of them returned to New Brunswick where they remain to this day. In writing a history of the Acadian people in Québec, Trépanier brings out their national and cultural distinctiveness. Following a description of how Acadians came to Québec, Trépanier devotes a large section to where they settled. Moreover, this book examines the landmarks in the edification of an Acadian identity distinct from the identities of Québec and Canada.

290 **Les Grecs du quartier Parc Extension: insertion linguistique dans la société d'accueil.** (The Greeks from the Parc Extension district: linguistic insertion into the host society.)
Calvin Veltman, Tina Ioannou. Montréal: Institut national de la Recherche scientifique, 1984. 106p.

A thorough study of the linguistic practices of Greeks in the Montréal area. This study attempts to fill the gap in empirical research related to the impact of Québec's language laws on the rate of linguistic assimilation. The results of this investigation reveal the shortcomings of the Canadian census in describing the real-life situation of the Greek community: regardless of whether French or English is declared as the principal language of use, Greek remains the language used in the home and among family members. Moreover, this study observes that the retention of the Greek language among Montréal Greeks is noticeably greater than the retention of the language by Greeks elsewhere in North America, perhaps suggesting that the environment of Montréal is more conducive than elsewhere to the retention of allophone languages.

291 **Remembrance of grandeur. The Anglo-Protestant élite of Montréal. 1900-1950.**
Margaret W. Westley. Montréal: Éditions Libre Expression, 1990. 311p.

Reveals the lives of the small minority of anglophone leaders who made Montréal the commercial capital of Canada for over a century. In the 1890s, some scholars estimated their collective wealth to have reached two-thirds of the nation's wealth, a staggering testament to their power. Westley examines the decline of this community between 1900 and 1950, marking the impact of two world wars and the many other economic and social transformations which slowly silenced the presence of this wealthy minority. Based in part on interviews of more than 100 descendants of the richest anglophone families of the early 20th century, the author argues that their decline was the result of the conservative nature of a society that was living in a closed world and that was unable to adapt to the profound changes taking place around it. Westley also argues that the children of this society did not have the respect of the francophone majority in part due to their self-imposed isolation from the francophone world. On the way of life in this neighbourhood see Donald MacKay's *The square mile* (Vancouver: Douglas and McIntyre Ltd., 1987. 223p.).

292 **The road to now. A history of blacks in Montréal.**
Dorothy W. Williams. Montréal: Véhicule Press, 1997. 235p. maps. bibliog.

Despite the fact that blacks have been part of Canadian and Québec history since the 16th century, few academic works have been written on their history. By virtue of its subject matter, therefore, this overview of the black presence in Montréal marks an important contribution to Québec historiography. Chapters are organized around the pivotal events which have shaped the community's experience in Montréal. In illustrating what it is to be a black Montréaler, Williams describes a community that is not homogeneous but is rather composed of a plurality of groups. In relating this historical process, Williams incorporates many untold stories, thereby giving a unique insight into the community's social history. This book stems from Williams' previous work entitled *Blacks in Montréal 1628-1986: an urban demography* (Cowansville, Québec: Éditions Yvon Blais, 1989. 147p.).

Emigration and Immigration

293 Immigrant odyssey: a French-Canadian habitant in New England.
Félix Albert, translated by Arthur L. Eno, Jr.   Orono, Maine:
University of Maine Press, 1991. 178p.

Rarely do readers enjoy the opportunity to read the autobiographies of illiterate, poor immigrants. In contrast to the monopoly held by the elite over the production of printed material, this work stands out as a historical gem revealing the material and cultural realities of Québec's rural population. This work also has empirical relevance to the established theories of the French Canadian mindset. As suggested by the introductory essay, 'we cannot muse over Félix's life without profoundly questioning the notion of nineteenth-century Québec as a traditional "folk" or "peasant" society comprised of backward, noncapitalist-minded farmers'.

294 Canadian Ethnic Studies = Études Éthniques au Canada.
Calgary, Alberta: Research Centre for Canadian Ethnic Studies,
University of Calgary for the Canadian Ethnic Studies Association,
1969- . 3 issues per year.

A scholarly journal covering ethnic issues and minority issues across Canada. There are many excellent articles on Québec in this journal as well. Another strength of this publication is the bibliographies it frequently includes in its issues.

295 Histoire des Franco-Américains de la Nouvelle-Angleterre,
1775-1990. (A history of Franco-Americans in New England,
1775-1990.)
Armand B. Chartier.   Sillery, Québec: Éditions du Septentrion, 1991.
436p. bibliog.

Written by a Franco-American, this book is a fair attempt to provide a solid history of francophones in New England. The time frame adopted in this work makes it indispensable by virtue of the absence of other research which extends so far into modern times. Focusing on the obstacles facing French-speaking people in their desire to preserve their culture, Chartier concludes this study by looking at the increasing lack of political solidarity among Franco-Americans.

296　**Les Français au Québec, 1765-1865: un mouvement migratoire méconnu.** (The French in Québec, 1765-1865: an underestimated migration.)
Marcel Fournier.　Sillery, Québec: Éditions du Septentrion, 1995. 387p. bibliog.

French immigration did not end with the English Conquest. Divided into two sections, this book begins with an explanation of the different waves of immigration that came from France. The author argues that those immigrants represented a bridge between France and its former colony and that this favoured the maintenance of French traditions in Québec. The second section of the book is a directory of 1,487 French immigrants who arrived in Québec between 1765 and 1865. Information on their region of origin, where they settled, their occupation and their civil status accompanies each entry. The book includes an index.

297　**L'immigration pour quoi faire?** (Immigration. What is the point?)
Denise Helly.　Québec: Institut québécois de Recherche sur la Culture, 1992. 229p.

Written by a recognized specialist on Québec immigration, this book is divided into two sections that discuss the processes preceding immigration and integration into a particular society. The first section deals with society's motivations to accept immigrants: the question of how many should be accepted; and on the bases of what criteria they should be chosen. The second section examines the question of identity and integration and asks what type of integration should be favoured and how should immigrants define themselves. The author also presents the state of the debate on these questions in Québec based on a series of interviews with bureaucrats, journalists and politicians involved in immigration. See also *Immigrés et création d'entreprise* (Immigrants and business creation) (Québec: Institut québécois de Recherche sur la Culture, 1994. 305p.) by Denise Helly and Alberte Ledoyen.

298　**From being uprooted to surviving. Resettlement of Vietnamese-Chinese 'Boat-people' in Montréal, 1980-1990.**
Lawrence Lam.　Toronto: York Lanes Press, 1996. 200p.

The presentation of a longitudinal study of the resettlement process experienced by Vietnamese-Chinese refugees living in Montréal. The book begins with an examination of the 'Boat People' phenomenon itself as described by media reports. This study is useful in revealing the structural barriers these refugees have attempted to overcome in trying to find a home for themselves and their families. Also on the Vietnamese community, see *Du Viêt-Nam au Québec: la valse des identités* (From Vietnam to Québec: the waltz of identities) (Québec: Institut québécois de la Recherche sur la Culture, 1995. 224p.) by Caroline Méthot.

299 **L'immigration et les communautés culturelles du Québec:**
1968-1990. (Immigration and cultural communities in Québec,
1968-90.)
Van Be Lam.   Québec: Documentor, 1991. 142p. bibliog.

Divided into three sections, this bibliography contains over 600 titles demonstrating the rich contribution made by cultural communities to Québec. The first section contains titles which deal with the economic and psycho-sociological impact cultural communities have had on Québec society. The second examines their integration into the host society. The third section, of use to educators, lists useful resources and reference tools for combating prejudices and racism. This last section is designed as a reference tool for teachers and students. For an expanded and updated edition of Lam's work, see item no. 300. Another relevant work is *Migration et communautés culturelles* (Migration and cultural communities) (Québec: Institut québécois de Recherche sur la Culture, 1982. 157p.) by Gary Caldwell and Fernand Harvey.

300 **L'immigration et les communautés culturelles du Québec:**
1990-1995. (Immigration and cultural communities in Québec,
1968-90.)
Van Be Lam.   Saint-Laurent, Québec: Éditions Sans Frontières, 1995.
198p. bibliog.

An expanded version of Lam's previous bibliography (see item no. 299). Over 400 titles, published between 1990 and the summer of 1995, are classified in this book. The first section lists titles which deal primarily with cultural communities and immigration in Québec and Canada. The titles in the second section are classified according to the various cultural communities in Québec and focus primarily on their socio-economic and sociocultural impact. The last section lists resources for teachers and students.

301 **Le Bazar, des anciens Canadiens aux nouveaux Québécois.**
(The bazaar: from old Canadians to new Quebecers.)
Daniel Latouche.   Montréal: Éditions du Boréal, 1990. 286p.

A humorous discourse on language, multiculturalism, demography and nationalism in present-day Québec. Latouche is one of Québec's most accessible and popular political commentators.

302 **L'émigration des Canadiens aux États-Unis avant 1930. Mesure**
du phénomène. (Assessing Canadian emigration to the United States
before 1930.)
Yolande Lavoie.   Montréal: Presses de l'Université de Montréal,
1972. 90p.

Poor record-keeping and the relative ease with which people could cross the Canadian American border have made it difficult to accurately assess the exodus of French Quebecers to the United States prior to 1930. In an effort to remedy this shortcoming, Lavoie critically assesses the statistical sources of the times in an effort to come to terms with the exodus. Lavoie's research remains among the most competent and respected on the subject.

303 **Montréal. Une société multiculturelle.** (Montréal. A multicultural society.)
Claire McNicoll.   Paris: Belin, 1993. 317p.

A thoughtful investigation into Montréal's original and unique approach to the integration of immigrants. Increased cultural diversity, due to large waves of immigration from the developing world following the 1960s, has forced North American society to question its method of integration. McNicoll highlights Montréal's exemplary approach towards accommodating new arrivals, an approach that avoids both cultural assimilation, on one hand, and ghettoization, on the other. The work focuses largely on the tensions between value systems and the process of social and economic integration.

304 **Textes de l'exode: recueil de textes sur l'émigration des Québécois aux États-Unis, XIXe et XXe siècles.** (Texts from the exodus: a collection of essays on Québec emigration to the United States during the 19th and 20th centuries.)
Edited by Maurice Poteet, Régis Normandeau.   Montréal: Guérin, 1987. 505p.

Why, during the latter half of the 19th century, hundreds of thousands of francophone Catholics emigrated to English-speaking Protestant New England comprises the central question of this book. Designed as an introduction to this important chapter in Québec's history, this book provides excerpts and reprints of articles and essays written since 1850 pertaining to the exodus. The first section contains essays on the phenomenon itself, culled from various newspapers and academic journals. The second part comprises excerpts from various texts written by the emigrants themselves, regarding the challenges they faced once in New England. The final section provides samples of Franco-American literature.

305 **Les Franco-Américains de la Nouvelle-Angleterre, 1776-1930.** (Franco-Americans of New England, 1776-1930.)
Yves Roby.   Sillery, Québec: Éditions du Septentrion, 1990. 434p.

A well-researched, wide-ranging portrait of Québec migration to New England prior to 1930. This synthesis is valuable for its consideration of research already published in the United States as well as in Québec. In addition, Roby provides the reader with new information regarding the religious and cultural life of Québec emigrants. The book's strong focus on social history also provides a balanced portrait of Quebecers' experiences.

306 **Le défi de l'immigration.** (The challenge of immigration.)
Jean-Pierre Rogel.   Québec: Institut québécois de Recherche sur la Culture, 1989. 122p. bibliog.

The author examines the possible ramifications of the newest wave of immigrants to Québec. In only eight years, the number of persons of Asian descent coming to the province increased from twenty-six to forty-two per cent of total immigrants. Such 'visible minorities', the author posits, may have greater trouble integrating into Québec society than earlier European immigrants. Rogel goes on to say that this fact, coupled with the low birth rate of francophone Quebecers, warrants a reconsideration of Québec's immigration and naturalization policy. Among his conclusions, the author emphasizes the importance of acculturizing immigrants through the school system and attracting more immigrants from French-speaking countries.

307 **Ah les États! Les travailleurs canadiens-français dans l'industrie textile de la Nouvelle-Angleterre d'après le témoignage des derniers migrants.** (The States! French Canadian workers in the New England textile industry based on the last migrants.)
Jacques Rouillard.   Montréal: Éditions du Boréal Express, 1985. 155p.

A rich analysis of francophone emigration to the United States from 1900 to 1930 based principally on interviews with rural francophone Quebecers who migrated to New England and later returned to Québec. Rouillard attempts to discover why over 400,000 Quebecers migrated despite the dire warnings of the clergy and elites of the times. The oral tradition, rediscovered by Rouillard in this work, provides fresh insight into the actual experiences of those Quebecers and stands in contrast to the 'official' interpretation of the elite. The second half of the book contains the transcripts of the more important interviews.

Women

308 **Pendant que les hommes travaillaient, les femmes elles. . . .**
(While the men were working, the women were . . . .)
Association féminine d'Éducation et d'Action sociale.   Montréal:
Guérin Éditeur, 1977. 405p.

A biographical reference work on 266 women who made an important contribution to
Québec society between 1820 and 1950. The biographical entries are arranged alphabetically and cross-referenced by theme (work, agriculture, etc.) and geography. Entries are
short and list important achievements, dates of birth and death, and areas of activity.

309 **Femmes et pouvoir dans l'église.** (Women and power in the Church.)
Edited by Anita Caron.   Outremont, Québec: VLB Éditeur, 1991.
254p. bibliog. (Études Québécoises, no. 19).

Thanks to the feminist movement, women became increasingly involved, following
the Second World War, in spheres of activity previously closed to them. But, despite
the increasing equality women experienced in society, the Church denied them a place
in the ecclesiastical power structure. This collection of essays seeks to understand why
women remained in a social structure which treated them as second-class citizens. In
answering this question, the authors suggest that there has been a trend within the
Québec Church for women to take on a greater role in the administration and management of parish activities.

310 **Femmes et politique.** (Women and politics.)
Edited by Yolande Cohen.   Montréal: Le Jour, 1981. 227p.

In addition to describing the growing politicization of women and the particular
visions of politics they espouse, the authors also address the role of the intellectual in
the feminist movement. These texts come from a variety of perspectives, and include
critical and empirical studies, history and writings by feminist militants. This collection
also demonstrates the dynamic debate over the future of the feminist movement that
occurs among its members. See also the author's more recent *Femmes et contre-pouvoir*
(Women and opposition force) (Montréal: Éditions du Boréal Express, 1987. 244p.).

311 **Ces femmes qui ont bâti Montréal: la petite et la grande histoire des femmes qui ont marqué la vie de Montréal depuis 350 ans.** (The women who built Montréal: the official and unofficial history of the women who have made their mark on Montréal life over the last 350 years.)
Edited by Maryse Darsigny, Francine Descarries, Lyne Kurtzman, Évelyne Tardy. Montréal: Éditions du Remue-Ménage, 1994. 627p.

This book reveals the significant contributions made by women, largely unknown, to Montréal's development and evolution. Over 350 short articles, many illustrated with photographs, are arranged in chronological order into five socio-historical sections which approximate the distinct periods in the social role of women in Montréal. Each of these five sections is preceded by a brief introductory paragraph relating the important events and milestones of each period. Several of the biographical entries suggest further reading.

312 **Une femme, mille enfants. Justine Lacoste Beaubien.** (One woman, a thousand children. Justine Lacoste Beaubien.)
Madeleine Des Rivières. Montréal: Éditions Bellarmin, 1987. 271p. bibliog.

A history of the founder of the Saint-Justine Hospital for Children, Justine Lacoste Beaubien (1877-1967). Founded for the care of sick children in 1907, the hospital was under Lacoste Beaubien's stewardship until 1966. This book recounts the life of one of Québec's most important women. It does not, however, deal with the hospital's history other than in relation to its founder.

313 **Québec women: a history.**
Micheline Dumont, Michèle Jean, Marie Lavigne, Jennifer Stoddart. Toronto: The Women's Press, 1987. 396p.

Unwilling to see women dispossessed of history, the authors describe the lives of the anonymous women who lived through history and have remained largely forgotten by a historiography that has focused almost exclusively on famous individuals. Much of the book examines changes in birthing techniques, raising children, pregnancy and delivery, and household work. Moreover, the authors emphasize the common experiences of women rather than just the experiences of those women who penetrated traditionally male-dominated spheres of activity. To contextualize these descriptions of women's lives, each chapter is preceded by a short summary of the important events during the period.

314 **Les religieuses sont-elles féministes?** (Are religious women feminists?)
Micheline Dumont. Montréal: Éditions Bellarmin, 1995. 204p.

Despite the seemingly ideological contradictions between feminism and religious thought, Dumont reveals how both have enhanced the role of women in society. This book suggests that women's religious orders belong to the same category of institutions that collectively attempted to influence political and economic life in order to improve women's situation in society. Dumont also examines new perspectives from which to understand women's history. Aside from the typical perspectives of oppression, domination, alienation and subordination, Dumont also considers women's experiences from the perspective of their individual and collective aspirations. Readers interested in further studies on religious orders and women should consult Marguerite Jean's *Évolution des communautés religieuses au Canada de 1639 à nos jours* (The evolution of religious communities in Canada from 1639 to the present) (Montréal: Fides, 1977. 324p.).

315 **Le Féminisme en Revue.** (Feminism in Review.)
Montréal: Fédération des Femmes du Québec, 1987-92. irregular.

This publication was the official press organ of the Québec Women's Federation, an important organization which has played a major role in the defence of the poor during the last few years. This magazine presents the results of member polls on various issues, articles on subjects that affect women, and information on different feminist demonstrations in Québec.

316 **Fragments et collages, essai sur le féminisme québécois des années 70.** (Fragments and collages, an essay on Québec feminism during the 1970s.)
Diane Lamoureux.   Montréal: Éditions du Remue-Ménage, 1986. 168p.

One of the very few book-length works on the relations between the feminist and nationalist movements in Québec.

317 **Travailleuses et féministes: les femmes dans la société québécoise.**
(Workers and feminists: women in Québec society.)
Edited by Marie Lavigne, Yolande Pinard.   Montréal: Éditions du Boréal Express, 1983. 430p. (Études d'Histoire du Québec, no. 13).

A collection of sixteen texts which take a thematic approach to the issues of salaried working women and the women's movement since the 19th century. These texts cover women involved in union movements, women labourers and farmers, and women in the Church who battled and fought in areas traditionally forbidden to them. Two women have especially marked the labour movement in Québec: Léa Roback and Madeleine Parent. Their experiences and thoughts have been published in Nicole Lacelle's *Madeleine Parent, Léa Roback: entretiens avec Nicole Lacelle* (Madeleine Parent, Léa Roback: conversations with Nicole Lacelle) (Montréal: Éditions du Remue-Ménage, 1988. 181p.). Domestic work, which remained the principal source of work for women during this century, is examined in Claudette Lacelle's *Urban domestic servants in nineteenth-century Canada* (Ottawa: National Historic Parks and Sites, Environment Canada, 1987. 254p.). The evolution of women's work in the 20th century is partially examined in Francine Barry's *Le travail de la femme au Québec. L'évolution de 1940 à 1970* (The evolution of women's work in Québec from 1940 to 1970) (Montréal: Presses de l'Université du Québec, 1977. 80p.).

318 **La recherche sur les femmes au Québec: bilan et bibliographie.**
(Research on women in Québec: assessment and bibliography.)
Denise Lemieux, Lucie Mercier.   Québec: Institut québécois de Recherche sur la Culture, 1982. 336p.

On the daily lives of women in Québec see: Denise Lemieux and Lucie Mercier's *Les femmes au tournant du siècle, 1880-1940* (Women at the turn of the century) (Institut québécois de Recherche sur la Culture, 1989. 398p.); and Denyse Baillargeon's *Ménagère au temps de la crise* (Housekeepers during the Depression) (Montréal: Éditions du Remue-Ménage, 1991. 311p.).

319 **Making and breaking the rules: women in Québec, 1919-1939.**
Andrée Lévesque, translated by Yvonne M. Klein. Toronto:
McClelland and Stewart, 1994. 170p. (Canadian Social History Series, no. 17).

Examines the degree to which the elite's standards on sexuality, maternity, and the role of women in society, were reflected in the population at large. Following a description of the ways in which doctors, politicians, and priests defined and enforced their moral code, Lévesque analyses the phenomena of contraception, abortion, infanticide, and prostitution as ways women transgressed the norm. Lévesque's detailed analysis and description of these practices reveals a society in the midst of transformation, which challenges the rather static view of pre-1960 Québec as characterized by an overarching and pervasive conservative consensus. According to Lévesque, the difference between the prescribed rules and reality illustrate the degree to which social expectations were changing. The perception of women according to male-defined ideology is well presented in Mona-Josée Gagnon's *Les femmes vues par le Québec des hommes. 30 ans d'histoire des idéologies, 1940-1970* (Women viewed by male Québec society. A history of thirty years of ideology) (Montréal: Éditions du Jour, 1974. 159p.). For a history of women during the Second World War, see Geneviève Auger and Raymond Lamothe's *De la poêle à frire à la ligne de feu: la vie quotidienne des Québécoises pendant la guerre '39-45* (From the frying pan to the firing line: the daily life of Québec women during the Second World War) (Montréal: Éditions du Boréal Express, 1982. 232p.).

320 **Les Québécoises et la conquête du pouvoir politique: enquête sur l'émergence d'une élite politique féminine au Québec.** (Québec women and the conquest of political power: a study of the emergence of a female political elite in Québec.)
Chantal Maillé.   Montréal: Éditions Saint-Martin, 1990. 194p.

Traces the origins and development of women's political power from the right to vote to their quest for representation and then to the establishment of a political elite. Maillé elaborates an original approach to the study of the emergence of political elites in incorporating gender relations into her argument. She suggests that the emergence of a female political elite is due to a rupture in society provoked by the transformation of attitudes regarding gender roles, the modification of social structures which granted women access to education and new job opportunities, and the growing willingness of political parties to nominate female candidates. Readers should also consult Constance Backhouse's *Petticoats and prejudice. Women and the law in nineteenth century Canada* (Toronto: Women's Educational Press, 1980. 467p.) which reveals the differences between the civil and common legal traditions and their impact on women's legal status and the rights they could and could not enjoy. Also see Irène Lépine's *Prendre sa place! Les femmes dans l'univers organisationnel* (Taking their place! Women in organizations) (Ottawa: Agence d'Arc, 1991. 365p.).

321 **Pionnières québécoises et regroupements de femmes d'hier à aujourd'hui.** (Women pioneers and women's groups in Québec from yesterday to today.)
Simonne Monet-Chartrand. Montréal: Éditions du Remue-Ménage, 1990. 470p. bibliog.

A history of women from the habitants (those who lived on the land in colonial times) to modern times. Chartrand, a founding member of the Québec Women's Federation, provides a social and political history of women in Québec. The work is structured as a chronological anthology and is primarily composed of excerpts and citations.

322 **Recherches Féministes.** (Feminist Research.)
Québec: Groupe de Recherche et d'Échange multidisciplinaire féministe, Université Laval, 1988- . 2 issues per year.

Contains original empirical studies which contribute towards the advancement of feminist research. This scholarly journal also publishes essays of a theoretical, epistemological and methodological nature, research notes, bibliographies, and book reviews.

323 **Droits des femmes en France et au Québec, 1940-1990.** (Women's rights in France and in Québec, 1940-90.)
Mariette Sineau, Évelyne Tardy. Montréal: Éditions du Remue-Ménage, 1993. 153p. bibliog.

A history of the legal rights gained by women in France and Québec and the different means each respective movement took to secure those rights. The authors attempt to demonstrate that, despite divergent historical paths, feminists in both countries are facing, for the first time, the same problems: an increasingly marginalized state role in social programmes and the issue of women's quality of life.

324 **Les bâtisseuses de la cité.** (The builders of the city.)
Edited by Évelyne Tardy. Montréal: Association canadienne-française pour l'Avancement des Sciences, 1992. 407p.

It is impossible to discuss Montréal's history without mentioning the names Jeanne Mance (1606-73) and Saint Marguerite Bourgeoys (1620-1700) among others. Women have been an integral force behind the economic, social and cultural development of the city. This work discusses their historical achievements in addition to the contemporary challenges facing them in the municipal context. The texts published in this volume comprise the proceedings of the women's studies seminars of the 1992 annual ACFAS (Association canadienne-française pour l'Avancement des Sciences – French Canadian Association for the Advancement of Sciences) Congress.

325   **Maires et mairesses du Québec: différences et ressemblances.**
(Mayors and women mayors in Québec: differences and similarities.)
Évelyne Tardy.   Montréal: Université du Québec à Montréal,
Département de Science politique, 1995. 58p. (Notes de Recherches,
no. 51).

A study of the presence of women in elected positions of power at the municipal level
of government. Aside from the similarities of age, motivation for seeking municipal
office, and degree of previous involvement in political activities, female and male
mayors are differentiated by the fact that female mayors do not hold a job outside of
the mayor's office, they are often more educated, and they face greater discrimination
in seeking office because of their gender. See also *Femmes et pouvoir* (Women and
power) (Montréal: Université du Québec à Montréal, Institut de Recherche et d'Études
féministes, 1995. 169p.) edited by Évelyne Tardy.

326   **Que font-elles en politique?** (What do women do in politics?)
Manon Tremblay, Réjean Pelletier.   Sainte-Foy, Québec: Presses de
l'Université Laval, 1995. 284p.

Compares the political experiences of women and men. Three stages of political
action are examined: entry into politics, the exercise of political power, and political
retirement. What is interesting in this study is the surprising conclusion that despite
contrasting backgrounds, obstacles and resources, once in politics the political
experiences of both sexes differ less than expected. In conclusion, this important study
poses the question of whether the achievement of power erases gender differences.

Language

Reference

327 **Dictionnaire de la langue québécoise.** (Dictionary of the Québec language.)
Léandre Bergeron. Montréal: VLB Éditeur, 1980. 574p.

A controversial dictionary which includes vocabulary derived from the inter-mixing of the French and aboriginal languages in addition to the particular slang expressions in use in Québec (a mix of French words with English syntax). The dictionary also includes a lot of expressions which are not in use any longer.

328 **Dictionnaire des difficultés de la langue francaise.** (Dictionary of difficult words and expressions in the French language.)
Gérard Dagenais. Québec: Éditions Pedagogia, 1967. 679p.

This dictionary informs the reader of the proper grammar and syntax to be used. The author uses history to explain the real meaning of certain words, thereby helping the reader to understand the words' proper usage. Whereas Léandre Bergeron's dictionary (see item no. 327) has been classified as populist, this work finds inspiration in a more elitist and structural conception of the French language.

329 **Régionalismes québécois usuels.** (Common Québec regionalisms.)
Robert Dubuc, Jean-Claude Boulanger. Paris: Conseil international de la Langue française, 1983. 227p.

Targeted at francophones outside of Québec, this work provides standard French definitions and examples of usage of over 250 uniquely Québec expressions. The reader can expect to find those expressions that are at once modern, creative, in frequent usage and universally understood across Québec. Consequently, this work does not include expressions exclusively used in particular regions of Québec.

330 **Dictionnaire des canadianismes.** (Dictionary of Canadianisms.)
Gaston Dulong. Montréal: Larousse Canada, 1985. 461p. maps.
Written by a well-known linguist, this dictionary deals with over 8,000 words or
expressions which belong to the oral language of French Canadians from Québec and
Acadia. The author gives a short definition of each word and the origin of the word.
This last information shows the influence aboriginal peoples and anglophones had in
the development of the oral language spoken in Québec.

331 **Le parler populaire du Québec et de ses régions voisines. Atlas
linguistique de l'Est du Canada.** (The popular dialects of Québec and
its neighbouring regions. A linguistic atlas of Eastern Canada.)
Gaston Dulong, Gaston Bergeron. Québec: Ministère des
Communications, Office de la Langue française, 1980. 10 vols.
With the idea that a people's history is intimately linked to the evolution of its
language, these ten volumes present the first scientific investigation of Québec's
linguistic heritage. This study provides statistics and information on the lexical, phonetic
and geographic trends and characteristics of Québec's popular dialects with reference
to standard French.

332 **Le Colpron. Le nouveau dictionnaire des anglicismes.**
(The Colpron. The new dictionary of Anglicisms.)
Constance Forest, Louis Forest. Laval, Québec: Éditions
Beauchemin, 1994. 289p.
An Anglicism is a word, expression, or compound word used in French and borrowed,
legitimately or not, from the English language. This book highlights only those
expressions which are incorrect. Thus while 'editorial' and 'football' remain legitimate, certain expressions such as 'point-de-vue' (for opinion) are not accepted as
correct usage. This dictionary explains the correct usage for the terms frequently
employed incorrectly by both anglophones and francophones. It is a useful and well-
presented tool for perfecting one's French.

333 **Dictionnaire du français québécois.** (Dictionary of Québec French.)
Edited by Claude Poirier. Sainte-Foy, Québec: Presses de
l'Université Laval, 1985. 169p.
A short but very detailed dictionary of words found in Québec and its regions. The
author not only provides definitions of the words but also cites newspaper articles,
novels and other dictionaries in which the words have been employed.

334 **Le français populaire au Québec et au Canada.** (Popular French in
Québec and Canada.)
Lorenzo Proteau. Boucherville, Québec: Les Publications Proteau,
1991. 1,116p.
A general inventory of common expressions used in Québec. Divided into thematic
sections (sports, business, etc.) each expression is presented by key word. This dictionary
does not pretend to provide correct French, but rather relates the terms and expressions
one will hear on the street and on television. Containing plentiful illustrations, this
book is aimed at the general public.

335   **Revue Québécoise de Linguistique.** (Québec Journal of Linguistics.)
Montréal: Département de Linguistique, Université du Québec à
Montréal, 1981- .
Deals with the major debates in the field of linguistics. This scholarly journal also
studies the state of the French language in Québec in relation to linguistic theory, and
it contains book reviews. It succeeds *Les Cahiers de Linguistique* (Linguistic Studies)
(Montréal: Département de Linguistique, Université du Québec à Montréal, 1971-80).

336   **Dictionnaire de la langue québécoise rurale.** (A dictionary of the
language of rural Québec.)
David Rogers.   Montréal: VLB Éditeur, 1977. 246p.
A very well put together dictionary of words used in rural Québec. The author
provides a good short definition of each word along with a reference to a novel in
which the word is used. This is a helpful tool for those who want to gain a better
understanding of novels set in, or about, rural Québec.

337   **Glossaire du parler français au Canada.** (A glossary of spoken
French in Canada.)
La Société du Parler français au Canada.   Sainte-Foy, Québec: Presses
de l'Université Laval, 1968. 709p.
Originally published in 1930, this dictionary of French is a scientific study of the
vocabulary employed in spoken French in Canada. It provides the phonetic pro-
nunciation, examples of usage and the etymology of each listed word.

General

338   **Le choc de patois en Nouvelle-France: essai sur l'histoire de la
francisation au Canada.** (The impact of patois in New France:
an essay on the history of Gallicization in Canada.)
Philippe Barbeau.   Sillery, Québec: Presses de l'Université du
Québec, 1984. 204p.
From a structural and historical hypothesis, the author attempts to understand what
defined the character of the French Canadian language during the French regime.
Tracing a parallel between the situation in France where more than thirty-three
dialects were spoken at the end of the 18th century, the author argues that the creation
of a homogeneous French Canadian language was the result of the assimilation of the
different dialects by the Île-de-France dialect.

339 **La lexicologie québécoise. Bilan et perspectives.** (Québec lexicology. Perspectives and assessment.)
Edited by Lionel Boisvert, Claude Poirier, Claude Verrault.
Sainte-Foy, Québec: Presses de l'Université Laval, 1986. 308p.

The production of Québec glossaries and dictionaries has undoubtedly increased Quebecers' awareness of their own linguistic specificity. This book comprises the proceedings of a conference uniting various researchers of the Québec lexicon. Beyond an assessment of researchers' activities, this work introduces the reader to the problems associated with the geographic and socio-political variations in the French language across the world. These essays provide an interesting portrait of the regionalization of French and the tension between these regionalisms and 'standard' French.

340 **Languages of the skies: the bilingual air traffic control conflict in Canada.**
Sandford F. Borins.   Montréal; Kingston, Ontario: McGill-Queen's University Press, 1983. 285p.

Describes and analyses the conflict between anglophones and francophones over the language to be used in air traffic control which took place in Québec in 1976. While most authors examining anglophone-francophone friction tend to focus on constitutional politics, Borins examines the degree to which this bureaucratic conflict reveals the fault lines of linguistic tension in the country. The roles of public opinion, the government, and leaders within each group testify to the extent to which the population was suddenly mobilized around this issue. Lasting from 1976 to 1980, the issue of language in air traffic control demonstrates many of the nuances of linguistic tension in Québec.

341 **Conflict and language planning in Québec.**
Edited by Richard Y. Bourhis.   Clevedon, England: Multilingual Matters Ltd., 1984. 304p. maps.

From a multidisciplinary perspective, these ten essays discuss various aspects of, and the impacts of, Québec's efforts to make French the sole official language of Québec. These essays attempt to explain the motives behind the adoption of Bill 101 in addition to investigating the manifold ways in which the Bill has touched almost all sectors of society. The Bill was ratified in 1977 and is alternatively known as the Charter of the French Language. Its primary goal was to allow the majority of Quebecers to live and develop in a French environment by bringing the French language to the forefront of public and economic life. Most importantly, it established the French language as the common language in Québec. Aspects of Bill 101 touched education, the economy and government. Several chapters of this book are devoted to discussing how the law has been received by those who opposed its implementation, such as members of the business community and the anglophone community.

342 **La qualité de la langue au Québec.** (The quality of French in Québec.)
Hélène Cajolet-Laganière, Pierre Martel.   Québec: Institut québécois de Recherche sur la Culture, 1995. 167p.

Once the euphoria surrounding the implementation of language laws subsided, many in Québec realized that the 1977 Charter of the French Language (Bill 101) did nothing to protect the integrity of the language. This work, written by a scholar in cooperation with a former president of the Conseil de la langue française (French Language Council), examines the evolution of French in Québec. Both authors suggest that the survival of French in Québec requires more than legal status and protection. They make a well-argued plea for the development of the quality of the language. This book discusses what is meant by 'quality of the language', a term which was created in Québec. In so doing, the authors assess how quality is perceived by the population at large. Over all, this is a good layman's introduction to the issues relating to the quality of French in Québec. Martel has also written *Le français québécois: usages, standard et aménagement* (Québec French: usage, standard and planning) (Sainte-Foy, Québec: Institut québécois de Recherche sur la Culture, 1996. 141p.).

343   **The position of the French language in Québec: report of the Commission of Inquiry on the position of the French language and on language rights in Québec.**
Commission d'Enquête sur la Situation de la Langue française et sur les Droits linguistiques au Québec.   Québec: Éditeur officiel du Québec, 1972. 3 vols. maps.

Generally known as the Gendron Commission, the Commission of Inquiry looked into the position of the French language and language rights between 1968 and 1972 and was part of the government's response to an increasingly complex problem – that of language. In attempting to understand contemporary language debates, the work of the Commission is especially useful in explaining the political and legal context within which the Québec government decided to expand its legislative role into the sector of language. The three volumes which comprise the Commissioners' final report (Language of work, Language rights, and The ethnic groups) have not lost their relevance in explaining the rights of the anglophone and allophone minorities as well as the rights of the francophone majority, in addition to elaborating the principles which should guide the government in its formulation of any language policy. The report's appendices, which contain the opinions of leading experts in the field of language rights, will be of special import to those interested in pursuing research in this area. For a recent history of the evolution of the French language in Québec and a policy position with respect to French as the common language, see the *Rapport du Comité interministériel sur la situation de la langue française: le français langue commune, enjeu de la société québécoise* (Report of the Interministerial Committee on francophone society: French as a common language, Québec's position) (Québec: Éditeur officiel, 1996. 319p.).

344   **Language rights in French Canada.**
Pierre A. Coulombe.   New York: Peter Lang Publishers, 1995. 176p. bibliog.

Combining political philosophy with public policy analysis, this book attempts to make a strong case in support of French language rights as a matter of justice in Québec. It argues for some reconciliation between liberal values and collective goals that aim to protect the French Canadian identity in, and outside, the province. The author is sensitive to the lingering resistance to language protection and official bilingualism across Canada.

345 **Les trois États de la politique linguistique au Québec: d'une société
traduite à une société d'expression.** (The three states of Québec's
linguistic policy: from a translated society to a society of expression.)
Jean-Claude Gémar.   Québec: Conseil de la Langue française, 1983.
201p.

Published by the Conseil de la Langue française (French Language Council), the
agency responsible for advising the Québec government on language, this book
examines Bill 101 (the Charter of the French Language) and compares it with previous
language laws. Gémar highlights the state's growing intervention in the language
debate in addition to the importance of language as a defining characteristic of the
Québec nation. While this book does not attempt to measure the relative success or
failure of these laws, interested readers will find Gémar's research useful in understanding the importance of language and its relationship with the state, as well as the
social and political events which gave popular support to the laws. The annex contains
the complete text of Bills 85, 63, 22, and 101.

346 **Contextes de la politique linguistique québécoise.** (The contexts of
linguistic policy in Québec.)
Edited by Marc V. Levine.   Québec: Conseil de la Langue française,
1993. 181p.

An important work on the language debate in the 1990s. The author identifies five
challenges facing the government in its continued involvement in language issues: the
political impact of legislation; the impact of demographic change; the judicial impact
of the Free Trade Agreement on existing legislation; market globalization and the
emergence of new technologies; and, finally, the cultural attraction of French for
young people. Every essay is well researched.

347 **The reconquest of Montreal: language policy and social change
in a bilingual city.**
Marc V. Levine.   Philadelphia: Temple University Press, 1990. 285p.
maps.

Levine examines the historical patterns of language dominance in Montréal, highlighting the uneasy coexistence of French and English speakers. The first part of the
book emphasizes the politicization of language in the 1960s and 1970s. During those
years, francophone nationalists advocated state intervention to alter Montréal's
linguistic balance of power. This culminated in the three language laws enacted
between 1969 and 1977: Bill 63 (1969), which aimed to promote the French language
as the predominant language in Québec but also gave all parents the right to choose
their children's language of instruction; Bill 22 (1974), which made French Québec's
official language; and Bill 101 (1977), otherwise known as the Charter of the French
Language (see item no. 341). The second part of the volume analyses the changes to
Montréal's linguistic landscape, particularly the changes relating to education, public
administration and business. Levine identifies the new linguistic challenge as arising
from beyond the island of Montréal, most notably from the new immigrants and the
pervasive American influence.

348 **Quebec's language policies: background and response.**
Edited by John R. Mallea.   Québec: Presses de l'Université Laval,
1977. 242p.

Though somewhat dated, this work provides an excellent introduction to language policy in Québec. Sections cover the politics of culture, demographic trends, education, and the status of French as a language of business. The appendix includes Bills 85, 63, and 22. For an outline of the background to the relations between the English and French in Québec and the language conflict before 1970 see Guy Bouthillier and Jean Meynaud (eds.), *Le choc des langues au Québec, 1760-1970* (The impact of languages in Québec, 1760-1970) (Montréal: Presses de l'Université du Québec, 1972. 739p.) and Pierre Godin's *La poudrière linguistique* (The linguistic powder-keg) (Montréal: Éditions du Boréal, 1990. 372p.).

349 **Les origines du français québécois.** (The origins of Québec French.)
Edited by Raymond Mougeon, Édouard Beniak.   Sainte-Foy, Québec:
Presses de l'Université Laval, 1994. 332p.

An attempt to reveal the conditions which shaped the development and evolution of the French language in Québec. What, for instance, contributed to the emergence of a single dialect in New France while multiple dialects were in existence in France until the 18th century? This book sets out to answer the preceding question by analysing the French language as spoken by the elite, in the regions, and by the general public. This book underscores an important part of Québec's linguistic specificity upon which much of contemporary Québec is built.

350 **La politique linguistique du Québec, 1977-1987.** (The politics of language in Québec, 1977-87.)
Michel Plourde.   Québec: Institut québécois de Recherche sur la Culture, 1988. 142p.

The author argues unabashedly for continued protection of the French language by the Québec government. Published ten years after the adoption of Bill 101 (the Charter of the French Language), this work also evaluates past, and more recent, attempts to bolster Québec's sense of linguistic security.

351 **Le débat linguistique au Québec. La communauté italienne et la langue d'enseignement.** (The linguistic debate in Québec. The Italian community and the language of education.)
Donat J. Taddeo, Raymond C. Taras, translated by Brigitte Morel-Nish.
Montréal: Presses de l'Université de Montréal, 1987. 243p. bibliog.

An examination of the Italian communities' position on the language of education from 1920 to the mid-1980s. In 1968, in what became known as the Saint-Léonard demonstrations, the Italian community captured the public's attention in a clash with francophones over the language of education. As the Italian community was the largest non-francophone, non-anglophone community in Québec, this event has become a reference point for the contemporary language issue and the debate over which language cultural communities should adopt when they arrive in Québec. This book is an academic first in revealing the historical development of the Italian community's institutions and organizations, ultimately leading to the affirmation of their political strength in 1968, and their political action up until the mid-1980s. It also relates the role played by the Catholic School Commission in the linguistic debate.

Health and Welfare

General

352 **Le système de santé au Québec: organisation, acteurs et enjeux.**
(Québec's health system: organization, actors and issues.)
Edited by Vincent Lemieux, Pierre Bergeron, Clermont Bégin, Gérard
Bélanger.   Sainte-Foy, Québec: Presses de l'Université Laval, 1994.
370p.

This collection of essays is certainly one of the best comprehensive analyses of the different aspects of Québec's health system. The first section of the book deals with the role of the state in the health sector. The book includes an excellent essay by Marc Ferland and Ginette Paquet on the impact of social factors on the welfare of different strata of the population. The second section is devoted to the health sector's administrative organization and the government's public policy in the field of health. The third section examines the medical and health professions and the last section describes the financial and technological resources of the industry.

353 **Santé et inégalités sociales. Un problème de distance culturelle.**
(Health and social inequality. A problem of cultural distance.)
Ginette Paquet.   Québec: Institut québécois de Recherche sur la
Culture, 1989. 133p.

Paquet suggests that the institutionalization of health services has contributed to the inequality among social classes with regard to their respective levels of general health. This book links this inequality with the lifestyles of the various social groups, and examines the efforts made by government agencies to encourage new, and healthier, lifestyles among the population. Paquet attributes the varying levels of health to differences in general culture among classes.

354 **Mental health and aboriginal people of Québec.**
Edited by Bella H. Petawabano, Éric Gourdeau, Francine Jourdain,
Aani Palliser-Tulugak, Jacquelin Cossette. Montréal: Gaëtan Morin
Éditeur, 1994. 304p.

A report commissioned by the Comité de la santé mentale du Québec (Committee on
Mental Health in Québec) seeking to discover the causes of mental illness among
aboriginal people. The report claims that aboriginals and their communities face
specific problems directly related to the tutelage they have experienced during the past
century. The report makes several recommendations to alleviate these problems,
including the adoption of a holistic and systemic approach towards treatment practices.

355 **Les CLSC . . . ce qu'il faut savoir.** (CLSCs . . . what you need to
know.)
Maurice Roy. Montréal: Éditions Saint-Martin, 1988. 2nd ed. 172p.

The CLSC (Centres locaux de services communautaires – Local community service
centres) system is an important actor in the health system in Québec. It encompasses a
series of services in local neighbourhoods and favours prevention over cure in dealing
with medical problems. This book provides a simple but effective overview of the
history, the role and the medical philosophy of the CLSC. Written by an employee of
the CLSC, the book also provides a good section on the challenges that faced the
CLSC system at the end of the 1980s. For a more analytical work on the CLSC
network see Louis Favreau and Yves Hurtubise's *CLSC et communautés locales* (The
CLSC and local communities) (Sainte-Foy, Québec: Presses de l'Université du
Québec, 1993. 211p.).

356 **Privatization: adopt or adapt?**
Lee Soderstrom. Québec: Commission d'Enquête sur les Services de
Santé et les Services sociaux, 1987. 242p.

In 1987, the Québec National Assembly set up a commission to examine all aspects of
the health and social services sector. This report discusses the issue of privatization and
its desirability in the Québec context. It is a scholarly examination of the feasibility of
privatization as a public policy solution to declining resources.

357 **L'évolution des politiques sociales au Québec, 1940-1960.**
(The evolution of social policy in Québec, 1940-60.)
Yves Vaillancourt. Montréal: Presses de l'Université de Montréal,
1988. 513p.

This is an important work that describes the evolution of the welfare state in Québec
during the Ottawa-Québec constitutional and ideological battles between 1940 and
1960. Divided into two sections, the book begins with an excellent explanation of
the ideological underpinnings of each order of government's respective social programmes. The motivations and interests behind these programmes are also revealed.
The second section focuses on the different programmes offered by both the federal and
provincial governments, namely the health system, public assistance, unemployment
insurance, pensions, etc. The author shows how the substance of these social programmes corresponds to the various interests of the particular social classes most
closely associated and protected by either the federal or Québec government. On the
social policies of the Duplessis regime see Gérard Boismenu's *Le Duplessisme: politique*

économique et rapports de force (item no. 128). On the state building process in Québec see James Iain Gow's *Histoire de l'administration publique québécoise, 1867-1970* (item no. 575).

History

358 **La médecine au Québec: naissance et évolution d'une profession.**
(Medicine in Québec: the origins and evolution of the profession.)
Jacques Bernier. Sainte-Foy, Québec: Presses de l'Université Laval,
1989. 207p. bibliog.

A historian's perspective on the development of the medical profession and how it secured virtual hegemony over Québec's health sector. Bernier focuses in on the medical community in Québec City, paying particular attention to its legal and economic status. In addition, Québec's medical profession is compared with those in Ontario and Western countries in order to contextualize the relatively early professionalization of medicine in Québec. In light of the significant degree of influence doctors had in Québec during the 19th century, this book provides a well-researched chronicle of how they got to this position in society and can therefore be classified among the important contributions to the social history of medicine. Women also played an essential role in the health sector as nurses. Moreover, during the 19th century, this role was largely filled by women's religious orders. The secularization of nursing is well presented in André Petitat's *Les infirmières, de la vocation à la profession* (Nurses, from vocation to profession) (Montréal: Éditions du Boréal, 1989. 408p.). For a survey of the medical profession, see Jean-Hughes Roy's *Profession: médecin* (Profession: doctor) (Montréal: Éditions du Boréal, 1993. 272p.).

359 **Histoire de la folie au Québec de 1600 à 1850.** (The history of
madness in Québec from 1600 to 1850.)
André Cellard. Montréal: Éditions du Boréal, 1991. 288p.

The process by which the diagnosis and treatment of mental illness was appropriated by the medical profession remained largely unknown and unchallenged until the pioneering work of Michel Foucault in the 1960s. Cellard builds on Foucault's critique in order to describe the process as it occurred in Québec. In attempting to link social, cultural, economic and scientific developments with conceptions of insanity and society's responses to this illness, this work provides a unique vantage point on Québec society as well as on the process of medicalization in Québec. The history of mental illness in Québec is also examined indirectly in Robert Viau's *Les fous de papier* (The fools of paper) (Montréal: Éditions du Méridien, 1989. 373p.) which examines the portrayal of mental illness in fiction written by Quebecers.

360 **L'aire du soupçon. Contributions à l'histoire de la psychiatrie au Québec.** (The zone of suspicion. Contributions to psychiatric history in Québec.)
Michel Clément. Montréal: Éditions Triptyque, 1990. 220p.

A general introduction to the history, sociology and anthropology of the psychiatric sciences in Québec during the latter half of the 19th century. The author traces the establishment of psychiatry in Québec through an examination of primary sources published by religious orders, reports from asylums, and the work of researchers. An analysis of these first manuals and reference works reveals the creation of a specific psychiatric tradition in Québec constructed from an amalgam of different theoretical traditions in the United States, France and Great Britain. In addition, Clément examines psychiatry as it was portrayed in the literature of the period.

361 **L'Hôpital-Général de Québec, 1692-1764.** (The Québec General Hospital, 1692-1764.)
Micheline D'Allaire. Montréal: Fides, 1971. 251p.

A detailed study of the religious order, Religieuses hospitalières de la miséricorde de Jésus (Religious Hospitallers of the Misericords of Jesus), which managed the Québec General Hospital in Monastère de Notre-Dame des Anges. This study attempts to unearth the social origins of those who ran the institution in addition to revealing whether any social change occurred within the institution between the time of its establishment in 1692 and the Conquest in 1760. The reader will also discover how the hospital was established.

362 **Histoire de la Faculté de Médecine de l'Université de Montréal, 1843-1993.** (The history of the Faculty of Medicine at the University of Montréal, 1843-1993.)
Denis Goulet. Montréal: VLB Éditeur, 1993. 502p. bibliog. (Collection Études Québécoises, no. 31).

A general history of the first francophone faculty of medicine in Montréal. In the first section, Goulet relates the institutional and professional history of the Faculty's predecessors, the Montréal School of Medicine and Surgery, and the Montréal branch of Laval University. In the sections covering the period from 1920 to 1993, Goulet examines the curriculum, the development of clinical teaching, the Faculty's association with other hospitals, and the research carried out within the Faculty. Overall, this study contributes to the history of medical training and research in French-speaking Canada.

363 **Histoire de l'Hôpital Notre-Dame de Montréal, 1880-1980.** (A history of Notre-Dame Hospital in Montréal, 1880-1980.)
Denis Goulet, François Hudon, Othmar Keel. Montréal: VLB Éditeur, 1993. 457p. bibliog. (Collection Études Québécoises, no. 32).

Notre-Dame Hospital has always been at the vanguard of fighting disease in Québec. The authors of this well-documented study reveal Notre-Dame's deep commitment to research in addition to its health services. The book is loosely structured around the internal and external factors that had an impact on the hospital's evolution. Among the internal factors discussed are the evolution of techniques and the financial situation of the hospital. The external factors are particularly well presented: the increasing role of the state; the evolution of educational techniques in Québec; and the utilization of new technologies, etc. In tracing the evolution of this important hospital, the authors present a brilliant picture of the evolution of Québec society.

364 **Trois siècles d'histoire médicale au Québec: chronologie des institutions et des pratiques, 1639-1939.** (Three centuries of medical history in Québec: a chronological account of institutions and practices from 1639-1939.)
Denis Goulet, André Paradis. Outremont, Québec: VLB Éditeur, 1992. 527p. bibliog.

An excellent chronology of events relating to the practice of medicine in Québec. The work is divided into five sections: the development of institutions; the impact of epidemics and the role of public health organizations; the evolution of the profession as illustrated by academic journals, associations and learned societies; the changes in medical teaching; and, finally, the progress of medical science. This information is presented chronologically in brief and descriptive paragraphs. The authors provide a useful introductory chapter which places their three-century study in historical context. For a more biographical look at how medicine was practised see Sylvio Leblond's *Médecine et médecins d'autrefois: pratiques traditionnelles et portraits québécois* (Medicine and doctors from yesteryear: traditional practice and Québec portraits) (Québec: Presses de l'Université Laval, 1986. 258p.).

365 **Santé et société au Québec, XIXe et XXe siècle.** (Health and society in Québec during the 19th and 20th centuries.)
Edited by Peter Keating, Othmar Keel. Montréal: Éditions du Boréal, 1995. 278p.

This collection of nine essays provides a summary of the principal themes of research in the history of health and welfare in Québec during the last two centuries. Themes covered include the general health of society, the emergence and development of state institutions in public health, sanitary practices, and the medical profession. This work will interest those in professions beyond the health industry due to its consideration of the practices used by society to prevent and combat disease. For an introductory history of public health in Québec see François Guérard's *Histoire de la santé au Québec* (A history of health in Québec) (Montréal: Éditions du Boréal Express, 1996. 123p.). Also see *Médecine et société: les années 80* (Medicine and society: the 1980s) (Montréal: Éditions Saint-Martin, 1981. 554p.), edited by Luciano Bozzini, Marc Renaud, Dominique Gaucher and Jaime Llambias-Wolff.

366 **Histoire de la sage-femme dans la région de Québec.** (A history of midwives in the Québec region.)
Hélène Laforce. Québec: Institut québécois de Recherche sur la Culture, 1985. 237p.

Explores the process and experience of childbirth during the 18th and 19th centuries in the region of Québec City. In this study, based on parish and archival documents, Laforce confirms the important place occupied by midwives at all levels of society in New France. Moreover, the reader will be impressed with Laforce's well-researched examination of the relationship between midwives, religious authorities and the gradual intrusion of doctors into the childbirth process. In demonstrating the degree to which midwifery was a social institution, Laforce reveals the network of alliances and organizations created by midwives, thereby constituting a medical elite. In this way the history of midwives sheds light on the evolution of Québec society.

367 **L'Hôtel-Dieu de Montréal, 1642-1973.** (Montréal's Hôtel-Dieu
Hospital, 1642-1973.)
Robert Lahaise. LaSalle, Québec: Éditions Hurtubise HMH, 1973.
346p. bibliog. (Les Cahiers du Québec, Collection Histoire, no. 13).
One of the more notable collections of studies on health and social services in Québec. The twelve essays in this volume discuss, among others, the following topics: the interrelated history of the Hôtel-Dieu Hospital and of Montréal; the roles of major personalities in the evolution of the institution, such as Joseph Benoît and Monseignor de Laval; the religious order; and the school of medicine.

368 **Something hidden: a biography of Wilder Penfield.**
Jefferson Lewis. Toronto: Doubleday, 1981. 311p.
Written by his grandson, this biography of Wilder Penfield benefits from the author's access to innumerable personal sources in narrating the life of Canada's pioneering neurosurgeon and one of McGill University's most famous professors. This work also presents the great scientific achievements of Dr. Penfield.

369 **La chirurgie à l'Hôtel-Dieu de Montréal au XIXe siècle.**
(19th-century surgery at Montréal's Hôtel-Dieu Hospital.)
Pierre Meunier. Montréal: Presses de l'Université de Montréal, 1989.
263p. bibliog.
Founded by Jeanne Mance in 1642 and originally established in Old Montréal, the Hôtel-Dieu Hospital remains an important francophone institution in Montréal. In 1860, it was moved north and built alongside what was then the Montréal School of Medicine and Surgery, creating one of the first teaching hospitals in North America by 1875. Based on medical archives and archives from the religious order charged with the running of the hospital, Meunier unites both history and medicine in recounting the hospital's surgical practices during the 19th century, relating both the innovations of the profession in addition to the history of the period itself.

370 **La croix et le scalpel. Histoire des Augustines et de l'Hôtel-Dieu de
Québec.** (The cross and the scalpel. The history of the Augustines and
the Hôtel-Dieu of Québec.)
François Rousseau. Sillery, Québec: Éditions du Septentrion, 1994.
2 vols.
From the arrival of the first Augustines in 1639 to the emergence and growth of the medical profession in the 19th century, the first volume describes the tension between tradition and the social change that was sweeping Québec. This tension was partially resolved with the medicalization of the Hôtel-Dieu Hospital of Québec City which affiliated itself with the Faculty of Medicine at Laval University in 1825. The transformation of the institution into a modern hospital is described in the second volume and reveals the extent to which these transformations presaged those of the Quiet Revolution. A related work, about the Hôtel-Dieu Hospital of Chicoutimi, is Normand Perron's *Un siècle de vie hospitalière au Québec. Les Augustines et*

l'Hôtel-Dieu de Chicoutimi, 1884-1984 (A century of hospital life in Québec. The Augustines and the Hôtel-Dieu Hospital of Chicoutimi, 1884-1984) (Montréal: Presses de l'Université du Québec, 1994. 439p.).

371 **The Royal Vic. The story of Montreal's Royal Victoria Hospital, 1894-1994.**
Neville Terry. Montréal; Kingston, Ontario: McGill-Queen's University Press, 1994. bibliog.

Commissioned by the Royal Victoria Hospital on the occasion of the institution's centenary, this book describes, with some pomp and circumstance, the history of one of Montréal's major hospitals from its establishment in 1894 up to 1994. This is an institutional history and describes, for the most part, the founders, doctors and staff who have contributed to the development of the hospital. This book is abundantly illustrated and aimed at the general public.

Social Trends

Reference

372 **Statistiques sociales: portrait social du Québec.** (Social statistics:
a social portrait of Québec.)
Suzanne Asselin. Québec: Bureau de la Statistique du Québec, 1992.
353p.
A comparative study of social statistics between Québec and other Western societies.
Eight themes ranging from demographics to housing and the environment provide a
fairly detailed picture of the standards of living in Québec over the past thirty years.
Moreover, this book is an interesting complement to macro-level economic statistics.

373 **Deux Québec dans un: rapport sur le développement social et
démographique.** (Two Québecs in one: a report on social and
demographic development.)
Conseil des Affaires sociales. Boucherville, Québec: Gaëtan Morin
Éditeur, 1989. 124p. maps. bibliog.
An examination of the nature of the demographic decline in Québec, and its potential
impact on Québec's economy and future growth, in addition to a thorough study of
emerging socio-economic cleavages. Alongside detailed maps, charts and tables, this
study reveals the growing divide between rich and poor and between the metropolis
and the regions. The first section draws a portrait of the demographic and migratory
patterns in Québec between the 1960s and the mid-1980s. This data is compared with
that for Ontario and Canada. The second section focuses on the socio-economic
disparities among cities, within their neighbourhoods and between Québec's larger
cities and their outlying regions. Overall, this study suggests that there is a need to
rethink and reformulate Québec's development strategy.

374 **Recent social trends in Québec, 1960-1990.**
Edited by Simon Langlois. Montréal; Kingston, Ontario:
McGill-Queen's University Press, 1992. 606p. bibliog.

An extremely valuable guide to the dominant socio-economic, institutional trends and attitudinal changes in Québec society since the Quiet Revolution. Chapters are well organized and contain statistical data and written summaries describing the dominant trends. Bibliographies at the end of each chapter alert the reader to the principal sources of study. The work was first published in French under the title, *La société québécoise en tendances, 1960-1990* (Trends in Québec society, 1960-90) (Québec: Institut québécois de Recherche sur la Culture, 1990. 667p.).

375 **Québec solidaire: rapport sur le développement.** (Solidarity in
Québec: report on development.)
Yvon Leclerc, Madeleine Blanchet, Paul Beaulieu. Boucherville,
Québec: Gaëtan Morin Éditeur, 1992. 182p.

Proposes the creation of a social pact that would contribute to the realization of a more equal and more just society. The report is divided into four sections. The first section discusses how to reconcile social change and the needs of the population. The second and third parts examine the obstacles that such projects will face, and the ideal way to implement the conditions necessary for the development of human potential. The last section is devoted to the conditions needed to motivate the population. In each section, the book provides examples of successful local initiatives in Québec.

General

376 **Être ou ne pas être Québécois.** (To be or not to be a Quebecer.)
Cahiers de Recherche sociologique. Montréal: Département de
Sociologie, Université du Québec à Montréal, 1995. 298p. (Cahiers de
Recherche Sociologique, no. 25).

Published on the eve of the 1995 referendum, this collection comprises an intellectual critical assessment and revision of the sovereignist project. In their discussion, the authors introduce the concepts of cultural pluralism, multiple identities and post-national identity to the debate on identity and nationalism in order to explain the complex issues facing an uncertain electorate. These issues manifest themselves in the public debate over who can claim to be a Quebecer, how one defines the Québec nation, the nation's relationship with modernity, and the battle between contradictory identities and competing nationalisms.

377 Le Québec en jeu. Comprendre les grands défis. (Québec in action.
     Understanding the major challenges.)
     Gérard Daigle, Guy Rocher. Montréal: Presses de l'Université de
     Montréal, 1992. 811p.

In an attempt to unearth the substance beneath the public debate and political discourse on a range of issues, forty-nine academics produced this twenty-eight-chapter
book on the transformations that have shaped Québec since 1960. Divided into four
sections (social, economic, cultural and political), this book contains a wealth of background information on the major issues that have surfaced since the Quiet Revolution
and charts their evolution across the last three decades. Each essay follows a similar
structure, focusing on the tensions, issues and challenges related to the evolution of
each topic.

378 Quebec: the unfinished revolution.
     Léon Dion. Montréal; Kingston, Ontario: McGill-Queen's
     University Press, 1976. 218p.

This work brings together a number of previously published papers and articles from
one of Québec's most respected social scientists. Taking a very broad approach, Dion
examines social change in the province and the development of a more strident
nationalism based on social democratic principles. He also looks at the crisis of
self-confidence that Québec and the whole Western world were perceived to be undergoing
during the 1960s and early 1970s. The author believes that these changes have been mis-
understood by English-speaking Canada. This is a translated and enlarged edition of
his 1973 work, *La prochaine révolution* (The next revolution) (Montréal: Leméac,
1973. 358p.).

379 Raisons communes. (Common reasons.)
     Fernand Dumont. Montréal: Éditions du Boréal, 1995. 255p.

This essay demonstrates the depth and brilliance of Dumont's thought as applied to
Québec. One of Québec's foremost intellectuals, Dumont reflects on issues such as
language, education and the welfare state with regard to the creation of a comprehensive
social project for Québec. In this book, Dumont makes his controversial claim that
Québec is a political community but not a nation. According to his argument, Québec
cannot be a nation since its territory is home to francophones, anglophones and the
aboriginal nations. Dumont nevertheless argues in favour of a sovereign Québec that
would recognize the diversity of its inhabitants. Dumont was awarded the City of
Montréal Award for this book.

380 La société québécoise après 30 ans de changements. (Québec
     society after thirty years of change.)
     Edited by Fernand Dumont. Québec: Institut québécois de
     Recherche sur la Culture, 1990. 358p.

Twenty-eight specialists suggest that Québec needs to turn a critical eye on the inherited legacies of the Quiet Revolution. Edited by one of Québec's most prominent
sociologists and intellectuals, this book is a refreshing analysis of recent transformations in the lifestyles, values and social relations of Quebecers. This collection is
important for those interested in the contemporary challenges facing Québec. Moreover,
the essays found herein demarcate themselves from the traditional interpretations
inherited from the Quiet Revolution.

381 **Traité des problèmes sociaux.** (A treatise on social problems.)
Edited by Fernand Dumont, Simon Langlois, Yves Martin.   Québec:
Institut québécois de Recherche sur la Culture, 1994. 1,264p.

A collection of fifty-four texts which discuss and describe various social problems, from poverty to the environment, which affect both the individual and society at large. In addition to providing an inventory of Québec's social ailments, this text also explains concepts, describes the process by which social norms are created, and discusses the institutions related to these problems.

382 **Histoire de familles et des réseaux. La sociabilité au Québec d'hier à demain.** (A history of families and networks. Social relations in Québec, past and future.)
Edited by Andrée Fortin.   Montréal: Éditions Saint-Martin, 1991. 260p.

A short but very interesting history of family in Québec from 19th-century rural Québec to 1990. The author, a sociologist, shows how these families were related to their environment and how these relations influenced the family's way of life. The author concludes with an analysis of contemporary challenges facing the family structure.

383 **Le défi des générations: enjeux sociaux et religieux du Québec d'aujourd'hui.** (The challenge of generations: social and religious issues in contemporary Québec.)
Jacques Grand'Maison.   Saint-Laurent, Québec: Fides, 1995. 496p.
(Cahiers d'Études Pastorales, no. 15).

This is the final report of a seven-year study whose goal was to define the ideal role the Church should play in society. Referring to changes in cultural, moral, social and spiritual values, inter-generational differences and changes within ecclesiastical institutions, the report suggests that the Church must focus on the battle for social justice. This work bears witness to the Québec Church's enduring and dynamic role in society in contrast to the more conservative interpretations of its social and historical impact.

384 **Quebec society: tradition, modernity, and nationhood.**
Hubert Guindon.   Toronto: University of Toronto Press, 1988. 180p.

This is a collection of Guindon's essays written between 1954 and 1987. One of Québec's most noted sociologists, Guindon examines Québec's bureaucratic revolution, social unrest, ethnic tension, the Church, the 1980 referendum, the Parti québécois, and the historical roots of nationalism. He argues that the growth of institutions in Québec altered its political culture.

385 **Action collective et démocratie locale. Les mouvements urbains de Montréal.** (Collective action and local democracy. Urban movements in Montréal.)
Pierre Hamel. Montréal: Presses de l'Université du Montréal, 1991. 239p. bibliog. (Politique et Économie, Tendances Actuelles, no. 4).

A study of Montréal's social movements as actors in the process of urban development between 1960 and 1980. Three aspects are studied: the financing of popular organizations; internal democracy; and issues involving local development.

386 **French Canada in transition.**
Everett C. Hughes. Chicago: University of Chicago Press, 1946. 227p. bibliog.

A seminal sociological study of a small Québec town as it confronted the effects of urbanization and industrialization. Hughes highlights the role played by traditional institutions of French-speaking Canada as they met the crisis of modernization. The author also stresses the ethnic tension that arose from English-speaking ownership of the new industries.

387 **Le social apprivoisé. Le mouvement associatif, l'État et le développement local.** (Taming society. The popular movement, the state and local development.)
Juan-Luis Klein, Christiane Gagnon. Hull, Québec: Éditions Asticou, 1989. 146p. (Collection Questionnements).

The continuing debate surrounding regional development in Québec remains an enduring legacy from the Quiet Revolution. Until the early 1980s, the invasion of technocrats, bureaucrats and economists into Québec's regions was viewed as essential to local development. This benevolent view of state intervention in regional economic development is discarded in this work in favour of one that places a premium on power for understanding patterns of local development. Klein and Gagnon's emphasis on the balance of power between local and institutional actors reveals a regional dynamic conditioned by the state, regional social movements and local power concentrations. This work demonstrates the important role played by popular movements in defining social relations and patterns of territorial management. Moreover, this work charts the emergence of regional social forces capable of greater involvement and proaction in the management of their own territory.

388 **Pluralism and inequality in Quebec.**
Leslie S. Laczko. Toronto: University of Toronto Press, 1995. 242p. bibliog.

The author examines ethnic pluralism and social change in Québec and compares the situation in Québec with that of other segmented societies (including Belgium, Switzerland, Israel, the United States and the former Soviet Union). Drawing upon functionalist and communal competitive perspectives, Laczko assesses the stability of cultural diversity and inequality in the province. This is a scholarly analysis that relies upon past cultural surveys and statistical data.

389 **L'avènement de la modernité culturelle au Québec.** (The advent of cultural modernity in Québec.)
Yvan Lamonde, Esther Trépanier.   Québec: Institut québécois de Recherche sur la Culture, 1986. 320p.

The period preceding the 1960s is often viewed in Québec as culturally backward in substance and monolithic in scope. This important collection of essays breaks with this myth by revealing the modern character of important cultural creations in pre-1960s Québec, demonstrating the relative pluralism of Québec society at the time.

390 **L'horizon de la culture: hommage à Fernand Dumont.** (The horizon of culture: essays in honour of Fernand Dumont.)
Simon Langlois, Yves Martin.   Sainte-Foy, Québec: Presses de l'Université Laval; Québec: Institut québécois de Recherche sur la Culture, 1995. 554p.

Fernand Dumont is certainly one of the greatest intellectuals of the post-war period in Québec. This collection of essays discusses the important themes of Dumont's work: the theory of culture; the epistemology of social science; theology; and Québec society. The book is not only a good introduction to Dumont's work but is also a good reflection of the role of language and culture in Québec society.

391 **Prison et ordre social au Québec.** (Prison and the social order in Québec.)
Jacques Laplante.   Ottawa: Presses de l'Université d'Ottawa, 1989. 211p.

Drawing from Michel Foucault's research on the origins of prison institutions, Laplante explores the events and circumstances which have favoured the emergence and maintenance of prisons in Québec from 1608 to the present. Unlike traditional studies, Laplante does not endorse an a priori conception of prisons as a rational re-action against crime. Moreover, he turns a critical eye on traditional conceptions and established stereotypes regarding current institutional practices. This book seeks to contextualize the phenomenon of incarceration in larger social, economic and political trends. In an effort to understand how prisons fit into the larger model of society, Laplante also examines societies without prisons.

392 **Animation sociale, entreprises communautaires et coopératives.** (Social leadership, community businesses and cooperatives.)
Edited by Benoit Lévesque.   Laval, Québec: Éditions coopératives Albert Saint-Martin, 1979. 380p.

Comprises the proceedings of a conference on social leadership, movements and cooperatives. Reuniting a large number of social activists and specialists from the regions of Québec, this conference symbolized a shift in the study of regional co-operatives, businesses and leaders. The concept of 'self-managing' cooperatives and social movements becomes prominent in the debate. Moreover, this book highlights the growing consciousness of social actors in the regions and their awareness of their relationship with the central Québec state.

393 **Statistiques: démographie, immigration et communautés culturelles au Québec depuis 1871.** (Statistics: demography, immigration and cultural communities in Québec since 1871.) Jean-François Manègre, Marie-Josée Raymond. Montréal: Conseil des Communautés culturelles et de l'Immigration, 1994. 109p.

A collection of statistics on various aspects of immigration and cultural communities in Québec since 1871. The work is divided into three parts. The first presents different aspects of Québec's population since 1871. The second section deals with immigration: the various ethnic communities found in Québec and their socio-economic profile. The last section presents data on immigrants' religious affiliations and levels of education. This is a good study for those interested in Québec's immigration demography.

394 **St-Denis: a French-Canadian parish.** Horace Miner. Chicago: University of Chicago Press, 1963. 299p. bibliog.

A sociological study of an isolated, family-oriented, self-sufficient community in Québec – St-Denis de Kamouraska. Miner provides an ethnographic description of old rural French Canadian folk culture in its least altered form. He also considers the factors responsible for social change in the direction of urbanization and Anglicization. Though this work has been criticized for portraying rural life akin to those of 'peasants' or 'folk societies', it nonetheless remains a classic in its field.

395 **French Canadian society.** Edited by Marcel Rioux, Yves Martin. Toronto: McClelland and Stewart, 1964. 405p. (Carleton Library, no. 18).

A sociological study of French Canadian society from its agricultural origins to its urban form in the late 1960s. The first section deals with the sociology of French-speaking Canada in historical perspective, examining such subjects as the family and the nature of the line village (le rang). The second deals with the social structure of contemporary Québec, including population and ecology, economic structure, social stratification and culture. The contributors include many of the pioneering sociologists from Québec and elsewhere, such as Léon Gérin, Horace Miner, Everett C. Hughes, Hubert Guindon and Fernand Dumont. The first of an intended two-volume work, this book also contains an especially important article by Albert Faucher and Maurice Lamontagne on Québec's industrial development which, in the tradition of Harold Innis, stressed the importance of geography and technology.

396 **La marche des Québécois: le temps des ruptures, 1945-1960.** (The march of Quebecers: a time of ruptures, 1945-60.) Jean-Louis Roy. Montréal: Leméac, 1976. 383p.

Many historians writing in the 1960s and 1970s turned their attention to the period between the Second World War and the Quiet Revolution in analysing Québec's modernization. Roy's book belongs to a corpus of literature which emphasizes the impact and manifestation of modernity in Québec during the period from the 1940s to the 1960s. An examination of various social groups in Québec (unions, cooperative movements, chambers of commerce) reveals a diversified society in the midst of transition and in search of an organizing principle. Moreover, Roy portrays Québec society as caught between both traditional and modern means of managing its development.

Periodicals

397   **Cahiers de Recherche Sociologique.** (Journal of Sociological Research.)
Montréal: Département de Sociologie, Université du Québec à Montréal, 1983- . 2 issues per year.

This publication, from one of Québec's most noted departments of sociology, at the University of Québec at Montréal, is not a journal in the strict sense. Each issue is thematic, dealing with the latest debates and research in the field. On average each volume exceeds 150 pages and comprises a dozen or so scholarly essays in addition to research notes.

398   **Possibles.** (Possibilities.)
Montréal: Possibles, 1976- . quarterly.

Focuses on social questions relating to Québec society. The mission of the publication is to initiate debate on topical social, political, economic and cultural issues. Each issue is thematic, but contains examples of promising photography, fiction and poetry, debates, and other non-thematic opinion pieces.

399   **Recherches Sociographiques.** (Sociographical Research.)
Sainte-Foy, Québec: Université Laval, 1960- . 3 issues per year.

This scholarly journal is dedicated to the study of the sociological, economic, political and cultural aspects of Québec and French-speaking Canada. Aside from publishing original research, this publication also includes book reviews and research notes.

400   **Sociologie et Sociétés.** (Sociology and Societies.)
Montréal: Université de Montréal, 1969- . 2 issues per year.

Published by the Department of Sociology at the University of Montréal, this publication is the only French-language scholarly journal in North America devoted to international sociological questions. While each issue is thematic, comprising a dozen or so essays on the given topic, there are typically at least one or two non-thematic essays included. Abstracts of articles are translated into English and Spanish.

Politics

Reference

401 **L'Année Politique au Québec.** (The Political Year in Québec.)
Montréal: Éditions Québec Amérique, 1987- . annual. Not published
in 1992-93.

Each edition comprises a thorough synopsis of the events that transpired in Québec
politics that year at the federal, provincial and municipal levels. In addition to examining the parties and their policies, the numerous contributors offer an analysis of
unions, public opinion and social movements. Each publication also includes statistical
tables on a variety of political, demographic and economic issues along with a chronology
of the year's events.

402 **Canadian Parliamentary Guide.**
Ottawa, 1867- . annual; Ottawa: Gale Canada, 1995- . annual.
Not published in 1911 and 1913.

An annual guide to Parliament, ministries, government departments, and parliamentarians.
This is the most complete and accessible guide to the 'Hill' to be found.

403 **Dictionnaire des parlementaires du Québec 1792-1992.**
(Dictionary of Québec parliamentarians 1792-1992.)
Edited by Gaston Deschênes. Sainte-Foy, Québec: Presses de
l'Université Laval, 1993. 859p.

Contains biographical information on 2,187 parliamentarians from the first House of
Assembly of Lower Canada to the members of the 1992 National Assembly. The
reader will also find biographies of: the members of the Legislative Council (Upper
House until 1838); the Crown's representatives, including Governors and Lieutenant-
Governors; and the members of Special Council (1838-40). A list of the deputies by
riding and a list of elections is also included in the appendix. This is the most accessible
and complete guide to Québec's parliamentarians.

404 **L'almanach politique du Québec.** (The Québec political almanac.)
Alain-G. Gagnon, James P. Bickerton, Munroe Eagles, Patrick J.
Smith, translated by Alain Desruisseaux. Montréal: Éditions Québec
Amérique, 1997. 251p. maps.

A comprehensive statistical overview of every federal riding in Québec. A written analysis of each riding relates the important events which have shaped the riding's electoral behaviour over the course of Québec's history. In addition, the results of the 1988 and 1993 federal elections are printed alongside statistical information on the demographic, ethno-linguistic, socio-economic, and industrial make-up of each riding. Appendices at the end of the book classify these ridings according to variables such as wealth, and largest and smallest majority victories, etc. Overall, this book is a useful guide explaining Québec's political heritage and it is undoubtedly a practical tool for policy analysts and students of political behaviour.

405 **Guide parlementaire québécois.** (Guide to the Québec Parliament.)
Gouvernement du Québec. Québec: Assemblée nationale, 1995.
3rd. revised printing. unpaginated.

Provides a complete listing of all ridings and their elected provincial representatives since 1867. The book also includes a list of all of the premiers and their cabinets.

406 **Aux origines du parlementarisme québécois 1791-1793.**
(Discovering the origins of Québec's parliamentary tradition,
1791-93.)
John Hare. Sillery, Québec: Éditions du Septentrion, 1993. 305p.
bibliog.

Québec retains the often forgotten distinction of being among the oldest practising democracies in the world. On 17 December 1791 deputies of the House of Assembly of Lower Canada gathered for the first time. While the majority of the first parliamentarians were French speakers and had no political experience, they embraced and adapted these British institutions and traditions for their own needs. Hare examines the role these first parliamentarians played in the creation of Québec's first constitution. He also examines the means used by various deputies to adapt these institutions to the French language. The book is also peppered with historical speeches and documents from this period.

407 **Politique et société au Québec: guide bibliographique.** (Politics and
society in Québec: bibliographic guide.)
Daniel Latouche. Montréal: Éditions du Boréal, 1993. 441p.

A bibliographical guide encompassing most important aspects of Québec society and politics. Both English and French documents are listed. Some 13,000 entries are classified according to 350 categories and accompanied by a very detailed table of contents and an index. Titles include published manuscripts, university theses, published articles in scholarly journals and books.

408   **Le Parti libéral du Québec: bibliographie rétrospective, 1867-1990.**
(The Parti libéral du Québec [Québec Liberal Party]: a retrospective
bibliography, 1867-1990.)
Michel Lévesque, Robert Comeau.   Québec: Bibliothèque de
l'Assemblée nationale, 1991. 198p.
A bibliography listing 2,224 books, chapters and articles relating to the provincial
Liberal Party, the PLQ (Parti libéral du Québec – Québec Liberal Party).

409   **Le Parti québécois: bibliographie retrospective.** (The Parti
québécois: a retrospective bibliography.)
Michel Lévesque, Robert Comeau.   Québec: Bibliothèque de
l'Assemblée nationale, 1991. 121p.
Contains 1,509 references to material relating to the PQ (Parti québécois), a provincially based political party founded in 1968 and still active today. The PQ is the
mainstream party which has traditionally argued in favour of Québec's sovereignty.

410   **L'Union nationale: bibliographie.** (The Union nationale: a
bibliography.)
Michel Lévesque.   Québec: Assemblée nationale, 1988. 51p.
Includes a listing of 325 titles related to the Union nationale, the provincially based
party which was founded in 1936 and was politically active until 1981. The book also
provides a useful synopsis and chronology of the party.

411   **Les programmes électoraux du Québec: un siècle de programmes
politiques québécois.** (Electoral platforms in Québec: a century of
Québec's political platforms.)
Jean-Louis Roy.   Montréal: Leméac, 1970. 2 vols.
Examines party programmes as indicators of the style and political salience of those
who wrote and presented these programmes to the electorate, and of the way politicians perceive the future of the polity. In two volumes, Roy briefly presents the
background to each federal election, and provides excerpts from party programmes
and campaign material. According to Roy, party programmes betray the motives
behind the political alliances between different parties, leaders' decisions and the way
these decisions were reached. Moreover, party programmes are interpreted in this
book as one of the only meaningful ways of evaluating the different conceptions of the
state posited by each political group or movement.

General

412 **La pratique de l'État au Québec.** (Statecraft in Québec.)
Gérard Bergeron. Montréal: Éditions Québec Amérique, 1984. 442p.

This work functions as both a history and a theory of state governance in Québec. Following a survey of the period between colonial times and the 1970s, the author concentrates on linguistic and labour policies and the 1980 referendum on sovereignty-association. In the second half of the book, Bergeron analyses the various functions of the state, interpreting them according to his own typology. For a critical examination of the power wielded by Québec civil service mandarins, readers should consult Pierre O'Neill and Jacques Benjamin's *Les mandarins du pouvoir* (The mandarins of power) (Montréal: Éditions Québec Amérique, 1978. 285p.), which examines the influence of high-placed advisors and civil servants between the governments of Jean Lesage (1960-66) and René Lévesque's first mandate (1976-81). Also see Bergeron's *Notre miroir à deux faces* (Our two-sided mirror) (Montréal: Éditions Québec Amérique, 1985. 340p.).

413 **Le Québec en textes: anthologie 1940-1986.** (Texts on Québec: an anthology, 1940-86.)
Edited by Gérard Boismenu, Laurent Mailhot, Jacques Rouillard.
Montréal: Éditions du Boréal, 1986. 622p. bibliog.

An excellent collection of essays, reports, manifestos and articles that highlights the multiplicity of voices which have existed in Québec over the past half century. The texts included, written by academics, artists, politicians and activists, were selected on their representativeness of the socio-economic transformation and ideological debates that have transpired between the 1940s and mid-1980s. Subjects are organized chronologically into the following thematic sections: the Second World War; urbanization the Duplessis regime; ideology; the development of the state; economy and work Montréal and regions; the national question; language and culture; and social movements. The book also includes a comprehensive bibliography and a chronology of major events.

414 **Social scientists and politics in Canada. Between clerisy and vanguard.**
Stephen Brooks, Alain-G. Gagnon. Montréal; Kingston, Ontario: McGill-Queen's University Press, 1988. 151p.

Provides a comparative analysis of social scientists in English-speaking Canada and Québec, demonstrating the extent to which their respective political roles and activities differ from one another. Commenting on the role of French Canadian intellectuals Brooks and Gagnon conclude that there is a unique relationship between the francophone social sciences and Québec nationalism. Brooks and Gagnon's case-studies are framed by a broader, theoretical debate on the class nature of intellectuals and whether they constitute a class unto themselves, are allied to a particular class, or remain classless See also Andrée Fortin's *Passage de la modernité: les intellectuels québécois et leurs revues* (Passage of modernity: Québec intellectuals and their journals) (Sainte-Foy, Québec: Presses de l'Université Laval, 1993. 406p.).

415 Québec: state and society.
Edited by Alain-G. Gagnon. Scarborough, Ontario: Nelson Canada,
1993. 507p. 2nd ed. bibliog.
This work is an expanded and updated version of a work which first appeared in 1984.
Both editions use a number of different analytical perspectives through which to view
Québec, chiefly political theory, political economy, history, demography and sociology.
The main areas covered include: the Québec economy; identity, symbols and visions;
Québec nationalism; state, society and politics; forms of representation; immigration,
ethnicity and language; and geopolitics. The work includes twenty-five essays from
many of Québec's most noted scholars. The second edition contains an annotated
bibliography and a reproduction of the Québec Charter of Human Rights and
Freedoms. An older text offering a similar interdisciplinary perspective is Édouard
Cloutier and Daniel Latouche, eds., *Le système politique québécois* (The Québec political
system) (LaSalle, Québec: Éditions Hurtubise HMH, 1979. 555p.).

416 **People, potholes, and city politics.**
Karen Herland. Montréal; New York: Black Rose Books, 1992. 222p.
Among the most comprehensive studies on Montréal municipal politics. Montréal's
city politics involve a tangled web of political parties and Herland is able to present an
incredible amount of information in a concise and user-friendly way. Following a
description of the city and its particular brand of party politics, Herland takes the
reader inside City Hall to illustrate how the bureaucracy and executive interact. The
book explains the history behind current political debates and how they are shaped by
city politics. A section on each of Montréal's districts provides researchers and students
with essential information on the distinct characteristics of each of the city's unique
neighbourhoods. Two other titles should also be mentioned: *The city and radical social
change* (Montréal; New York: Black Rose Books, 1982. 344p.), edited by Dimitri
Rossopoulos, which looks at municipal politics in general but makes references to
Montréal; and Andrew Sancton's *Governing the island of Montréal: language differences and metropolitan politics* (Berkeley, California: University of California Press,
1985. 213p.). The latter also touches on Montréal's distinct position in Québec,
regarding its linguistic composition. For an account of one of Montréal's most important
municipal political parties, see Timothy Lloyd Thomas's *A city with a difference: the
rise and fall of Montreal Citizen's Movement* (Montréal: Véhicule Press, 1997. 214p.).

417 **La société distincte de l'État: Québec-Canada, 1930-1980.** (The
distinct character of the state: Québec-Canada, 1930-80.)
Anne Legaré, Nicole Morf. Montréal: Éditions Hurtubise HMH,
1989. 237p.
Taking a structuralist approach, the authors analyse Canada's passage from a classic
liberal laissez-faire state to its more interventionist form following the Depression.
They highlight the antagonism between the Canadian state and federalism, and the
increasing tension between the federal government and the Québec provincial government.

418　An option for Quebec.
René Lévesque.　Toronto: McClelland and Stewart, 1968. 128p.
Published after Lévesque's resignation from the PLQ (Parti libéral du Québec –
Québec Liberal Party) in 1967 and following his decision to sit as an independent, this
work outlines his vision and arguments in favour of an independent Québec. Lévesque
rejects the idea of according special status to Québec within the Canadian Federation
and the idea that the Québec economy could only be viable in Canada. He also looks
at the Scandinavian Union and the European Economic Community as possible future
models for Québec in its relationship with Canada. This is one of the clearest and earliest
attempts to formulate an idea about Québec as an associated-sovereign state.

419　Quebec: social change and political crisis.
Kenneth McRoberts.　Toronto: McClelland and Stewart, 1993. 3rd ed.
556p. bibliog.
One of the best texts on Québec politics and society yet published. McRoberts
analyses the transformation of Québec from the Duplessis era to the present day from
a developmental perspective. Unique factors affecting Québec's modernization are
highlighted: the political and economic dependence of Québec on Ontario and the
United States; the cultural division of labour and skewed class structure within the
francophone community; Canadian federal institutions; and the historical national
consciousness of Québec francophones. McRoberts adequately accounts for the
transformation of Québec from a conservative rurally based society to a secular
modernized state. The third edition brings the analysis up to the rejection of the 1992
Charlottetown Accord, and the emergence of the Bloc québécois (Québec Bloc) in
federal politics. This work is intended for the specialist and general reader alike.

420　Politics in the new Quebec.
Henry Milner.　Toronto: McClelland and Stewart, 1978. 257p.
bibliog.
Published shortly after the election of the PQ (Parti québécois) in 1976, this work
makes use of Marxist analysis to examine the political dynamic in the province.
Beginning with the premise that Québec constitutes a nation, the author examines: the
evolution of national consciousness; the economy and social classes; the Right and the
extra-Parliamentary Left; the PLQ (Parti libéral du Québec – Québec Liberal Party)
and the PQ; and the new politics in Montréal.

421　Mes premiers ministres: Lesage, Johnson, Bertrand, Bourassa et
Lévesque. (My Prime Ministers: Lesage, Johnson, Bertrand, Bourassa
and Lévesque.)
Claude Morin.　Montréal: Éditions du Boréal, 1991. 632p.
Morin served as a deputy minister in the first four of these administrations and as a
cabinet minister in the last. Morin's memoirs afford an insider's perspective on such
important political events as the Federal-Provincial conference of 1967, the Victoria
conference of 1971 and the Québec referendum of 1980. The book evaluates the
leadership styles of these five Québec premiers and their policies and administrative
abilities. Of related interest is Morin's autobiography spanning the period between his
youth and the end of his political career, Les choses comme elles étaient (Things as
they were) (Montréal: Éditions du Boréal, 1994. 494p.).

422 **L'espace québécois.** (Québec: defining boundaries.)
Edited by Alain Noël, Alain-G. Gagnon. Montréal: Éditions Québec
Amérique, 1995. 305p.

An examination of Québec from various theoretical perspectives. The first section
looks at Québec within the new world order, focusing on the effects of continentalization
and globalization. The second section analyses the regions in Québec with an emphasis
on economic development and political representation. The final section deals with the
interaction between identity and territory, with chapters examining the native communities and ethnic pluralism. The twelve essays provide a useful understanding of
Québec society following the end of the Cold War and the ratification of NAFTA
(North American Free Trade Agreement).

423 **Montréal. A citizen's guide to politics.**
Edited by Jean-Hughes Roy, Brendan Weston. Montréal; New York:
Black Rose Books, 1990. 215p.

Twenty-seven essays divided into eight major themes scrutinize the various manifestations of municipal public policy between the reigns of Jean Drapeau (Mayor of
Montréal, 1968-86) and Jean Doré (Mayor of Montréal, 1986-94). Chosen from
among the city's most informed journalists, economists and social activists, the
authors whose work is included in this book not only deconstruct the maze of city
politics, but they also posit solutions to the city's current and future problems. This is
an important book for anyone interested in municipal public policy and analysis.

Social and political movements

424 **Classes sociales et mouvements sociaux au Québec et au Canada.**
(Social classes and social movements in Québec and Canada.)
David Descent, Louis Maheu, Martin Robitaille, Gilles Simard.
Montréal: Éditions Saint-Martin, 1989. 207p.

Comprises both a history of sociological scholarship in Québec as well as a selective
inventory of published titles on class issues. The useful introductory essay on the
evolution of sociological study in Canada and Québec is followed by a lengthy inventory of related published works. The essay outlines the progress of academic research
on social movements and social classes. This work is the closest bibliographical
source to works on social class and social movements from a historical perspective.
Related works include: *La société québécoise en tendances 1960-1990* (Trends in
Québec society, 1960-90) (Québec: Institut québécois de Recherche sur la Culture,
1990. 667p.), by Simon Langlois; and *Les classes sociales au Canada et au Québec:
bibliographie annotée* (Social classes in Canada and Québec: an annotated bibliography), written by Fernand Harvey and Gilles Houde (Québec: Institut supérieur des
Sciences humaines, Université Laval, 1979. 288p.).

425 **Quebec, only the beginning: the manifestoes of the Common Front.**
Edited by Daniel Drache. Toronto: New Press, 1972. 272p.

This work includes the manifestos of three of Québec's largest and most militant unions during the early 1970s: the CSN (Confédération des syndicats nationaux – Confederation of National Trade Unions); the FTQ (Fédération du travail de Québec – Québec Federation of Labour); and the CEQ (Corporation des enseignants de Québec – Québec Teachers' Corporation). In 1971, they formed a common front issuing a call for working-class politicization. According to the unions, Québec nationalism could not be achieved without a realignment of class forces, especially in the light of the ascendancy of the middle class during and following the Quiet Revolution. Though the unions were unsuccessful in building a socialist society, their ideas helped impart a new dynamic to the Québec independence movement. This work documents the urgency of their message during the period. For a study of the Common Front, the reader should also consult Jean-Marc Piotte, Diane Éthier and Jean Reynolds' *Les travailleurs contre l'État bourgeois: avril et mai 1972* (Workers against the bourgeois state: April and May 1972) (Montréal: L'Aurore, 1975. 274p.).

426 **Mouvement populaire et intervention communautaire de 1960 à nos jours.** (Popular movements and community intervention from 1960 to the present.)
Louis Favreau. Montréal: Le Centre de Formation populaire/ Les Éditions du Fleuve, 1989. 307p. bibliog.

A detailed study of local community groups and activists from a historical and geo-political perspective. Favreau specifically looks at the inter-generational relationships and cooperative efforts within individual groups in addition to the partnerships between groups, their areas of activity, and the conditions surrounding their emergence. Overall, the author suggests that community movements are strong enough to influence political activity and occasionally sufficiently self-confident to have a direct effect in the creation of local economies. Aside from these micro-level relationships, Favreau also reveals the power struggles between community groups and the state. A thematic bibliography is included.

427 **FLQ: the anatomy of an underground movement.**
Louis Fournier, translated by Edward Baxter. Toronto: NC Press Limited, 1984. 362p. bibliog.

A well-researched study of the FLQ (Front de libération du Québec – Québec Liberation Front), a militant group calling for the independence of Québec. Relying upon information from former FLQ activists, Fournier provides a vivid account of the group's networks along with the anti-terrorist operations of the police and politicians. As a chronicle of the FLQ's history from its founding in 1963 up to 1980, the work provides a detailed study of the October Crisis of 1970 which culminated in a double kidnapping and the murder of Québec Labour Minister Pierre Laporte. For a compilation of FLQ writings, including manifestos, letters, and autobiographical accounts, see Robert Comeau, Daniel Cooper and Pierre Vallières' *FLQ: un projet révolutionnaire, lettres et écrits felquistes 1963-1982* (The FLQ: a revolutionary project, letters and FLQ writings, 1963-82) (Outremont, Québec: VLB Éditeur, 1990. 275p.). Ron Haggart and Aubrey Golden's *Rumours of war* (Toronto: James Lorimer & Co., 1979. 311p.) focuses on the constitutional legality of the War Measures Act of October 1970. Also see Marc Laurendeau's *Les Québécois violents: un ouvrage sur les causes et la rentabilité de la violence d'inspiration politique au Québec, 2e édition, revue et augmentée* (Violent Quebecers: a work on the causes and profitability of politically inspired violence in Québec, 2nd edition, revised and expanded) (Sillery, Québec: Éditions du Boréal Express, 1974. 240p.).

428 **Action collective et démocratie locale. Les mouvements urbains montréalais.** (Collective action and local democracy. Montréal's urban social movements.)
Pierre Hamel. Montréal: Presses de l'Université de Montréal, 1991. 239p.

Demonstrates the role of Montréal's social movements in the development of the city in the early 1960s and the late 1980s. Using the sociology of mobilization theory, the author argues that the credibility acquired by Montréal's social movements and their progressive institutionalization in Québec's political systems were the consequence of their ability to fully participate in the development of Montréal. The book also provides a good picture of Montréal's social movements.

429 **Les organisations populaires, l'état et la démocratie.** (Popular organizations, the state, and democracy.)
Pierre Hamel, Jean-François Léonard. Montréal: Nouvelle Optique, 1981. 208p.

Popular movements have played an important role in Québec since 1960 in their role as government critics and as bearers of alternative solutions to public policy issues. The authors of this study demonstrate how the crisis of socialism and liberal democracy can lead to new initiatives for collective action outside the realm of the state. Citing the example of the Canadian political system, the authors demonstrate why these new forms of solidarity should be adopted.

430 **Community action: organizing for social change.**
Henri Lamoureux, Robert Mayer, Jean Panet-Raymond, translated by Phyllis Aronoff, Howard Scott. Montréal; New York: Black Rose Books, 1989. 215p.

While this book is principally a manual for organizing community action, it also provides a useful introduction to this activity in Québec. The first part is devoted to a historical survey of community organization in Québec since the 1960s. Although brief, this overview reveals the peculiarities of the distinct Québec context, e.g., the CLSC (Centres locaux de services communautaires – Local Community Service Centres) and their importance in the development of Québec society. The remaining three sections address issues relating to organization such as mobilization and group functions. A comprehensive list of groups is provided at the end of the book.

431 **Old passions, new visions: social movements and political activism in Quebec.**
Edited by Marc Raboy, translated by Robert Chodos. Toronto: Between the Lines, 1986. 250p.

A collection of critical, polemical and activist writings on socio-political issues in contemporary Québec. The selections, written between 1980 and 1985, include essays, group statements and round-table discussions by feminists, environmentalists, pacifists, socialists, and union activists. The work provides an insight into the diverse ideological perspectives and mobilizing forces in Québec. For a similar work, written in French, which examines new social movements in the province, see Serge Proulx and Pierre Vallières' *Changer de société: déclin du nationalisme, crise culturelle, et alternatives sociales au Québec* (Changing society: the decline of nationalism, cultural crisis, and social alternatives in Québec) (Montréal: Éditions Québec Amérique, 1982. 298p.).

432 **Power corrupted: the October Crisis and the repression of Québec.**
Edited by Abraham Rotstein. Toronto: New Press, 1971. 127p.

A reprint of the January 1971 issue of *Canadian Forum*. This work provides a series of commentaries by English Canadian authors on the long-term implications of the October Crisis. For another assessment of this crisis, see Germain Dion's *Un tornade de 60 jours: la crise d'octobre 1970 à la Chambre des communes* (A sixty-day tornado: the October Crisis in the House of Commons) (Hull, Québec: Éditions Asticou, 1985. 222p.) which focuses on how the 1970 FLQ (Front de libération du Québec – Québec Liberation Front) October Crisis affected the Ottawa-Hull region. Jean-François Cardin's *Comprendre Octobre 1970: le FLQ, la crise et le syndicalisme* (Understanding October 1970: the FLQ, the crisis, and the labour movement) (Montréal: Éditions du Méridien, 1990. 226p.) highlights the FLQ's relationship with unions in Québec. Francis Simard's *Talking it out: the October Crisis from inside* (Montréal: Guernica, 1987. 191p.) relates the events from the perspective of one of Pierre Laporte's kidnappers.

433 **The asbestos strike.**
Edited by Pierre Elliott Trudeau. Toronto: James Lewis & Samuel, 1974. 382p.

The asbestos strike of 1949 in the Eastern Townships constituted the most serious incident of labour conflict in Québec's post-war era. It also represented the first time that a strong and independent unionism confronted a foreign-owned corporation and unsympathetic political establishment. More than heightening class consciousness, the strike, according to Pierre Trudeau, was a 'turning point in the entire religious, political, social, and economic history of the Province of Québec'. Trudeau's essay describes the ideological and institutional forces that impeded Québec's development up to the 1960s. Other essays examine the financial history of the asbestos industry, the history of the trade union movement, the history of the strike and the roles of the Church, press, and judicial system during the conflict.

Political parties

434 **Provincial party financing in Québec.**
Harold M. Angell. Lanham, Maryland: University Press of America, 1996. 113p. bibliog.

A good overview of the evolution of party financing in Québec from the system used during the premiership of Taschereau (1920-36) to the party financing system which is currently still in place, and qualified by the author as a pioneer of its day. Forbidding corporate donations, the party financing system that was put in place in 1977 favoured the maintenance of a two-party system. This book reveals the motives behind, and the consequences of, the different party financing laws in Québec. The author also presents the impact of financing strategy on political parties' electoral success. The book includes data on the evolution of political donations in Québec.

435 **Le virage: l'évolution de l'opinion politique au Québec depuis 1960 ou comment le Québec est devenu souverainiste.** (The turning-point: evolution of public opinion in Québec since 1960, or, how Québec became sovereignist.)
Édouard Cloutier, Daniel Latouche, Jean-Hamelin Guay. Montréal: Éditions Québec Amérique, 1992. 181p.

The failure of the Meech Lake Accord in 1990 was followed by a large increase in the support for Québec sovereignty among the population. In studying the evolution of public opinion regarding various constitutional options since the 1960s and the socio-economic characteristics of their supporters, the authors explain this incremental increase. This book provides an excellent typology of the many 'sovereignist' options as well as a good analysis of the movement's evolution.

436 **Le Bloc populaire, 1942-1948.** (The Bloc populaire, 1942-48.)
Paul-André Comeau. Montréal: Éditions Québec Amérique, 1982. 478p.

Born of the conscription crisis and the war effort, the Bloc populaire came to life in 1942 in the months that followed a federal plebiscite on conscription which tore the country apart and pitted French-speaking Canada against English-speaking Canada. This book describes the history and historical context which gave birth to the Bloc populaire in addition to outlining the party's formation and organization. Aside from its strong position against conscription, the Bloc populaire also adopted a social and economic platform addressing the problems facing French Canadians as a result of the dirty 1930s. Although the Bloc's electoral success was brief at both the federal and provincial level, the emergence of a united nationalist political force in Ottawa signalled the emergence of neo-nationalism. For a study of the political thought behind the party see: Denis Monière's *André Laurendeau et le destin d'un peuple* (André Laurendeau and the destiny of a nation) (Montréal: Éditions Québec Amérique, 1983. 347p.); and Robert Comeau and Lucille Beaudry's *André Laurendeau, un intellectuel d'ici* (André Laurendeau, a native intellectual) (Sillery, Québec: Presses de l'Université du Québec, 1990. 310p.).

437 The Bloc.

Manon Cornellier, translated by Robert Chodos, Simon Horn, Wanda Taylor. Toronto: James Lorimer & Co., 1995. 180p.

This work serves as both a history of the Bloc québécois and a short biography of its founder Lucien Bouchard (1938-). It covers the period from the party's birth in 1990 following the failure of the Meech Lake Accord, until just before the 1995 Québec referendum on sovereignty. Cornellier, a journalist based in Ottawa, describes the Bloc as a skilful opposition party and characterizes Bouchard as a controlling but competent leader. This is one of the few books available in English about the first separatist party ever elected to Canada's federal Parliament. See also Lucien Bouchard's autobiography, entitled *On the record* (Toronto: Stoddart, 1994. 288p.), for an account of his life and his involvement in politics. Bouchard left the Bloc québécois to become the leader of the Parti québécois and Premier of Québec in 1996.

438 Le RIN de 1960 à 1963: étude d'un groupe de pression au Québec.

(The RIN from 1960 to 1963: study of a pressure group in Québec.)
André d'Allemagne. Montréal: Édition l'Étincelle, 1974. 160p.

From its creation in March 1963 to its dissolution in October 1968, the RIN (Rassemblement pour l'indépendance nationale – Coalition for National Independence) reflected the growing popular support for Québec's independence. Despite its short life, the RIN remains an indelible part of Québec political history as one of the constituent groups that gave life to the PQ (Parti québécois). D'Allemagne, a founding member of the RIN, analyses the organization as a pressure group. In choosing this method of analysis, the author compares the RIN with other pressure groups in order to demonstrate its initial neutrality on ideological issues. The bulk of this study, however, is devoted to the structural changes which marked the evolution of the RIN from a pressure group to a political party. See also Réjean Pelletier's *Les militants du RIN* (RIN activists) (Ottawa: Éditions de l'Université d'Ottawa, 1974. 82p.).

439 The failure of l'Action libérale nationale.

Patricia Dirks. Montréal; Kingston, Ontario: McGill-Queen's University Press, 1991. 191p. bibliog.

This work studies the rise and fall of the ALN (Action libérale nationale), a Depression-born third party in Québec. Started by dissident PLQ (Parti libéral du Québec) reformers and nationalists in 1934, the ALN called for the creation of a francophone-controlled Québec economy and the preservation of French-speaking Canada's traditional social order. This platform attracted widespread religious and popular support and led to rapid disillusionment within the reformist wing of the party. The party faced its demise by the end of the 1939 Québec election. Though primarily historical in nature, this work draws upon a number of theoretical studies on third parties that help explain the ephemeral nature of this movement as well as the lingering legacy of its ideas.

440 PQ: René Lévesque and the Parti québécois.

Graham Fraser. Toronto: Macmillan, 1984. 434p. bibliog.

One of the best biographies of René Lévesque (1922-87) written in English. The work also provides a thorough analysis of the PQ (Parti québécois) and the rise of nationalism in Québec. Other works on Lévesque include Jean Provencher's *René Lévesque, portrait d'un Québécois* (René Lévesque, portrait of a Quebecer) (Markham, Ontario: Paper

Jacks Ltd., 1975. 270p.) and Peter Desbarats' *René: a Canadian in search of a country* (Toronto: McClelland and Stewart, 1976. 223p.).

441 **L'impact référendaire.** (The referendum factor.)
Edited by Guy Lachapelle, Pierre P. Tremblay, John E. Trent.
Montréal: Presses de l'Université du Québec, 1995. 420p.
Published in anticipation of the 1995 Québec referendum, the principal objective of this collection was to discern the challenges that would face Quebecers and Canadians the day after the referendum regardless of the result. In so doing, this collection describes the economic, structural, political and demographic factors which contributed to the actual state of affairs between Québec and Canada up to the eve of the referendum. Those interested in the philosophical and sociological issues at stake during the referendum should read *Être ou ne pas être Québécois* (see item no. 376).

442 **Le NPD et le Québec, 1958-1985.** (The NPD and Québec, 1958-85.)
André Lamoureux. Montréal: Éditions du Parc, 1985. 230p. bibliog.
One of the few book-length accounts of the NPD (Nouveau parti démocratique – New Democratic Party) in Québec. The author focuses on the founding of the NPD in Québec in 1961, and on the party's subsequent inability to achieve political success. Unlike most English Canadian accounts, Lamoureux denies that the NPD was necessarily doomed to failure in the province. The party's decline was more likely to have stemmed from the loss of support from key unions as early as 1963, coupled with the party's inability to accept Québec nationalist perspectives. This is a scholarly account with a useful bibliography.

443 **Pour une politique: le programme de la Révolution tranquille.**
(Towards a policy: the programme of the Quiet Revolution.)
Georges-Émile Lapalme. Outremont, Québec: VLB Éditeur, 1988. 348p.
Georges-Émile Lapalme (1907-85), as leader of the PLQ (Parti libéral du Québec – Québec Liberal Party) between 1950 and 1958, was considered by some as the father of the Quiet Revolution. This book, written in 1959 and published posthumously, illustrates Lapalme's vision of the social and institutional changes that were about to occur in Québec. For Lapalme, the PLQ was the main instrument of reform in the province. The appendix includes the 1960 policy platform statement of the PLQ and its 1962 manifesto.

444 **Une élection de réalignement. L'élection générale du 29 avril 1970 au Québec.** (The realigning election. The general election of 29 April 1970.)
Vincent Lemieux, Marcel Gilbert, André Blais. Montréal: Éditions du Jour, 1970. 182p. (Cahiers de Cité Libre).
Argues that the 1970 general election constitutes the second political and electoral realignment in Québec's history in addition to describing what variables contributed to the final vote result. According to the authors, four factors (partisan, political, socio-economic, and personality) and two mechanisms (electoral laws and the electoral map) influence the final decision of any given voter. An analysis of these factors following the 1970 Québec general election reveals a distinct change in voter loyalties

in comparison to earlier elections, and the emergence of a new set of party alignments: the rapid rise of the PQ (Parti québécois) at the expense of the provincial Liberal Party, the PLQ (Parti libéral du Québec), which in turn profited from the rapid decrease of support for the Union nationale. These changes in electoral preferences are related to the polarization of the parties along two axes: the external axis representing the parties' position on federalism; and the internal axis representing the growing dissatisfaction among voters with the outgoing Union nationale Government.

445 **Le Parti libéral du Québec: alliances, rivalités et neutralités.**
(The Parti libéral du Québec: alliances, rivalries and neutrality.)
Vincent Lemieux. Sainte-Foy, Québec: Presses de l'Université Laval, 1993. 257p.

A study of the PLQ (Parti libéral du Québec – Québec Liberal Party) in the 20th century. Lemieux examines five distinct periods in the party's history: its hegemony between 1897 and 1936; its weakness between 1936 and 1960; the leadership of Lesage and Bourassa between 1960 and 1976; the party's role in opposition between 1976 and 1985; and the return of Bourassa from 1985 to 1992. Lemieux uses a typology that focuses on the party's relations with various groups in society and within the state.

446 **Personnel et partis politiques au Québec: aspects historiques.**
(Québec political parties and their personnel: a historical perspective.)
Edited by Vincent Lemieux. Montréal: Éditions du Boréal Express, 1982. 350p. (Études d'Histoire du Québec, no. 11).

A historical overview of Québec political parties and, specifically, their internal organization and behaviour once in government. The essays contained in this collection focus mainly on the leaders and upper echelons of party organizations. Of interest are two articles on the predecessors of the PQ (Parti québécois) in addition to two articles on the municipal political parties of Québec and Montréal. This book does not, however, provide a comprehensive synthesis of Québec political parties.

447 **Les sondages et la démocratie.** (Opinion polls and democracy.)
Vincent Lemieux. Québec: Institut québécois de Recherche sur la Culture, 1988. 122p. (Diagnostic, no. 7).

At a general level, this book attempts to discern whether the proliferation of opinion polls has had a positive impact on the democratic process. Lemieux borrows E. E. Shattschneider's definition of democracy and then attempts to describe the conditions under which opinion polls would improve the democratic process. Along the way, Lemieux describes how opinion polls are designed, implemented and used.

448 **Le référendum confisqué.** (The confiscated referendum.)
Claude-V. Marsolais. Outremont, Québec: VLB Éditeur, 1992. 272p. bibliog. (Études Québécoises, no. 23).

A critical analysis of the events leading to the defeat of the 'Yes' forces during the referendum on sovereignty-association held in May 1980. This defeat resulted in the 'patriation' (transfer to Canada), against Québec's will, of the Canadian Constitution, which entailed the adoption of a centralizing federal principle. Marsolais' central question is examining how status-quo federalism won out over the renewed federalism as posited by the provincial Liberals, the PLQ (Parti libéral du Québec – Québec

Liberal Party), and sovereignty-association as put forward by the PQ (Parti québécois – Québec Party). Marsolais criticizes the vagueness of the PQ's attitude to its own project. He concludes by suggesting that the desire for power corrupted political leaders within both provincial parties, thereby enabling the federal Liberals, the Parti libéral du Canada (Liberal Party of Canada) to impose their constitutional project. Although the book focuses on politicians and political parties, it analyses secondary actors such as labour unions and pro-federalist business leaders and associations.

449 **La bataille du Québec. Deuxième épisode: les élections québécoises de 1994.** (The battle of Québec. The second chapter: the 1994 Québec election.)
Denis Monière, Jean-Hamelin Guay. Montréal: Éditions Fides, 1995. 268p.

In examining the electoral platforms, media coverage, electoral strategies and political messages employed during the 1994 Québec general election, the authors attempt to account for the victory of the PQ (Parti québécois) over the PLQ (Parti libéral du Québec). Moreover, the authors emphasize the unique events which rendered the election historic in the eyes of many commentators; namely, the polarization between two distinct programmes for government and two distinct conceptions of Québec's place within Canada. Of related interest are Monière and Guay's two other works entitled *La bataille du Québec. Premier épisode: les élections fédérales de 1993* (The battle of Québec. First chapter: the 1993 federal general election) (Saint-Laurent, Québec: Fides, 1994. 193p.) and *La bataille du Québec. Troisième épisode: 30 jours qui ébranlèrent le Canada* (The battle of Québec. Third chapter: thirty days that shook Canada) (Saint-Laurent, Québec: Fides, 1996. 266p.).

450 **Québec in a new world. The PQ's plan for sovereignty.**
National Executive of the Parti québécois, translated by Robert Chodos. Toronto: James Lorimer & Co., 1994. 160p.

Written for the general public, this book was published prior to the 1994 provincial election and outlined what to expect from a PQ (Parti québécois) government. Aside from outlining the PQ's plans for economic development, culture and social policy, etc., this book describes the PQ's position on sovereignty, territorial boundaries, aboriginal issues and how the party intends to achieve its political project.

451 **Partis politiques et société québécoise: de Duplessis à Bourassa, 1944-1970.** (Political parties and Québec society: from Duplessis to Bourassa, 1944-70.)
Réjean Pelletier. Montréal: Éditions Québec Amérique, 1989. 397p.

An analysis of Québec political parties during the quarter century following the Second World War. The author covers the social conservatism of the Duplessis era, economic and institutional changes during the 1960s, the interventionist PLQ (Parti libéral du Québec) under Lesage, the decline of the Union nationale, and the realignment of parties following the 1968 election. The work focuses primarily on political parties, election campaigns, and party programmes.

452 The rise of a third party.
Maurice Pinard. Montréal; Kingston, Ontario: McGill-Queen's University Press, 1975. 285p.

Drawing upon his sociological background, Pinard examines the sudden rise of Réal Caouette and the Social Credit Party of Québec in the 1962 federal election. Using this as a case-study, the author formulates a general hypothesis to explain the rise of new political movements both in Canada and elsewhere. Pinard examines economic conditions, the resistance of the poor to rising movements, the problems of mobilizing a mass following, and the high susceptibility of youth to new movements. Though first published in 1971, this remains an influential theoretical work.

453 The Union nationale: Québec nationalism from Duplessis to Lévesque.
Herbert Quinn. Toronto: University of Toronto Press, 1979. 2nd ed. 342p. bibliog.

Though chiefly concerned with the Union nationale – Québec's dominant provincial party between the 1930s and 1950s – Quinn's work also serves as a political history of the province during this period and beyond. According to the author, the nationalism of the 1920s led to the formation, and rise to power, of Maurice Duplessis' Union nationale party in the 1930s. Quinn brings his analysis up to the rise of the PQ (Parti québécois) during the 1970s, which he demonstrates as being the ascendancy of a radical, over a more conservative, nationalism.

454 The rise of the Parti québécois, 1967-1976.
John Saywell. Toronto: University of Toronto Press, 1977. 174p.

Published shortly after the election of the PQ (Parti québécois) in 1976, this work provides a chronological account of the party's rise between 1967 and 1976. The narrative relies largely upon commentary provided by the major Canadian daily newspapers. Also see Vera Murray's *Le Parti québécois: de la fondation à la prise du pouvoir* (The Parti québécois: from its foundation to its electoral victory) (Montréal: Éditions Hurtubise HMH, 1976. 242p.).

455 The dynamics of right-wing protest: a political analysis of Social Credit in Quebec.
Michael B. Stein. Toronto: University of Toronto Press, 1973. 256p.

Stein describes the evolution of the Social Credit movement in Québec from its founding in 1936 until 1970, stressing the social transformation and revolutionary turmoil of this period in Québec political life. By analysing the social, attitudinal and behavioural profile of the party's leaders, the author attempts to formulate a general theory of right-wing protest movements. For a similar treatment of this phenomenon in Québec, see Maurice Pinard's *The rise of a third party* (see item no. 452).

Periodicals

456 **Canadian Journal of Political Science = Revue Canadienne de Science Politique.**
Ottawa: Canadian Political Science Association, 1968- . quarterly.
This bilingual publication of the Canadian Political Science Association includes articles comprising the most recent research carried out by Canadianists.

457 **Politique et Sociétés.** (Politics and Societies.)
Montréal: Société québécoise de Science politique, 1980- . 3 issues per year.
The official publication of the SQSP (Société québécoise de science politique – Québec Political Science Association). Formerly entitled the *Revue Québécoise de Science Politique* (Québec Review of Political Science) (Montréal: Société québécoise de Science politique, 1980-96. semi-annual), this journal focuses primarily on Québec politics from a comparative perspective.

Identity and Political Culture

458   **Action Nationale.** (National Action.)
       Montréal: Ligue d'Action nationale, 1933- . monthly.

This journal is as much a part of Québec history as it is about Québec history. The mandate of *Action Nationale* (National Action), however, extends beyond history to include articles, essays, and opinion pieces on everything relating to the 'national question'. While many academics sit on the journal's editorial board, its content includes pieces from all sectors of society: academics, youth, and experts in the field. Each issue typically includes research-length articles, short articles on current political events, and book reviews. *Action Nationale* is recognized as having a nationalist political orientation, making this journal all the more important for readers interested in the pulse of nationalist thought.

459   **L'archipel identitaire.** (The identity archipelago.)
       Marcos Ancelovici, Francis Dupuis-Déri.   Montréal: Éditions du
       Boréal, 1997. 215p.

A series of interviews with major intellectuals such as Liah Greenfeld and Alain Finkielkraut who are researching the question of cultural identity. The book also includes interviews with prominent Québec intellectuals, including Charles Taylor, Jean Larose, Lise Bissonnette, Neil Bissoondath and David Homel, which deal more directly with the question of Québec's identity. Other themes of this work include federalism, nationalism, language, art, and religion. See also the equally recent, yet more scholarly, discussion of Québec identity in Mikaël Elbaz, Andrée Fortin and Guy Laforest's *Les frontières de l'identité* (The frontiers of identity) (Sainte-Foy, Québec: Presses de l'Université Laval/L'Harmattan, 1996. 374p.).

460 **Espace régional et nation: pour un nouveau débat sur le Québec.**
(Regional space and nation: towards a new debate on Québec.)
Gérard Boismenu, Gilles Bourque, Roch Denis, Jules Duchastel,
Lizette Jalbert, Daniel Salée. Montréal: Éditions du Boréal Express,
1983. 217p.

This work suggests an analytical and conceptual model of studying Québec that seeks to understand the national question in Québec within the Canadian context. The authors are critical of those who have analysed Québec as a global society with its own distinct social structure, institutions and political traditions, to the exclusion of referring to the Canadian reality apart from as an example to demonstrate the differences between English-speaking Canadian society and Québec society. The authors argue that the regional approach to studying Québec nationalism proposed in this work avoids political bias in favour of either federalism or sovereignty.

461 **Québec and the American dream.**
Robert Chodos, Eric Hamovitch. Toronto: Between the Lines, 1991.
251p.

Examines the somewhat paradoxical tension between the objective of those in favour of sovereignty to protect their culture, on one hand, and their concomitant desire to maintain close relations with the United States, the world's largest cultural assimilator, on the other. In the process of discussing contemporary Québec-US relations, this book relates how the French came to possess, and subsequently lose, the continent. The authors also discuss the noticeable influence American culture, particularly the 'American dream', has had on Québec's distinctive North American character. Another relevant study is Yvan Lamondes' *Ni avec eux ni sans eux: le Québec et les États-Unis* (Neither with them nor without them: Québec and the United States) (Montréal: Nuit Blanche, 1996. 120p.).

462 **Citoyenneté et nationalité. Perspectives en France et au Québec.**
(Citizenship and nationality. Perspectives from France and Québec.)
Dominique Colas, Claude Émeri, Jacques Zylberberg. Paris: Presses
universitaires de France, 1991. 505p.

A collection of essays whose publication stems from a symposium that compared the political systems of Québec and France. This volume deals exclusively with issues of citizenship and nationality, and the different manner in which they have manifested themselves in Québec and France. Essays are divided into thematic sections such as philosophy, history, law, and social politics. Overall, this book presents a contemporary comparative analysis of Québec's national project (the cultural, political, social and economic activities of the nationalist movement).

463 **Boundaries of identity: a Quebec reader.**
Edited by William Dodge. Toronto: Lester Publishing Limited, 1992.
290p.

This work includes a multitude of varied opinions on Québec sovereignty, chosen from newspaper articles, essays, interviews, poetry, manifestos, literary excerpts and film scripts. In addition to the political and constitutional issues associated with sovereignty, Dodge's edited work examines aboriginal, gender, anglophone and immigrant perspectives. Selections are included from over fifty prominent individuals, both anglophone and francophone.

464   **A Canadian challenge = Le défi québécois.**
      Christian Dufour.   Lantzville, British Columbia: Oolichan Books,
      1990. 173p. bibliog. (The Institute for Research on Public Policy).
A thoughtful essay that calls for a fundamental change in the attitudes within, and
relationships between, English- and French-speaking Canada. Condensing over 200
years of history, Dufour argues that both linguistic groups have been unable to overcome the 'psychological' consequences of the Conquest. According to Dufour,
English-speaking Canada must establish a new nationalism that encompasses the
aspirations of contemporary Québec. Similarly, Québec must recognize the Canadian
component in its identity. Dufour argues convincingly in favour of a modicum of
convergence between Québec, and English Canadian, nationalism in order to ensure
that both cultures survive their confrontation with increasing Americanization. See
also Christian Dufour's *La rupture tranquille* (The quiet rupture) (Montréal: Éditions
du Boréal Express, 1992. 170p.).

465   **Genèse de la société québécoise.** (The genesis of Québec society.)
      Fernand Dumont.   Montréal: Éditions du Boréal, 1993. 393p.
Attempts to locate the point in history when Québec society developed a self-
consciousness as a distinct political and cultural entity. The book begins its search
with Québec's colonization and continues through to the mid-19th century. Focusing
mainly on literature and historical works written in Québec, Dumont demonstrates
how the population successively perceived itself through different periods, how it
evolved, and how it was shaped by formative events. The book not only presents an
original vision of Québec's early identity, but it also reveals the need societies have to
understand themselves. The book is extremely well written and its eloquence testifies to
Dumont's accomplishments as a writer and poet. This work won Dumont the 1994
France-Québec Award.

466   **The vigil of Quebec.**
      Fernand Dumont, translated by Sheila Fischman and Richard Howard.
      Toronto: University of Toronto Press, 1971. 131p.
A noted Québec sociologist and intellectual, Dumont discusses a number of themes in
this book: the nature of the Quiet Revolution; the cultural dominance of the United
States *vis-à-vis* Québec; the viability of socialism in Québec; and the nature of the
FLQ (Front de libération du Québec) as well as the October Crisis in 1970. Also
included is 'A letter to my English-speaking friends' in which he urges both English
and French-speaking Canadians to end their mutual indifference.

467   **La liberté n'est pas une marque de yogourt.** (Liberty is not a yogurt
      brand name.)
      Pierre Falardeau.   Montréal: Stanké, 1995. 239p.
Written by one of Québec's most influential film-makers, this book presents a collection of Pierre Falardeau's texts, letters and film projects written since the 1970s. In
this collection, Falardeau denounces the intellectual dishonesty of some intellectuals,
journalists and public figures, the political interference in decisions regarding the
funding of the arts, and the increasing superficiality of the way independence is marketed
by political parties. Falardeau's films are typically historical: the first is entitled
Octobre (October) (Montréal: Stanké, 1994. 190p.) and presents a sympathetic view of
the FLQ during the 1970 October Crisis; the second, *15 février 1839* (15 February

1839) (Montréal: Stanké, 1996. 169p.), chronicles the last hours of Chevalier de Lorimier who was sentenced to death and hanged by Lower Canadian authorities for his role in the rebellions of 1837-38.

468   **Une planète nommée Québec. Chroniques sociales et politiques, 1991-1995.** (A planet called Québec. Social and political columns between 1991 and 1995.)
       Pierre Graveline.   Outremont, Québec: VLB Éditeur, 1996. 346p.

One of *Le Devoir*'s regular columnists between 1991 and 1995, Pierre Graveline is also known for his leading role in the Québec Writers' Union's support for sovereignty during the 1995 referendum. His columns, which are organized thematically, extend beyond a lament for unachieved national dreams. Graveline, whose writing style has won him accolades from Québec's leading academics and journalists, turns a critical eye to the major issues and challenges facing contemporary Québec. In addition to his call for national independence, Graveline makes a just and well-reasoned argument in favour of social solidarity and a solid, well-researched criticism of neo-liberal politics and policies.

469   **Hommage à Marcel Rioux.** (In honour of Marcel Rioux.)
       Edited by Jacques Hamel, Louis Maheu.   Montréal: Éditions Saint-Martin, 1992. 228p. bibliog.

A collection of essays in honour of one of Québec's most respected sociologists and intellectuals. Written by social scientists, artists and writers, this work provides a critical analysis of Rioux's theories and his intellectual thought on culture, art, education, youth and the Québec national question, thereby touching on the major questions and issues facing modern Québec. A bibliography of Rioux's works is also included.

470   **Nationalism and the politics of culture in Québec.**
       Richard Handler.   Madison, Wisconsin: University of Wisconsin Press, 1988. 217p. bibliog.

An interdisciplinary study of Québec nationalism during the PQ's two mandates (1976-84). Handler focuses on the cultural aspects of Québec nationalism: he provides a sketch of folkloric research in Québec, scrutinizes the Québec Department of Cultural Affairs, assesses the government's role in the protection of cultural heritage, and examines language legislation and immigration policies. More generally, this book is concerned with the way nations establish boundaries through rhetoric and writing. In the conclusion, Handler suggests that culture is not limited to tightly defined nations. He argues that nationalism that seeks to create exclusive cultural boundaries is futile.

471   **Québécois et Américains: la culture québécoise aux XIXe et XXe siècles.** (Quebecers and Americans: Québec culture during the 19th and 20th centuries.)
       Edited by Yvan Lamonde, Gérard Bouchard.   Saint-Laurent, Québec: Éditions Fides, 1995. 418p. bibliog.

An examination of Québec's place in the American continental 'cultural space'. The collection's primary objective is to analyse Québec's entrance into this 'cultural space' as a distinct North American francophone community and its corresponding abandonment of traditional European cultural referents. This rupture began, according to the authors, with the rise of a territorial consciousness within Quebecers' collective imagination. In their examination, the authors pay special attention to three cleavages (the split between intellectuals and masses, intra-intellectual differences, and east-west divisions within the province) which result in different attitudes regarding Québec's place in the American 'cultural space'. The authors also attempt to compare Quebecers' experiences with those of Americans, Canadians and Mexicans. A related work is Dean Louder's *Le Québec et les francophones de la Nouvelle-Angleterre* (Québec and New England francophones) (Sainte-Foy, Québec: Presses de l'Université Laval, 1991. 309p.).

472 **Territoires de la culture québécoise.** (Territories of Québec culture.)
Yvan Lamonde.   Sainte-Foy, Québec: Presses de l'Université Laval, 1991. 293p.

A collection of Lamonde's articles published over the course of his career. This collection presents his research over the past fifteen years on Québec's sociocultural history. The social history of ideas and intellectuals figure among the principal themes in his work.

473 **La petite noirceur.** (The little darkness.)
Jean Larose.   Montréal: Éditions du Boréal, 1987. 206p.

Written by one of the most influential intellectuals in Québec, this collection of polemical essays discusses topics such as Québec's artistic output, the 1980 referendum, and Québec's distinctiveness. In these essays, as in his other works, Larose rejects what he interprets as Québec society's 'anti-intellectualism' and excessive nationalism. Also see Larose's *La souveraineté rampante* (Rampant sovereignty) (Montréal: Éditions du Boréal, 1994. 112p.).

474 **La question identitaire au Canada francophone: récits, parcours, enjeux, hors-lieux.** (The question of identity in francophone Canada: stories, meanderings, stakes and placelessness.)
Edited by Jocelyn Létourneau.   Sainte-Foy, Québec: Presses de l'Université Laval, 1994. 292p.

An examination of identity as it pertains to minority francophone communities in Canada, outside of Québec. The authors focus on the way identity issues have been shaped and transformed by globalization and regionalism. In light of new theories of identity, which stress the dynamic nature of individuals' loyalties, these essays map the recent transformations of identity within Canadian francophone communities.

475 **La mémoire dans la culture.** (Memory in culture.)
Edited by Jacques Mathieu.   Sainte-Foy, Québec: Presses de l'Université Laval, 1995. 344p.

Using the past to understand the role of culture, this collection of essays attempts to give meaning to history in its role as mediator between the individual and the community in francophone North America. Two methods are used in analysing the past: the first is based on empirical evidence; the second attempts to discover how the past has been perceived and analysed by social actors.

476   **Les mémoires québécoises.** (Québec memories.)
       Jacques Mathieu, Jacques Lacoursière.   Sainte-Foy, Québec: Presses
       de l'Université Laval, 1991. 383p.

A comprehensive examination of the Québec identity that touches upon its myths, territory, ethnicity, the family, the Church, arts and symbolic representations. Useful illustrations are included from various archival sources.

477   **Québec Studies.**
       Hanover, New Hampshire: American Council of Québec Studies,
       1983- . 2 issues per year.

Focuses on French Canadian literature and civilization, but any given issue typically includes a broad range of articles on all aspects of Québec society and culture. The journal is interdisciplinary and bilingual, and includes book reviews and brief research notes.

478   **Un peuple dans le siècle.** (A people in the century.)
       Marcel Rioux.   Montréal: Éditions du Boréal, 1990. 452p.

A remarkable and very persuasive essay in favour of a more humanitarian and reinforced Québec society. In this book, Rioux's last publication before his death, Rioux uses his personal experiences to illustrate the evolution of Québec society. The last section of the book is devoted to the challenges that face the people of Québec: the loss of a distinct cultural identity; the domination of capitalism; and American hegemony. This work is particularly notable for its lucidity and rich analysis.

479   **Quebec in question.**
       Marcel Rioux, translated by James Boake.   Toronto: James Lorimer &
       Co., 1978. rev. ed. 209p.

An important work from one of Québec's most noted sociologists and intellectuals. It provides a broad interpretation of the ideological context which fuelled the neo-nationalism of the 1960s. As a socialist and 'sovereignist', Rioux offers a perspective that opposes much of Québec's pre-Quiet Revolution discourse.

480   **Les rapports culturels entre le Québec et les États-Unis.** (Cultural
       relations between Québec and the United States.)
       Edited by Claude Savary.   Québec: Institut québécois de Recherche
       sur la Culture, 1984. 353p.

Comprises the proceedings of a conference on Québec-American cultural relations. Specifically, this work examines the impact of American culture on the way Quebecers perceive themselves in addition to measuring the impact American culture has had on Québec society. These texts use an anthropological definition of culture, based on morals, behaviour and values. Rather than espousing typically negative interpretations of American influences on Québec, the authors of these texts perceive American influence as part of a larger dynamic fuelled by the interaction and meeting of two societies.

481 **The race question in Canada.**
André Siegfried. Toronto: McClelland and Stewart, 1966. 247p.
(Carleton Library, no. 29).
Frank Underhill, in the introduction to this book, appropriately refers to Siegfried as the 'Tocqueville of Canada'. First published under the title *La Canada, les deux races: problèmes politiques contemporains* (Canada, the two races: contemporary political problems) (Paris: Librairie Armand Colin, 1906), Siegfried offers an incisive analysis of the relations between the English and French in Canada. He looks at the Catholic Church in Québec, the school system, French sentiment towards outside powers (Britain, France and the United States), political parties, external relations and the nature of French Canadian nationalism. Most startling is the remarkable durability of his insights. See also Gérard Bergeron's *Quand Tocqueville et Siegfried nous observaient* (When Tocqueville and Siegfried where watching us) (Sillery, Québec: Presses de l'Université du Québec, 1990. 183p.).

482 **Le Québec: un pays, une culture.** (Québec: one country, one culture.)
Françoise Tétu de Labsade. Montréal: Éditions du Boréal, 1990.
458p. bibliog.
Demonstrates a more nuanced and complex vision of Québec's cultural and artistic production, revealing Québec's resistance to being defined in broad terms. Through a historical, artistic, and social synthesis of events, the author demonstrates what makes Québec a distinct society. This work is designed for students wishing to examine particular aspects of Québec and it is consequently written in accessible prose. Each chapter is relatively autonomous thereby facilitating selective reading.

483 **Les problèmes culturels du Québec.** (Québec's cultural problems.)
Edited by Giuseppe Turry. Ottawa: Éditions La Presse, 1974. 127p.
This book contains the various declarations regarding the protection of Québec's culture made by four Québec premiers during the 1960s and early 1970s (Jean Lesage, Daniel Johnson, Jean-Jacques Bertrand and Robert Bourassa). From the Lesage's political slogan 'Maîtres chez nous' (Masters of our own house) to Johnson's 'Equality or Independence' and Bourassa's concept of 'cultural sovereignty', Québec has experienced important changes at the level of its identity. The book pertains to Quebecers' changing identity as it manifested itself in the official speeches of the province's political leaders.

484 **La ligne du risque.** (Risk line.)
Pierre Vadeboncœur. Montréal: Bibliothèque québécoise, 1994.
2nd ed. 288p.
Written by a former contributor to the *Cité Libre* magazine, this collection of six essays, animated by a spirit of revolt, is a profound statement in favour of a sovereign Québec. Vadeboncœur presents Québec sovereignty as an act that would allow Québec to break with its tradition of conformity. These essays are profoundly anticlerical and they present a political project based on the rejection of the past in favour of the total liberty and full autonomy of the individual.

Nationalism

485   **Nationalism and the national question.**
Nicole Arnaud, Jacques Dofny, translated by Penelope Williams.
Montréal; New York: Black Rose Books, 1977. 133p.

A dialogue between two authors on the subject of nationalism in Québec and
Occitanie, a southern region of France housing thirteen million inhabitants. Viewing
both regions as distinct national entities, the authors assess the dynamics of nationalism
in both national groupings.

486   **Bilan du nationalisme au Québec.** (An appraisal of nationalism in
Québec.)
Louis Balthazar.   Montréal: L'Hexagone, 1986. 212p.

A general account of the evolution of nationalism in Québec from the French regime
to the 1980 referendum. The purpose of the book is to distinguish the different forms
and orientations of Québec nationalism. Rejecting a Marxist approach to studying
nationalism in Québec, the author analyses nationalism in light of the theories of
authors such as Hans Köhn, Karl Deutsch and Anthony Smith. For a general account
see Gilles Gougeon's *A history of Québec nationalism* (Toronto: James Lorimer &
Co., 1994. 118p.).

487   **Prelude to Quebec's Quiet Revolution: liberalism versus
neo-nationalism, 1945-1960.**
Michael D. Behiels.   Montréal; Kingston, Ontario: McGill-Queen's
University Press, 1985. 366p.

One of the best accounts of the ideological undercurrents during this period. Behiels
looks at the main competing intellectual movements that immediately predated
Québec's institutional modernization of the 1960s. Behiels suggests that the initial
spark that gave life to the Quiet Revolution resulted from the dynamic created by
two competing ideological groups. The first included social democrats and liberals
associated with the *Cité Libre* magazine and organized labour, such as Pierre Trudeau,

Gérard Pelletier and Jean Marchand. The other group comprised young journalists and intellectuals associated with *L'Action Nationale* (National Action) and *Le Devoir*. In revealing the historical antecedents to the Quiet Revolution, Behiels also dispels the monolithic image often associated with the pre-1960 period, too often characterized as the 'Grande noirceur' (the Great Darkness). This book is essential reading for all students of modern Québec.

488 **Le Québec: la question nationale.** (Québec: the national question.)
Gilles Bourque, Anne Legaré. Paris: Maspero, 1979. 232p.

This work attempts to explain contemporary events as the natural products of particular historical experiences. Moreover, Bourque and Legaré argue that national tensions are intimately related to Québec's experience in the federal system, highlighting the historical importance of the national question which they believed, in 1979, to be undervalued. This book constitutes an expanded version of Bourque's earlier work, *Question nationale et classes sociales au Québec, 1760-1840* (see item no. 489).

489 **Question nationale et classes sociales au Québec, 1760-1840.** (The national question and social classes in Québec, 1760-1840.)
Gilles Bourque. Montréal: Éditions Parti Pris, 1970. 350p.

At the heart of this Marxist interpretation of Québec history is a structuralist approach based on the relationship between social classes and the national question. While Marxists typically emphasize the social over the national, Bourque attempts to combine the two. He suggests that the Conquest was a formative event in the historical experience of Québec because it imposed a new social structure on the French colony. He then describes Québec's history in the context of the battle between two ethnically differentiable social structures within which social classes competed for domination. This is a scholarly and theoretical work written for an academic audience.

490 **Is Quebec nationalism just? Perspectives from anglophone Canada.**
Edited by Joseph H. Carens. Montréal; Kingston, Ontario: McGill-Queen's University Press, 1995. 240p.

A series of thoughtful essays that examine the compatibility of Québec nationalism and the liberal principles of freedom, justice, equality and democracy. Unlike many English Canadians, the authors share the view that the aspirations of Quebecers to control their own political destiny is not fuelled by a hostility towards liberalism. This book constitutes the most progressive English Canadian contribution to the study of liberal nationalism in Québec to date, and is an essential read for those interested in Québec's quest for increased sovereignty.

491 **Quebec nationalism in crisis.**
Dominique Clift. Montréal; Kingston, Ontario: McGill-Queen's University Press, 1982. 151p. bibliog.

Prematurely, the author pronounces the decline of nationalism in Québec, as evidenced by the shift in popular sentiment towards individualism and the weakening of social control by various intellectual elites. The author believes that following the re-election of René Lévesque in 1981, nationalism has increasingly become a matter of mere rhetoric; it is now identified with conformity rather than social change. Although

Clift's prognosis was disproved by the historic rise in Québec nationalism in 1990 (at this time there was a great consensus among federalist and 'sovereignist' nationalists), his work nevertheless represents a recurring opinion among a minority of analysts that Québec nationalism will one day expire.

492 The independence movement in Quebec, 1945-1980.
William D. Coleman.   Toronto: University of Toronto Press, 1988. 274p.

An excellent and somewhat controversial analysis of the Quiet Revolution and the subsequent rise of the independence movement. Coleman examines the shifting coalition of classes that helped bring about modernization in the 1960s followed by the rise of support for sovereignty in the 1970s and 1980s. He claims that the independence coalition united organized labour, the francophone business class, and parts of the new middle class. According to the author, the changes during this period, along with the collapse of traditional French Canadian culture, merely hastened the integration of Québec into the North American economy. This continentalization may portend insurmountable difficulties in maintaining a distinct Québec culture. Related works include Jean-Claude Robert's *Du Canada français au Québec libre: histoire d'un mouvement indépendantiste* (From French Canada to a free Québec: the history of the independence movement) (Paris: Flammarion, 1975. 323p.).

493 Canada, Québec, and the uses of nationalism.
Ramsay Cook.   Toronto: McClelland and Stewart, 1995. 2nd ed. 294p.

A revised and updated edition of Cook's 1986 work by the same title, bringing together a number of the author's previously published essays. As one of Canada's most noted historians, Cook grapples with the challenges of reconciling Québec nationalism with the idea of the modern nation state. He also traces the development of English Canadian and aboriginal nationalism. Cook argues that a 'civic society', enshrining the duality of languages and diversity of cultures, represents the best solution to the ongoing unity crisis in Canada.

494 Two nations: an essay on the culture and politics of Canada in a world of American pre-eminence.
Susan M. Crean, Marcel Rioux.   Toronto: James Lorimer & Co., 1983. 167p.

The authors call for the national autonomy of both Canada and Québec in order to stem the perceived cultural and economic threat from the United States. They examine the relationship between Québec and Canada as well as the troubled history of US-Canadian relations.

495 Nationalismes et politique au Québec. (Nationalism and politics in Québec.)
Léon Dion.   Montréal: Hurtubise HMH, 1975. 177p. bibliog.

In this work, the noted political analyst Léon Dion attempts to unravel three distinct types of nationalism in Québec: conservative nationalism, personified in the political careers of Henri Bourassa, Lionel Groulx and André Laurendeau; liberal nationalism, exemplified by Pierre Trudeau and Gérard Pelletier; and social democratic nationalism, as espoused by the PQ (Parti québécois). Dion traces the roots, evolution, and political implications, of each of these nationalist traditions. Readers interested in a different interpretation of what Dion has characterized as the 'conservative nationalism' of Bourassa and Laurendeau should consult Michael Oliver's *The passionate debate. The social and political ideas of Québec nationalism, 1920-1945* (see item no. 502).

496 **The question of separatism: Quebec and the struggle over sovereignty.**
Jane Jacobs.   New York: Random House, 1980. 134p.

A thoughtful work, examining the implications of separation for Québec. Jacobs looks at the political economies of Montréal and Toronto, the peaceful secession of Norway from Sweden in 1905, and the project of sovereignty-association. Jacobs takes the view that the independence movement in Québec is in part a political response to the decline of Montréal's role in Canadian economic affairs. Underpinning Jacob's analysis is a disdain for large bureaucratic states and an appreciation for technological innovation. Always the iconoclast, the author attempts to dispel the myths of federalists and separatists alike.

497 **Community in crisis: French-Canadian nationalism in perspective.**
Richard Jones.   Toronto: McClelland and Stewart, 1972. 2nd ed.
192p. bibliog. (Carleton Library, no. 59).

In the foreword to the book, the author expresses his desire 'to discover how the French Canadian looks at himself'. Jones believes that Quebecers' perception of themselves as a colonized minority fuels their sense of nationalism. As in similar books published by English Canadians during this period, the author attempts to trace the roots of the new nationalism of the early 1970s by looking to Canada's colonial history. A common mistake made by many analysts during the early days of the independence movement was the failure to recognize the growing tendency for French Canadians to see themselves as 'Quebecers' as opposed to French Canadians. Nevertheless, historical explanations for the contemporary nationalist movement are still held by a number of academics and analysts.

498 **Nations against the state. The new politics of nationalism in Québec, Catalonia and Scotland.**
Michael Keating.   New York: St. Martin's Press, 1996. 260p.

Keating suggests that the increasing indifference manifested by these three minority peoples towards either full independence or the status quo as potential political solutions is the result of important transformations in the form and content of the traditional concept of the nation state. This book explores the meaning of identity and nationalism in industrialized countries in an attempt to understand the changes that are occurring in the modern nation state. Looking specifically at the content of nationalist messages, Keating argues that the nation state is undergoing a transformation and that 'civil society is as important a sphere as the state for the nation-building project'. Moreover, Keating's refreshing interpretation of minority nationalism as a potentially problem-solving mechanism breaks with the frequent hostility several academics have directed at nationalist movements.

499   **Canada and Quebec, past and future: an essay.**
Daniel Latouche.   Toronto: University of Toronto Press, 1986. 157p.
bibliog. (Macdonald Commission Research Study, no. 70).

In an iconoclastic fashion, Latouche highlights what he sees as English-speaking Canada's non-existence as a distinct society and the threat of Québec society's slow disintegration. Latouche also remarks on the mutual dependence of Québec and Canada, believing that what serves the development of one is also beneficial for the other. In addition, he takes a revisionist look at the past, stressing the continuity of events in the 1960s with earlier periods.

500   **The decolonization of Quebec: an analysis of left-wing nationalism.**
Henry Milner, Sheilagh Hodgins Milner.   Toronto: McClelland and
Stewart, 1973. 257p. bibliog.

The authors examine the rise of a left-wing separatist ideology in Québec during the 1960s and 1970s. Sympathetic to the goals of this movement, the authors emphasize Québec's socio-economic dependence on both Ontario and the United States. The first part of the book considers the effects of imperialism on Québec's economy and culture by analysing patterns of trade and ownership. The second part looks at factors since the 1930s that have led to the development of a left-leaning nationalism. See also André d'Allemagne's *Le colonialisme au Québec* (Colonialism in Québec) (Montréal: Les Éditions R.-B., 1966. 191p.).

501   **Le Québec, une nation opprimée.** (Québec: an oppressed nation.)
François Moreau.   Hull, Québec: Éditions Vents d'Ouest, 1993. 181p.

Suggesting that Québec is an oppressed nation, the author of this book advocates Québec independence as the only way to reject the Canadian neo-liberal agenda. Moreover, Moreau believes that independence is a precondition for a more socialist and humanitarian society. The book focuses principally on the historical nature of Québec's oppression from the Conquest to the present day. Moreau is mainly concerned with economic oppression, highlighting the fact that, even today, franco-phones, on average, are less well remunerated than anglophones.

502   **The passionate debate. The social and political ideas of Québec nationalism, 1920-1945.**
Michael Oliver.   Montréal: Vehicule Press, 1991. 284p.

This study of Québec nationalism was originally written in 1956 but not published for over thirty-five years. Oliver shows how Québec nationalism has acted as a vehicle for change and also how it has joined itself with both right- and left-wing ideologies. This is one of the few analyses of Québec nationalism written in English which reveals the progressive ideology of the early left-wing nationalists such as Olivar Asselin and André Laurendeau. The work is an essential piece of literature for the reader who wants a more nuanced portrait of early 20th-century Québec nationalism.

503   **The shouting signpainters: a literary and political account of Québec revolutionary nationalism.**
Malcolm Reid.   Toronto: McClelland and Stewart, 1972. 315p.

Reid provides a narrative account of political events in Québec, filling in the backdrop to the events he describes with his personal experience of popular language, literature and politics in the province. Easy to read and personal, this book provides the reader with an anglophone's perspective of the period from the late 1960s to the October Crisis of 1970.

504 **Letters to a Québécois friend (with a reply by Daniel Latouche).**
Philip Resnick. Montréal; Kingston, Ontario: McGill-Queen's University Press, 1990. 125p.

Written in December 1988 in the aftermath of the Canadian general election and the Supreme Court rulings over language laws in Québec, this collection of letters was addressed to an imaginary Québec friend. Resnick is widely associated with a growing group of English Canadian left-wing nationalists. His letters reveal an English Canadian interpretation of Free Trade (the Free Trade Agreement of 1988), the Meech Lake Accord (1987-90), and Québec's place within Canada. Daniel Latouche, a well-known academic and columnist for *Le Devoir* plays the role of the imaginary Québec friend in the second half of the book and answers Resnick's letters, thereby presenting a Québec nationalist's interpretation of the same events.

505 **First world nationalism: class and ethnic politics in Northern Ireland and Quebec.**
Katherine O'Sullivan See. Chicago: University of Chicago Press, 1986. 215p. bibliog.

An important study of nationalism that develops a theory of the origin and evolution of nationalist movements in advanced industrial settings, specifically Northern Ireland and Québec. See's model of resource competition (the competition between various political actors) focuses on the way class elites develop and use ethnic institutions to control and mobilize groups. For example, a nationalist movement without access to political capital (such as town councils) will find its ability to mobilize its support base more difficult than if it had greater access to political capital. Resources can take the form of political institutions (assemblies, councils, parliaments) and organizations within civil society (ethnic groups, interest groups, media groups, unions, etc.). The author focuses on Québec's isolationism prior to the Second World War, the emergence of competing types of nationalism following the war, and the emergence of the PQ (Parti québécois) in the 1970s. Written for an academic audience, this book is part of the growing literature on nationalism in post-industrial settings.

506 **Abbé Groulx: variations on a nationalist theme.**
Edited by Susan Mann Trofimenkoff. Vancouver: Copp Clark, 1973. 256p. bibliog.

Abbot Lionel Groulx has been described by some as the 'spiritual father of modern Québec'. As a priest, polemicist, and professor of history, Groulx provided a guiding hand behind the *Action Française* movement in the 1920s, an important nationalist movement in the province during this period. This work brings together selections of Groulx's writing in the form of poetry, essays, articles and biography. The last section contains assessments of Groulx's contribution to Québec society by prominent journalists and intellectuals. This is the best compilation of Groulx's work ever translated into English.

507　Action française: French Canadian nationalism in the twenties.
　　Susan Mann Trofimenkoff.　Toronto: University of Toronto Press,
　　1975. 157p. bibliog.

The *Action Française* was a Montréal-based nationalist movement and publication which developed in the aftermath of the First World War, and reached its height in the 1920s under the guiding hand of Lionel Groulx. The movement urged its followers to recognize and confront the linguistic, economic, social and political threats to their distinctive existence in North America. Although *Action Française* collapsed in 1928, some of its ideas resurfaced in subsequent manifestations of Québec nationalism. This work focuses on the origins, founders, organizations, publications, and concerns, of this movement.

508　White niggers of America.
　　Pierre Vallières, translated by Joan Pinkham.　Toronto: McClelland
　　and Stewart, 1971. 281p.

Condemning the capitalist system, Vallières advocates revolution as a way of achieving a more equitable class system. Though the author strongly supports Québec independence, he believes that liberating Québec society from the oppression of the Church and the American 'predators of industry' should remain pre-eminent objectives. The book reflects some of the more radical leftist ideas that helped fuel the Quiet Revolution of the 1960s.

Secession

509 **Secession. The morality of political divorce from Fort Sumter to Lithuania and Québec.**
Allen Buchanan.   Boulder, Colorado: Westview Press, 1991. 174p. bibliog.

Although not exclusively about Québec, this work merits a mention for the way it brings political philosophy to bear on the concrete political debate over sovereignty and self-determination. Since Québec figures as one of Buchanan's references, this book will interest readers who want to examine Québec's moral claims for self-determination in contrast to the constraining legal and judicial arguments often raised in English-speaking Canada against Québec's bid for separation. Buchanan not only proposes a theory which outlines the conditions under which political separation is morally justifiable, but he also glosses over the various counter-arguments that do not constitute a legitimate justification of separation.

510 **La partition du Québec: de Lord Durham à Stéphane Dion.**
(The partition of Québec: from Lord Durham to Stéphane Dion.)
Claude G. Charron.   Montréal: VLB Éditeur, 1996. 205p. (Collection Partis Pris Actuels).

Since the 1995 referendum, the partition of Québec's territory has become an increasingly attractive solution for some members of the anglophone community and political elite who want to remain in Canada in the advent of an independent Québec. Denouncing this option as dangerous and anti-democratic, the author of this essay traces the historical roots of the idea of partition in Québec. He argues that the idea of partition dates from the Conquest and that it is the political expression of anglophones' fear of becoming a minority governed by a francophone majority. The author points to Northern Ireland, India and Cyprus as examples of the dangers of partition. There is a good chapter on how advocates of partition have appropriated aboriginals' quest for self-determination in a dangerous game of divide and conquer.

511 **Exposés et études, vol. 1: les attributs d'un Québec souverain.**
(Presentations and studies, volume 1: characteristics of a sovereign Québec.)
Commission d'Étude des Questions afférentes à la Sécession du Québec à la Souveraineté. Québec: Assemblée nationale, 1992.

These four volumes include presentations made to the Bélanger-Campeau Commission (November 1990 to February 1991) in charge of examining all questions relating to Québec sovereignty. The presentations contained herein, many of which are by Québec's leading experts and academics, provide important sources of information on Québec society. Two volumes focus exclusively on the judicial and economic issues relating to Québec sovereignty. Moreover, these documents comprise essential information for the reader who wants to understand the desire for self-determination shared by many Quebecers.

512 **Parting as friends: the economic consequences for Quebec.**
John McCallum, Chris Green. Toronto: C. D. Howe Institute, 1991. 110p.

Assuming a non-acrimonious separation of Québec from the rest of Canada, the authors examine the possible implications of secession for the Québec economy. The authors foresee negative consequences in both the short and long term, predicting higher taxes, emigration and reduced investment in the province. The most vulnerable areas include the Québec dairy industry, the head offices of foreign firms, the city of Hull, and the clothing and textile industries. Another work on this subject is Daniel Drache and Roberto Perin's *Negotiating with a sovereign Québec* (see item no. 543).

513 **Le syndrome des plaines d'Abraham.** (The syndrome of the Plains of Abraham.)
Éric Schwimmer. Montréal: Éditions du Boréal, 1996. 205p.

This is an ethnographic study of Québec nationalism that uses observation and interviews to analyse attitudes towards sovereignty at a micro-level. The study is divided into two parts. The first is devoted to a comparative analysis of secessionist movements (e.g., those in New Guinea and those in New Zealand) and national minorities (e.g., Scotland in the United Kingdom, and the Maoris in New Zealand). The second part focuses on the political thought of Quebecers. Three models of discourse are identified: the assimilationist, the dualist, and the secessionist. The overall image is one of ambiguity which explains why Quebecers tend to prefer sovereignty-association and other forms of political partnership and association to full-blown independence. The author underlines the fact that a majority 'Yes' vote would only be the first step towards independence.

514 **The secession of Quebec and the future of Canada.**
Robert A. Young. Montréal; Kingston, Ontario: McGill-Queen's University Press, 1995. 376p. bibliog.

Starting with the premise that Québec has opted for sovereignty, this work provides a comparative analysis of cases of peaceful secession. This is followed by an assessment of the constitutional options available for a Canada 'without Québec'. Young minutely examines the transition towards sovereignty and its long-term implications. This is the best and most thorough work on the potential dynamics of the negotiation of sovereignty.

Secession

On English-speaking Canada's vision of Québec sovereignty, see Michel Sarra-Bournet's *Le Canada anglais et la souveraineté du Québec* (English-speaking Canada and Québec sovereignty) (Montréal: VLB Éditeur, 1995. 215p.), which presents a 'Who's who' of English-speaking Canada and opinions on Québec's possible separation. Christian Dufour's *La rupture tranquille* (The quiet rupture) (Montréal: Éditions du Boréal Express, 1992. 170p.) discusses the potential positive impacts that might result from Québec's separation. Based in part on his *A Canadian challenge = Le défi québécois* (see item no. 464), Dufour focuses on Québec's specificity and the failure of the Meech Lake Accord in 1990 as precursors of the inevitability of Québec separation.

Ideology

515 **Un Québec corporatiste? Corporatisme et néo-corporatisme, du passage d'une idéologie corporatiste sociale à une idéologie corporatiste politique: le Québec de 1930 à nos jours.**
(A corporatist Québec? Corporatism and neo-corporatism, the evolution from a social corporatist ideology to a political corporatist ideology: Québec from 1930 to the present.)
Clinton Archibald.   Hull, Québec: Éditions Asticou, 1983. 429p.

Though Québec has always had corporatist tendencies in the design and function of its political institutions, the author argues that the province has never been a corporatist state. Archibald begins by defining corporatism and then offers an analysis of corporatist models in the Western world. He goes on to examine incidences of corporative structures and ideologies during three distinct periods in Québec: 1930 to 1960; the Quiet Revolution between 1960 and 1970; and the decade from 1970-80. This work is a comprehensive study of Québec's political and ideological development during the 20th century.

516 **L'apolitisme des idéologies québécoises. Le grand tournant de 1934-1936.** (The apoliticism of Québec ideologies. The turning-point of 1934-36.)
André-J. Bélanger.   Québec: Presses de l'Université Laval, 1974. 392p.

In 1974 this book made waves due to its re-interpretation of the ideological dynamic in Québec prior to the Quiet Revolution. In very structured and theoretical prose, Bélanger analyses ideologies in Québec in parallel with the economic, political and social movements of the mid-1930s. He argues that the apoliticism of ideological movements at the time aborted a possible 'Quiet Revolution of the 1930s', which was favoured by the political, social and economic juncture. Moreover, he claims that the apoliticism of such publications and groups as *Le Devoir* (see item no. 1026), *La Relève*, *Action Nationale* (see item no. 458), Jeune-Canada (Young Canada), and the École sociale populaire (Social Popular School) hindered the realization of their own social projects. Among other analysts of Québec's ideologies are Michel Brunet, Fernand Dumont and Gérard Bergeron.

517 **Ruptures et constantes: quatre idéologies du Québec en éclatement: La Relève, La JEC, Cité Libre, Parti Pris.** (Rupture and continuity: the explosion of four ideologies: *La Relève, La JEC, Cité Libre,* and *Parti Pris.*)
André-J. Bélanger. Montréal: Éditions Hurtubise HMH, 1977. 219p.

Emphasizes the role of the press as a barometer of the intellectual changes and developments that occurred prior to the Quiet Revolution. Moreover, Bélanger praises these case-studies for opening the political debate which had, until then, been under the firm control of clerical authorities. The evidence put forward in this work challenges the conservative notion that Québec's entry into modernity did not occur before 1960.

518 **La société libérale duplessiste, 1944-1960.** (The liberal society under Duplessis, 1944-60.)
Gilles Bourque, Jules Duchastel, Jacques Beauchemin. Montréal: Presses de l'Université de Montréal, 1994. 435p.

One of several recent works that reassesses state and society under the Duplessis regime in Québec. It attempts to evaluate the leadership of the Union nationale in the light of social thought during this period. For a more conventional interpretation of the Duplessis era, see Robert Rumilly's *Maurice Duplessis et son temps* (Maurice Duplessis and his times) (Montréal: Fides, 1978. 2 vols.).

519 **Idéologies au Canada français.** (Ideology in French-speaking Canada.)
Edited by Fernand Dumont, Jean Hamelin, Jean-Paul Montminy. Sainte-Foy, Québec: Presses de l'Université Laval, 1971- . 4 vols. (Histoire et Sociologie de la Culture, nos. 1, 5, 11-12).

This indispensable four-volume collection of scholarly essays provides a wide-ranging view of the ideologies that dominated French-speaking Canada and Québec between 1850 and 1976. However, this series cannot be described as a comprehensive synthesis of Québec ideologies. Nevertheless, each volume provides a thought-provoking reflection of the various ideological trends of each period examined. It should also be noted that these essays occasionally emphasize the more progressive ideological groups and individuals in Québec.

520 **Quebec: the challenge of independence.**
Anne Griffin. London; Toronto: Associated University Presses, 1984. 220p.

Based primarily on a series of interviews, Griffin provides an explanation of the social, historical and psychological factors that have contributed to the emergence of a separatist movement in Québec. In the last part of the book, the author examines the implications of Quebecers' experience for other bi- and multi-ethnic states.

521 **Cité Libre: une anthologie.** (*Cité Libre*: an anthology.)
Yvan Lamonde, Gérard Pelletier.   Montréal: Éditions internationales
Alain Stanké, 1991. 413p. bibliog.

Cité Libre, founded in the 1950s by former Prime Minister Pierre Trudeau and Gérard Pelletier, along with other liberals and social democrats, was one of Québec's most important intellectual outlets for ideological protest at the time. It was established as a vehicle for expressing dissatisfaction with Duplessis and conservative institutions such as the clericalism of the Catholic Church, which the founders believed to be obstacles to the establishment of a modern, francophone society. Moreover, the publication was one representation of the intellectual changes occurring at the time which subsequently formed part of the foundation for the Quiet Revolution of 1960-66. This anthology comprises forty-two essays and articles that appeared in *Cité Libre* between 1950 and 1965. Authors include Pierre Trudeau, Gérard Pelletier, René Lévesque, Pierre Vadeboncœur, Marcel Rioux, and other important intellectuals. These essays are organized into ten thematic sections ranging from *Cité Libre's* mission to nationalism and democracy.

522 **Combats libéraux au tournant du XXe siècle.** (Liberal battles at the turn of the 20th century.)
Edited by Yvan Lamonde.   Montréal: Fides, 1995. 288p.

This book breaks with the widely held view that conservatism dominated Québec society and was unchallenged at the turn of the century. Citing the works of liberal thinkers, these authors give nuances to the history of a time widely believed to be devoid of ideological competition. Aspects of liberal thought are examined in such individuals as: the journalist Arthur Buies (1840-1901); the well-known poet Louis-Honoré Fréchette (1839-1908); and Godfroy Langlois, a writer and a radical element within the Québec Liberal Party at the turn of the century, and a remnant of the Parti rouge (Red Party). The Parti rouge was the Liberal Party in Canada East (i.e. Québec) which was formed in 1848 as the ideological successor to the Patriots (the party of Louis-Joseph Papineau). The Parti rouge would later dissolve and become one of the founding members of the Liberal Party in 1873. This work also examines the content of liberal debates such as those on secular education, liberal nationalism, changes in judicial thought and resistance to censorship.

523 **Gens de parole. Conférences publiques, essais et débats à l'Institut canadien de Montréal, 1845-1871.** (People of words. Public conferences, essays and debates at the Montréal Canadian Institute, 1845-71.)
Yvan Lamonde.   Montréal: Éditions du Boréal, 1991. 176p.

Of the many social and cultural associations which sprung up in cities following 1840, the Montréal Canadian Institute is the most well known. Frequently in disagreement with the Church, the Institute was one of the significant sources of radical ideology and was responsible in part for Montréal's cultural renaissance. Not only does Lamonde provide an exhaustive analysis of the debates and speeches, but his unfailing commitment to minute detail brings them to life for the reader.

524 **L'histoire des idées au Québec, 1760-1960: bibliographie des études.** (The history of ideas in Québec: a bibliography.) Yvan Lamonde. Montréal: Bibliothèque nationale du Québec, 1989. 167p.

This bibliography lists 795 scholarly articles, books and bibliographies, classified into 6 sections which roughly approximate the 6 phases of Québec's intellectual history. Of particular import, this bibliography contains relevant biographical entries found in the *Dictionary of Canadian biography* (see item no. 179). It should be noted that original manuscripts and primary sources are not covered in this book.

525 **Ideologies in Quebec: the historical development.** Denis Monière, translated by Richard Howard. Toronto: University of Toronto Press, 1981. 312p. bibliog.

In this award-winning volume, the author examines Québec's ideological evolution beginning with colonial times and ending with the 1980 referendum. Adopting a class interpretation and eschewing an elitist vision of history, Monière looks at those ideologies most closely associated with the working classes of Québec. During the century following the 1837 Patriot rebellions, Québec experienced the ideologies of survival, agriculturalism, Messianism, and anti-statism. These were not challenged until the advent of industrialization in the late 19th century. By adopting such a perspective, Monière highlights the economic and political liberation of Québec labour.

526 **Histoire des idéologies au Québec aux XIXe et XXe siècles.** (A history of ideologies in Québec during the 19th and 20th centuries.) Fernande Roy. Montréal: Éditions du Boréal, 1993. 128p.

Special attention to the interaction between social classes and nationalism renders this history of Québec ideologies especially interesting. Aside from an analysis of ideologies themselves, Roy investigates how ideology is used by different social groups. In examining the evolution of ideology, the author pays close attention to the ways in which ideology and nationalism have interacted to produce different outcomes. The book's brief and concise form makes it ideal for the non-specialist.

527 **Le Jour: émergence du libéralisme moderne au Québec.** (*Le Jour* [The Day]: the emergence of modern liberalism in Québec.) Victor Teboul. Montréal: Éditions Hurtubise HMH, 1984. 436p. bibliog. (Les Cahiers du Québec, Collection Communications, no. 80).

Unlike anywhere else in Canada, the press has played a key role in the historical evolution of ideas in Québec. Not only has there been an intimate connection between the press and most of Québec's leading intellectuals, but the press has also acted as a central theatre of public debate. This work belongs to a small corpus of literature on Québec's left-wing, radical liberals. The book traces the opinions espoused by *Le Jour* (The Day) on a variety of issues such as culture and the arts, ideology and politics, thereby providing the reader with a wide view of the weekly's intellectual position. Teboul's interpretation of Québec liberalism, however, is open to criticism.

528 **Histoire des idées au Québec: des troubles de 1837 au référendum de 1980.** (A history of ideas in Québec: from the troubles of 1837 to the 1980 referendum.)
Edited by Georges Vincenthier.   Outremont, Québec: VLB Éditeur, 1983. 468p. bibliog.

An anthology of excerpts and reprints from speeches and articles drawn from prominent intellectual leaders and thinkers of Québec. Each entry bears witness to the intellectual elite's reaction to the events that were transforming Québec society. Nineteen chapters are divided into three sections which loosely correspond to the three dominant ideological periods in Québec's history: the first section deals with the early to late 19th century, which was characterized by liberal, democratic and secular ideas; the second part covers the late 19th century to the mid-20th century, distinguished by the ascendancy of nationalism and its ties to conservatism along with the changes engendered by the economic crisis of the 1930s; and the third section examines the contemporary period (from the mid-20th century to the present), which is marked by the rejection of traditional thought and the adoption of secular values.

529 **Du Canada au Québec: généalogie d'une histoire.** (From Canada to Québec: a genealogy of history.)
Heinz Weinmann.   Montréal: Éditions de L'Hexagone, 1987. 477p. bibliog.

An excellent study of the political thought of Québec. Inspired by the work of Freud and René Girard, Weinmann traces many of the historical 'moments' that have defined the modern psyche in Québec, including the first encounters with the land and aboriginal peoples, and the Conquest.

Constitution and Federalism

Reference

530 **Canadian Royal Commission on Bilingualism and Biculturalism.**
Report of the Royal Commission.
Ottawa: Queen's Printer, 1967. 6 vols.

Created in 1963 at a time when Québec nationalism was rising in Québec, the Laurendeau-Dunton Commission was charged with reporting on the situation of bilingualism and biculturalism in Canada. Inspired by a 'dualist' vision of Canada, which was based on the interpretation of the 1867 British North American Act as a compact between the two founding nations, the Commission recognized that true equality of the individual can only be achieved through equality of the two principal linguistic communities. The Commission's recommendations on bilingualism were only partially followed. The Trudeau Government ignored the report's recommendations on biculturalism; multiculturalism was introduced in its place.

531 **The Tremblay Report.**
Edited by David Kwavnick.   Toronto: McClelland and Stewart, 1973.
229p.

Fully titled 'The Report of the Royal Commission of Inquiry on Constitutional Problems', the Tremblay Commission was originally charged in 1953 with examining the fiscal relations between the federal government and the provinces. In the end, the document, which outlined the Commission's findings, provided a remarkable picture of the philosophical and moral foundation of a Catholic French Canadian society prior to the Quiet Revolution and an elaborate interpretation of federalism. Additionally, in order to bolster their position *vis-à-vis* the federal government, the authors of the report espouse a compact theory of Confederation, wherein any changes to the Constitution must be approved by Québec – one of the four original provinces in 1867. Kwavnick provides an excellent abridgement of the original five-volume report.

532 **Les constitutions du Canada et du Québec: du régime français à nos jours.** (The Canadian and Québec constitutions from the French regime to today.)
Jacques-Yvan Morin, José Woehrling.   Montréal: Éditions Thémis, 1994. 2nd ed. 2 vols. bibliog.

Written for law students, this two-volume work describes the evolution of constitutional institutions in a wide-ranging manner which will appeal to any reader interested in Québec's constitutional history. In their analysis of various constitutional documents, a large number of which are printed in the second volume, Morin and Woehrling avoid considering each document separately. Relating the evolution of Québec and Canadian constitutional law and institutions, in addition to the socio-political context of each document, their analysis enables the reader to understand each document as it fits into a larger historical context. This work covers the period from 1534 to 1992. It does not, however, deal with those aspects of the Constitution that govern the division of powers between the federal and provincial governments and the protection of the rights and freedoms of individuals and linguistic groups, etc. There is a section on the Meech Lake Accord (1987-90) and its failure, and the Charlottetown Accord (1992). Moreover, there is an interesting chapter on the relations between English-speaking Canada and Québec. For a briefer summary which focuses on the legal changes to the Constitution, see Lorraine Pilette's *La constitution canadienne* (The Canadian Constitution) (Montréal: Éditions du Boréal Express, 1993. 124p.).

533 **Une nouvelle fédération canadienne: la Commission constitutionnelle du Parti libéral du Québec.** (A new Canadian federation: the Constitutional Committee of the Parti libéral du Québec.)
Montréal: Parti libéral du Québec, 1980. 145p.

Also known as the Beige Paper, this is the final report of a committee set up in 1977 to advise the PLQ (Parti libéral du Québec – Québec Liberal Party) on the Canadian constitutional dilemma. Among the various recommendations are: the establishment of a Canadian charter of inalienable rights; the principle of dualism espoused by the explicit recognition of Canada's two founding peoples; and a new division of legislative powers which would guarantee Québec power over the management of human and natural resources in the province.

534 **Québec Commission parlementaire sur l'avenir politique et constitutionnel du Québec. Report of the Commission and the political and constitutional future of Québec.**
Québec: The Commission, 1991. 171p.

Formed after the failure of the Meech Lake Accord in 1990, the Bélanger-Campeau Commission was charged with the task of studying the political and constitutional status of Québec and formulating recommendations on the political measures that should be taken by the Québec Government. After public hearings throughout Québec, and after the solicitation of expert studies, the Commission recommended the holding of a referendum on Québec sovereignty and the offering of a new partnership with the rest of Canada. This report constitutes precious information on the potential consequences of Québec's independence for its economy, constitution and territory, which renders it essential reading for those who want to understand the political situation in Québec.

535 **A Quebec free to choose.**
Québec: Parti libéral du Québec, 1991. 62p.

Written by the Constitutional Committee of the PLQ (Parti libéral du Québec – Québec Liberal Party) and popularly referred to as the Allaire Report, this is perhaps one of the most important documents to surface from within the provincial Liberal Party structure. Following the death of the Meech Lake Accord (1990) and a significant rise in nationalist sentiments in Québec, Premier Robert Bourassa set up the Committee to examine all options for Québec's future, with the exception of the status quo and annexation to the United States. The final report, adopted by a large majority of PLQ MNAs (Members of the National Assembly, Québec's parliament) in 1991, proposed independence if federalism was not drastically reformed. Among the changes demanded was the retreat of the federal government from eleven provincial fields of responsibility, and the cession to Québec of eleven other jurisdictions. This document soon came to represent the minimum standard that many Quebecers demanded (and continue to demand) in order to remain in Canada.

536 **Québec-Canada: a new deal. The Québec Government proposal for a new partnership between equals: sovereignty-association.**
Québec: Éditeur officiel, 1979. 109p.

This document outlines the basis of what Quebecers voted on in the 1980 referendum, proposing the establishment of an economic and monetary union between Canada and Québec. Inspired by the collective experience of history and the will of Quebecers to decide their future, this document explains, from the Québec Government's perspective, Québec's experience of federalism as one characterized by centralization and federal intrusion in the province's exclusive areas of jurisdiction. Referring to the failed attempts at national reconciliation, the document suggests sovereignty-association as the best means to 'ensure for Québec a maximum of autonomy while maintaining the natural interdependence and the historical and human links that exist between Québec and the rest of Canada'.

537 **Task force on Canadian unity. Coming to terms: the words of the debate (Jean-Luc Pepin & John P. Robarts).**
Hull, Québec: Ministry of Supply and Services Canada, 1979. 111p.

Better known as the Pepin-Robarts Commission, this Royal Commission was set up by Pierre Trudeau in 1978 to 'support, encourage and publicize the efforts of the general public . . . and contribute its own initiatives and views . . . to the general awareness with regard to unity'. When the Commission reported in 1979 that the Government should consider an important decentralization of powers in certain key areas of interest to Québec, Trudeau ignored the recommendations. This volume is the final report of the Commission. Aside from its explanations of general, social and political terms and descriptions of the Canadian system of government, it outlines various constitutional options and variants that might have satisfied some of Québec's demands.

General

538 **L'accession à la souveraineté et le cas du Québec.** (The accession of
sovereignty and the case of Québec.)
Jacques Brossard, Daniel Turp. Montréal: Presses de l'Université de
Montréal, 1995. 853p. bibliog.
First published in 1976 (Montréal: Presses de l'Université de Montréal, 1976. 800p.),
Brossard's work remains one of the rare, and surely the most significant, politico-legal
treatises on the right to self-determination and sovereignty for Québec. This book
attempts to answer many of the legal questions and considerations associated with
Québec's desire to become a sovereign nation, namely: the issue of citizenship; the
right to secession; borders; federal pension funds and other federally administered
programmes; international treaties; and the national debt. This updated edition also
includes an essay by the respected constitutionalist and Member of Parliament, Daniel
Turp. His essay updates Brossard's seminal work by taking into account recent
developments in international and Canadian law. Both Brossard's and Turp's bibliographies provide excellent reference sources. For an examination of Québec's
constitutional positions throughout history, see Jean-Pierre Charbonneau and Gilles
Paquette's *L'option* (see item no. 540).

539 **Le mal canadien.** (The Canadian problem.)
André Burelle. Saint-Laurent, Québec: Fides, 1995. 239p.
Former advisor to the Trudeau and Mulroney governments on constitutional matters,
André Burelle tackles the issue of renewed federalism in describing not only what
Québec wants but also what it would be prepared to negotiate in a new Canada.
According to Burelle, the Meech and Charlottetown experiences are evidence that, as
long as Canadians subscribe to Trudeau's unitary nation-building heritage, national
reconciliation will remain inaccessible. Burelle suggests that a feasible compromise
might entail negotiations among the constituent states of the federation on an
'Economic and Social Pact', which would abandon the liberal individualist model for
one inspired by the European Community model.

540 **L'option.** (The option.)
Jean-Pierre Charbonneau, Gilles Paquette. Montréal: Éditions de
l'Homme, 1978. 620p.
This book attempts to provide Canadians and Quebecers with a detailed summary of
the major issues, realities, concepts and choices relating to the national question
during the first PQ (Parti québécois) mandate (1976-81). While this book served as a
source document for those PQ militants who wanted to deepen their understanding of
sovereignty-association, this document was also designed to open a dialogue with
Canadians opposed to the PQ project. As such, this book touches on Québec and
Canadian history, the federal system, Québec identity, as well as the basic characteristics
of the sovereignty-association model.

541 **Québec: dix ans de crise constitutionnelle.** (Québec: ten years of constitutional crisis.)
Roch Denis.   Outremont, Québec: VLB Éditeur, 1990. 306p. (Études Québécoises, no. 16).

To mark the ten years since the 1980 referendum on sovereignty-association and a promise by federal politicians to renew Canadian federalism, Denis compiled this selection of editorials, newspaper columns, speeches, party manifestos, declarations, and legislation representative of the progression of the constitutional debate from 1980 to 1990. The texts are divided into three sections: the first deals with the aftermath of the referendum, internal transformations within the PQ (Parti québécois), and the rise of nationalism; the second group of texts illustrates the constitutional crisis, from the debate over the 'patriation' of the Constitution (transfer of the Canadian Constitution to Canada) as set out in the Canada Act of 1982, to the Meech Lake Accord (1987-90); and the third section presents various interpretations of the status quo and different perspectives on Québec nationalism.

542 **Le duel constitutionnel Québec-Canada.** (The Québec-Canada constitutional duel.)
Léon Dion.   Montréal: Éditions du Boréal, 1995. 378p.

A collection of essays dealing with the various constitutional conflicts in Canada since the beginning of the 1980s: the 1982 'patriation' of the Constitution; the Meech Lake Accord (1987-90); the 1990 Bélanger-Campeau Commission; and the 1992 Charlottetown Accord. The author often uses his own personal experience to explain the evolution of Québec-Canada relations.

543 **Negotiating with a sovereign Québec.**
Edited by Daniel Drache, Roberto Perin.   Toronto: James Lorimer & Co., 1992. 296p. bibliog.

Published just before the defeat of the Charlottetown Accord in the autumn of 1992, this book examines the viability of a sovereign Québec, aboriginal autonomy, and a restructured English-speaking Canada. The book begins with the premise that Québec will assert its sovereignty and seek to negotiate a new relationship with Canada. The sixteen contributors address such issues as the possibility of re-association following separation, aboriginal rights, trade and monetary association, and potential cross-border policies.

544 **Canada, adieu? Quebec debates its future.**
Edited by Richard Fidler.   Lantzville, British Columbia: Oolichan Books, in association with the Institute for Research on Public Policy, 1991. 328p.

This book consists of selected submissions to the Québec Government's Bélanger-Campeau Commission which was held several months after the failure of the Meech Lake Accord in June 1990. Formally called the 'Commission on the Political and Constitutional Future of Québec', this forum provided an occasion for Quebecers to discuss a range of controversial historical and political issues. Fidler has selected 35 briefs (out of the nearly 600), representing political parties, business, labour, women, immigrant groups, anglophones and francophones. The final report of the Commission is also included.

545   Québec and Canada, past, present and future.
      John Fitzmaurice.   London: C. Hurst & Co., 1985. 343p.
A useful survey of Québec history and politics for the general reader. The author
attempts to underscore the distinctiveness of Québec in comparison with the other
Canadian provinces. For evidence, he points to Québec's complex relations with the
British before 1867 and the history of federal-provincial relations thereafter. Most of
the author's attention is focused on the period of, and preceding, the Quiet Revolution.
The author closes with a careful analysis of the party political system and the major
political actors.

546   A Meech Lake post-mortem: is Quebec sovereignty inevitable?
      Pierre Fournier, translated by Sheila Fischman.   Montréal; Kingston,
      Ontario: McGill-Queen's University Press, 1991. 154p.
A strong criticism of both the Meech Lake Accord (1987-90) and those who opposed
constitutional reform, most notably Pierre Trudeau, Jean Chrétien and Clyde Wells.
The author outlines the reasons underlying the failure of the Accord along with the
growing opposition in English-speaking Canada to Québec's vision. Fournier's preference
for Québec sovereignty is readily apparent throughout the book.

547   Allaire, Bélanger, Campeau et les autres. (Allaire, Bélanger,
      Campeau and the rest.)
      Alain-G. Gagnon, Daniel Latouche.   Montréal: Éditions Québec
      Amérique, 1991. 602p.
1991 was a determining year in Québec's political history. Following the failure of the
Meech Lake Accord (1990), two important reports were released: the Bélanger-
Campeau Report and the Allaire Report. This book first presents a summary of the
most important political commissions in the histories of Canada and Québec. The second
section of the book introduces the principal briefs tabled before the Bélanger-
Campeau Commission on a wide range of subjects: from Québec minorities to the
economic viability of a sovereign Québec.

548   Répliques aux détracteurs de la souveraineté du Québec. (Replies
      to the critics of Québec sovereignty.)
      Edited by Alain-G. Gagnon, François Rocher.   Outremont, Québec:
      VLB Éditeur, 1992. 507p. (Études Québécoises, no. 27).
This collection of essays by prominent Québec intellectuals deals with the major
obstacles that the Québec government and society would have to face in the eventuality
of a democratic vote in favour of sovereignty. The authors deal with the most common
federalist objections to the 'sovereignist' project. The editors conclude with an original
essay on the evolution of Québec nationalism from an ethnic nationalism to a nationalism
based on civic values and open to pluralism. This is a book for those who want to
know more about the different motivations behind the 'sovereignist' project. See also
two collections of letters published during the 1995 referendum: *Je me souverain* (I
remember sovereignty) (Montréal: Éditions des Intouchables, 1995. 158p.); and *Trente
lettres pour un oui* (Thirty letters for a 'Yes') (Montréal: Stanké, 1995. 170p.).

549 **Égalité ou indépendance.** (Equality or independence.)
Daniel Johnson. Montréal: Les Éditions de l'Homme, 1965. 125p.

The publication of this essay by the leader of the Union nationale in 1965 had an important impact on Québec's political community. It was the first time that a leader of a major political party lent credence to the idea of an independent Québec. Johnson's argument was based on his conviction that the British North America Act of 1867 was a pact between two nations – a pact which has often been broken – and that Canada must recognize the binational and bicultural character of the country in order for Québec to consider remaining in the federation. This essay is essential reading for an understanding of the political situation of the 1960s and the continued evolution of Québec nationalism.

550 **Le Québec et la restructuration du Canada, 1980-1992: enjeux et perspectives.** (Québec and the restructuring of Canada, 1980-92: stakes and perspectives.)
Edited by Guy Laforest, Louis Balthazar, Vincent Lemieux. Sillery, Québec: Éditions du Septentrion, 1991. 312p.

This collection of essays examines the consequences of the 'patriation' of the Canadian Constitution in 1982 without Québec's consent. Until 1982 all amendments to the Canadian Constitution had to be passed by the UK Parliament. In addition to a host of other issues, one significance of the 1982 'patriation' was the adoption of an amendment formula. The principal topics discussed in this work are: the evolution of the Québec state since 1980; the national identity conflict; the interpretation of the 1982 constitutional reform; the 1990 Meech Lake Accord; and the role of intellectuals in the actual political debate. The essays provide a good overview of the political evolution of Québec in the 1980s in relation to the constitutional events which have transpired since 1982.

551 **Trudeau and the end of a Canadian dream.**
Guy Laforest, translated by Paul Leduc Browne, Michelle Weinroth. Montréal; Kingston, Ontario: McGill-Queen's University Press, 1995. 217p.

A critical assessment of the Canadian constitutional reform of 1982. Laforest provides an excellent analysis of the symbolic and ideological significance of the Charter of Human Rights and Freedoms and the act of 'patriation' as they influence Québec's dream of dualism as defended by André Laurendeau. The demise of the Meech Lake Accord in 1990, which is portrayed in this work as an effort to reintroduce biculturalism, is seen as the final blow to Canadian dualism and the definitive victory of Pierre Elliott Trudeau's conception of a bilingual and multicultural Canada. This is a useful account of the intellectual roots of the Canadian constitutional debate. See also Laforest's *De l'urgence: textes politiques* (Of urgency: political texts) (Montréal: Éditions du Boréal, 1995. 200p.).

552   **Le fédéralisme canadien: évolution et problèmes.** (Canadian
        federalism: evolution and problems.)
        Maurice Lamontagne.   Québec: Presses de l'Université Laval, 1954.
        298p.

A classic study examining the relative power relations between the federal government and the provinces. Written from a political economy perspective, the author
evaluates the efficacy of the federal system in dealing with economic development,
labour relations, monopolies, social security and culture. The author argues that the
country must maintain its bicultural status and that Québec must participate actively in
the new post-war federalism.

553   **Plaidoyer pour le Québec.** (A plea for Québec.)
        Daniel Latouche.   Montréal: Éditions du Boréal, 1995. 244p.

A reasoned discourse on the political future of Québec. For Latouche, the defence of
democracy, as well as federalism, is essential in mitigating the intolerance inherent in
tribal nationalism. The author examines the constitutional impasse in Canada, the
social and economic costs of separation, and the challenges that would confront
Québec the day after proclaiming sovereignty. This sociological and political analysis
is an important work for understanding current debates in Québec society.

554   **English Canada and Québec: avoiding the issue.**
        Kenneth McRoberts.   North York, Ontario: Robarts Centre for
        Canadian Studies, 1991. 64p.

McRoberts brings to light the ironies of the past thirty years between English-speaking
Canada's attempts to stave off independence and the resulting opposite result, in the
form of the growing support for sovereignty in Québec, in order to illustrate the crisis
facing English-speaking Canada. McRoberts suggests that in refusing to deal directly
with the Québec issue, English-speaking Canada now faces its own identity crisis.
Moreover, the only way English-speaking Canada will be able to discover itself is by
facing the Québec issue head-on.

555   **Misconceiving Canada: the struggle for national unity.**
        Kenneth McRoberts.   Don Mills, Ontario: Oxford University Press,
        1997. 395p.

After almost forty years of constitutional debate over national unity, Canada is divided
more than ever. McRoberts, one of the most prominent English Canadian specialists
on Québec, argues that this division is the result of Trudeau's citizenship project (the
tools used by the government to shape the identity of the people, including symbolic
actions such as flag waving and civic holidays, as well as substantial actions such as
immigration policies and education policies). According to McRoberts, this idea
implies the equality of individuals and provinces, thereby rendering accommodation to
Québec's aspirations impossible. In order to resolve the crisis, McRoberts argues that
Canadians must abandon Trudeau's vision and embrace the spirit of the Laurendeau-
Dunton Commission (the Bilingualism and Bicultural Commission, 1963-67) which
supported the spirit of dualism and accommodation.

556   **Quebec and the Constitution, 1960-1978.**
      Edward McWhinney.   Toronto: University of Toronto Press, 1979.
      170p.

This book provides a thorough analysis of Canada's constitutional development during the 1960s and 1970s, particularly Québec's demands for increased social, economic, linguistic and political power. It also examines Québec's efforts to transfer power to a new social and economic francophone elite, largely through changes in language legislation. Though McWhinney's study predates the 1982 constitutional amendments, the author does suggest several new ways of achieving a 'cooperative federalism' and a 'renewed' Confederation.

557   **Les lendemains piégés. Du référendum à la nuit des longs couteaux.** (A booby-trapped future. From the referendum to the 'Night of the long knives'.)
      Claude Morin.   Montréal: Éditions du Boréal, 1988. 395p.

A former Québec minister responsible for constitutional negotiations, Morin provides a unique and personal account of the constitutional negotiations leading up to the 1982 Canada Act. His privileged position and first-hand knowledge of the issues provide the reader with a detailed account of the events that led to the 'patriation' of the Constitution (transfer of the Canadian Constitution to Canada), beginning with the defeat of the PQ (Parti québécois) Government's proposal in the 1980 referendum. The book offers a chronological 'behind the scenes' recollection based on the author's personal notes and unpublished materials, some of which are included in the appendix. Morin's stated intent is 'to reveal how the result of the referendum was deliberately deviated of its true significance to allow an upheaval of the political rules of the game'.

558   **Quebec versus Ottawa: the struggle for self-government, 1960-1972.**
      Claude Morin, translated by Richard Howard.   Toronto: University of Toronto Press, 1976. 164p.

Between 1963 and 1971, Claude Morin served as the Deputy Minister of Intergovernmental Affairs in the Québec Government. This book chronicles the issues and predominant conflicts between Québec and Ottawa during the 1960s and early 1970s. Through an examination of the rules and structures of the federal system, Morin shows how many Quebecers now believe that only sovereignty can safeguard their interests. This is an excellent analysis of attitudes towards federalism in Québec.

559   **Demain, le Québec: choix politiques et constitutionnels d'un pays en devenir.** (Tomorrow, Québec: the political and constitutional choices of a country in the making.)
      Jacques-Yvan Morin, José Woehrling.   Sillery, Québec: Éditions du Septentrion, 1994. 316p.

After evaluating the history of Québec-Ottawa relations, the authors sketch an outline of a new constitution for Québec, assess the rights of linguistic minorities, and examine the economic and institutional choices available for a sovereign Québec. The authors call for an arrangement between Québec and Canada along the lines of the European Union.

560 **Le fédéralisme canadien.** (Canadian federalism.)
Gil Rémillard. Montréal: Éditions Québec Amérique, 1983. 2 vols.
2nd ed. bibliog.

This major work relates the evolution of Canadian federalism in terms of its historical judicial evolution. The first volume of the book deals with the constitutional law of 1867, its formation and its evolution through judicial decisions. The author demonstrates the different interests behind both the type of federalism favoured and the various interpretations of these decisions. Rémillard suggests that the 1867 British North America Act was the result of a historic compromise that was beneficial for French-speaking Canada. In the second volume Rémillard is more critical of the Canada Act of 1982, describing it as an incomplete compromise. The second volume is divided into two sections. The first part begins with an introduction to the 'patriation' process. As the author demonstrates, the events leading up to 1982 are related to the evolution of federal-provincial relations. The evolution of these relations comprise the subject matter of the second section. The conclusion of the second volume is essential for those who want to understand the constitutional position of the PLQ (Parti libéral du Québec) which formed the Government during the second half of the 1980s. Both volumes include an index.

561 **Toward a Canada-Quebec union.**
Philip Resnick. Montréal; Kingston, Ontario: McGill-Queen's
University Press, 1991. 119p.

Following the failure of the Meech Lake Accord in 1990, a myriad of books were published, all of which proposed a new Québec-Canada relationship. In this work, Resnick rejects both status-quo federalism and sovereignty-association as viable constitutional alternatives. For other works proposing a new institutional structure, see *Seeking a new Canadian partnership: asymmetrical and confederal options* (Montréal: Institute for Research on Public Policy, 1994), edited by F. Leslie Seidle, and André Burelle's *Le mal canadien* (see item no. 539). Another work which outlines various ways of redefining Canada to include Québec is by Jeremy Webber, a noted and respected constitutional law professor: *Reimagining Canada. Language, culture, community and the Canadian constitution* (Montréal; Kingston, Ontario: McGill-Queen's University Press, 1994. 373p.) makes one of the most eloquent and well-argued defences of asymmetry.

562 **Bilan québécois du fédéralisme canadien.** (A Québec assessment of
Canadian federalism.)
Edited by François Rocher. Outremont, Québec: VLB Éditeur, 1992.
405p.

This work takes a critical look at the Canadian polity from a Québec perspective, examining the costs and benefits to Québec of membership in the federal system. The contributing authors assess a wide array of issues, including the impact of the Canadian Charter of Rights and Freedoms (1982), regional development strategies, bilingualism policy, and economic interdependence.

563 **Le choix d'un pays. Le débat constitutionnel Québec-Canada, 1960-1976.** (The choice of a country. The Québec-Canada constitutional debate, 1960-76.)
Jean-Louis Roy. Montréal: Leméac, 1978. 366p.

From a Québec perspective, Roy provides a solid overview of the events, and the principal actors and their discourse, concerning the constitutional issue between 1960 and 1976. This period of constitutional debate ultimately led to the 1980 referendum and the 'patriation' of the Constitution in the Canada Act of 1982. Roy suggests that this period, which was characterized by Québec's search for a major redefinition of the institutions and processes of the federation, marks a turning-point in Canada's constitutional history.

564 **Souveraineté-association: l'urgence de réfléchir.** (Sovereignty-association: the need to reflect.)
Panayotis Soldatos. Montréal: France-Amérique, 1979. 207p.

An early attempt to demystify the ambiguous meaning of 'sovereignty-association'. The author examines the potential advantages and disadvantages of restructuring Québec's relationship with the rest of Canada along lines suggested by the PQ (Parti québécois). Many of his arguments remain relevant to the current debate.

565 **Reconciling the solitudes. Essays on Canadian federalism and nationalism.**
Charles Taylor. Montréal; Kingston, Ontario: McGill-Queen's University Press, 1993. 208p.

A collection of essays written by the renowned anglophone Québec philosopher on the national issue in Canada and Québec. This book is a major contribution on the issues of liberalism and federalism, collective rights and recognition. It includes an introduction by Guy Laforest and an index.

566 **Federalism and the French Canadians.**
Pierre Elliott Trudeau. Toronto: Macmillan, 1968. 212p.

A series of articles and addresses by Pierre Trudeau who, shortly after the publication of this book, became Prime Minister of Canada. The essays, many of which were published in *Cité Libre*, present a coherent philosophical defence of federalism, a form of government which Trudeau believes is best able to protect the liberty of the citizen in general and French Canadian society in particular. As an opponent of the perceived injustices of the Duplessis Government in the 1940s and 1950s, Trudeau is adamantly opposed to a political society based along ethnic or national lines. The thinking behind Trudeau's conception of federalism still has resonance for many today who oppose Québec separatism or a radical alteration of Canada's federal institutions. For book-length accounts on Trudeau's life and thought, see: Stephen Clarkson and Christina McCall's *Trudeau and our times* (Toronto: McClelland and Stewart, 1990. 2 vols.); George Radwanski's *Trudeau* (Toronto: Macmillan, 1978. 372p.); and Richard Gwyn's *The Northern Magus* (Toronto: McClelland and Stewart, 1980. 399p.). Additional examples of Trudeau's thought can be found in *Against the current, selected writings, 1939 à 1996* (Toronto: McClelland and Stewart, 1996 340p.). For an analysis of Trudeau's thought as it relates to liberalism in Canada, see Claude Couture's *La loyauté d'un laïque. Pierre Elliott Trudeau et le libéralisme canadien* (The loyalty of a layman. Pierre Elliott Trudeau and Canadian liberalism) (Montréal: L'Harmattan, 1997. 160p.).

Administration and Government

567 **L'administration publique québécoise: évolutions sectorielles, 1960-1985.** (Québec's public administration: the evolution of administrative sectors, 1960-85.)
Edited by Yves Bélanger, Laurent Lepage.   Sillery, Québec: Presses de l'Université du Québec, 1989. 226p.

In an attempt to gauge the current trends in Québec's public administration, this collection examines those who occupy top-level civil service jobs and their administrative policies. Second, this collection looks at the main political and administrative issues which have marked the five most important state sectors: education, health and social services, manpower training, culture, and municipal affairs. Although these texts do confirm the oft-noted centralizing tendency within the Québec civil service, they also reveal the exceptional cases where the civil service has demonstrated a certain spontaneity and innovation in adapting to unique administrative circumstances.

568 **La politique au Canada et au Québec.** (Politics in Canada and Québec.)
André Bernard.   Montréal: Presses de l'Université du Québec, 1986. 2nd ed. 535p. bibliog.

A useful primer on Canadian and Québec politics that emphasizes the role of political institutions and public administration. The book is structured along four major themes: the social environment, political parties and interest groups, federal negotiations, and political legitimization through representative institutions. The text is supplemented by over seventy tables and graphs.

569 **Politique et gestion des finances publiques: Québec et Canada.**
(The politics and management of public finance: Québec and Canada.)
André Bernard.   Sillery, Québec: Presses de l'Université du Québec,
1992. 470p.

A handbook on state budgeting, fiscal expenditure and public sector growth in Canada
and Québec, this also examines the institutional constraints involved in public financial management.

570 **Réflexions sur l'art de se gouverner: essai d'un praticien.**
(Reflections on the art of governing: an essay by a practitioner.)
Louis Bernard.   Montréal: Éditions Québec Amérique–ÉNAP, 1987.
132p.

A very thorough analysis of the state apparatus in Québec from a career public servant.
The author examines such issues as parliamentary reform, the influence of MNAs
(Members of the National Assembly, Québec's parliament), and the role of the
ministerial council. This is a good primer on state organization and management in the
province.

571 **Un état réduit? = A downsized state?**
Edited by Robert Bernier, James Iain Gow.   Montréal: Presses de
l'Université de Montréal, 1994. 435p.

A bilingual collection that examines the trend of deficit reduction in Canada and
Québec from the mid-1980s to the mid-1990s. In contrast to the majority of studies
published on the reduction of government spending, which have tended to be descriptive,
prescriptive or concerned only with downsizing's impact on the civil service, this
collection adopts a wider perspective. The first group of essays examine the evolution
of revenues, expenditures and deficits, and the public service. Others focus on the
transformations of the state in the process of downsizing, with regard to accountability,
transparency and access to information laws. The machinery and processes of central
management itself are scrutinized. Overall, this work reveals the forces that sustain
elevated spending in addition to the philosophies and processes that states have
recently employed to restrain their interventions.

572 **Bibliographie du Parlement du Québec.** (Bibliography of the
Québec Parliament.)
Québec: Publications du Québec, 1992. 119p. bibliog.

A list of the major academic publications pertaining to the institutions associated with
the Québec parliament, the Assemblée nationale (National Assembly). The Québec
legislature comprised, until 1968, a lower, elected house called the Assemblée législative
(Legislative Assembly) and an upper, appointed house called the Conseil législati
(Legislative Council). In 1968, the upper house was abolished and the term
'Assemblée nationale' was used to refer to the lower, elected house.

573 **Documents déposés à l'Assemblée nationale.** (Documents deposited in the National Assembly.)
Québec: Bibliothèque de l'Assemblée nationale, 1992- . 4 vols.

These volumes list all the documents deposited in the National Assembly between 1979 and 1994. Each volume has two parts. The first section lists documents by date of deposition in the Assembly, and contains the following information: the document's number, the name of the depositor, and a brief description of the document's nature. The second section is a subject index. This series continues the work contained in *Documents sessionnels de l'Assemblée législative du Québec, 1961-1970* (Sessional documents of the Legislative Assembly of Québec, 1961-70) (Québec: Bibliothèque de l'Assemblée nationale, 1982. 277p.). This resource is an ideal reference tool for the researcher or student.

574 **A financial profile of Québec.**
Québec: Ministère des Finances, 1990- . annual.

A very brief summary of the major characteristics of the Québec economy, government spending, major industries and investment.

575 **Histoire de l'administration publique québécoise, 1867-1970.** (A history of public administration in Québec, 1867-1970.)
James Iain Gow. Montréal: Presses de l'Université de Montréal, 1986. 443p. bibliog.

A comprehensive study of Québec's administrative structures. In each of the three periods examined (1867-96, 1896-1936, 1936-19), Gow highlights the changes in bureaucratic organization and the growth of the welfare state. The author also analyses the missions of each successive government in the areas of sovereignty, the economy, social welfare and cultural policy. Gow concludes that the link between state intervention and administrative reform has not always been as strong as originally posited by other analysts. The work also includes historical data on state revenue and expenditures as well as a useful bibliography.

576 **Les institutions administratives locales au Québec: structures et fonctions.** (Local administrative institutions in Québec: structures and functions.)
Robert J. Gravel. Sillery, Québec: Presses de l'Université du Québec, 1987. 110p. bibliog.

A survey of local and regional administrative institutions in Québec. This introductory and practical guide describes the structure and functions of local and regional institutions in addition to their relationship with various provincial departments and organizations. Using charts and organigrams, the author presents a portrait of municipal government in Québec, lists its responsibilities, and reveals the source of municipal and regional power. Despite its consideration of historical and sociological aspects of local government, this concise study is an ideal introduction to the institutional aspects of local administration.

577 **Les institutions québécoises: leur rôle, leur avenir.** (Québec institutions: their function and their future.)
Edited by Vincent Lemieux. Sainte-Foy, Québec: Presses de l'Université Laval, 1990. 330p.

With contributions from over twenty Québec scholars, journalists and politicians, this work covers a number of topics relating to social institutions in Québec. Both historical and theoretical in content, topics include the Church, the family, the education system, labour unions, human resources, health services, and the legal system. Related works include Vincent Lemieux's *Les relations de pouvoir dans les lois: comparaison entre les gouvernements du Québec de 1944 à 1985* (Power relations in the laws: a comparison of Québec governments between 1944 and 1985) (Sainte-Foy, Québec: Presses de l'Université Laval, 1991. 247p.).

578 **Patronage et politique au Québec, 1944-1972.** (Patronage and politics in Québec, 1944-72.)
Vincent Lemieux, Raymond Hudon. Sillery, Québec: Éditions du Boréal Express, 1975. 187p.

A study of patronage as practised by the two major provincial political parties during the post-war period, the PLQ (Parti libéral du Québec – Québec Liberal Party) and the UN (Union nationale). Based on the results of a series of interviews conducted in small Québec towns, the authors attempt to establish a theory of patronage relationships inherent in politics. This is a useful study of the evolution of patronage and the differences between political parties.

579 **La modernisation politique du Québec.** (Political modernization in Québec.)
Edited by Edmond Orban. Montréal: Éditions du Boréal Express, 1976. 249p.

A collection of essays that examine, from a variety of perspectives, the rapid transformation experienced by Québec during the Quiet Revolution. The book attempts to answer three questions: in what way were the institutions under observation equipped to respond to the rapid social transformation; what conditions were necessary to bring about successful modernization and secure the maximum benefits for society; and what the future held as this process continued to unfold.

580 **La crise des finances publiques et le désengagement de l'État.** (The crisis of public finance and the disengagement of the state.)
Edited by Gilles Paquet, Jean-Pierre Voyer. Montréal: Association des Économistes québécois, 1993. 366p.

The early 1990s brought both the Canadian and Québec governments face to face with a financial crisis characterized by rising debt and deficit problems. This in turn led to a public debate over the ideal role of the state in public affairs. This collection attempts to unearth the causes of this high level of debt and reveal the consequences for both governments. The majority of the authors advocate a neo-liberal vision of the state's ideal economic role. With regard to Québec, these essays discuss the health system, the underground economy, welfare programmes and the repercussions of the Québec government's intervention in economic affairs.

581 **Regards sur la décentralisation gouvernementale au Québec.**
(Observations on government decentralization in Québec.)
Edited by Marc-Urbain Proulx. Chicoutimi, Québec: Groupe de
Recherche et d'Intervention régionales, 1995. 422p.

Predicated on the belief that Canada is 'over-governed', this work calls for greater
decentralization of powers to, and within, Québec. The authors analyse the issues
involved in devolving greater powers to the municipal level of government, as well as
the structural changes such devolution would require. Areas such as political institutions,
economic development, and the labour market are examined.

582 **À l'ombre du rationalisme: la société québécoise de sa dépendance
à sa quotidienneté.** (In the shadow of rationality: Québec society from
dependency to everyday life.)
Gilbert Renaud. Montréal: Éditions Coopératives Albert
Saint-Martin, 1984. 278p. bibliog.

An attempt to understand Québec's social structures using two seemingly contradictory methods. The first section of the book analyses social relations and the national
question in order to discover those factors which contribute to the structure of Québec
society. The second section examines the human passions and other 'irrational' forces
that are also involved in the definition of Québec society.

583 **L'administration publique.** (Public administration.)
Carole Simard, Luc Bernier. Montréal: Éditions du Boréal, 1992.
122p. bibliog.

A work premised on the view that knowledge of the role played by the civil service is
essential for an understanding of society at large. This book focuses on the role, staff,
and organization, of the Québec and Canadian civil services. Simard and Bernier have
also included an important chapter on the challenges facing the civil service. This
book provides a solid and comprehensive introduction to the discipline and includes
graphs, tables and a comprehensive bibliography.

584 **La longue marche des technocrates.** (The long march of the
technocrats.)
Jean-Jacques Simard. Montréal: Éditions Coopératives Albert
Saint-Martin, 1979. 198p.

This book is interested in analysing the basis of the Quiet Revolution. The author
argues that the 1960s marked the ascendancy of a technocratic bourgeoisie which was
allied to certain fragments of the native business class. Adopting a sociological
approach, Simard suggests that the major goal of the Quiet Revolution was to create a
modern advanced capitalist state.

Foreign Relations

General

585 **Trente ans de politique extérieure du Québec, 1960-1990.**
(Thirty years of Québec external affairs, 1960-90.)
Edited by Louis Balthazar, Louis Bélanger, Gordon Mace et al.
Sainte-Foy, Québec: Centre québécois de Relations
internationales/Éditions du Septentrion, 1993. 412p.

This collection of essays by political scientists demonstrates the increasing role played by the Québec government on the international stage over the last thirty years. The book focuses on the diplomatic, economic, and political relations between Québec and different regions and countries of the world and the Agence de la Francophonie (Francophone Agency). While the study of Québec's external activities is relatively new, this work provides the widest and most complete overview of the subject.

586 **Incertitudes d'un certain pays: le Québec et le Canada dans le monde, 1958-1978.** (The uncertainties of a certain country: Québec and Canada in the world, 1958-78.)
Gérard Bergeron. Sainte-Foy, Québec: Presses de l'Université Laval, 1979. 270p.

A series of essays by one of Québec's most prominent political scientists. The first section analyses the following: the influence of international events on Québec and Canadian politics; the history of Québec's foreign affairs; and the consequences of American economic hegemony on Québec's political and economic development. The second section deals with the internal evolution of Québec and Canada's respective political systems during the 1960s and 1970s.

587 **De Paris à Washington. La politique internationale du Québec.**
(From Paris to Washington. Québec's international policy.)
Luc Bernier.   Sainte-Foy, Québec: Presses de l'Université du Québec,
1996. 173p. bibliog.

One of the most recent and well-researched investigations into the unique status enjoyed by Québec as a player on the international stage, from a domestic perspective. Thanks in part to the actions of de Gaulle – the French leader recognized French-speaking Canada in 1940 and made a speech in Montréal in 1967, declaring 'Vive le Québec libre' (Long live free Québec) – Québec experienced a significant expansion of its international role despite the hostility from the federal government. This expanded international role has produced a unique case-study among federal countries. Bernier examines the evolution of Québec's international role over the past three decades, from bilateral to multilateral negotiations, with a critical eye to the internal forces which have shaped external policy. This book is therefore particularly useful in revealing the ways in which international policy has been used in Québec state-building, for example.

588 **Études Internationales.** (International Studies.)
Sainte-Foy, Québec: Institut québécois des Hautes Études
internationales, 1970- . quarterly.

A multidisciplinary scholarly journal covering international commerce, development and relations. See also the *Revue Québécoise de Droit International* (Québec Journal of International Law) (Montréal: Éditions Thémis, 1985-) for Québec-based analyses of international law.

589 **Contemporary Québec and the United States, 1960-1985.**
Alfred Olivier Hero, Jr., Louis Balthazar.   Boston, Massachusetts:
University Press of America, 1988. 532p.

Despite its title, this work is not limited to an examination of elite bilateral relations between Québec and the United States. The authors examine Québec's relations within Canada and also America's cultural influence on Québec. In addition, the authors approach the study of economic relations with a focus on trade and investment trends and their likely impact on Québec's nationalist aspirations. As much of the study relies upon attitudinal surveys, several useful tables are included in the appendix. Hero published an interesting study of the relations between Louisiana and Québec in his *Louisiana and Québec: bilateral relations and comparative sociopolitical evolution, 1673-1993* (Lanham, Maryland: University Press of America, 1995. 381p.). Another study of the relations between Québec and New England can be found in Stephen J. Hornsby, Victor A. Konrad and James J. Herlan's *The northeastern borderlands: four centuries of interaction* (Fredericton, New Brunswick: Canadian-American Center, University of Maine/Acadiensis Press, 1989. 160p.). A bilingual work on relations between Ontario and Québec is *Vingt ans de relations entre le Québec et l'Ontario, 1969-1989: actes du Colloque de Glendon, 11 novembre 1989* (Twenty years of Ontario-Québec relations, 1969-89: proceedings of the Glendon Colloquium, 11 November 1989) (Toronto: Éditions du GREF, 1991. 167p.).

590 **Présence internationale du Québec: chronique des années 1978-1983.** (Québec's international presence: an account of the period 1978-83.)
Edited by Gérard Hervouet, Hélène Galarneau. Québec: Centre québécois de Relations internationales, 1984. 368p.

A detailed description of the international activities of the government at a time when Québec was affirming its presence on the international stage. Specifically, this book provides an excellent source of information on Québec's commercial policy, immigration policy, and its relations with the Agence de la Francophonie (Francophone Agency) and different regions and countries of the world.

591 **In the eye of the eagle.**
Jean-François Lisée. Toronto: Harper Collins, 1990. 353p.

An important work about American governments' interest in, and policy on, the Québec question, during the past fifty years. Written by an acclaimed journalist, this book describes previously hidden events, based on thousands of documents culled from over a dozen government agencies, 240 interviews, and other sources. Lisée predicts that while American interests will always desire 'a strong and united Canada', they will 'live with it' if Québec decides it wants to be separate. This book is perhaps the best source for understanding the way American statesmen and bureaucrats perceive, and have perceived, Québec nationalism, politics and independence. Related works include Alfred O. Hero, Jr. and Marcel Daneau's excellent *Problems and opportunities in U.S.-Québec relations* (Boulder, Colorado: Westview Press, 1984. 320p.).

592 **L'art de l'impossible: la diplomatie québécoise depuis 1960.** (The art of the impossible: Québec diplomacy since 1960.)
Claude Morin. Montréal: Éditions du Boréal Express, 1987. 470p.

Describes the motives behind Québec's external affairs strategy between 1964 and 1985. The book also provides a good overview of the obstacles faced by successive governments in their efforts to increase Québec's presence on the international stage. Written by the former intergovernmental affairs minister of the first PQ (Parti québécois) Government (1976-81), this work includes many anecdotes relating to Morin's years in office.

593 **Le Canada et le Québec sur la scène internationale.** (Canada and Québec on the international stage.)
Edited by Paul Painchaud. Montréal: Presses de l'Université du Québec, 1977. 643p.

A general overview of the evolution of Canada's and Québec's international activities since 1945 with regard to the power relationships and interactions within, and between, these societies. The book explores organizations, international systems and Québec's place in the international relations network. The first part of the book provides a good analysis of the motives behind, and limits of, Canadian international relations.

594 **Le Québec dans le monde.** (Québec in the world.)
André Patry. Montréal: Leméac, 1980. 167p.

A personal account of the tension between the federal and Québec governments over foreign relations during the four decades leading up to 1980. While this book has not been written as a history of international affairs in Québec, the author describes, and places in historical perspective, Québec's quest for the right to sign international agreements.

595 **Le Québec et les accords de l'Uruguay Round. Du GATT à l'Organisation mondiale du commerce.** (Québec and the agreements of the Uruguay Round. From GATT to the World Trade Organization.)
Québec: Ministère des Relations internationales, 1996. 100p.

Briefly summarizes Québec's commercial position on the world stage. Specifically, this book examines the negotiation processes of the Uruguay Round of the GATT (General Agreement on Tariffs and Trade) talks in 1994, and analyses their impact on Québec. The interpretation of how GATT affects Québec commerce is preceded by a brief description of Québec's place in the world market.

596 **Géopolitique et avenir du Québec.** (Geopolitics and the future of Québec.)
J. R. M. Sauvé. Montréal: Guérin Éditeur, 1994. 349p. bibliog.

Describes Québec's geography and geopolitical role. In the first chapter, the author presents the geographic factors which have characterized and shaped Québec's historical development. The following five chapters are devoted to the history of five countries which have similar geopolitical situations: Denmark, Sweden, Holland, Portugal, and Norway. The final two chapters present the positive and negative aspects of Québec's geopolitical position with special regard to the impact of these factors on the province's political future. The author insists that Québec independence is far from 'geopolitical nonsense'; especially since Québec has a similar geopolitical situation to other independent countries. Also see *Environnement stratégique et modèles de défense: une perspective québécoise* (Strategic environment and defence models: a Québec perspective) (Montréal: Méridien, 1996. 288p.) by Charles-Philippe David and Stéphane Roussel.

The French-speaking world

597 **Le Québec dans la Francophonie et sa contribution au sommet de Québec.** (Québec in the Agence de la Francophonie [Francophone Agency] and its contribution to the Québec summit.)
Maité Le Goff Jay-Rayon. Québec: Ministère des Relations internationales, 1988. 172p. maps.

This volume was published following the Québec summit of the Agence de la Francophonie (Francophone Agency) in 1987. The first chapter examines the historical development of this organization, which was created in 1970 to bring together French-speaking countries for the purpose of creating a worldwide dialogue. The second and third chapters discuss the organization and work of the first and second Conférences des chefs d'État et de gouvernement (Conferences of the heads-of-state of [French-speaking] countries). See also Jean-Marc Léger's *La Francophonie: grand dessin, grande ambiguité* (The Francophonie: grand design, a lot of ambiguity) (LaSalle, Québec: Éditions Hurtubise HMH, 1987. 242p.) and Jean-Louis Roy's *La francophonie: l'émergence d'une alliance* (The Francophonie: the emergence of an alliance) (LaSalle, Québec: Éditions Hurtubise HMH, 1989. 131p.).

598 **Le pari québécois du Général de Gaulle.** (General de Gaulle's gamble on Québec.)
Renée Lescop. Montréal: Éditions du Boréal Express, 1981. 218p.

Charts the relationship between General de Gaulle and Québec, from the French leader's recognition of French-speaking Canada in 1940, and his 'Vive le Québec libre' (Long live free Québec) speech in Montréal in 1967, to his death in 1970. Lescop provides a well-researched analysis of the motives behind de Gaulle's policy decisions with regard to Québec. This study places many of de Gaulle's statements and actions in the context of the contemporary diplomatic situation, demonstrating the complex relations which existed between France, Canada and Québec. Half of the book is comprised of a detailed chronology, covering the period from 1940 to 1970, and providing key dates and descriptions of significant events which shaped relations between Québec and France.

599 **Québec's relations with Francophonie: a political geographic perspective.**
Colin Old. Ottawa: Carleton University Press, 1984. 55p. bibliog.

Attempts to evaluate Québec's contacts and interaction within the Agence de la Francophonie (Francophone Agency). This work does not examine any of Québec's bilateral agreements with other countries. Rather, the value of this work is in identifying Québec's association with an extensive network of non-governmental organizations within the Agence de la Francophonie. While this work is dated, it provides a good and concise portrait of Québec's relations within this agency up to 1984.

600 **De Gaulle et le Québec.** (De Gaulle and Québec.)
Dale C. Thomson. Saint-Laurent, Québec: Éditions du Trécarré, 1990. 410p.

Written as a supplement to Thomson's *Jean Lesage & the Quiet Revolution* (see item no. 150), this work attempts to explain the events surrounding General de Gaulle's now famous remark, 'Vive le Québec libre' (Long live free Québec), uttered from the balcony of Montréal City Hall in 1967. Moreover, Thomson analyses de Gaulle's statement in the framework of the tripartite relations involving Canada, France and Québec that were developing during the 1960s. Thomson relates the evolution of Canada-Québec-France relations in an engaging manner. A well-prepared index is also provided. Related works include Sylvie and Pierre Guillaume's *Paris-Québec-Ottawa: un ménage à trois* (Paris-Québec-Ottawa: a ménage à trois) (Paris: Éditions Entente, 1987. 227p.).

Political Economy

601 **Québec Inc. and the temptation of state capitalism.**
Pierre Arbour. Montréal: R. Davies Publishing, 1993. 165p.
Written by a former manager of the Caisse de dépôt et placement du Québec (Québec Deposit and Investment Fund – Québec's largest investment fund), this work takes a critical view of state economic management since the 1960s. Arbour examines such companies as the Asbestos Corporation, Québecair and Sidbec, proclaiming that the state is best left to 'govern', rather than manage, these enterprises. In the final chapter, the author analyses the state's language policies over the same period. Written for the non-specialist, this book is an insider's account of bureaucratic management within several of Québec's state-owned firms.

602 **Structure and change: an economic history of Québec.**
Robert Armstrong, Terry-Lee Wheelband. Toronto: Gage Publishing, 1984. 295p. bibliog.
Easily accessible for the non-economist, this work traces Québec economic history from the 16th century to the Second World War. The author builds upon the traditional staples approach to Canadian economic history. The role of institutions in shaping the province's economic development is highlighted.

603 **Le défi technologique.** (The technological challenge.)
Robert Bourassa. Montréal: Éditions Québec Amérique, 1985. 161p. bibliog.
Published just before Robert Bourassa's political return as Prime Minister of Québec in 1985, this book outlines the economic vision that would mark his first years back in office. He argues that Québec must take a decisive step towards technological innovation in order to develop along the lines of other industrialized countries. Following a summary of the advantages of a technologically based economy, for example, California's Silicon Valley and North Carolina's Research Triangle Park, Bourassa proposes a 'liberal vision' of how to meet these new challenges. Bourassa suggests that the private sector, rather than the state, must be the engine of innovation; the role of the latter, moreover, must be reduced to create a favourable fiscal climate.

177

604   **The empire of the St. Lawrence.**
Donald G. Creighton.   Toronto: Macmillan, 1956. 441p. maps.

An unabridged edition of Creighton's original thesis which was first published in 1937 as *The commercial empire of the St. Lawrence, 1760-1850* (Toronto: Ryerson, 1937. 441p.). His interpretation of Canadian history finds inspiration in the idea that the Saint-Lawrence is the 'basis of a transcontinental, east-west system, both commercial and political in character'. His thesis attempts to link Canada's transcontinental political structure to the economic importance of the Saint-Lawrence River.

605   **Économie du Québec: une économie à la remorque de ses groupes.**
(The economy of Québec: an economy tagging behind its groups.)
Roma Dauphin.   Laval, Québec: Beauchemin, 1994. 291p. bibliog.

A basic text examining the bases of the Québec economy, its resources, industrial structure, the role of the state, and Québec's relations with Canada and the world.

606   **Le modèle québécois de développement économique.** (Québec's model of economic development.)
Edited by Jean-Pierre Dupuis.   Québec: Presses Inter-Universitaires, 1995. 183p.

A series of essays by sociologists, economists and political scientists on Québec's economic development strategy. The first section of the book discusses the content and the efficacy of Québec's particular strategy; essays in this section offer both positive and critical reactions to the model. The second section assesses the impact of this model on managerial strategies in Québec. The editor concludes with an excellent synthesis of the different authors' arguments. This is an excellent book for those interested in Québec's economic development.

607   **Éléments d'analyse économique pertinents à la révision du statut politique et constitutionnel du Québec.** (Elements of an economic analysis concerning the revision of Québec's political and constitutional status.)
Québec: Commission sur l'Avenir constitutionnel du Québec, 1991. 566p.

Prepared under the auspices of the 1990 Bélanger-Campeau Commission, one of whose recommendations was the holding of a referendum on Québec sovereignty, this volume contains nine studies and texts on the economic impact and characteristics of Québec separation. The following issues are discussed: Québec's access to world and Canadian markets in the event of sovereignty; current trade patterns between Québec, Canada, the United States and the world; employment; integration into international finance and the corresponding budgetary and fiscal standards Québec would have to meet; federal transfer programmes; and forecasts of Québec's public spending in the event of sovereignty.

608   **Histoire économique et unité canadienne.** (Economic history and
Canadian unity.)
Albert Faucher.   Montréal: Fides, 1970. 296p. bibliog. (Histoire
Économique et Sociale du Canada Français).

In contrast to the majority of analysts of the 1950s who used the concept of 'folk
society' to explain the economic inferiority of French Canadians, Faucher interprets
Québec's economic development by analysing the limits imposed by physical geography,
the type of resources exploited, and the required investment, highlighting the importance
of these factors is the main objective of this anthology. The first section of the book
summarizes Faucher's thought on Canadian economic history. The second section
stresses the impact of Québec's location on the North American continent which
contributed to its stunted development. The book includes tables, charts and graphs
and a comprehensive bibliography of Faucher's publications. See also Faucher's
Québec en Amérique au XIXe siècle (Québec in America during the 19th century)
(Montréal: Fides, 1973. 247p.). For a critical assessment of Faucher's arguments, see
René Durocher and Paul-André Linteau's *Le retard du Québec et l'infériorité
économique des Canadiens français* (The backwardness of Québec and the economic
inferiority of French Canadians) (Montréal: Éditions du Boréal, 1971. 127p.).

609   **La Caisse de dépôt et placement du Québec. Sa mission, son impact
et sa performance.** (The Québec Deposit and Investment Fund. Its
mission, its impact, and its performance.)
Edited by Claude E. Forget.   Toronto: C. D. Howe Institute, 1984.
162p. bibliog.

Published by a private-sector, right-of-centre Canadian think-tank, this collection of
thirteen essays examines the successful performance of the Caisse de dépôt et placement du Québec, the largest pension-fund manager in Canada. The authors of this
work examine the Caisse's mission and management from a pragmatic and economic
perspective. The last section offers experts' opinions on how the Caisse should orient
itself for the future.

610   **Capitalisme et politique au Québec.** (Capitalism and politics in
Québec.)
Edited by Pierre Fournier.   Montréal: Éditions cooperatives Albert
Saint-Martin, 1981. 292p.

A critical assessment of the first mandate of the PQ (Parti québécois) (1976-81),
which focuses on the government's economic and social policies. For a study of the
government's role in economic planning and development before the PQ, and more
specifically on the 1940s and 1950s, the reader should consult Gilles Bourque and
Jules Duchastel's work, entitled *Restons traditionnels et progressifs* (Let us remain
traditional and progressive) (Montréal: Éditions du Boréal, 1988). During the 1980s, at
the same time as the PQ was turning towards neo-liberal economic policies, the federal
government became increasingly involved in Québec's development through its
spending power. This period is well documented in Gérard Bélanger's *Croissance du
secteur public et fédéralisme: perspective économique* (Federalism and the growth of
the public sector: an economic perspective) (Montréal: Éditions Agence d'Arc, 1988.
361p.).

611 **Québec beyond the Quiet Revolution.**
Alain-G. Gagnon, Mary Beth Montcalm.   Scarborough, Ontario:
Nelson Canada, 1990. 221p.

A political economic assessment of Québec's transformation since the 1960s. The authors argue that Québec's declining importance within Canadian and continental capital markets, as early as the turn of the century, placed significant political pressure on the provincial government to stimulate the Québec economy. Among the authors' main premises is the idea that the province's economic peripheralization, more than language policy or nationalism, has provided the major stimulus for institutional change in Québec. More recently, by acting to strengthen indigenous entrepreneurial activities, the Québec state has ironically made the private sector more suspicious of government intervention, fuelling the emergence of a neo-liberal nationalism. This is a solid introduction to the links between Québec's political activity and its economic development. The work also provides an analysis of the province's union movement, language legislation and constitutional relations with the rest of Canada.

612 **Histoire économique du Québec, 1851-1896.** (Economic history of Québec, 1851-96.)
Jean Hamelin, Yves Roby.   Montréal: Fides, 1971. 436p.

Mainly focused on the period covering Québec's rapid industrialization, this work examines five central phenomena: demographic pressure; the transportation revolution; the transition away from farming; urbanization; and trade.

613 **S'appauvrir dans un pays riche.** (Impoverishing ourselves in a rich country.)
Richard Langlois.   Montréal: Éditions Saint-Martin, 1990. 142p.

Against the backdrop of significant economic growth in the late 1980s, Langlois highlights the growing problem of poverty in Québec. More than a mere overview of poverty and its various manifestations, this book pays special attention to the growing disparities between regions, the deteriorating job market, the persistence of educational inequality, and the profound mutation of the state. This book also reveals the new faces of poverty: growing poverty among youth and single parents, and among those who, despite being active members of the workforce, fall below the poverty line.

614 **L'autre économie, une économie alternative.** (The other economy, an alternative economy.)
Edited by Benoit Lévesque, André Joyal, Omer Chouinard.   Sillery, Québec: Presses de l'Université du Québec, 1989.

A collection of essays on the social economy; an economy which exists apart from the traditional forces of the market. The different authors look at two fields of this alternative economy: the alternative enterprises, and the experiences of local and regional development. The various authors look at different economies including Québec. See also Louis Favreau and Benoit Lévesque's *Le développement économique communautaire: économie sociale et intervention* (Community economic development: social economy and intervention) (Sainte-Foy, Québec: Presses de l'Université du Québec, 1996. 230p.).

615   **The silent surrender. The multinational corporation in Canada.**
Kari Levitt.   Toronto: Macmillan, 1970. 185p.

The 1960s and 1970s witnessed an increase in concern among English Canadians regarding the effects of American ownership of capital in Canada. Defending Canadian national interests, this book is the most popular work attacking foreign ownership. Levitt's work belongs to a larger collection of literature written by left-leaning English Canadian economists who argued Canadian national interests could only be protected by a positive policy on foreign ownership. With regard to Québec, Levitt's desire for a strong federal government must come at the expense of provincial autonomy. She claims that 'the provinces will reinforce the continentalist trend by joining the competitive scramble for foreign investment'. In this sense we witness the tension within the English Canadian Left: caught between their sensitivity for Québec's desire for self-determination and their own desire to strengthen the 'Canadian nation' through its economy.

616   **Unequal beginnings. Agriculture and economic development in Québec and Ontario until 1870.**
John McCallum.   Toronto: University of Toronto Press, 1980. 148p.
(The State and Economic Life Series no. 2).

An important analysis which breaks with the many cultural hypotheses traditionally used in explaining Ontario's economic lead over Québec. Basing his research on the role of agriculture in capital accumulation, the author argues that this discrepancy resulted from the wealth provided by Ontario's superior agricultural land rather than from the conservatism of the habitants and the Church in Québec. The greater yield of Ontario's land enabled the province to accumulate capital which was then reinvested into the construction of transport, industrial, and urban, infrastructures. McCallum argues that the relative speed with which both provinces' infrastructures developed had a large impact on their economic growth. This book is of tremendous importance to anyone who wants to understand the economic history of Québec and Canada. It includes many tables.

617   **Economic and social history of Québec, 1760-1850: structures and conjunctures.**
Fernand Ouellet.   Ottawa: Gage Publishing Limited, 1980. 696p.
maps. bibliog. (Carleton Library no. 120).

When the French edition was first published in 1966 – *Histoire économique et sociale du Québec 1760-1850: structures et conjonctures* (Montréal: Fides, 1966. 639p.) – Ouellet placed himself in the middle of a historical controversy. Ouellet argues that the cession of New France to Great Britain had no significant influence on the colony's social, economic, or institutional, structures. Instead, the author emphasizes the slow development of the Québec economy during the ninety years of British domination. 'Beyond the change of Empire', Ouellet writes, 'the permanence of the colonial framework was accompanied by a remarkable stability in the economic structure and the principal activities of which it was composed'. Perhaps most contentious is his conclusion that the 'trauma' of the Conquest was largely a fabrication of the defensive psychology employed by later generations. This book remains a classic social and economic history. It includes tables, maps, graphs and a comprehensive bibliography.

618   **L'État interventionniste: le gouvernement provincial et l'économie du Québec.** (The interventionist state: the provincial government and the Québec economy.)
Edited by Filip Palda.   Vancouver: The Fraser Institute, 1994. 216p.

This work examines the role played by the Québec government in fostering economic development within the province. As might be expected from an avowedly conservative research institute, it takes a critical view of past attempts at state planning, and argues that such interventions have placed an unfair financial burden on the population. The book contains contributions by seven authors on several aspects of the Québec economy, namely: research and development, innovation, competitiveness, education, the labour market, financing, and hydro-electricity. Most of the studies rely on economic data from the 1980s and the early 1990s. For a similar, though less scholarly treatment of state interventionism in Québec, see Pierre Arbour's *Québec Inc. and the temptation of state capitalism* (item no. 601).

619   **La pensée économique au Québec français. Témoignages et perspectives.** (Economic thought in French Québec. Testimonies and perspectives.)
Directed by Gilles Paquet.   Montréal: Association canadienne-française pour l'Avancement des Sciences, 1989. 364p.

A collection of the writings of the major economists who have shaped the interpretation of political economy and economic history. Thirty-four interviews with different generations of economists are also transcribed and presented in this work. Finally, the third section comprises three texts which reveal the contemporary tendencies in economic research during the 1980s, and the progress made in the discipline.

620   **La machine à milliards: l'histoire de la Caisse de dépôt et placement du Québec.** (The billion-dollar machine: a history of the Québec Deposit and Investment Fund.)
Mario Pelletier.   Montréal: Éditions Québec Amérique, 1989. 330p.

Since its establishment in 1965, the Caisse de dépôt et placement in Québec has accumulated over thirty billion dollars in assets, making it the most important shareholder in Canada. The author examines three distinct periods in the company's history: the founding years (1966-73), the years of consolidation (1973-80), and the years of expansion (1980-89).

621   **Unequal union: roots of crisis in the Canadas: 1815-1873.**
Stanley Bréhaut Ryerson.   Toronto: Progress Books, 1973. 2nd ed. 477p.

Ryerson was the first historian to apply Marxist analysis to the history of Québec. Yet, in his earlier works, he distinguished himself from other Marxist historians in his consideration of social and national phenomena. It was the ascendancy of the neo-nationalist school in Québec history and the advent of the Quiet Revolution that led Ryerson to criticize the assumption that the Union of the Canadas (1840) constituted the moment when French Canadians gained political equality. Rather, Ryerson demonstrates how the Union represented the institutionalization of colonialism and the imposition of the 'unequal union' of the Conquest. Confederation in 1867 is also seen as the imposition of a centralized colonial union which never properly

eradicated the problem of national inequality which still pervades the political landscape.

622 **Une économie à libérer: le Québec analysé dans ses structures
économiques.** (An economy to liberate: an analysis of Québec through
its economic structures.)
Maurice Saint-Germain. Montréal: Presses de l'Université de
Montréal, 1973. 471p. bibliog.

A very thorough analysis of the economic development of Québec from the period of
French colonization to the late 1960s. The study focuses on the degree of autonomy
and the homogeneity of Québec's economy – the overall portrait presented in this
work is one of dependency and dualism. The explanation stresses sociological and
historical factors and calls for a political reorganization (i.e. sovereignty) in order to
develop a more autonomous and integrated economy. The author makes extensive use
of Québec scholarly works and, in so doing, he introduces the reader to the debates and
issues that animate discussions relating to Québec's political economy and economic
history. The work contains an index, a very detailed table of contents, and an
extensive bibliography.

623 **L'économie du Québec et de ses régions.** (The economy of Québec
and its regions.)
Diane-Gabrielle Tremblay, Vincent Van Schendel. Montréal:
Éditions Saint-Martin, 1991. 649p.

A macroeconomic study of Québec's present and past economic structure. Areas
covered include developmental theories, business cycles, productivity, demography,
regional economies, and financial institutions. For a similar, but less recent, study, see
Rodrigue Tremblay's *L'économie québécoise* (The Québec economy) (Montréal:
Presses de l'Université du Québec, 1979. 493p.). Another widely used macroeconomic
study of Québec is Pierre Fréchette and Jean-P. Vézina's *L'économie du Québec*
(Québec's economy) (Montréal: Éditions HRW, 1985. 641p.).

Finance and Banking

624 La Laurentienne. La passionnante aventure d'un groupe financier à la conquête du monde. (La Laurentienne. The exciting adventure of a financial group trying to conquer the world.)
Pierre Godin. Montréal: Éditions Québec Amérique, 1988. 482p. (Collection Succès d'Amérique).

Established in 1938 in Lévis as a small insurance company, the Laurentienne Group has since become a major financial and banking institution. With a presence on three continents, the Laurentienne Group represents the early difficulties and subsequent success of Québec's francophone entrepreneurs. In this financial biography, Pierre Godin relates the story of the evolution of the group, its president, its acquisitions, and the conflicts and obstacles it has faced. The book focuses on the personalities of the important members of the Laurentienne. In doing so, Godin traces a picture of the 'economic and social mutation of Québec' since the 1960s, and its influence on the creation of a francophone bourgeoisie.

625 La saga des Caisses populaires. (The Caisses populaires [Credit Union] saga.)
Jacques Lamarche. Montréal: Éditions La Presse, 1985. 271p.

A short history of the Caisses populaires Desjardins (Desjardins Credit Union), a cooperative financial group owned by more then four million Quebecers, which was set up in 1900. The author retraces the origins of the Mouvement Desjardins (Desjardins Movement), as it is now called, and presents a brief portrait of the founder, Alphonse Desjardins (1854-1920). Lamarche also writes of the Desjardins beginnings in the city of Lévis, where the first Caisse populaire was set up, and the later creation of the federation. The rest of the book is mainly devoted to a description of the different components of the Mouvement Desjardins. For more recent information pertaining to the Mouvement Desjardins, see Lamarche's *Le Président Béland* (President Béland) (Montréal: Guérin Éditeur, 1997. 356p.).

626 **Le capital financier québécois.** (Québec's finance capital.)
François Moreau. Montréal: Éditions Saint-Martin, 1981. 155p.
bibliog.

An examination of the roles played by the savings and credit cooperatives, private banks, insurance companies, and state investment companies in Québec. These include such companies as the Mouvement Desjardins (Desjardins Movement), the National Bank, the Caisse de dépôt et placement du Québec (Québec Deposit and Investment Fund), and the Laurentienne Group. From a Marxist perspective, the author analyses how these institutions have helped shape Québec's economic development. Moreau also assesses how a ready supply of French-owned capital has bolstered Québec's political position *vis-à-vis* the federal government.

627 **Histoire du Mouvement Desjardins. Tome 1: Desjardins et la naissance des Caisses populaires, 1900-1920.** (A history of the Mouvement Desjardins [Desjardins Movement]. Volume 1: Desjardins and the birth of the Caisses populaires [Credit Unions], 1900-20.)
Pierre Poulin. Montréal: Éditions Québec Amérique, 1990. 373p.
bibliog.

In examining the birth of the Mouvement Desjardins (Desjardins Movement) in 1900, Poulin pays close attention to the social context in Québec during the first two decades of the 20th century. This contextualization highlights the degree to which the fortunes of the Mouvement Desjardins were linked with the progression of other social movements such as the Catholic social action movement and the nationalist movement, organized and managed by Henri Bourassa and Olivar Asselin. Moreover, the genesis of the Mouvement Desjardins must be understood as part of a larger movement within a society caught between the national question, the social impact of liberal economic policies, and the development of capitalism. In this context, the cooperative movement is presented as a remedy that benefited from the broad support of social leaders. Related works include *L'émergence de l'idéal coopératif et l'État au Québec: 1850-1914* (The emergence of the cooperative ideal and the Québec state: 1850-1914) by Jean-Marie Fecteau and Isabelle Dupuis (Montréal: Chaire de Coopération, Université du Québec à Montréal, 1989. 110p.).

628 **Du comptoir au réseau financier. L'expérience historique du Mouvement Desjardins dans la région du centre du Québec, 1909-1970.** (From the counter to a financial empire. The historical experience of the Mouvement Desjardins [Desjardins Movement] in the centre region of Québec from 1909-70.)
Yvan Rousseau, Roger Levasseur. Montréal: Éditions du Boréal, 1995. 388p.

This book traces the history of the URTR (Union régionale des Caisses populaires Desjardins de Trois-Rivières – Trois-Rivières Regional Federation of Desjardins Credit Unions), the oldest of the eleven regional federations of the Mouvement Desjardins (Desjardins Movement), from the birth of the first Caisses populaires (Credit Unions) in 1909 to the 1970s. Moreover, in analysing the URTR's network of affiliated Caisses populaires and its relationship with the other members of the Mouvement Desjardins, the authors are able to trace the growth and evolution of the Mouvement Desjardins itself.

629 **Banking en français: the French banks of Québec: 1835-1925.**
Ronald Rudin. Toronto: University of Toronto Press, 1985. 188p.

This work examines the operations of the nine French-run chartered banks in Québec between 1835 and 1925, beginning with the Banque du peuple (People's Bank) and ending with the Banque canadienne nationale (National Bank of Canada). The author argues that these francophone enterprises were not hindered by any lack of business sense among their managers, but rather by problems associated with gaining access to larger capital markets. This is one of the best institutional and historical studies of the province's financial sector.

630 **In whose interest? Québec's Caisses populaires, 1900-1945.**
Ronald Rudin. Montréal; Kingston, Ontario: McGill-Queen's University Press, 1990. 224p.

The Caisses populaires (Credit Unions) in Québec have been one of the most important French-run business enterprises throughout the 20th century. Through their lending to local businesses, the Caisses have played an influential role in the economic development of the province. According to the author, over three quarters of French-speaking Quebecers belonged to one of these funds in 1986. This work looks at the class composition of the Caisses populaires, highlighting the role played by the *petit bourgeois* founders of the Caisses in 1900, and the rise of the new middle class prior to the Quiet Revolution of the 1960s. Rudin's revisionist thesis suggests that the movement's founders, threatened by large capital, were less concerned with helping the masses than they were interested in maintaining and consolidating their own influence.

Trade

631 **Le libre-échange par défaut.** (Free trade by default.)
Dorval Brunelle, Christian Deblock. Montréal: VLB Éditeur, 1989.
302p.

Discusses the historical and economic contexts of the North American Free Trade Agreement (NAFTA) of 1993, while taking Québec's special place into account. In examining the process of continentalization and the current trends in economic relations between Canada and the United States, the authors are able to interpret NAFTA as the institutionalization of a new economic bloc. The book's strength is its ability to analyse NAFTA as part of a growing trend of economic integration. This analysis escapes the polemical debates in which NAFTA is simply judged according to its potential impact on English-speaking Canadian culture. Rather, NAFTA is viewed through the lens of ideology which emphasizes Canada's shift away from state intervention and Keynesian economic theory, and towards economic policies dominated by a neo-liberal agenda.

632 **L'impact de l'Accord du libre-échange sur le commerce bilatéral entre le Québec et les États-Unis.** (The impact of the Free Trade Agreement on bilateral commerce between Québec and the United States.)
Gilles Duruflé, Benoit Tétrault. Montréal: Research Institute on Public Policy, 1994. 43p.

Six years after the ratification of the Canada-US Free Trade Agreement of 1988, the authors analyse the agreement's effect on Québec-US bilateral commerce. They conclude that this accord has been more beneficial for Québec than for the rest of Canada. Their conclusion is based on the aggregate export/import ratio and on an analysis of several sectors of Québec's economy. The book includes tables, charts and graphs.

633 **Québec. Le défi économique.** (Québec. The economic challenge.)
Jacques Fortin. Sillery, Québec: Presses de l'Université du Québec,
1990. 242p. bibliog.

Examines the challenges facing Québec's economy within the context of increased
international competition and the emergence of large, regional economic trading
blocs. Québec's economic development from the Conquest to the late 1980s is presented in a brief, introductory chapter. The remainder of the first section is dedicated
to Québec's place within the international context. Various aspects of the economy are
examined, such as: international trade treaties; technological change; Québec's
competitiveness in productivity; manpower and investment; and university research
and training. The author's own suggestions for improving Québec's competitiveness
are summarized in the second half of the book.

634 **Québec 1960-1980: la crise du développement.** (Québec 1960-80:
the crisis of development.)
Edited by Gabriel Gagnon, Luc Martin. Montréal: Éditions Hurtubise
HMH, 1973. 500p. map. (Collection l'Homme dans la Société no. 1).

An anthology of texts written by Quebecers during the 1960s on the topic of development. The book attempts to illustrate how changes during the Quiet Revolution did not
occur uniquely at the level of politics and government action. In examining popular
participation, this anthology aims to show that the rise in the collective consciousness
of Québec's autonomy stretched beyond the elite circle of politicians. While the state
did play an important role in reorganizing society, this work suggests that other actors,
such as the unions, students' and citizens' groups, also influenced the decision-making
process which shaped Québec's development over the course of the decade. This
dynamic interpretation illustrates the reactions state development policies engendered,
the mobilization they assumed, and how this mobilization developed according to
power relations, ideological debates, and experiences at the level of the regions.

635 **Un siècle à entreprendre. La Chambre de commerce de Montréal,
1887-1987.** (A century of enterprise. The Montréal Chamber of
Commerce, 1887-1987.)
Yves Guérard, Madeleine Saint-Jacques, Pierre Shooner. Montréal:
Éditions Libre Expression, 1987. 191p.

A popular history of both the business elite and the general economic development of
Montréal. The book contains excellent illustrations.

636 **Mondialisation de l'économie et PME québécoises.** (Globalization
of the economy and small and medium-sized businesses in Québec.)
Pierre-André Julien, Martin Morin. Sainte-Foy, Québec: Presses de
l'Université du Québec, 1995. 204p. bibliog.

Over the past twenty years, there has been a simultaneous development in the dynamics
of small and medium-sized businesses (SMBs) and the opening of Québec markets to
international competition. These businesses constitute the heart of the Québec economy
and their adaptation to these new trade patterns is of significance. This work focuses
on some of the sectors several analysts thought would be most hard-hit by the transformation of the markets. A study of the strategies employed in the manufacturing sector
(from increased specialization to expansion into the world market) reveals that these

companies have adapted fairly well to globalization and its impact. Julien has written a typology of SMBs' strategic choices in reaction to globalization, entitled *Typologie des comportements stratégiques des PME exportatrices* (Typology of exporting SMB strategic behaviour) (Trois-Rivières, Québec: GREPME, Université du Québec à Trois-Rivières, 1994). Information on Québec SMBs can occasionally be found in the *Journal of Small Business and Entrepreneurship* (Toronto: International Council for Small Business-Canada, 1985- . quarterly), a Canadian periodical 'devoted to fostering entrepreneurship and small business development'.

637 **Québec under free trade: making public policy in North America.**
Edited by Guy Lachapelle. Montréal: Presses de l'Université du Québec, 1995. 420p.

Supported by both the PLQ (Parti libéral du Québec – Québec Liberal Party) and the PQ (Parti québécois), the Canada-US FTA (Free Trade Agreement) of 1988 has consistently been embraced by Québec governments. Anxious to extend its economic, social and political relationships with the rest of the continent, Québec has distinguished itself from other Canadian regions whose governments have adopted a more cautious approach to free trade. This collection of scholarly articles examines Québec's desire to be integrated into the North American economy from a variety of perspectives: historical, political, social and economic. Several articles discuss the impact of NAFTA (North American Free Trade Agreement) on the Québec economy in addition to the challenges facing Québec public policy in the context of NAFTA. This is an excellent and revealing book on Québec's unique relationship with North America. See also *La libéralisation des échanges Canada-États-Unis et les relations industrielles au Québec: négocier l'avenir* (Trade liberalization between Canada and the United States and industrial relations in Québec: negotiating the future), edited by Michel Brossard (Montréal: Presses de l'Université de Montréal/École de Relations industrielles, 1989. 250p.).

638 **Le commerce extérieur du Québec.** (Québec's international trade.)
François Moreau. Hull, Québec: Éditions Critiques, 1988. 158p.

A critical assessment of the neo-classical arguments in favour of free trade. The author stresses the short-term social costs of free trade particularly to small and medium-sized enterprises, arguing that, in general, the benefits of liberalized trade can only be expected at a much later date. This work is one of many published before the implementation of the 1988 Canada-US Free Trade Agreement that analyse the likely impact of trade liberalization. See also Jean Blouin's *Le libre-échange vraiment libre?* (Is free trade really free) (Québec: Institut québécois de Recherche sur la Culture, 1986. 134p.) which provides a useful summary of the most prevalent forms of trade protection. Blouin argues that the achievement of a fair trade system may require reforms that go beyond free trade between Canada and the United States.

639 **Histoire de la Chambre de commerce de Québec: 1809-1959.**
(A history of Québec's Chamber of Commerce.)
Fernand Ouellet. Québec: Centre de Recherche de la Faculté de Commerce de l'Université Laval, 1959. 105p. (Histoire Économique).

Describes the evolution of the Québec City Chamber of Commerce between 1809 and 1959. Ouellet suggests that the Chamber of Commerce, as an organization dedicated to economic promotion, is a unique tool through which one can witness the trends and development of Québec's regional economy. To illustrate this, Ouellet explains the official positions adopted by the Chamber on a variety of issues like free trade and the Great Depression. The book also describes the importance of Québec City to the Canadian economy throughout this period.

640 **Québec International.**
Québec: Ministère des Affaires internationales, de l'Immigration et des Communautés culturelles, 1995- . annual.

A comprehensive directory of the major international associations based in Québec, of the associations based outside Québec which study Québec and Canada, and of all associations which contribute to the promotion of Québec on the international stage. The directory includes the address of each association and a short annotation on its objectives.

641 **Autonomie et mondialisation: le Québec et la Catalogne à l'heure du libre échange et de la Communauté européenne.** (Autonomy and globalization: Québec and Catalonia facing free trade and the European Community.)
Edited by Gaëtan Tremblay, Manuel Parès i Maicas. Sillery, Québec: Presses de l'Université du Québec, 1990. 352p.

A comparison of Québec and Catalonia, what the authors term 'small enclave societies'. This book examines the likely implications of the European Community's common market for Catalonia, as well as the 1988 Canada-US Free Trade Agreement's impact on Québec. The many contributors to this work share the hope that this internationalization will provide more autonomy for their national institutions, thereby diminishing the power of their respective central governments. The book stems from a symposium held in Montréal in April 1987 which brought together scholars from Québec and Catalonia.

Business and Industry

General

642 **Lavalin. Les ficelles du pouvoir.** (Lavalin. The threads of power.)
Carole-Marie Allard. Ottawa: Éditions JCL, 1990. 317p. bibliog.
Examines the history of Lavalin, the largest engineering consultancy firm in Canada in
the late 1980s, its president, Bernard Lamarre, and the company's industrial strategy.
From 50 employees in 1961 to 7,500 in 1988, and business worth close to a billion
dollars, Lavalin represented one of Québec's success stories of the time, thanks in part
to the James Bay hydro-electric projects of the 1970s.

643 **L'entreprise québécoise: développement historique et dynamique
contemporaine.** (Québec businesses: historical development and
contemporary dynamics.)
Yves Bélanger, Pierre Fournier. LaSalle, Québec: Éditions Hurtubise
HMH, 1987. 187p. (Les Cahiers du Québec, Collection Science
Politique no. 90).
This work provides a history of francophone business in the province, starting in the
early 19th century and focusing on the period just before, and immediately following,
the Quiet Revolution (1960-66). For this latter period, the authors acknowledge the
pre-eminent role played by the Québec government as a motor of economic development.
In contrast, they argue that federal politics has largely impeded Québec's growth.
According to the authors, francophone-controlled businesses in Québec are now poised
for success in both the Canadian and world markets.

644   Le Québec militaire: les dessous de l'industrie militaire québécoise.
      (Military Québec: the hidden side of the Québec military industry.)
      Yves Bélanger, Pierre Fournier.   Montréal: Éditions Québec
      Amérique, 1989. 202p.

As the authors indicate, the military industry in Québec employs 50,000 workers and
involves over 300 businesses, representing 3 billion dollars in sales per year. They
argue, however, that further development of this industry would be harmful given the
decline in military procurement worldwide. By carefully examining five sectors within
the military industry, a clearer picture of Québec's contribution emerges.

645   Les conquérants. (The conquerors.)
      Jean Côté, François-Xavier Simard.   Montréal: Éditions Béluga,
      1989. 239p.

A series of biographical portraits on a selection of owners of important small and
medium-sized businesses in Québec. The authors relate the evolution of each in
addition to their visions of the future.

646   Le mouvement coopératif québécois. Guide bibliographique.
      (The Québec cooperative movement: a bibliographical guide.)
      Gaston Deschênes.   Montréal: Éditions du Jour, 1980. 291p.

This reference book lists 1,551 works related to cooperative movements in Québec. It is
organized according to sector (savings and credit, agriculture, forestry, etc.), principles
and philosophy, and management.

647   The Québec establishment: the ruling class and the state.
      Pierre Fournier.   Montréal; New York: Black Rose Books, 1976.
      228p. bibliog.

A class-based interpretation of the relations between business and government in
Québec from 1960 to 1974. Relying primarily upon an exhaustive set of interviews
with business leaders, this work examines the structure of business, the corporate elite
and its ideology, associations such as the Chambre de commerce (Chamber of
Commerce) and the Conseil du patronat, and business access to the Québec government.
Fournier stresses the dominant role played by the capitalist class in the development
and welfare of Québec society.

648   Québec Inc.: French Canadian entrepreneurs and the new business
      élite.
      Mathew Fraser.   Toronto: Key Porter Books, 1987. 280p. bibliog.

The author examines the rise of the French-speaking corporate elite in Québec. He
identifies its ascendancy with a new credo in the province – one that is both highly
individualistic and market-oriented. After outlining the main classes of the French
Canadian business elite, Fraser examines the political support that ignited this entrepreneurial dynamism. This new business revolution, he argues, represents the second
stage of the Quiet Revolution, which is now led by entrepreneurs, not bureaucrats.
This is a well-written account based upon extensive interviews. See also Thomas
Courchene's *Québec Inc.: foreign takeovers, competition/merger policy and universal
banking* (Kingston, Ontario: School of Policy Studies, Queen's University, 1990.
53p.).

649 **The value-added enterprise. The Québec model.**
Edited by Pierrette Gagné, Michel Lefebvre. Montréal: Publi-Relais, 1993. 310p.
A guide to new management concepts relevant to the challenges of globalization, written in simple and clear language. Designed for students, executives, workers and teachers, this book also gives examples of how to put concepts into action, and how to develop a successful corporate mission, business plan and export strategy.

650 **Steinberg. The breakup of a family empire.**
Ann Gibbon, Peter Hadekel. Toronto: Macmillan Canada, 1990. 284p.
At the forefront of the Canadian supermarket industry, the Steinberg empire was one of Québec's major employers. This work charts the development of the Steinberg family business in Québec from its beginnings in the second decade of the 20th century to its decline in the 1980s. The authors illustrate Sam Steinberg's contribution to Québec's economy and the various elements which led to the unravelling of his company following his death.

651 **Les Québécois, entre l'État et l'entreprise.** (Quebecers, between the state and business.)
Jean Mercier. Montréal: L'Hexagone, 1988. 192p.
A wide-ranging analysis of private and public sector management in Québec. After examining the historical experience of organizations in Québec from colonial times to the present, the author proposes various management reforms within these businesses. He focuses on attitudes, budgetary restrictions, and the remarkable growth of information technology during the 1980s. Also see *Valeurs de l'entreprise québécoise* (Values of Québec business), edited by Roderick J. Macdonald (Montréal: Guérin Éditeur, 1995).

652 **La bourgeoisie industrielle au Québec.** (The industrial bourgeoisie in Québec.)
Arnaud Sales. Montréal: Presses de l'Université de Montréal, 1979. 322p. bibliog.
Given the significant influence of economic power in the development of social policy in Québec society, Sales' objective is to discover why the Québec population, despite its demographic weight, has been unable to secure control over the majority of private and public economic levers. Francophone under-representation within the industrial bourgeoisie was originally attributed to English and French cultural differences. Sales refutes this claim by demonstrating how structural differences in Canadian industry, some of which can be traced back as far as the Conquest and Confederation, are responsible for this under-representation. This sociological study first examines the development of industry in Canada and its major transformations. The second section is devoted to an analysis of the national and ethnic stratification within the industrial bourgeoisie.

653 **Pierre Péladeau. Biographie.** (Pierre Péladeau. A biography.)
François-Xavier Simard, Jean Côté. Outremont, Québec: Éditions
Quebecor, 1996. 199p.

A light-hearted look at one of the most powerful men in Québec. Péladeau founded
the publishing empire, Quebecor, which remains the flagship success story of the
emergent francophone business elite. This book chronicles his rise to power.

654 **The river barons: Montréal businessmen and the growth of
industry and transportation, 1837-1853.**
Gerald Tulchinsky. Toronto; Buffalo, New York: University of
Toronto Press, 1977. 310p. bibliog.

This work charts the development of the business community in Montréal, focusing on
the innovations in the field of transportation. The years between 1837 and 1853
witnessed the rapid extension of railway lines outside Montréal, and the concentration
of large industrial plants along the shores of the Lachine Canal. The author examines
the French, English, Scottish and American entrepreneurs who were involved in the
city's development during this period.

655 **In its corporate capacity: the Seminary of Montréal as a business
institution, 1816-1876.**
Brian Young. Montréal; Kingston, Ontario: McGill-Queen's
University Press, 1986. 295p. bibliog.

An important contribution to the economic history of Montréal, this work examines
the Seminary of Montréal against Québec's contemporary transition from feudalism to
capitalism. The economic activities of the Seminary's members, who were both the
seigneurs of Montréal as well as priests, represent the evolution of their management
style, from traditional to professional. The capital accumulation of the Seminary after
the 1837-38 insurrections and its progressive alliance with the state and the bourgeoisie
were used to ensure the development of social institutions that would assist in controlling
the masses and serve to legitimize the transformations brought about by industrialization.
See also Gabriel Dussault's *Charisme et économie. Les cinq premières communautés
masculines établies au Québec sous le régime anglais, 1837-1870* (Charisma and
economics. The first five male religious orders established during the English regime,
1837-70) (Québec: Université Laval, Department of Sociology, 1981. 149p.).

Periodicals

656 **Les Affaires.** (Business.)
Montréal: Transcontinental, 1981- . weekly.

The most comprehensive business and finance newspaper in Québec. *Les Affaires*,
which continues *Le Journal des Affaires* (Montréal: Le Journal des Affaires, 1928-81),
provides weekly summaries of Québec's key financial, banking and economic indicators.
In addition, the newspaper includes company profiles, industry sector analyses, and
analytical articles on management strategies, resource management, and marketing

etc. *Les Affaires* is referred to by policy analysts, social scientists and most of Québec's business leaders. The periodical also annually publishes the equivalent of a *Fortune 500* for Québec companies.

657 **Les Affaires Plus.** (Business Plus Magazine.)
Montréal: Transcontinental, 1991- . 10 issues per year.

This is the companion magazine to the weekly *Les Affaires* newspaper (see item no. 656). Published ten times a year (double issues in December-January and July-August), this magazine comprises articles on the most influential people in Québec, feature stories on companies and social trends, and financial advice columns.

658 **Forces.**
Montréal: Société d'Éditions de la Revue forces, 1994- . quarterly.

Forces is a bilingual magazine that publishes articles on Québec's major economic, social and cultural challenges. The magazine often showcases articles by leading Québec opinion leaders (e.g., newspaper editors, labour and business leaders), providing insights into the opinions of Québec's movers and shakers. Articles tend to focus on current events and the magazine typically includes an in-depth interview with an important leader from Québec's economic, cultural or political milieu.

659 **Relations Industrielles.** (Industrial Relations.)
Québec: Department of Industrial Relations, Laval University, 1945- . quarterly.

An excellent bilingual journal of academic research and opinion in the area of industrial relations, unions, and the job market.

Resources

Energy

660 **Hydro-Québec: autres temps, autres défis.** (Hydro-Québec: different times, different challenges.)
Edited by Yves Bélanger, Robert Comeau. Montréal: Presses de l'Université du Québec, 1995. 372p.

The history of the public utility company, Hydro-Québec, necessarily entails the history of Québec. Based on a conference held to mark Hydro-Québec's fiftieth anniversary, this work is an interdisciplinary collection of thirty-six essays which examine the current challenges facing this public utility in the context of its historic economic mission and its relationship with Québec society. The essays are grouped according to six topics: issues and future choices; fifty years of history; economic development and innovation; northern politics and relations with aboriginal peoples; energy and the environment; and privatization. Recognizing the important link between Hydro-Québec and Québec society as a whole, this work looks at the impact of today's social and economic problems (deficit reduction, First Nations demands, environmental concerns) on this public utility.

661 **Shawinigan Water and Power, 1898-1963. Formation et déclin d'un groupe industriel au Québec.** (Shawinigan Water and Power, 1898-1963. Formation and decline of an industrial group in Québec.)
Claude Bellavance. Montréal: Éditions du Boréal, 1994. 446p. bibliog.

Provides a history and analysis of the Shawinigan Water and Power (SWP) company, one of Québec's largest industrial groups, up to the second round of hydro-electric power nationalization in the 1960s. This work highlights the importance of analysing the history of the hydro-electric power industry before nationalization by examining the role played by SWP in Québec's development. The last two chapters are devoted to the structure of the company and its industrial activities. This work begins with a historiography of the hydro-electric industry and ends with an impressive and well-organized bibliography useful to anyone seeking a greater understanding of the industry.

662 **Hydroelectricity and industrial development: Québec, 1898-1940.**
John Harkness Dales. Cambridge, Massachusetts: Harvard University Press, 1957. 269p.

A seminal work within the literature on hydro-electricity and its role in Québec. This book is important to students attempting to understand the role of the hydro-electric industry in Québec's industrialization at the turn of the century. Beyond a comparison of Québec's major hydro-electric firms and their practices, Dales examines how hydro-electricity, in comparison with coal and other fuels, influenced the structure of the Québec economy. Highlighting the significant potential hydro-electric power had to decentralize industry, Dales argues that individual private firms did not take advantage of, or develop, this resource. Dales argues further that the possibility of creating consumer demand for hydro-electric power was not exploited adequately by private companies.

663 **Énergie et fédéralisme au Canada.** (Energy and federalism in Canada.)
Michel Duquette, Kevin Fitzgibbons, Élaine Gauthier. Montréal: Presses de l'Université de Montréal, 1992. 242p.

This work places the uniqueness of Canadian energy management within the context of energy management in three other federations: the United States, Germany and Switzerland. A detailed description is provided of the institutions in question and of the links between government and industry. Provincial energy management is also distinguished from its federal counterpart through the examination of three case-studies: the natural gas industry in Québec; the nuclear industry in Ontario; and the hydrocarbon industry in the Prairies. Moreover, the development of the federal energy policy under the Conservative Government of 1988-93 provides an insight into the process of reconciliation between the provinces and Ottawa, in addition to tracing the ideological origins of such a policy.

664 **Hydro-Québec: la société de l'heure de pointe.** (Hydro-Québec: the rapid-transit company.)
Philippe Faucher, Johanne Bergeron. Montréal: Presses de l'Université de Montréal, 1986. 221p.

This work focuses on Hydro-Québec's management strategies since the second wave of nationalization in 1963. Through an examination of the political and economic choices and limits facing this government corporation, the authors present a wide-ranging portrait of the major economic challenges facing post-industrial societies. Hydro-Québec has been chosen as the object of this study due to its symbolic and economic importance for Québec in addition to its status as one of the major motors of Québec's modern consumer-based society. The second part of the book examines the role of Hydro-Québec as an economic policy tool. In the context of limited resources, unsatisfied demand, increasing maintenance costs and decreasing investment, Faucher and Bergeron examine the balance between Hydro-Québec's role as a profit-making corporation and its obligation to provide benefits for Québec society. Overall, this book stands out as a detailed assessment of the industrial development of Québec's most important state-owned enterprise.

665   **Les enjeux économiques de la nationalisation de l'électricité.**
(The economic issues behind the nationalization of electricity.)
Carol Jobin.   Montréal: Éditions coopératives Albert Saint-Martin,
1978. 206p.

Inspired by the capitalist development theory, Jobin seeks to demonstrate that the nationalization of electricity in Québec – more specifically, hydro-electricity, from which most of the province's electric power is derived – was secretly desired by the large Québec monopolies that wanted the state to assume the management of the hydro-electricity sector which was becoming increasingly less profitable. This work is useful because it examines the origins of the industry, and also because it provides a critical analysis of the Quiet Revolution from the point of view of class. The first chapter paints a picture of the industry in Québec prior to nationalization by assessing Québec in relation to other provinces and comparing the importance of hydro-electric power with other energy sources available in Québec. The second chapter uses economic theory to analyse nationalization by applying the concept of monopolistic competition. The last chapter examines the political aspect of nationalization, its implementation and financing, and the transfer from the private to the public sector.

666   **Electric rivers: the story of the James Bay project.**
Sean McCutcheon.   Montréal; New York: Black Rose Books, 1991.
194p.

A work that examines both the natural and human history of the James Bay hydro-electric project (1971-84), one of the largest projects of its kind in the world. When completed, the James Bay complex could generate some 27,000 megawatts of power, equivalent to the output of 35 or more nuclear power plants. McCutcheon also mentions the potential repercussions on the natural environment and on aboriginal communities. Though the author's opposition towards this project is evident throughout, he does present a synopsis of views from Québec aboriginals and provincial bureaucrats.

667   **Hydro-Québec: navire amiral ou bateau ivre? Avec une dette de
trois milliards.** (Hydro-Québec: flagship or drunken boat? With a
debt of three billion.)
Yvon Pageau.   Boucherville, Québec: G. Vermette, 1993. 171p.

Proposing the creation of a national energy policy on hydro-electricity, the author argues that Hydro-Québec has made economic decisions harmful to Québec's future consumers. The author believes that Hydro-Québec's long-term provisions are wrong, due to an overestimation of the demand for electricity. Pageau believes that this mistake could be dangerous for Québec's economic health and disastrous for the environment.

668   **James Bay: the plot to drown the North Woods.**
Boyce Richardson.   San Francisco: Sierra Club, 1972. 190p.

A strong criticism of the James Bay hydro-electric project and its impact on the environment and the aboriginals' way of life. The author discusses the motives of the opposing political forces which fought in favour of, or against, the project. Beyond the James Bay project, this book provides a good critique of the obsession with progress in industrialized societies. Written by a former journalist, this book is an engaging piece of social commentary.

Agriculture

669 **Anthropologie et Sociétés.** (Anthropology and Society.)
Sainte-Foy, Québec: Université Laval, 1977- . 3 issues per year.
Published by the Department of Anthropology at Laval University, this scholarly journal publishes three thematic issues per year. Themes focus primarily on the practical and theoretical debates surrounding anthropology in Québec. Within each issue, essays unrelated to the issue's theme are also included.

670 **L'histoire de l'agriculture au Québec.** (Agricultural history of Québec.)
Colette Chatillon. Montréal: Étincelle, 1976. 125p.
This work analyses the agricultural industry through the lens of economic history, from French colonialism to the mid-1970s. Adopting a class-based approach, this work seeks to answer two questions. The first is general, attempting to discover how to analyse society from the point of view of class conflict and materialism. Consequently, the evolution of agriculture in Québec is seen as the dispossession of one class (small commodity producers) for the benefit of larger producers. The second question attempts to situate Québec and Canada within the international context. This work focuses on the dialectical relationships between production, industry and agriculture.

671 **Agriculture et développement dans l'est du Québec.** (Agriculture and development in eastern Québec.)
Bruno Jean. Montréal: Presses de l'Université du Québec, 1985. 431p. bibliog.
This study encompasses the area south of the Saint-Lawrence River, including the southern Gaspé, Bonaventure and Lower Saint-Lawrence. The author examines the industrial development of this peripheral region of Québec, focusing on the structure of local community enterprises. This is a thorough study containing an excellent bibliography and tables.

672 **Histoire de l'agriculture.** (A history of agriculture.)
Firmin Létourneau. Montréal: Imprimerie Populaire, 1950. 325p.
This is a classic among the corpus of literature on Québec agriculture. In an occasionally passionate prose, Létourneau extols the virtues of the men and women who ploughed Québec into existence and, against all odds, remained farmers and true to the land. Rural life is associated with strength of character and survival, a popular and recurring theme in nationalist ideology between 1870 and 1960. The book itself is divided into six chapters, reflecting political events such as the Conquest and Confederation and betraying the political message behind this history. Agriculture and religion, according to Létourneau, comprise the central institutions and elements in French-speaking Canada's history.

673 **L'agriculture familiale au Québec.** (Family agriculture in Québec.)
Michel Morisset. Paris: L'Harmattan, 1987. 203p.

Describes the development of family agriculture in Québec since the the mid-19th century. The author discusses the stages that led to the creation of a viable commercial agriculture. Morisset demonstrates how family agriculture was driven by forces that the traditional elites could not control: economic cycles, rural exodus, and agricultural policies.

674 **La nation canadienne et l'agriculture.** (The Canadian nation and agriculture.)
Maurice Séguin. Trois-Rivières, Québec: Éditions du Boréal Express, 1970. 279p. maps.

A historian from the 'neo-nationalist' school of Québec history, Séguin's analysis of agriculture is intimately related to the national question. Séguin argues that the Conquest (1760) forfeited the economic, political and social levers of power to the British, leaving the French Canadians in a state of oppression. This crisis forced French Canadians into the unprofitable and unforgiving agricultural sector in order to survive. This oppression continued with the advent of industrialization in Québec which resulted in the creation of a pool of cheap labour comprised overwhelmingly of French Canadians. Séguin concludes that French Canadians' inferiority derives not from a lack of dynamism or cultural backwardness but rather from British colonization itself. Séguin's thoughts on the national question and the role of the Conquest and the Act of Union are elaborated in his *L'idée de l'indépendance au Québec: genèse et historique* (The idea of independence in Québec: origins and history) (Trois-Rivières, Québec: Éditions du Boréal Express, 1968. 66p.).

675 **Agriculture et colonisation au Québec.** (Agriculture and colonization in Québec.)
Edited by Normand Séguin. Montréal: Éditions du Boréal Express, 1980. 222p.

This collection of eleven historical essays examines the main aspects of agriculture and colonization and their interrelation since 1850. It is an important contribution to the development of agriculture as a field worthy of study in itself. Topics in this work include: the social repercussions of agricultural industrialization; capitalism and agriculture; demographic trends within rural milieus; the myth of the agricultural vocation; the dairy industry; causes of population migration; the agro-forestry industry; and mechanization in the agricultural industry.

676 **La conquête du sol au 19e siècle.** (The conquest of the land during the 19th century.)
Normand Séguin. Sillery, Québec: Éditions du Boréal Express, 1977. 295p.

A meticulous inquiry into the colonization and evolution of the Notre-Dame d'Hébertville parish in the Saguenay region during the second half of the 19th century. Through this particular case-study, the author aims to illustrate the socio-economic problems associated with colonization in Québec. Séguin argues that the labour needs of the forestry magnates, reinforced by the state's laissez-faire development policies, presided over the colonization of the region despite the lack of fertile farming land.

which, in turn, led to the predominance of subsistence farming and poverty. This work provides an excellent analysis of Québec's land development policy as well as a thorough description of community organizations which struggled to build infrastructures for their towns.

Fisheries

677 **Les pêches maritimes au Québec: enjeux économiques et intervention de l'État.** (Maritime fisheries in Québec: economic stakes and state intervention.)
Marcel Daneau.   Québec: Presses de l'Université Laval, 1991. 214p.
This book provides both a history of the sector and an outline of the state of the industry in general. The author demonstrates how the legislative action of the different governments has often been motivated by short-term imperatives rather than by a global and comprehensive approach to the industry. See also *D'hier à demain: la pêche maritime au Québec* (From past to future: maritime fishing in Québec), by O. Cloutier (Rimouski, Québec: Université du Québec à Rimouski, Groupe de Recherche interdisciplinaire en Développement de l'Est du Québec, 1991. 116p.). For a technical and scientific investigation of the fisheries industry in Québec, see the following two periodicals published by the government: *Analyse Économique et Commerciale du Poisson de Fond au Québec* (Economic and Commercial Analysis of Deep Water Fish in Québec) (Ottawa: Pêches et Océans Canada, 1991- . annual); and *Analyse Économique et Commerciale du Poisson Pélagique au Québec* (Economic and Commercial Analysis of Pelagic Fish in Québec) (Ottawa: Pêches et Océans Canada, 1991- . annual).

678 **Pêche et coopération au Québec.** (Fishing and cooperation in Québec.)
Paul Larocque.   Montréal: Éditions du Jour, 1978. 379p.
Québec's fisheries have almost always been among the principal economic activities of the Gaspé region. Consequently, difficulties in the fisheries industry translate into difficulties for the region. In order to increase solidarity among the inhabitants, the members of the fisheries industry created a cooperative in the late 1930s. The author relates the obstacles they faced and the impact the cooperative had on Gaspesian society. The book provides a very good overview of the living and working conditions of fisheries workers in Québec.

679 **La pêche sur le Saint-Laurent: répertoire des méthodes et des engins de capture.** (Fishing on the Saint-Lawrence: directory of harvest means and mechanisms.)
Marcel Moussette.   Montréal: Éditions du Boréal Express, 1979. 213p. bibliog.
The contact between French fishermen and aboriginals since the foundation of the French colony to the present has produced innovative fishing techniques in Québec.

The author demonstrates in this essay the constant evolution in technology that has marked Québec's fisheries industry.

Forestry

680 **Les pâtes et papiers au Québec, 1880-1980. Technologie, travail et travailleurs.** (Pulp and paper in Québec, 1880-1980. Technology, work and labour.)
Jean-Pierre Charland. Québec: Institut québécois de Recherche sur la Culture, 1990. 447p. bibliog.

A thematic analysis of the technological, economic and social histories of the pulp and paper industry and those involved in it. Aside from providing a history of the industry's economic development, this work examines the evolution of technology, its impact on the industry and society, and its uses in the industry. The social history of the pulp and paper labour force is also examined. The work contains an impressive bibliography. See also Jean Désy and Gisèle Bélanger's *Des forêts pour les hommes et les arbres* (Forests for men and for trees) (Laval, Québec: Éditions du Méridien, 1995. 369p.).

681 **Forêt et société en Mauricie.** (Forests and society in Mauricie.)
René Hardy, Normand Séguin. Montréal: Éditions du Boréal, 1984. 223p.

The authors use the forestry industry as a launchpad for a discussion of the Mauricie region's social and historical development. This book examines the birth of the industry in the region and analyses the transformations that occurred in light of economic factors such as the American demand for lumber and changing technology, in order to explain the character of the region. The region's colonization as well as its industrial history are also examined.

682 **Enjeux forestiers.** (Forestry issues.)
Edited by Paul Larocque, Jean Larrivée. Rimouski, Québec: Les Cahiers du GRIDEQ 20, 1991. 220p.

A work examining forestry in Québec, with emphasis on economics, regulatory policy, and conservation management. The authors assess the difficulties of sustaining a viable forestry industry and offer several suggestions for its maintenance.

683 **Gestion forestière.** (Forest management.)
Damien Saint-Amand, Robert Jobidon. Mont-Royal, Québec: Modulo, 1986. 197p.

Even if this book is mainly theoretical, it provides important insights into the state of the forestry industry in Québec. The government also publishes a periodical on the forestry industry which contains vital statistics, *Portrait Forestier du Québec* (Portrait of the Forestry Industry in Québec) (Québec: Ministère des Forêts, 1990- . annual).

684 **Les interrelations entre les industries des pâtes et papiers et du sciage et le développement économique de l'est du Québec: 1950 à 1980.** (The interrelations between the pulp and paper industry, and sawmill, and the economic development of eastern Québec between 1950 and 1980.)
Jean Saint-Onge. Rimouski, Québec: Université du Québec à Rimouski, Groupe de Recherche interdisciplinaire en Développement de l'Est du Québec, 1982. 167p. bibliog. (Cahiers du GRIDEQ, no. 10).
Demonstrates how the pulp and paper industry dominated the sawing industry and reveals the impact of this domination on the economic development of eastern Québec. Using a class-based method of analysis, the author describes in detail the role of the state in supporting this domination. This work constitutes an important contribution to the literature on core-periphery relations. The book includes a comprehensive bibliography.

Mining

685 **Géologie du Québec.** (Québec's Geology.)
Québec: Ministère des Ressources naturelles, 1994- . 2 issues per year.
Designed for the informed reader as well as the general public, this government publication provides general information on Québec's geological characteristics. For easy access, this publication is divided into chapters dealing with particular regions of the province.

686 **Cain's legacy: the building of the Iron Ore Company of Canada.**
Richard Geren. Sept-Îles, Québec: Iron Ore Co. of Canada, 1990. 351p.
Commissioned by the Hanna Mining Company, this is a narrative account of the history of the Iron Ore Company. While this book reveals a clear bias in favour of the company, it provides a glimpse into the exploration and development of New Québec and Labrador which the reader will find useful. This work was written for the general public.

687 **La sidérurgie dans le monde rural: les hauts fourneaux du Québec au XIXe siècle.** (Steel and iron metallurgy in the rural world: wood furnaces in Québec during the 19th century.)
René Hardy. Sainte-Foy, Québec: Presses de l'Université Laval, 1995. 303p. maps. bibliog.
An impressive bibliography sustains this analysis of the iron industry in Québec and its impact on the development of the Trois-Rivières region. The author examines the reasons behind the industry's disappearance from the region at the turn of the century and, in so doing, analyses Canadian economic policy, demonstrating the role played by Québec within the country's steel and iron industry as a whole. This work also

focuses on the rural environment, and on the way wood burning metallurgy diversified rural society and contributed towards the creation of industrial towns.

688 **L'industrie minérale du Québec: bilan et faits saillants.** (Mining industry in Québec: appraisal and salient points.)
Québec: Ministère des Ressources naturelles, 1994.

The 1994 edition of this annual publication presents a wide-ranging portrait of the mining industry in Québec. Different aspects of the industry, such as investment, environmental impact, financing, research and development, security and manpower are summarized and accompanied by graphs and statistics. A section on each of Québec's regions is also presented. A summary of Québec's main mineral products (from copper to cadmium) closes the issue.

689 **L'entrepreneurship minier: la révolution tranquille du Québec minier.** (Mining entrepreneurship: the Quiet Revolution in Québec's mining industry.)
Edited by Gilles Saint-Pierre.   Boucherville, Québec: Gaëtan Morin Éditeur, 1989. 252p.

This collection of seventeen essays, written by academics and business leaders, presents the entrepreneurial successes of the mining industry and examines their positive economic impact on the Québec economy. Topics discussed include: the evolution of the industry and famous prospectors; the role of state-owned agencies in the development of the industry; and the needs of small and medium-sized mining enterprises. Also included is an essay on the principal metals mined and their characteristics, and descriptions of the making of successful mining companies. This work has been written for specialists in the industry as well as for investors.

690 **Des mines et des hommes: histoire de l'industrie minérale québécoise: des origines au début des années 1980.** (Of mines and men: a history of the mining industry in Quebec: from the origins to the beginning of the 1980s.)
Marc Vallières.   Québec: Ministère de l'Énergie et des Ressources, 1989. 439p. maps.

This scholarly work looks at the historical, socio-economic and political forces which have motivated the expansion and development of this sector. Throughout, the author explains the impact the Québec mining industry had, and continues to have, on society.

Transport

691 **Railways of southern Québec.**
John Derek Booth. West Hill, Ontario: Railfare Enterprises, 1982.
2 vols.

These two volumes illustrate the organization, construction and impact of certain railway lines in the Eastern Townships of Québec. The railway network in this region provides a microcosm of the Canadian railway experience in addition to illustrating the varied roles played by railways in Canada. More specifically, this work affords the reader a more profound understanding of the economic geography of the Townships: the origins of the railway concept in the region, the process of its construction, and its role in providing transport services. While the rail industry no longer enjoys the transport monopoly it once had, the following books are worthy of mention simply because they deal with railway companies once based in Québec: A. W. Currie's *The Grand-Trunk railway of Canada* (Toronto: University of Toronto Press, 1957. 556p.), and G. R. Stevens' *History of the Canadian National Railways* (New York: Macmillan, 1973. 538p.).

692 **Bulletin Économique du Transport au Québec.** (Economic Bulletin of Transport in Québec.)
Québec: Ministère des Transports, 1992- . quarterly.

Published by the Department of Transport, this journal provides important statistical data on the transport industry in Québec. Among the indicators which are examined are the labour market, and varied data regarding the railways, aviation and maritime industries. Each issue contains a dossier on a particular challenge faced by the transport industry.

693 **À la remorque des transports.** (Transport in tow.)
Daniel Latouche. Sillery, Québec: Québec Science Éditeur, 1980.
282p.

Provides a sociological examination of transport in Québec. The first three chapters situate the importance of transport in both the histories of Québec and Canada by describing the political and economic aspects of transport, such as: federal-provincial jurisdictions, the economics of transport, and the political pressures of state-building. The remaining chapters deal with various modes of transport and the challenges that face them: the automobile, public transport, aviation, railways, marine shipping, and trucking.

694   **Le Saint-Laurent et ses pilotes. 1805-1860.** (The Saint-Lawrence and its navigators, 1805-60.)
Jean Leclerc.   Montréal: Leméac, 1990. 236p.

Portrays the central place the Saint-Lawrence occupied during its heyday as the most important means of communication and commerce between 1805 and 1860. This book examines the administrative, technical and human aspects of the river. More specifically, the book focuses on the increasingly important role played by government, and on the proliferation of navigators offering their services to European vessels. The maritime history of Québec City's port takes precedence over that of other Québec ports in this work.

695   **Recherches Transport: Bulletin Scientifique et Technologique.**
(Transport Research: Scientific and Technological Bulletin.)
Québec: Ministère des Transports, 1994-97. quarterly.

Published by the Ministry of Transport, this bulletin focused on the state of research on transport in Québec and on the legislation regarding the industry. It has since been superseded by *Innovation Transport: Bulletin Scientifique et Technique* (Transport Innovations: Scientific and Technical Bulletin) (Québec: Transports Québec, 1998- . quarterly).

696   **Nos aviateurs: des "fous de l'air" aux pilotes de ligne.** (Our aviators: from the 'clowns of the air' to commercial pilots.)
Jacques Rivart.   Montréal: Les Éditions de l'Homme, 1981. 271p. maps.

Describes the contributions made to aviation by Quebecers. In addition to anecdotes regarding famous aviators such as Jean-Marie Landry and the four Vachon brothers, Rivart also describes the emergence and establishment of the larger airline carriers. This is a thorough and well-researched work on aviation history in Québec up to the late 1970s. Rivart also touches on the use of aeroplanes in the development of Québec's natural resources, and their role in providing services to inhabitants of Québec's large territory.

697   **Le vieux prince.** (The old prince.)
Léon-A. Robidoux.   Montréal: Guérin Éditeur, 1988. 189p.

A history of the 'raftsmen' who plied Québec's rivers until the turn of the century, transporting lumber. This accessible book describes the social conditions in which the raftsmen lived and the historical development of the trade from the 17th century to the beginning of the 20th century. The author also examines the lives of two famous raftsmen, Jos Montferrand and Aimé Guérin.

698 **Québec and the St-Lawrence Seaway.**
Gennifer Sussman. Montréal: C. D. Howe Institute, 1979. 46p.
This brief research study examines the economic impact of the Saint-Lawrence Seaway which enabled ocean-going vessels to enter the Great Lakes without having to stop in Montréal or Québec. Stopping short of using a full-scale cost-benefit analysis, the author concludes that the Seaway did benefit ports in Québec. The essay reveals the impact which federal transport policy can have on Québec's economy. By extension, policy developments in this field also play an important role in provincial-federal negotiations. For information regarding Québec's position on the issue of federal-regional conflicts, the reader should consult Luc-Normand Tellier's *Économie et indépendance* (Economics and independence) (Montréal: Éditions Quinze, 1977. 331p.). See also Mabel Tinkiss Good's *Chevrier: politician, statesman, diplomat and entrepreneur of the St. Lawrence Seaway* (Montréal: Stanké, 1987. 214p.) for a look at the politics behind the Seaway.

699 **Promoters and politicians: the North-Shore railways in the history of Québec, 1854-1885.**
Brian J. Young. Toronto: University of Toronto Press, 1978. 192p. maps.
Railway mania only came to Québec following Confederation. This work analyses the political battles that occurred as a result of the development of North Shore railways in Montréal. Young reveals the degree of state intervention in Québec as well as the destabilizing impact railways had on politics. This approach is in contrast to the central role often given to ideological battles and the role of the Church in explaining these same phenomena. This book traces the diversity of clerical, business, and political interests that came together to develop the railways into a public venture which cut across linguistic lines.

Labour

700 **Les relations industrielles au Québec: 50 ans d'évolution.**
(Industrial relations in Québec: fifty years of evolution.)
Edited by Rodrigue Blouin. Sainte-Foy, Québec: Presses de
l'Université Laval, 1994. 842p.

This collection of thirty-five essays identifies and explains major landmarks in the
development of industrial relations in Québec in the context of five topics: the concept
and discipline of industrial relations; the actors, state, unions and business leaders;
work relations, including collective bargaining, strikes, the democratization of the
workplace and the impact of free trade; the management of human resources; and public
policy in the areas of manpower training, employment equity, working conditions,
health and safety, collective bargaining and remuneration. This is a useful interdisciplinary tool for those wishing to understand the field and the history of industrial
relations in Québec.

701 **Histoire de la FTQ: des tout débuts jusqu'en 1965.** (A history
of the FTQ: from its origins until 1965.)
Edited by Émile Boudreau. Montréal: Fédération des Travailleurs
et Travailleuses du Québec, 1988. 384p.

Commissioned by the FTQ (Fédération des travailleurs et travailleuses du Québec –
Québec Federation of Labour), this history traces the traditions and legacy of one of
Québec's most important labour federations from its inception until 1965. The evident
bias of this work is mitigated by the participation and cooperation of several noted
academics in its production, notably that of Léa Roback. Accessible to a wide
readership, the book is aimed at providing a journalistic account of the institutional
development of the FTQ, in addition to providing a broad synthesis of the origins of
the labour movement in Québec. For the history of the FTQ after 1965, see *Histoire de
la FTQ: 1965-1992: la plus grande centrale syndicale au Québec* (A history of the
FTQ, 1965-92: the largest union in Québec) (Montréal: Éditions Québec Amérique,
1994. 291p.) by Louis Fournier.

702 **The anatomy of poverty: the condition of the working class in Montréal, 1896-1929.**
Terry Copp. Toronto: McClelland and Stewart, 1974. 192p.
(Canadian Social History Series).

At the turn of the century, a time roughly associated with national expansion and prosperity, over two thirds of Montréal's population derived their income from hourly wages and their welfare, as a group, improved little between 1896 and 1929. This work attempts to describe the socio-economic system within which the working class lived, and also sets out to determine which aspects of the socio-economic system were indigenous to Montréal and Québec. This methodology arises from the author's personal belief that historians have focused too much on cultural differences between Québec and the rest of Canada at the expense of analysing economic questions. Citing evidence from public health sources, housing and welfare conditions, and industrial conflict, this work argues that improvements in the welfare of the working class during this period only occurred when social or health problems afflicted the entire society, reflecting the inability of political and social institutions to provide needed relief.

703 **The history of labor movements in Québec.**
CSN, CEQ, translated by Arnold Bennett. Montréal; New York:
Black Rose Books, 1987. rev. ed. 299p. bibliog.

Originally published in 1979 by the education committees of the two largest unions in Québec – the CSN (Confédération des syndicats nationaux) and the CEQ (Centrale de l'enseignement du Québec) – this revised edition provides a synthesis of the labour movement from its beginnings to the late 1970s, with the aim of providing a collective memory for the labour movement. Divided into six chronological sections, this work describes the economy, political life, the conditions of the working class, the union movement, and labour political action for each period, paying particular attention to the conditions of working women, child labour, strikes, and collective bargaining achievements. A chronology and bibliography are provided at the end of the book, making it an ideal source for quick reference. For a good overview of the internal organization of the different labour unions see Bernard Dionne's *Le syndicalisme au Québec* (Unionism in Québec) (Montréal: Éditions du Boréal, 1991. 126p.).

704 **Éléments d'histoire de la FTQ: la Fédération des travailleurs du Québec et la question nationale.** (Historical fragments of the FTQ: the Québec Federation of Labour and the national question.)
François Cyr, Rémi Roy. Montréal: Éditions coopératives Albert Saint-Martin, 1981. 205p.

This work examines the relationship between class and national consciousness within the FTQ (Fédération des travailleurs et travailleuses du Québec). Drawing from empirical evidence, the authors trace the impact of the national question on the development of the FTQ during three 'periods': the linguistic debate; the emergence of the independence movement; and the rise of PQ (Parti québécois) members within the organization. See also Louis Fournier's *Louis Laberge: le syndicalisme c'est ma vie* (Louis Laberge: unionism is my life) (Montréal: Éditions Québec Amérique, 1992. 418p.).

705 **Luttes de classes et question nationale au Québec, 1948-1968.**
(Class conflicts and the national question in Québec, 1948-68.)
Roch Denis. Montréal; Paris: Presses socialistes internationales,
Études et documentation internationales, 1979. 601p. bibliog.

Taking a class-based approach, Denis argues that the development of the national question cannot be understood solely as the product of conflict among the bourgeois classes. Instead, the author concludes that the nature of the national question was largely determined by the conflict between an organized working class, conscious of its demographic leverage, and the old political regime under which it was suffocating. From his examination of the twin battles of national independence and social democratization, and how they interrelate, in the period 1948-68, Denis concludes that the working class had a decisive impact on the evolution of the national question. This work proposes an alternative hypothesis to that of Gilles Bourque and Anne Legaré's *Le Québec: la question nationale* (see item no. 488). This work also contains an extended bibliography and a chronological summary of events between 1948 and 1968.

706 **Les syndicats face au pouvoir: syndicalisme et politique au Québec de 1960 à 1992.** (Unions confronting power: unionism and politics in Québec between 1960 and 1992.)
Roch Denis, Serge Denis. Ottawa: Éditions du Vermillon, 1992. 196p.

Describes the external and internal circumstances of the labour market in order to explain the political action of labour unions in Québec since the Quiet Revolution. Among the factors explored are those of nationalism, institutionalization and cooperation. The authors compare labour unions in Québec with those in the rest of Canada. See also Jean-Marc Piotte, Diane Éthier and Jean Reynolds' *Les travailleurs contre l'État bourgeois: avril et mai 1972* (Workers against the bourgeois state: April and May 1972) (Montréal: L'Aurore, 1975. 274p.). For a more minute analysis of state-union relations involving the CEQ (Centrale de l'enseignement du Québec), the reader should consult Jean-Claude Tardif's *Le mouvement syndical et l'État: entre l'intégration et l'opposition: le cas de la CEQ, 1960-1992* (The union movement and the state: between integration and opposition: the case of the CEQ, 1960-1992) (Sainte-Foy, Québec: Université Laval, 1995. 210p.).

707 **Solidarité Inc. Un nouveau syndicalisme créateur d'emplois.**
(Solidarity Inc.: a new unionism that creates jobs.)
Louis Fournier. Montréal: Éditions Québec Amérique, 1991. 287p.

A detailed account of Le Fonds de solidarité (The Solidarity Fund) of the FTQ (Fédération des travailleurs et travailleuses du Québec – Québec Federation of Labour), Québec's largest union. Fournier examines the creation of this union-owned financial institution which was set up in 1983 and which, as of 1991, has over 110,000 shareholders and assets worth more than 500 million dollars. Most importantly, the author argues, the fund has supported economic development within Québec and has helped to maintain employment within domestic enterprises.

708   **Le syndicalisme: état des lieux et enjeux.** (Unionism: an inventory
of the current situation and issues.)
Mona-Josée Gagnon.   Québec: Institut québécois de Recherche sur
la Culture, 1994. 140p.

A solid introduction to the role and place of labour unions in Québec society. The
author suggests that labour union crises are the product of the state's incapacity to
deal with new challenges such as the globalization of the economy. This study
provides a new interpretation of the problems facing labour movements in Québec and
Western economies. The author provides a good account of the interaction in Québec
between the labour movement and the state.

709   **Les Métallos, 1936-1981.** (The Métallos, 1936-81.)
Jean Gérin-Lajoie.   Montréal: Éditions du Boréal Express, 1982.
347p.

Written by the former director of the Métallos union, which represented steelworkers,
this work provides a popular history of one of Québec's most important unions both in
terms of membership and its impact on the union movement in general. In examining
the Métallos, this work also deals with the rise of mass industrial unions which sought
to incorporate all workers of an industry into an organized front against employers.

710   **Les relations de travail au Québec.** (Labour relations in Québec.)
Jean Gérin-Lajoie.   Boucherville, Québec: Gaëtan Morin Éditeur,
1992. 375p.

An introductory work to the field of industrial relations which focuses significantly on
the relationship between managers, and unionized and non-unionized workers. The
largest chapters are devoted to the processes of collective negotiation, the collective
agreement, and arbitration. The book's approach is institutional, examining the actors,
their motivations and their actions.

711   **Le mouvement ouvrier au Québec.** (The workers' movement in
Québec.)
Edited by Fernand Harvey.   Montréal: Éditions du Boréal Express,
1980. 330p.

Published at a time when research on the labour movement and unions was gaining in
popularity, this is a collection of ten essays on the history of the Québec labour movement. It includes mainly works on the labour movement and its political action rather
than texts on the labour conditions of the working class. Themes covered include: the
historiography of the labour movement; the political action of unions; the evolution of
unions; class conflict; and mechanisms of collective bargaining. For an analysis of the
Catholic workers' union, see Jean-Pierre Collins's *La Ligue ouvrière catholique
canadienne, 1938-1954* (The Canadian Catholic Workers' League) (Montréal: Éditions
du Boréal, 1996. 253p.).

712 **Révolution industrielle et travailleurs: une enquête sur les rapports entre le capital et le travail au Québec à la fin du XIXe siècle.** (Industrial revolution and workers: a study of the relationships between capital and labour in Québec in the late 19th century.)
Fernand Harvey.   Montréal: Éditions du Boréal Express, 1978. 347p.

The problems associated with industrialization in Canada and Québec were in full force during the 1880s. In response, Prime Minister John A. Macdonald inaugurated a Royal Commission whose mandate was to examine the relationship between capital and labour. The minutes of this Commission provide a unique insight into labour conditions at the time when Québec was entering the Industrial Revolution. Harvey's work examines the foundations of the social, cultural, economic and technical transformations occurring in Québec at the time. Based on these observations, this work looks at the political structure of the Commission and its Commissioners, labour conditions and class conflict, and finally the Commission's report.

713 **La culture ouvrière à Montréal, 1880-1920: bilan historiographique.** (Working-class culture in Montréal, 1880-1920: historiographical assessment.)
Yvan Lamonde, Lucia Ferretti, Daniel Leblanc.   Québec: Institut québécois de Recherche sur la Culture, 1982. 178p.

Describes the popular culture of the working class in Montréal between 1880 and 1920 with the aim of determining whether the study of cultural phenomena enlightens one's understanding of social classes. This work examines the convergence between labour history, urban history, and sociocultural history through the following themes: class, living and working conditions, family life, and social life.

714 **Les relations du travail au Québec: une analyse de la situation dans le secteur public.** (Labour relations in Québec: an analysis of the situation in the public sector.)
Michel Leclerc, Michel Quimper.   Sainte-Foy, Québec: Presses de l'Université du Québec, 1994. 336p.

Adopting a multidisciplinary approach, this work provides a broad analysis of labour relations in the public sector through the lenses of history, management, sociology and economics, thereby contributing to the study of industrial relations as a separate academic discipline. Following an introductory discussion on the field of industrial relations and its theories, the authors divide their work into four sections: a comparative history of labour relations in Great Britain, the United States, France, Canada, and Québec; an examination of labour laws in the context of the Canadian Constitution and the Charter of Rights and Freedoms; a look at the political structure of unions, the process of collective bargaining, and the management of collective conventions; and a section devoted to the future of labour relations, new trends in management and the workforce, and recent economic trends (such as NAFTA) and their impact.

715 **Syndicalisme, législation ouvrière et régime social au Québec avant 1940.** (Unionism, labour legislation and the social system in Québec before 1940.)
Esdras Minville, edited by François-Albert Angers. Montréal: Presses HÉC; Fides, 1986. 619p.

This work is part of a larger series containing the complete works of Esdras Minville (b.1896), a noted Québec economist. The present volume reproduces two unedited manuscripts that Minville prepared for the 1937-40 Rowell-Sirois Commission (a.k.a. the Royal Commission on Dominion-Provincial Relations): the first on labour law and union history in Québec, and the second on Québec's social system. The Commission's mandate to examine the relationship between Canada and the provinces provides the backdrop to Minville's work and the ensuing debate regarding the division of powers between Ottawa and the provinces. Consequently, Minville's work was partially prepared with specific political goals and solutions in mind regarding the degree of autonomy Québec should be accorded as a result of its specificity.

716 **Histoire de la CSN, 1921-1981.** (A history of the CSN, 1921-81.)
Jacques Rouillard. Montréal: Éditions du Boréal Express, 1982. 335p.

Published for the sixtieth anniversary of the CSN (Confédération des syndicats nationaux – Confederation of National Unions), this work adds to an important corpus of literature on Québec's history from the perspective of workers. It presents CSN's institutional evolution from its inception as a Catholic-dominated union to its current place as one of Québec's largest unions. In examining this institution, however, Rouillard also enlightens our understanding of the Québec working class. This work is designed for the general public; individual chapters are supplemented by excerpts from primary sources.

717 **Histoire du syndicalisme au Québec: des origines à nos jours.** (A history of the union movement in Québec: from its inception to the present.)
Jacques Rouillard. Montréal: Éditions du Boréal, 1989. 535p.

This work presents an institutional history of unions and suggests that continental economics were more important in their development than the specificity of French culture and its religious legacy. Critical of the popular belief that union history only began during the Quiet Revolution, Rouillard argues that unions can trace their roots as far back as the 1850s when Québec was experiencing the first effects of industrialization. He reasons that the same economic factors which explain the rise and fall of unions across North America are salient to Québec unions as well. Citing primary sources from union archives and federal and provincial departments of labour, this text also examines the ideological role played by unions as critics of the status quo and as agents of social change.

718   **Le monde du travail au Québec: bibliographie = The world of labour in Québec: bibliography.**
James D. Thwaites, André E. Leblanc.   Sainte-Foy, Québec: Presses de l'Université du Québec, 1995. 589p.

A greatly expanded and reorganized version of an earlier work by the same authors, *Le monde ouvrier au Québec: bibliographie retrospective* (The working-class world in Québec: a retrospective bibliography) (Montréal: Presses de l'Université du Québec, 1973. 283p.). This bilingual bibliography contains over 5,700 titles in both French and English on the subject of labour history in Québec. Unlike the previous edition, this reference work is organized according to source type rather than subject matter. Sources listed in this book include articles, full-length books, theses, journals, magazines and audio-visual resources. An author and thematic index are presented at the end of the book. See also Thwaites' *Travail et syndicalisme: naissance et évolution d'une action sociale* (Labour and unionism: the birth and evolution of a social action) (Sainte-Foy, Québec: Presses de l'Université Laval, 1996. 405p.).

Environment

Architecture

719   **ARQ-Architecture Québec.**
Montréal: Groupe culturel préfontaine, 1981- . 6 issues per year.
The official journal of the Order of Québec Architects. It deals with questions relevant to the practice of architecture in Québec, for example, administrative, legal and technological aspects of the profession. The journal also contains pictures of major projects of the Order's members.

720   **Pignon sur rue. Les quartiers de Montréal.** (A home of one's own. The neighbourhood of Montreal.)
Michèle Benoît, Roger Gratton.   Montréal: Guérin Éditeur, 1991. 393p.
A series of chapters on the architectural history of Montréal's neighbourhoods. This book provides historical context to explain the way that the city was built, making it an excellent introduction to Montréal's history and architectural heritage. An abundance of drawings, photographs and graphs renders it accessible to the general reader.

721   **Architectures du XXe siècle au Québec.** (20th-century architecture in Québec.)
Claude Bergeron.   Montréal: Éditions du Méridien, 1989. 271p.
One of the first books dedicated to a synthesis of Québec's architecture over the past century. In relating the predominant styles of each period, Bergeron links architectural practice with the socio-economic evolution of society. Consequently, chapters are divided into the following sections: pre-Depression, the inter-war period, the post-war period, and the 1970s to the present. Each chapter reviews the architectural styles unique to that period. A lexicon is provided for those readers not familiar with basic architectural terms.

722 **L'architecture des églises protestantes des Cantons de l'Est et des Bois-Francs au XIXe siècle.** (The architecture of Protestant churches in the Eastern Townships and the Bois-Francs during the 19th century.) Hélène Bergevin. Sainte-Foy, Québec: Université Laval, 1981. 182p. bibliog. (Art Ancien du Québec no. 3).

A study of 180 Protestant churches which sets out to establish an architectural pattern. The first section of the book examines architectural aspects of the churches (bell towers, facades, etc.) while the second examines their value in relation to stylistic trends of 19th-century architecture in Québec.

723 **La maison de faubourg. L'architecture domestique des faubourgs Saint-Jean et Saint-Roch avant 1845.** (The suburban home. Domestic architecture of the Saint-Jean and Saint-Roch suburbs before 1845.)
Hélène Bourque. Québec: Institut québécois de Recherche sur la Culture, 1991. 199p.

Describes the process of architectural development in the Saint-Jean and Saint-Roch suburbs of Québec City before the great fire of 1845. The author attempts to uncover the reasons behind the homogeneous character of the architectural style of both suburbs: she argues that it is the result of the influence of the form of suburban development.

724 **Architectures: la culture dans l'espace.** (Architecture: culture in space.)
Edited by Jean-Charles Falardeau. Québec: Institut québécois de Recherche sur la Culture, 1983. 210p. (Questions de Culture no. 4).

The authors examine and analyse the links between architecture and culture in Québec. These essays suggest that culture must be understood and analysed from a pluralistic perspective: Falardeau writes, 'Every culture is exposed to the winds of many civilizations'. Several essays address the importance of the home and its place in Québec culture. Among the other themes addressed in this collection are the manifold elements that have influenced Québec's architectural tradition, and the way art has portrayed and interpreted Québec's architecture.

725 **Construire une église au Québec. L'architecture religieuse avant 1939.** (Building a church in Québec. Religious architecture before 1939.)
Raymonde Gauthier. Montréal: Éditions Libre Expression, 1994. 244p.

Combining architectural and social history, Gauthier examines the building of churches in Québec. This book brings to light how Québec churches have benefited from their proximity to English, French and American architectural traditions. In addition, in paying special attention to the socio-economic conditions of the times Gauthier is also able to identify factors which limited the creativity of architects.

726 **La tradition en architecture québécoise: le XXe siècle.** (Tradition in Québec architecture: the 20th century.)
Raymonde Gauthier. Montréal: Éditions du Méridien, 1989. 104p.
Examines the existence of traditional architecture in 20th-century Québec. Divided into three sections, Gauthier analyses the architects themselves, how they were trained and how traditional styles were transmitted through education and job contracts, and finally the perpetuation of this traditional style through architectural preservation and the creation of new architectural styles inspired by American neo-colonialism.

727 **Évolution de la maison rurale traditionnelle dans la région de Québec.** (Evolution of the traditional rural house in the Québec region.)
Georges Gauthier-Larouche. Sainte-Foy, Québec: Presses de l'Université Laval, 1974. 321p. bibliog. (Les Archives de Folklore no. 15).
Studies the evolution of the rural house from its origins through to the 1940s. This book focuses on stone houses and the architectural evolution of their various components, such as roofs, walls and heating. Also examined is the impact of Québec's climate on the design of homes.

728 **Loin du soleil. Architectural practice in Québec City during the French regime.**
Marc Grignon. New York: Peter Lang Publishing, 1997. 295p. bibliog.
An interesting study of architectural production in Québec City during the reign of Louis XIV, the Sun King, from the 1680s to the 1730s. At this time, Québec City's status as colonial capital was strengthened by a diversified economy, a growing population base and the French King's decision to establish basic institutions in the city. Grignon's approach is novel in its attempt to bridge the traditional gap between architectural objects and the documents related to them. This work focuses on the relationship between builders and clients and the tensions between them which collectively reveal the political and social importance of different projects. Moreover, this approach inevitably enlightens one's understanding of certain social issues during this period and will therefore also be of particular interest to the social historian.

729 **Opening the gates of eighteenth-century Montréal.**
Edited by Phyllis Lambert, Alan Stewart. Montréal: Canadian Centre for Architecture, 1992. 93p.
A study of the interrelationship of Montréal's fortifications, their ownership, the use of space within the walls, and the nature of the buildings during the 18th century. Particular attention to the role of history, in addition to the use of illustrations, renders this book accessible to the general public.

730   **La maison traditionnelle au Québec.** (The traditional house in
       Québec.)
       Michel Lessard, Gilles Vilandré.   Montréal: Éditions de l'Homme,
       1974. 493p. bibliog.

Examines Québec's architectural heritage through a study of various restoration
projects. Written by a professional architect and a historian, this work benefits from a
multidisciplinary approach.

731   **La présence anglicane à Québec. Holy Trinity Cathedral,
       1796-1996.** (The Anglican presence in Québec. Holy Trinity Cathedral,
       1796-1996.)
       Luc Noppen, Lucie K. Morisset.   Sillery, Québec: Éditions du
       Septentrion, 1995. 189p.

A history of the oldest church still standing in Québec City and counted among the
most important monuments in the city. This book relates the history and construction
of Holy Trinity Cathedral, the lives of its builders and promoters, and its architectural
heritage. Erected to consolidate and symbolize the British State in North America, the
history of this institution necessarily reveals the sociocultural transformations occurring
at the time.

732   **Québec monumental.** (Monumental Québec.)
       Luc Noppen, Hélène Jobidon, Paul Trépanier.   Sillery, Québec:
       Éditions du Septentrion; Montréal: Ordre des Architectes du Québec,
       1990. 191p. bibliog.

From the construction of the now famous hotel Château Frontenac to the recent
projects of the early 1990s, this book studies the history of architectural creation in the
Québec City area between 1890 and 1990. Abundantly illustrated with photographs
and drawings, each of the more than 150 buildings discussed is accompanied by
a brief history of the building and its architectural significance. Brief biographies
are provided of the architects cited throughout the book, along with an impressive
bibliography.

733   **Québec, trois siècles d'architecture.** (Québec, three centuries of
       architecture.)
       Luc Noppen, Claude Paulette, Michel Tremblay.   Montréal: Éditions
       Libre Expression, 1979. 447p.

Founded in 1608 by Samuel De Champlain, Québec City is well known for the beauty
of its architecture. This book studies the evolution of architecture in the city and the
architecture of important structures, such as churches, hospitals, and City Hall. The
book includes many photographs, rendering it very accessible to the non-specialist.

734   **Country houses for Montréalers, 1892-1924. The architecture of
       E. and W. S. Maxwell.**
       France Gagnon Pratte.   Montréal: Éditions du Méridien, 1987. 214p.

Aside from building some of Canada's most important commercial and public buildings, architects Edward and William S. Maxwell were also commissioned by

Montréal's wealthiest citizens to build their country homes in the environs of Montréal and in St. Andrews, New Brunswick. Pratte performs a meticulous study of the Maxwells' architectural drawings between 1892 and 1923. Trained overseas and in the United States, the Maxwells become two of Canada's leading architects which testifies to Montréal's prominent economic position in North America during the late 18th and early 19th centuries. After a brief history of the architects, Pratte classifies the summer homes they designed according to location: the Laurentians, the Atlantic coast, the West Island, Saint-Bruno and other neighbouring areas. Particular attention is paid to the Maxwells' designs in the context of the architectural trends of the day. This work is abundantly illustrated with drawings and photographs.

735 **The Church of Notre-Dame in Montréal: an architectural history.**
Franklin Toker.   Montréal; Kingston, Ontario: McGill-Queen's University Press, 1970. 124p. bibliog.
A history of the building and the renovation of Notre-Dame de Montréal. Toker focuses on the original architect rather than the people who financed and built the Church. In this history, Toker attempts to understand Notre-Dame's legacy as the symbol of French-speaking Canada.

Urban environment

736 **Shelter, housing and homes. A social right.**
Arnold Bennett.   Montréal: Black Rose Books, 1997. 236p.
An indispensable guide to housing policy in Québec. It begins with an anecdotal history of popular struggles for social housing in Montréal during the 20th century. The following chapters contain policy documents from two of Montréal's main housing rights organizations. There is also a chapter on the impact of the 1994 Civil Code changes on housing rights. Readers should note that the second half of the book discusses housing in other provinces. Nevertheless, the wealth of information on Québec contained in this book makes it a unique and practical source.

737 **Les grandes places publiques de Montréal.** (Principal public places in Montréal.)
Marc H. Choko.   Montréal: Éditions du Méridien, 1990. 215p.
An exceptional book on the history of four well-known public squares in Montréal: Victoria, Viger, Dorchester, and Place d'Armes. Illustrated with 213 historical and contemporary photographs and drawings, the work introduces the evolution of these historic squares from their inception to the present day. Moreover, Choko presents the architectural changes these squares experienced in the context of Montréal's socio-economic history, linking urban planning with the greater transformations of the city and its people.

738 **Paroisses et municipalités de la région de Montréal au XIXe siècle, 1825-1861.** (Parishes and municipalities in the Montréal region during the 19th century, 1825-61.)
Serge Courville. Québec: Presses de l'Université du Québec, 1988. 350p.

Describes the civil and Catholic administrative units of what was then the district of Montréal (covering much of western Lower Canada). The primary goal of this book is to fill the gap in the literature on the geographical evolution of administrative units in the region. This work will be of particular interest to those researchers studying rural Québec.

739 **L'ordre urbain.** (The urban order.)
Pierre Delorme. Hull, Québec: Éditions Asticou, 1986. 220p. bibliog.

A theoretical study of urban development in Québec which communicates the author's call for the state to stem and control urban disorder.

740 **Villes industrielles planifiées.** (Planned industrial cities.)
Edited by Robert Fortier. Montréal: Éditions du Boréal, 1996. 328p.

An interdisciplinary work on the subject of city planning in Québec which analyses three case-studies: the towns of Shawinigan Falls, Témiscamingue, and Arvida. Each city's socio-economic, cultural and political aspects are examined in detail. All three cities developed alongside major hydro-electric sources and bear witness to the ways in which urban city planning adapted to local environments.

741 **L'aménagement urbain: promesses et défis.** (Urban development: promises and challenges.)
Edited by Annick Germain. Québec: Institut québécois de Recherche sur la Culture, 1991. 267p.

The seven essays contained in this collection are united by their common vision of urban planning as a discipline constantly in flux. Moreover, through an examination of urban planning cases in Montréal and other towns, this collection charts the major trends in Québec urban planning and development. Other topics include the social, political, and cultural aspects of urban planning. This collection also demonstrates the relationship between cultural activity and urban renewal.

742 **Aménager l'urbain de Montréal à San Francisco. Politiques et design urbains.** (Organizing and managing urban spaces from Montréal to San Francisco. Urban design and policies.)
Annick Germain, Jean-Claude Marsan. Montréal: Éditions du Méridien, 1987. 191p.

The revitalization of run-down areas of cities is the central focus of this collection of essays. Written by urban planners, politicians, architects and academics, these essays discuss the renewed interest by politicians and urban planners in urban regeneration. While only a few of the essays touch directly on Montréal, this book is valuable in attempting to situate Montréal's experience in an international and comparative context.

743 **Arvida au Saguenay. Naissance d'une ville industrielle.** (Arvida on the Saguenay. The birth of an industrial town.)
José E. Igartua. Montréal; Kingston, Ontario: McGill-Queen's University Press, 1996. 273p.

Although Arvida's streets bear the names of the aluminium magnates who built the city, such as Andrew Mellon and Arthur Vining Davis (then president of Alcoa), the history of the workers who lived and worked there remains largely untold. Built by Alcoa, the largest aluminium producer in the world at the time, Arvida represents the significant and powerful role played by bourgeois industrialists at the turn of the century in the development of Québec's interior and its economy. Igartua blends two historical approaches: that concerned with regional under-development; and that labelled 'new social history', concerned with the lives of the working class. Aside from an account of the mind-boggling amount of planning that went into every aspect of the town's construction, the reader will be impressed by Igartua's detailed description of the people who lived there. This book is one of the finest examples of industrial and social history on Québec's recent past.

744 **Les parcs de Montréal des origines à nos jours.** (Montréal's parks from their origins to the present day.)
Jean de Laplante. Montréal: Éditions du Méridien, 1990. 255p.

A history of the Montréal parks network from the early 18th century to the late 1980s. In looking at the management of Montréal's parks, de Laplante discusses how their functions have changed over time. From simple green spaces to organized playing fields, Montréal has not escaped the greater North American trends governing park management. The book is organized chronologically, and begins with the proliferation of public squares during the 1840s. The city's acquisition and construction of larger parks between 1874 and the present day is examined in a chapter dealing with the Parc Lafontaine. The association of sports and park space during the early 20th century and into the 1950s is also discussed.

745 **Montréal in evolution: historical analysis of the development of Montréal's architecture and urban environment.**
Jean-Claude Marsan. Montréal; Kingston, Ontario: McGill-Queen's University Press, 1990. 456p. maps.

Reflections on Montréal's architectural development and urban evolution are intertwined with a discussion of the influences which contributed to these developments and evolution: namely, the limits imposed by geography and those imposed by humans in accordance with their needs, technologies, and ideologies. This work is divided into four sections: the first discusses the climate, substratum and soil characteristics of the city; the second deals with the pre-industrial period and the influence of French and British architecture; the third analyses the impact of the Industrial Revolution on economics, culture, and society; and the last section looks at 20th-century Montréal and contemporary projects (Place Ville Marie, Place Bonaventure and Place Victoria). This book is designed for the general public and provides an essential reference point for readers interested in the historical context of Montréal's environment. See also Guy Pinard's *Montréal: son histoire, son architecture* (Montréal: its history, its architecture) (Montréal: Éditions La Presse, 1987. 345p.).

746 **Montréal – tableaux d'un espace en transformation.** (Montréal essays on an area in transformation.)
Edited by Frank W. Remiggi, Gilles Sénécal. Montréal: ACFAS, 1992. 498p. maps.

In anticipation of Montréal's 350th birthday, this work presents the proceedings of the 57th Annual ACFAS (Association canadienne-française pour l'avancement des sciences) Conference whose principal theme was Montréal. Comprising thirty-four essays, this work is perhaps one of the few which unites an often scattered group of disciplines, each offering their unique perspective on the issues affecting – and afflicting – Montréal. An overarching theme of the work is Montréal's continual capacity for change and rebirth. In light of this, many of the texts discuss Montréal's urban development and territorial management.

747 **Revue Québécoise d'Urbanisme.** (Québec Urban Studies Review.)
Montréal: Association québécoise d'Urbanisme, 1987- . quarterly.

Formerly entitled *Contact*, this journal focuses primarily on urban policies. Another useful source is *Urban History Review = Revue d'Histoire Urbaine* (Ottawa: History Division, National Museum of Man, 1972- . 2 issues per year).

748 **Les bâtisseurs du siècle.** (Builders of the 20th century.)
Pierre Turgeon. Outremont, Québec: Lanctôt Éditeur, 1996. 195p.

Published on the occasion of the 100th anniversary of the Builders' Exchange of Montréal, this work is an illustrated presentation of Montréal's major construction projects completed between 1897 and 1996. Chapters are organized chronologically and present an uncritical analysis of the city's development from the perspective of those who built the railways, bridges and skyscrapers which mark Montréal's landscape. This book has been written for the general public.

Rural environment

749 **La désintégration des régions: le sous-développement durable au Québec.** (The disintegration of the regions: sustainable under-development in Québec.)
Charles Côté. Chicoutimi, Québec: Éditions JCL, 1991. 261p. maps.

A sociological evaluation of government policy and its effect on Québec's regions, focusing primarily on the Saguenay-Lac-Saint-Jean area. Re-evaluating economic and demographic data over the past twenty years, this work paints a picture of Québec's regions in the process of being systematically stripped of those human resources most needed for demographic and economic growth: a trend which produces under-development in many regions to the benefit of few others. The author reveals how current Québec policy in the health and social services sectors has led to counter-productive competition among regional municipalities who are fighting for the same scarce resources. This book was written for a wide audience. Related works include *Deux Québec dans un: rapport sur le développement social et démographique* (see item no. 373).

750   **Aménagement intégré des ressources et luttes en milieu rural.**
(Integrated resource planning and struggles in the rural milieu.)
Edited by Hugues Dionne.   Rimouski, Québec: GRIDEQ (Groupe de
Recherche interdisciplinaire en Développement de l'Est du Québec –
Interdisciplinary Research Group for the Development of Eastern
Québec), Université du Québec à Rimouski, 1983. 351p. (Cahiers du
GRIDEQ no. 11).

This work is the result of several years of research on popular movements in the
eastern part of Québec. In the wake of the Quiet Revolution, many local and regional
communities formed popular protest movements in reaction to state-centric development plans. These movements not only reacted against the intrusion of state planners,
but they also proposed their own solutions and articulated their own development
plans. This work presents a study and analysis of three endogenous regional movements, demonstrating that popular resistance to the state policy was not monolithic
and homogeneous. This work places their internal power struggles, democratic decision-making processes, and public positions *vis-à-vis* the state into context, illustrating
the diversity of regional political protest.

751   **Développement régional, État et groupes populaires.** (Regional
development, the state and popular movements.)
Alain-G. Gagnon.   Hull, Québec: Éditions Asticou, 1985. 286p.

Constitutes an important contribution to the study of Québec's regions, a field often
eclipsed by the wide perspectives of national and social debates in Québec. More
specifically, this work examines the development of three popular movements in the
Gaspésie and Bas-Saint-Laurent regions and attempts to situate their activity within
the social, political and administrative changes taking place in these regions during the
1970s and early 1980s. This work reveals the complexity of social relations at the
regional level, and the particular economic development conditions which produced
these movements. The author also examines relations between the state and regions
and concludes that these popular movements have helped to highlight the growing distance between the central state and local interests.

752   **Les partenaires du développement face aux défis du local.**
(Partners in development and local challenges.)
Edited by Christiane Gagnon, Juan-Luis Klein.   Chicoutimi, Québec:
Université du Québec à Chicoutimi, GRIR, 1992. 401p.

An important contribution to the study of local community development, this book
demonstrates the consequences of partnership in the 'New World Order'. Dealing with
such subjects as multinational powers, social rights and the creation of a new social
contract, the authors demonstrate both the advantages and disadvantages of various
local development strategies. Using empirical information, the authors illustrate the
challenges facing Québec's regions.

753 **Région, régionalisme et développement régional. Le cas de l'est du Québec.** (Region, regionalism and regional development. The case of eastern Québec.)
Bruno Jean, Danielle Lafontaine. Rimouski, Québec: GRIDEQ, Université du Québec à Rimouski, 1984. 358p. (Cahiers du GRIDEQ no. 14).

A diverse collection of essays dealing with the socio-economic and historical development of eastern Québec. The book contains no overarching argument other than to present the regional question as an inherently complex one, defying interpretation according to any single theory or any single discipline. The book is loosely organized into two sections: the first contains essays concerning regional economic structures and relations; the second discusses the social and political relations of the region.

754 **La pratique du développement régional.** (The art of regional development.)
Rimouski, Québec: GRIDEQ, Université du Québec à Rimouski, 1995. 134p. (Cahiers du GRIDEQ).

A series of essays dealing with the practice of regional development in Québec. Among the topics discussed are the history of regional development, planning, regionalization, and decentralization. This book also provides a general overview of the research undertaken on this topic in Québec.

755 **Le phénomène régional au Québec.** (The regional phenomenon in Québec.)
Edited by Marc-Urbain Proulx. Rimouski, Québec: Presses de l'Université du Québec, 1996. 317p.

Economic globalization presents a series of new challenges for Québec's regions whose solutions require more than economic and political analysis. This important collection of essays attempts to understand regionalism in Québec with regard to other disciplines such as geography, sociology, ethnology and history. The strength of the book is its multidisciplinary vision of the regional reality in Québec and its theoretical discussion of these issues.

756 **Le Québec rural dans tous ses états.** (Rural Québec under stress.)
Edited by Bernard Vachon. Montréal: Éditions du Boréal, 1991. 311p.

The authors of this collection believe that rural Québec is 'sick' due to neglect, exclusion, and proximity to urban life. They believe that rural coalitions and solidarity movements are the means by which Québec can develop into a post-industrial, post-economic society which would place a greater emphasis on individual development through collective action. The book discusses the social, historical and geographical context of the regions, analyses patterns of rural development, and proposes a new rural master plan.

Environmental protection

757 Gestion des ressources renouvelables: secteurs agricole et forestier.
(Management of renewable resources: agricultural and forestry
industries.)
Pierre Chevalier. Sainte-Foy, Québec: Télé-Université, 1993. 557p.
maps.
A descriptive piece of work on the various disruptions facing the agricultural and
forestry sectors. The author uses Québec as his main empirical case-study, providing
substantial information on the environmental situation in Québec.

758 Contre-temps. (Off-beat.)
Montréal: Coopérative d'Information et de Recherche écologiste du
Québec, 1984-95. 4 issues per year.
Focused on different environmental scandals and on alternative measures to protect
the environment. This journal was certainly the Québec publication which dealt the
most with the political question in relation to conservation.

**759 Le pouvoir du citoyen en environnement: guide d'intervention
québécois.** (The power of the citizen in environmental issues:
Québec action guide.)
Yves Corriveau, Andréanne Foucault. Montréal: VLB Éditeur, 1990.
425p.
A useful work for all of those interested in both the history of environmental
protection in Québec and the opportunities for the citizen to get involved. Following
an introduction to the major actors, the authors describe the different political and
judicial means that citizens can employ to oppose a project they believe to be potentially harmful to the environment. The book describes the tangled web of political
forums where environmental issues can be addressed. Moreover, this guide explains
the procedures of these forums and suggests how to use these opportunities for public
debate efficiently. The authors argue that the best way to defend a cause is to use both
political and judicial means. Also see *L'état de l'environnement au Québec: un bilan
des milieux agricole, forestier et aquatique* (The state of the environment in Québec:
an assessment of the agricultural, forestry and aquatic milieus), edited by Harvey
Linwood Mead (Montréal: Association canadienne-française pour l'Avancement des
Sciences, 1987. 212p.).

760 Franc-Vert.
Charlesbourg, Québec: Union québécoise pour la Conservation de la
Nature, 1991- . 6 issues per year.
Published six times a year, *Franc-Vert* is a journal on nature and environmental
questions, written for the general public. The majority of the articles it carries deal
with environmental protection in Québec.

761 **Instituer le développement durable: éthique de l'écodécision et sociologie de l'environnement.** (Institutionalizing sustainable development: ethics of environmental sociology and 'ecodecisions'.) Edited by José A. Prades, Robert Tessier, Jean-Guy Vaillancourt. Montréal: Fides, 1994. 310p.

Discusses how economic imperatives often conflict with environmental concerns. This collection of essays deals with the social, economic and political impacts of sustainable development. Special attention is paid to the problem of acid rain and to the environmental policies of Québec governments.

762 **Guide des sites naturels du Québec.** (Guide to natural sites in Québec.) Serge Tanguay. Waterloo, Ontario: M. Quintin, 1988. 251p. maps.

This simple and easy-to-use guide provides important information for amateur nature lovers. Each chapter covers a particular region and includes information on how to access the sites, descriptions of the sites, and the activities that can be practised there. The book includes maps and pictures.

763 **Des animaux malades de l'homme.** (Animals sick of man.) Claude Villeneuve. Sillery, Québec: Québec Science, 1983. 350p. maps.

The author suggests that economic decisions must be based on a deep knowledge of the state of the environment in Québec. In order for decisions which would be harmful to the environment to be avoided, this book presents the demographic and health conditions of a series of animals in Québec and the impact of man on their development. The book includes a large number of tables and statistical data that provide a good overview of the environmental situation in Québec with regard to animal conservation.

Education

General

764 **L'école détournée.** (Leading schools astray.)
Louis Balthazar, Jules Bélanger.   Montréal: Éditions du Boréal
Express, 1993. 169p.

These authors describe their personal solutions to the problems currently afflicting Québec's education system. They make a passionate argument in favour of including certain basic morals and values, and certain core disciplines, in the curriculum. Although the judgements and conclusions presented in this work are not supported by statistics, they represent an interpretation of what values should guide future education reforms. Also see Gaston Chalifoux's *L'école à recréer. Décrochage: réalités et défis* (Recreating school. Dropping out: realities and challenges) (Montréal: Éditions Saint-Martin, 1996. 169p.).

765 **L'enseignement spécialisé au Québec, 1867 à 1982.** (Technical
education in Québec, 1867 to 1982.)
Jean-Pierre Charland.   Québec: Institut québécois de Recherche sur
la Culture, 1982. 485p.

A historical examination of technical education in Québec, this work looks at two aspects of the technical education system: its history as a separate education system; and its history as it relates to society at large. The first two parts of this book chart the origins of technical education institutions through the initiatives of provincial and local governments, school commissions, and industrialists. The third section examines the role played by technical education in the government's larger plans of economic development. The last section examines the impact of the Parent Commission (see item no. 766) on the development of technical education.

766 **Report of the Royal Commission of Inquiry on Education in the Province of Québec.**
Commission royale d'Enquête sur l'Enseignement dans la Province de Québec. Québec: Gouvernement du Québec, 1967. 5 vols.

The most important study of education in modern-day Québec. The Commission royale d'enquête sur l'enseignement dans la province du Québec (Royal Commission of Inquiry on Education in the Province of Québec) was launched by Mgr. Alphonse-Marie Parent in 1961. This all-encompassing report elaborated upon the idea of a two-year 'junior college' system which was finally implemented in 1967 with the establishment of the first CEGEP (College d'enseignement général et professionel – school offering general and vocational education). The reader should also consult Guy Rocher's *Le Québec en mutation* (Québec in mutation) (Montréal: Éditions Hurtubise HMH, 1973. 345p.) and Rocher's defence of the Parent report in *Entre les rêves et l'histoire: entretiens avec Georges Khal* (Between dreams and history: conversations with Georges Khal) (Montréal: VLB Éditeur, 1989. 230p.).

767 **Les écoles de rang au Québec.** (Countryside schools in Québec.)
Jacques Dorion. Montréal: Éditions de l'Homme, 1979. 436p.

Small countryside schools were often the only community institution in the Québec 'rang' (line village), and they promoted an ideology inspired by religious and agrarian family values. Archival evidence of their existence is scarce and consequently this work draws on personal interviews and on correspondence between the Department of Public Instruction and the various municipalities in an attempt to provide a material and spiritual picture of what countryside schools were like. This book is divided into two parts: the first section describes the physical aspects of these schools, where they were situated, and how they were built, etc.; and the second examines the socio-economic characteristics of the teachers, their values, and their working conditions.

768 **L'éducation, 25 ans plus tard! Et après?** (Education twenty-five years later! And the future?)
Edited by Fernand Dumont, Yves Martin. Québec: Institut québécois de Recherche sur la Culture, 1990. 432p.

Provides a general overview of the major questions facing educators and students following twenty-five years of profound changes in the Québec educational system. Critical of the gradual bureaucratization of the school system, Dumont reflects on the growing inability of the public to judge the quality of their education system. This collection provides an assessment of the past quarter-century with an eye to the changes educational institutions will be required to make in the future if they are to remain learning institutions of quality. Topics covered include: cultural diversity and school organization; adult education; redefining the role of universities; the teaching of French and history; and the training of educators. These texts have been written with the general public in mind.

769 **Between past and future: Québec education in transition.**
Norman Henchey, Donald Burgess. Calgary, Alberta: Detselig Enterprises, 1987. 294p.

This is an excellent study of education in Québec from the 1960s to the mid-1980s. The topics include: social and historical contexts; the structure of elementary, secondary, post-secondary and adult education; the teaching profession; educational financing; and past and present policy issues. In suggesting policy concerns for the future, the authors show much sensitivity regarding the political dimension of Québec society. A number of useful appendices are included.

770 **Lois, structures et fonctionnement du milieu scolaire québécois.**
(Laws, structures and operation of the educational system in Québec.)
Directed by André Lemieux. Montréal: Éditions Nouvelles, 1995.
545p. (Collection Éducation).

A useful guide to the legal characteristics of the Québec educational system. Written especially for educators, this book contains the work of sixteen experts in the field. Topics include teacher training, the role and missions of the various educational sectors (primary, secondary, CEGEP [College d'enseignement général et professionel – school offering general and vocational education], and university), and the foundations of the education system in Québec from the French regime to the recent pedagogical changes of 1995. This is a very comprehensive work which is suitable for the student of education or the specialist. See also Robert Gagnon's *Histoire de la Commission des écoles catholiques de Montréal* (History of the Montréal Catholic School Board) (Montréal: Éditions du Boréal, 1996. 400p.).

771 **Education in New France.**
Roger Magnuson. Montréal; Kingston, Ontario: McGill-Queen's University Press, 1992. 223p. bibliog.

The school system at the time of the French regime faced many difficulties. Heir of a European tradition of education, the Church had to adapt to the presence of the aboriginal population which did not identify with this tradition. The Church also had to educate and prepare young men and women who would be useful and well-suited to the colony. This important work demonstrates that the Church was unable to create a coherent system of education. Instead, the informal character of the educational system fostered the diversity of various ways of learning.

772 **Le corps enseignant du Québec de 1845 à 1992: formation et développement.** (Québec teachers from 1845 to 1992: training and development.)
M'hammed Mellouki, François Melançon. Montréal: Éditions Logiques, 1995. 351p. bibliog.

A study of the development of the teaching profession in Québec's Protestant and Catholic school systems. This work discusses the education of teachers, their working conditions, their labour organizations, and their relationship with the administrative authorities of the times. The work also provides a comparison of the development of the two systems. A substantial bibliography and helpful tables complement the analysis. Readers should also consult Micheline Dumont and Nadia Fahmy-Eid's *Maîtresses de maison, maîtresses d'école* (Mistresses of the home, mistresses of the school) (Montréal: Éditions du Boréal, 1983. 413p.) for a study of the role of women in education. On women's education, see Dumont and Fahmy-Eid's *Les couventines. L'éducation des filles au Québec dans les congrégations religieuses enseignantes, 1840-1960* (Convent schoolgirls. The education of girls in Québec by religious teaching orders, 1840-1960) (Montréal: Éditions du Boréal, 1986. 315p.).

773 **The long road to reform: restructuring public education in Québec.**
Henry Milner. Montréal; Kingston, Ontario: McGill-Queen's
University Press, 1986. 165p.

Milner looks at the move towards sectarianism in the Québec school system and, more specifically, at the fate of the Parti québécois's 1982 White Paper on education. This plan proposed that individual schools be given considerable autonomy in place of the existing confessional school board organization. Milner documents the strong opposition to this proposal and the vested interests which erected formidable obstacles to educational reform during this period. He also examines the foundations of public education in Québec.

774 **Penser l'éducation: nouveaux dialogues avec André Laurendeau.**
(Thinking education: new conversations with André Laurendeau.)
Edited by Nadine Pirotte. Montréal: Éditions du Boréal, 1989. 233p.

This collection is the result of a colloquium that followed the twentieth anniversary of the death of André Laurendeau (1912-68). The collection undertakes an original investigation of Laurendeau's work, looking at Laurendeau's views on education from a humanist point of view. The second section of the book is particularly interesting: both Fernand Dumont and Charles Taylor provide commentaries on the intellectual traditions in Québec. Dumont makes an important distinction between an 'intellectual tradition' and a 'tradition of intellectuals'. The last two sections describe the ideal educational system based on Laurendeau's philosophy.

775 **Le système d'éducation du Québec.** (The educational system of
Québec.)
Edited by Micheline Poirier-Després, Philippe Dupuis. Montréal:
Gaëtan Morin Éditeur, 1995. 324p. bibliog.

A descriptive overview of the educational system in Québec. The author explores the history of education in Québec since New France, its administrative structures, and the main actors in the system. Emphasis is placed on the important documents that have shaped the world of education in Québec. The book includes a short bibliography after each section. See also *L'organisation de l'éducation au Québec: structure et fonctionnement* (Organization of education in Québec: structure and operation) (Laval, Québec: Agence d'Arc, 1992. 466p.), edited by André Lemieux.

776 **Les loups sont-ils québécois? Les mutations sociales à l'école
primaire.** (Are the big, bad wolves Quebecers? Social transformations
in primary school.)
Yuki Shiose. Sainte-Foy, Québec: Presses de l'Université Laval,
1995. 226p.

This work can be situated within the theoretical framework of cultural exclusion and inclusion; it examines this issue as it applies to Québec by examining a Catholic, francophone public school as a socializing institution. The book is divided into two parts: the first deals with the theory of cultural identity, inclusion, and exclusion as it relates to the education sector; and the second, drawing on government documents published since the Gendron Commission (a.k.a. the Commission d'enquête sur la situation de la langue française et sur les droits linguistiques au Québec – Commission of Inquiry on the Situation of the French Language and Linguistic Rights in Québec),

1968-72, compares the reality of francophone Catholic schools with the state's interpretation of cultural identity. The second section investigates one classroom and the
teacher-student relationships therein in order to construct the boundaries of cultural
exclusion and inclusion. For other works considering minorities see Linda Susan Khan's
Schooling, jobs, and cultural identity: minority education in Québec (New York:
Garland, 1992).

777 **Le Ministère de l'éducation et le Conseil supérieur.** (The
Department of Education and the High Council of Education.)
Arthur Tremblay, with the collaboration of Robert Blais, Marc Simard.
Sainte-Foy, Québec: Presses de l'Université Laval, 1989. 2 vols.
Québec did not have a Department of Education until 1964. This work, written by the
first Deputy Minister of Education, relates the different obstacles that faced the creation
of this Department from the time of Confederation to the beginning of the 1960s. The
authors demonstrate how the domination of the conservative elites in Québec hampered
the establishment of a centralized and secular school system in the province.

Higher education

778 **L'Université de Montréal. La quête du savoir.** (The University of
Montréal. The pursuit of knowledge.)
Hélène-Andrée Bizier.   Montréal: Éditions Libre Expression, 1993.
311p.
A general, illustrated overview of the history of the Université de Montréal which
highlights the major contributions made to the institution's evolution and its architectural transformations. The author describes the evolution of the educational
philosophy of the university, and the prevailing ideologies. The book includes a very
detailed chronology of the events that have marked the history of the university.

779 **Matériaux fragmentaires pour une histoire de l'UQAM: d'une
descente aux enfers à l'UQAM de l'an 2000.** (Fragments of material
towards a history of UQAM: from a descent into hell to UQAM of the
year 2000.)
Claude Corbo.   Montréal: Éditions Logiques, 1994. 367p.
The creation of UQAM (Université du Québec à Montréal – University of Québec at
Montréal) in the late 1960s was an important step towards the democratization of
Québec's university system. The author, a former principal of the university, relates
the different stages of the construction and development of UQAM. Based on his own
personal experience, Corbo underlines UQAM's originality while stressing the university's need for better government financing. For a wider perspective on UQAM's
emergence and development see Lucia Ferretti's *L'université en réseau. Les 25 ans de
l'Université du Québec* (The networked university. The past twenty-five years of the
Québec University system) (Sainte-Foy, Québec: Presses de l'Université du Québec,
1994. 328p.).

780 **Cinquante ans de sciences sociales à l'Université Laval: l'histoire de la Faculté des sciences sociales, 1938-1988.** (Fifty years of social sciences at Laval University: a history of the Faculty of Social Sciences, 1938-88.)
Edited by Albert Faucher.   Sainte-Foy, Québec: Université Laval, Faculté des Sciences sociales, 1988. 390p.

A collection of essays which traces the evolution of Laval University's Faculty of Social Sciences. Organized chronologically, this work examines the Faculty's institutional history from the perspective of teaching and research. Most of the essays focus on specific departments of the Faculty, their mandates, and their impact on Québec society, charting the importance of academic research in Québec's history. This book also brings out the significant role intellectuals had in Québec. For a more general history of Laval University as a whole, see Jean Hamelin's *Histoire de l'Université Laval: les péripéties d'une idée* (item no. 782).

781 **McGill University, for the advancement of learning.**
Stanley Brice Frost.   Montréal; Kingston, Ontario: McGill-Queen's University Press, 1980, 1984. 2 vols.

Esteemed historian Stanley Brice Frost has written extensively on the history of McGill University. Established in 1821, McGill is Montréal's oldest university. In two volumes, Frost chronicles the evolution and expansion of the University from its benefactor, Sir James McGill, to the turbulent 1960s, and culminating with the University's Sesquicentennial celebration in 1971. Frost is adept at including important contextual information, and relating the University's concomitant development with that of Montréal. Moreover, McGill's history is organized into chapters corresponding to the major events and stages of its rich heritage. A related work by the same author is *The man in the ivory tower. F. Cyril James of McGill* (Montréal; Kingston, Ontario: McGill-Queen's University Press, 1991. 314p.). In anticipation of its 175th anniversary, the University published a brief, illustrated introduction to its history, entitled *McGill, a celebration* (Montréal; Kingston, Ontario: McGill-Queen's University Press, 1991. 211p.). Edgar Andrew Collard edited a series of anecdotes from McGill graduates, professors and administrators, entitled *The McGill you knew. An anthology of memories, 1920-1960* (Don Mills, Ontario: Longman Canada, 1975. 269p.).

782 **Histoire de l'Université Laval: les péripéties d'une idée.** (The history of Laval University: the evolution of an idea.)
Jean Hamelin.   Sainte-Foy, Québec: Presses de l'Université Laval, 1995. 341p. bibliog.

Commissioned by graduates of Laval, this history is written in a narrative style designed for the general reader rather than for the professional historian. It is, however, the only complete history of the University and constitutes an important addition to the collective memory of the graduates, teachers and employees of Laval University. An impressive bibliography provides additional sources of information for the reader interested in specific aspects of the University.

783 **Histoire de l'École des hautes études commerciales de Montréal, tome 1: 1887-1926.** (A history of the School of Commercial Studies of Montréal, tome 1: 1887-1926.)
Pierre Harvey.   Montréal: Éditions Québec Amérique; Presses HÉC, 1994. 382p.

Established towards the end of the 19th century, Montréal's HÉC (l'École des hautes études commerciales – School of Commercial Studies), as it is commonly called, was an important instrument in the development of a francophone business class in Québec. Written by a former director of the HÉC, this volume relates the story of the school from its founding to 1926. The author presents the major events that shaped the school in those years: the creation of the Chambre de commerce de Montréal (Montréal Chamber of Commerce) and the origin of the idea of a francophone school of business; the choice of a location; and the process of affiliation with Laval University. The history of the school is presented mainly through the stories of important individuals who have shaped its past.

784 **L'université. Questions et défis.** (The University. Questions and challenges.)
Laurent Laplante.   Québec: Institut québécois de Recherche sur la Culture, 1988. 141p.

A journalist's perspective on the major issues facing Québec's universities, such as tuition fees, academic freedom, and the under-funding of Québec's universities. Overall, the author challenges the notion that Québec universities' largest problem is lack of funding. This is not meant to be an academic evaluation of university education but it does discuss many of the major challenges and questions relating to university education in Québec.

785 **Continuité et rupture: les sciences sociales au Québec.** (Continuity and rupture: social sciences in Québec.)
Edited by Georges-Henri Lévesque.   Montréal: Presses de l'Université de Montréal, 1984. 2 vols.

These two volumes are the result of an important symposium held in 1981 that brought together four generations of social scientists (from the 1930s to the 1980s) to discuss and assess the strengths and weaknesses of fifty years of research in economics, political science, sociology, history and other related disciplines. For the first time, the reader can appreciate the work of the intellectuals, professors and researchers who developed the teaching of the social sciences in Québec and their impact on Québec's social development.

786 **The science of social redemption. McGill, the Chicago School and the origins of social research in Canada.**
Marlene Shore.   Toronto: University of Toronto Press, 1987. 340p.

McGill University's Department of Sociology during the inter-war years serves as the background to Shore's attempt to discern how institutions shape the character of academic disciplines. This study seeks to examine the intellectual and social history of the times by examining issues such as the academic influence of the Chicago School, issues of academic freedom, and academic politics within the Department. In charting the evolution of the Department's intellectual content, Shore attempts to reveal the discipline's overlooked contributions to Canadian intellectual life.

Science and Technology

787 **La recherche sur l'innovation: une boîte de Pandore?** (Research on innovation: a Pandora's box?)
Edited by Lysette Boucher. Montréal: Association canadienne-française pour l'Avancement des Sciences, 1995. 261p.

Provides an account of the state of research and development in Québec. If the first two sections deal principally with theoretical consequences of technological innovations, the various authors make use of Québec firms as examples. The third section deals directly with the question of the environment surrounding the actors involved in research and industrial development. Among the topics dealt with are government intervention, productivity, and technological cooperation among different sectors in Québec and Canada.

788 **Histoire des sciences au Québec.** (A history of the sciences in Québec.)
Luc Chartrand, Raymond Duchesne, Yves Gingras. Montréal: Éditions du Boréal, 1987. 487p. bibliog.

Written for the non-specialist, this book provides a thorough history of the sciences in Québec from the surveyors and navigators of New France to contemporary physicists and neurologists. Institutions and scientists with both English and French backgrounds are considered in this study.

789 **La politique technologique au Québec.** (Québec's policy on technology.)
Edited by Robert Dalpé, Réjean Landry. Montréal: Presses de l'Université de Montréal, 1993. 247p. bibliog. (Collection Politique & Économie).

Analyses government intervention in the development and promotion of technological innovation in Québec. Increasingly targeted as a key to economic growth by post-industrial societies, technological innovation in Québec has experienced an expansion of government intervention. The content of this book is structured according to two goals: the first is to facilitate the public's understanding of government action in the area of technological innovation; and the second is to provide an assessment of government activity and the particular problems associated with the drafting and implementation of public policy. The first section looks at the way Québec industrialists use and have used technology, and the second contains essays which examine specific government actions over the past twenty years, covering such initiatives as the shift towards technology. Overall, this work achieves the feat of uniting both industrial and political analyses in the study of technological innovation.

790 **L'entrée dans la modernité. Science, culture et société au Québec.**
(Entering modernity. Science, culture and society in Québec.)
Marcel Fournier. Montréal: Éditions Saint-Martin, 1986. 246p.

Modernization in Québec has either been too fast for some, or too slow for others. Regardless, the process of modernization was the result of the efforts of men and women who gradually challenged the dominant forces. This interesting book by Marcel Fournier presents a portrait of five important intellectuals who, in their respective fields of research, contributed to the advent of Québec's modernization. The intellectuals examined are: Édouard Montpetit (1881-1954) (business), Frère Marie-Victorin (1855-1944) (biology), Father Georges-Henri Lévesque (b.1903) (social science), Jean-Charles Falardeau (b.1914) (social science), and Paul-Émile Borduas (1905-60) (fine arts). The author presents short biographies of these intellectuals, and descriptions of their philosophies and the impact they had on the intellectual landscape. This book provides a good overview of the evolution of science in Québec and of Québec society in general.

791 **Sciences et médecine au Québec: perspectives socio-historiques.**
(Science and medicine in Québec: socio-historical perspectives.)
Edited by Marcel Fournier, Yves Gingras, Othmar Keel. Québec:
Institut québécois de Recherche sur la Culture, 1987. 210p.

This collection of six essays adds to a growing body of literature on the social history of medicine and the sciences: the publication of this work seeks to redress the relative absence of academic research in this area. This collection attempts to provide a more nuanced portrait of the development of the sciences in Québec by demonstrating how different social, institutional, economic and political conditions favoured the emergence of different scientific practices. In addition, the authors seek to situate Québec's scientific development in the Canadian and international contexts. The following topics are examined: the relationship between ultramontanism, liberalism and science in education in the second half of the 19th century; the administrative, political and economic implementation of vaccinations in 19th-century Montréal; the social composition of students in the sciences in the first half of the 20th century; and an institutional analysis of the obstacles and development of the Montréal Cancer Institute.

792 **Histoire de l'École Polytechnique. La montée des ingénieurs**
francophones. (History of the Polytechnic. The rise of francophone engineers.)
Robert Gagnon. Montréal: Éditions du Boréal, 1991. 526p. bibliog.

Engineers have played a major role in the development of Québec's economy. In fact, the largest engineering firm in Canada has its headquarters in Québec. The success of these firms contributed, in turn, to the development and expansion of the Polytechnique, Québec's most important and renowned francophone school of engineering. Robert Gagnon relates the evolution of the Polytechnique from 1873 to 1990. This book has the merit of relating both the social context that contributed to the evolution of the school and the school's role in the creation of a new social group (i.e., francophone engineers).

793 **Les premières inventions québécoises.** (Québec's first inventions.)
Guy Giguère.   Outremont, Québec: Quebecor, 1994. 382p.

Provides a list and illustrations of inventions designed and built by Quebecers since 1824. For each invention, the author provides the name of the inventor, the year of its creation, and the place where it was invented.

794 **Pour l'avancement des sciences: histoire de l'ACFAS, 1923-1993.**
(For the advancement of science: a history of the ACFAS, 1923-93.)
Yves Gingras.   Montréal: Éditions du Boréal, 1994. 268p.

Challenging the widely held myth that Québec society was trapped in the dark ages until the Quiet Revolution, this work provides evidence to the contrary by examining the history of the ACFAS (Association canadienne-française pour l'avancement des sciences – French Canadian Association for the Advancement of Science). In the form of an institutional biography, this book looks at the central role played by this organization in developing and supporting the scientific and academic community in Québec, presents evidence from great Québec scientists and thinkers, and examines ACFAS' institutional links with other organizations. Also of interest is Gingras' conclusion that the achievements of the Quiet Revolution can be traced to thinkers and other scientific pioneers from thirty years earlier.

795 **Science, culture et nation.** (Science, culture and nation.)
Edited by Yves Gingras.   Montréal: Éditions du Boréal, 1996. 179p.

Well known for his book on Laurentian flora (see item no. 66) and credited with the establishment of Montréal's botanical gardens, the Frère Marie-Victorin was also one of Québec's most brilliant intellectual figures during the 1920s and 1930s. This collection of Marie-Victorin's essays, presented and edited by Yves Gingras, discuss various questions such as the history of science in Québec, the economic liberation of French-speaking Canadians, and the world of education. These essays reveal a radical thinker who had an important impact on Québec society at that time. For more information on Marie-Victorin, see Gilles Beaudet's *Frère Marie-Victorin* (Montréal: Lidec, 1985. 64p.). For a comprehensive synthesis of the history of scientific research in Canada, including Québec, see Gingras' *Physics and the rise of scientific research in Canada* (Montréal; Kingston, Ontario: McGill-Queen's University Press, 1991. 203p.).

796 **McGill medicine. Volume 1: the first half century, 1829-85.**
Joseph Hannaway, Richard Cruess.   Montréal; Kingston, Ontario: McGill-Queen's University Press, 1996. 219p.

A history of Canada's first medical school from its establishment in 1829 by four conservative Scottish physicians, to 1885 and the concomitant scientific and academic reforms in its teaching programme. By virtue of the comprehensive lists of graduates, faculty prize-winners, and biographical sketches of faculty members, this work offers a concise and unique reference tool to one of McGill's most notable faculties.

Moreover, this book is all the more unique thanks to the attention it devotes to the important changes in the way medicine was taught at McGill and, by extension, in Québec and Canada.

797 **SNC. Engineering beyond frontiers.**
Suzanne Lalande, translated by Dominique Clift. Montréal: Éditions Libre Expression, 1992. 280p.

SNC, now called SNC-Lavalin, based in Montréal, is the largest engineering firm in Canada and an important actor on the world stage. This book describes the evolution of the firm from its foundation in 1911 to its fusion with Lavalin at the beginning of the 1990s. The author focuses mainly on the important individuals and leaders in the development of SNC and on their values and ambitions. The book also closely examines the company's particular management style and its specific qualities.

798 **Les dynamismes de la recherche au Québec.** (The dynamics of research in Québec.)
Edited by Jacques Mathieu. Québec: Presses de l'Université Laval, 1991. 272p.

A collection of sixteen essays which examines the evolution and current state of scientific research in Québec in the social sciences and humanities; the authors argue that scientific research is never completely isolated from its environment. Despite the varied academic backgrounds of the authors, they each contribute to a more general understanding of how sociocultural factors affect the conditions under which research is conducted in Québec.

799 **Les chercheurs de la mer. Les débuts de la recherche en océanographie et en biologie des pêches du Saint-Laurent.**
(Researchers of the sea. The beginnings of oceanography and fisheries biology in the Saint-Lawrence.)
Jacques Saint-Pierre. Québec: Institut québécois de Recherche sur la Culture, 1994. 255p. bibliog.

Québec has a long tradition of studying the sea and its denizens. This book presents the evolution of oceanographic research in Québec from the 1920s to the 1960s. Arguing that research had a deep impact on fishing techniques, the author demonstrates how oceanographic research in Québec has changed from having a fundamentalist approach to being more oriented towards economic imperatives. A comprehensive bibliography is included.

800 **John William Dawson. Faith, hope, and science.**
Susan Sheets-Pyenson. Montréal; Kingston, Ontario: McGill-Queen's University Press, 1996. 274p.

While this book focuses on Dawson 'the scientist', it also chronicles his brilliant career as educator, administrator, palaeontologist, and geologist. Dawson spent thirty-eight years as Principal of McGill University during which time the University experienced a surge of academic growth and reputation. Over the course of a decade, Sheets-Pyenson canvassed and analysed thousands of letters, articles, books, minutes and other records to write what is the most definitive biography of the man credited with transforming McGill into 'the Canadian Oxford'. Moreover, the author's research reveals the important role Dawson played in putting Montréal on the scientific map. As he extended McGill's 'scientific fortunes' he also brought fame and fortune to the Natural History Society of Montréal. Dawson himself wrote an autobiography, *Fifty years of work in Canada, scientific and educational* (London, Edinburgh: Ballantyne, Hanson & Co., 1901. 308p.). Another biography of Dawson is Charles F. O'Brien's *Sir William Dawson: a life in science and religion* (Philadelphia: American Philosophical Society, 1971. 207p.).

801 **L'aventure de la fusion nucléaire au Québec: la politique de la *Big Science* au Québec.** (The adventure of nuclear fusion in Québec: the politics of Big Science in Québec.)
Michel Trépanier. Montréal: Éditions du Boréal, 1995. 304p.

Research on nuclear fusion occupies an important place in Québec, particularly since the construction of the tokamak, a powerful instrument used in the study of nuclear fusion. The author argues that this project is a good example of the evolution of research since the Second World War: it represents the dependence of the scientific community on the government for funds to pursue its projects. The author believes that the main effects of this dependence are the necessity for scientists to adapt to the government's priorities and the creation of a scientific lobby group that tries to 'sell' their projects to the population.

Literature

Reference

802 **La littérature québécoise du XXe siècle.** (Québec literature during the 20th century.)
Luc Bouvier, Max Roy.   Montréal: Guérin, 1996. 499p.

This introduction to 20th-century Québec literature brings together approximately 100 representative texts, including poems, songs, essays and plays, in a practical anthology containing biographical notes, reading suggestions and introductions to each section. The book is intended to introduce readers to Québec authors.

803 **Anthologie de la nouvelle et du conte fantastiques québécois au XXe siècle.** (An anthology of fantastic short stories and tales in 20th-century Québec.)
Edited by Maurice Émond.   Montréal: Fides, 1987. 276p.

This compact anthology is the first devoted exclusively to the genre of the fantastic such as it is practised in Québec. Twelve authors and twenty texts are covered by the anthology. It takes into account the fascination of this genre among readers and Québec short story writers/tellers. The book also considers the transformation of this genre while in contact with a society which feeds upon its own anxieties and fantasies.

804 **Littérature canadienne-française et québécoise, anthologie critique.** (French Canadian and Québec literature, a critical anthology.)
Michel Erman.   Montréal: Éditions Beauchemin, 1992. 592p.

A historical and critical anthology which aims to offer not only a general overview of various themes in French Canadian and Québec literature, but also to present extracts of works which correspond to intrinsic literary criteria. The sections of the book, divided into literary genres, underline the evolution of this literature as it oscillated between its European and North American influences.

805   Études Françaises. (French Studies.)
Montréal: Presses de l'Université de Montréal, 1965- . 3 issues per
year.
A scholarly journal dealing with French Canadian literature and French literature.

806   **Le roman contemporain au Québec, 1960-1985.** (The contemporary
novel in Québec, 1960-85.)
Edited by François Gallays, Sylvain Simard, Robert Vigneault.
Ottawa: Centre de Recherche en Civilisation canadienne-française,
University of Ottawa; Montréal: Fides, 1992. 548p. bibliog.
(Archives des Lettres Canadiennes).
The scope of studies offered in this latest volume from the 'Archives des lettres
canadiennes' (Archive of Canadian Literature) series reflects the diversity and prodigious
acceleration in the production of Québec novels after 1960. Even though the majority
of articles concern either a rereading and critical review of a specific novel or novelist,
or a sort of reading/synthesis of a specific work, there are three general articles which
contextualize the novel in question in the period it was written. This volume contains
a chronological bibliography of Québec novels published each year from 1970-85.

807   **Écrivains contemporains du Québec depuis 1950.** (Contemporary
writers of Québec since 1950.)
Lise Gauvin, Gaston Miron.   Paris: P. Sehhers, 1989. 579p. bibliog.
The first anthology in France to present an impressive number of francophone Québec
writers, poets, novelists, playwrights, and literary essayists. It covers the period from
1950 to 1980. The passages are organized alphabetically by author, along with
biographical notes. Lists of authors' works are included at the end of the anthology.

808   **Dictionnaire des auteurs de langue française en Amérique du
Nord.** (Dictionary of French-language authors in North America.)
Réginald Hamel, John Hare, Paul Wyczynski.   Montréal: Fides, 1989.
rev. ed. 1,364p.
This updated and enlarged edition presents clear information on over 1,600 francophone authors in North America. The dictionary is in large part devoted to
French-language authors from Québec, Acadia, Ontario, Western Canada and a certain
number of Franco-American and Louisiana authors. The succinct biographical notes
and chronological organization allow for quick consultation.

809   **Romanciers immigrés: biographies et œuvres publiées au Québec
entre 1970 et 1990.** (Immigrant novelists: biographies and works
published in Québec between 1970 and 1990.)
Denise Helly, Anne Vassal.   Québec: Institut québécois de Recherche
sur la Culture, Centre interuniversitaire d'Analyse du Discours et
Sociocritique des Textes, 1993. 122p.
This bio-bibliographical dictionary deals with immigrant novelists in Québec from
1970 to 1990. Information on 140 writers, and some 400 works, is organized according
to whether the authors have: written novels or collections of short stories; immigrated

to Québec or to another province in Canada; published at least one novel or collection of short stories in Québec; published in Québec between 1970 and 1990; and published in English and French.

810 **Le Québec, 1830-1939: bibliographie thématique: histoire et littérature.** (Québec, 1830-1939: thematic bibliography: history and literature.)
Robert Lahaise. LaSalle, Québec: Éditions Hurtubise HMH, 1990. 173p.

Lahaise presents a bibliography on Québec, exploring history and literature. He provides a vivid historical study, and a literary essay which situates writers and works in their socio-historical contexts. This is a very innovative interdisciplinary bibliography. (Two other bibliographies will follow, covering the colonial period, 1534-1830, and contemporary Québec, 1939 to the present.)

811 **Dictionnaire des œuvres littéraires du Québec.** (A dictionary of literary works from Québec.)
Edited by Maurice Lemire. Montréal: Fides, 1978-87. 6 vols.

In addition to reflecting on the literary climate across different periods, this dictionary aims to establish the corpus of works and to provide first-hand bibliographical information on Québec production. There are six volumes, covering the following periods: origins to 1900; 1900-39; 1940-59; 1960-69; 1970-75; and 1976-80. Each volume contains analyses of works, biographical notes and bibliographical references. This is a fundamental research tool; the dictionary provides a significant amount of information and stimulates research by providing a key to understanding the development of literary and meta-literary discourse in Québec.

812 **Liberté.** (Liberty.)
Montréal: Liberté, 1959- . monthly.

Founded in 1959, *Liberté* is a literary review that showcases short novels, poems, current debates, and book reviews. Identified with the secularization movement in the 1960s, *Liberté* has continued to concern itself with the many intellectual debates in Québec. Prior to 1962, *Liberté* was published bi-monthly.

813 **Anthologie de la littérature québécoise.** (Anthology of Québec literature.)
Edited by Gilles Marcotte. Montréal: L'Hexagone, 1994. 2 vols.

This anthology espouses the idea that, in order to present an accurate portrait of Québec literature, one must examine, in addition to French Canadian works published after the 19th century, works published prior to the 19th century, despite their status which has often been considered non-literary. By examining older works which have traditionally fallen well beyond what has properly been considered 'literature' in a modern sense, we are able to observe signs of a tradition upon which rest contemporary literary movements in Québec. The work is divided into two volumes and four parts: 'Écrits de la Nouvelle France: 1534-1760'; 'La Patrie littéraire: 1760-1895'; 'Vaisseau d'or et croix du chemin: 1895-1935'; and 'L'âge de l'interrogation: 1937-1952'. Each section places the literary motivation behind the writings in historical context.

814 **Moebius.**
Montréal: Éditions Triptyque, 1977- . quarterly.

A review meant to awake, animate and stimulate Québec's cultural universe. Its pages are open to creation, essays and opinions relating to literature both from Québec and from further afield. Past thematic issues include: *The writers*, on migrant writers in Québec; and *Between risk and violence*, on feminist writing in Québec.

815 **Nuit Blanche.** (Sleepless Night.)
Québec: s.n., 1982- . quarterly.

A journal whose articles deal with modern 20th-century Québec literature. It publishes book reviews, history and criticism.

816 **Stop.**
Montréal: PAJE, 1986- . quarterly.

Published four times a year, *Stop* is a journal dedicated to French Canadian prose. This journal favours 'personal, inventive and free' writing; it often publishes work by young and promising authors. Also see *XYZ* (Montréal: XYZ, 1985- . quarterly), another quality prose journal.

817 **Chronologie littéraire du Québec.** (A literary chronology of Québec.)
Sylvie Tellier. Québec: Institut québécois de Recherche sur la Culture, 1982. 352p. (Instruments de Travail, no. 6).

This repertory constitutes a substantial instrument for the DOLQ (Dictionnaire des œuvres littéraires au Québec – Dictionary of literary works in Québec). Three main parts cover the periods, 1761-1899, 1900-39, and 1940-59. Each section is divided into four categories of major literary genres: the novel, theatre, poetry, and the essay. This chronological guide allows the reader to observe, over the course of Québec's literary history, the strong periods of certain subjects and the spreading of ideologies.

818 **Voix et Images.** (Voice and Images.)
Montréal: Presses de l'Université du Québec, 1975- . quarterly.

A scholarly journal devoted entirely to French Canadian literature.

819 **Littérature québécoise. Des origines à nos jours. Textes et méthode.** (Québec literature from its origins to the present: texts and method.)
Edited by Heinz Weinmann, Roger Chamberland. Montréal: Éditions Hurtubise HMH, 1996. 350p.

Covers the history of francophone literature in Québec from its origins until the present. The book takes a pedagogical approach, and includes elements such as a constant association of literary works and artistic works, historical references and numerous pedagogical tools, such as methodological guidelines and lexicons. The book creates an 'intertextuality' which compares extracts from Québec French-language literature with extracts from the works of other francophone authors. There are many colour illustrations and photographs, which complement the perspective offered by the texts.

General

820 **Naissance d'une littérature: essai sur le messianisme et les débuts de la littérature canadienne-française, 1850-1890.** (The birth of a literature: an essay on Messianism and the beginnings of French Canadian literature, 1850-90.)
Réjean Beaudoin. Montréal: Éditions du Boréal, 1989. 209p.

Beaudoin's study explores the following questions: how literature was considered in the second half of the 19th century, during which time the first 'national' works were written; expectations of literary discourse; and what writing meant to the first Québec writers. This book offers a new and personal look at Québec's literary tradition, contributing to a better understanding of Québec literature today. For a more general survey of Québec's 19th-century literature, see *Les meilleurs romans québécois du XIXe siècle* (The best Québec novels of the 19th century), edited by Gilles Dorion (Montréal: Fides, 1996. 2 vols.).

821 **Mélanges de littérature canadienne-française et québécoise offerts à Réjean Robidoux.** (A selection of French Canadian and Québec literature in honour of Réjean Robidoux.)
Edited by Yolande Grisé, Robert Major. Ottawa: Presses de l'Université d'Ottawa, 1992. 430p.

This book contains a collection of both critical and original texts, all linked to, or representing, French Canadian and Québec literature. It was published in honour of Réjean Robidoux, whose areas of interest in research were so diverse. Written by various specialists in Québec literature – Gabrielle Roy and Émile Nelligan being at the forefront – many of the texts included in this work shed light on some elements and constants of this diversity. Others examine the historical period of the beginnings of French Canadian literature, which was the object of Robidoux's first forays into literary research. This panorama of studies covers a broad spectrum of Québec literature from the end of the 19th century to the present.

822 **Je me souviens. La littérature personnelle au Québec, 1860-1980.** (I remember. Personal literature in Québec, 1860-1980.)
Yvan Lamonde. Québec: Institut québécois de Recherche sur la Culture, 1983. 278p. bibliog.

Lamonde explores the collective experience of memory in a province whose motto is 'Je me souviens' (I remember). This work examines specific literary genres of 'personal' literature in Québec, including the personal journal, memoirs and the autobiography. An extensive analytical bibliography of personal documents from Québec is included to cover the period 1860-1980. This selection is intended to reveal how Quebecers went about recounting their personal and collective experiences.

823 **L'institution littéraire.** (The institution of literature.)
Maurice Lemire. Québec: Institut québécois de Recherche sur la
Culture, 1986. 217p.

Based on a colloquium held in 1985, this book aims to probe the coming of age of
Québec literature with respect to French literature and the process of the institutionalization of literature insofar as it has played a cultural role. Moreover, the very notion
of literature as an institution is studied. The existence and identity of Québec literature
in the 19th and 20th centuries is also analysed. A very pertinent compilation of studies
is included, which naturally leads to discussions on the survival and flourishing of
'minor literatures' written in international languages.

824 **La littérature québécoise en projet.** (Québec literature: a work in
progress.)
Maurice Lemire. Montréal: Fides, 1993. 277p.

Lemire analyses the changes occurring in literature in Québec during the 1840s and
the 1850s. Reconstructing a sketch of the era, he shows how significant these decades
were for the future. In his analysis, he looks at the idea of a national literature, the
relationships between art and morals and both so-called 'legitimate' and 'illegitimate'
genres.

825 **La vie littéraire au Québec.** (Literary life in Québec.)
Edited by Maurice Lemire, Aurélien Boivin et al. Sainte-Foy,
Québec: Presses de l'Université Laval, 1991-96. 3 vols.

A reference tool of a scientific nature. The three volumes aim to explore the phenomenon
of literature in Québec, not only by examining the texts themselves, but also by
exploring the process of their production and the conditions defining their reception.
This is a three-part literary history of Québec literature, which is concerned first of all
with studying the conditions of its emergence and of the development by which the literature acquired its social recognition. Each volume covers a different period:
1764-1805; 1806-39; and 1840-69. These three volumes provide an excellent resource,
pertaining to the conditions defining Québec literature.

826 **La littérature pour la jeunesse au Québec.** (Children's literature in
Québec.)
Édith Madore. Montréal: Éditions du Boréal, 1994. 126p. bibliog.

Madore aims to fill the gap in the research carried out on this young literary tradition
in Québec, children's literature. The aim of the first part of the book is to examine the
history of children's literature in Québec from the 1920s to the present. The second
part looks at the works of major authors of this genre. The book is extremely concise
and very informative. The bibliography and annexes which list collections and editors
are also very helpful, in that they help to further consolidate the presence of this
genre.

827 **Les 100 romans québécois qu'il faut lire.** (The 100 Québec novels that must be read.)
Jacques Martineau. Montréal: Nuit Blanche Éditeur, 1994. 153p.

This compact guide is useful for students and academics, as well as general readers with an interest in Québec novels, who want to familiarize themselves with a body of work which is expanding at a rate of more than 200 titles a year. This guide meticulously aims to provide the reader with a means of choice. Each novel is characterized in various ways according to the nature of the story, the style, the theme, etc.

828 **Littérature et société: anthologie.** (Literature and society: anthology.)
Edited by Jacques Pelletier, Jean-François Chassay, Lucie Robert.
Montréal: VLB Éditeur, 1994. 446p.

This anthology contains important essays dealing with the relationship between literature and society. There is significant variety in the texts; included are some well-known analyses by the 'founders' of literary sociology, such as Lukács, Goldmann, Sartre, Auerbach and Bakhtine. This work also contains more recent articles on social discourse analysis, sociocriticism, the study of the literature as an institution, and new feminist perspectives. It is addressed to anyone interested in the social meaning of works of fiction.

829 **Le poids de l'histoire: littérature, idéologies, société du Québec moderne.** (The weight of history: literature, ideologies, modern Québec society.)
Jacques Pelletier. Montréal: Nuit Blanche Éditeur, 1995. 346p.

The studies presented in this book aim to answer how the bonds between literature and society were established over the long period extending from the mid-1930s to the 1980s, the era which marks Québec's initiation into what has come to be called 'modernity'. Pelletier examines literature in terms of a social phenomenon arising from critical historical moments. Among the subjects he studies are the novel from the Duplessis era and the Quiet Revolution, and avant-garde art and poetry from 1970 to 1980. He considers these texts as 'dynamic factors' in a living culture of which they constitute a part – expressions of the social discourse from which they are drawn and which they nourish from within.

830 **L'institution du littéraire au Québec.** (Literature as an institution in Québec.)
Lucie Robert. Québec: Presses de l'Université Laval, 1989. 272p.

Confining her study to the Québec context, Robert examines the relationship between the written text and 'literature', looking at the canonization process which transforms a text into literature. The corpus that Robert studies includes mainly newspaper and journal articles which may be characterized by their non-literary status. She examines issues relating to the concept of literature as an institution in the public arena and the triumph of the written word.

831 **Fonder une littérature nationale: notes d'histoire littéraire.** (Founding a national literature: notes on literary history.)
Réjean Robidoux. Ottawa: Éditions David, 1994. 208p.
Published in this volume are texts which reflect the great passion of Réjean Robidoux: 19th-century Québec literature. These essays, or notes and quoted passages, examine: the publications, *Les Soirées Canadiennes* (Canadian Evenings) and *Le Foyer Canadien* (Canadian Home), in the Québec literary movement of the 1860s; and the writers, abbé Casgrain and Octave Crémazie. The reader will notice Robidoux's appreciation for the religious and political approaches of the authors and texts studied.

832 **Chronique d'une académie: 1944-1994: de l'Académie canadienne-française à l'Académie des lettres du Québec.**
(Chronicle of an academy, 1944-94: from the Académie canadienne-française [French Canadian Academy] to the Académie des lettres du Québec [Québec Academy of Letters].)
Jean Royer. Montréal: L'Hexagone, 1995. 150p.
This book chronicles the life and activities (e.g. verbal proceedings) of the Académie des lettres du Québec (Québec Academy of Letters) between 1944 and 1994. Based on meticulous research of the Academy's archives, this book provides a historical portrait of the institution which is at the core of Québec's literary existence and production. Jean Royer deciphers, analyses, and summarizes the facts and gestures of the academics recorded in the verbal proceedings of the first half-century of the institution's existence. Such a chronicle is a useful resource for understanding the literary life of modern Québec. Comprehensive appendices contain names of members, Academy records, annual colloquia and current publications.

833 **Développement et rayonnement de la littérature québécoise.**
(The development and the influence of Québec literature.)
Edited by the Union des écrivaines et écrivains québécois. Québec: Nuit Blanche Éditeur, 1994. 444p.
Comprises the proceedings of a major conference on the influence of Québec's literature, edited by the Union of Québec Writers. Writers, editors, publishers, journalists, librarians and others discussed, over the course of this conference, all aspects of the industry from literary creation to reviews. Fifty essays are divided into five sections on the following themes: the distinct character of Québec literature; the distribution of, and the growing influence of the media on, Québec literature; the evolution of the writer; the future of reading; and the book industry.

Criticism

834 **Traverses de la critique littéraire au Québec.** (An overview of
literary criticism in Québec.)
Jacques Allard. Montréal: Éditions du Boréal, 1991. 212p.

The essays contained in this book deal with the 'critical space' in Québec. Allard
provides a brief history of literary criticism in Québec, and examines recent studies on
the literary individual or critic in Québec. Finally, he studies criticism as its own
object of criticism. For a critical view of the latest literary output see Allard's *Roman
mauve: microlectures de la fiction au Québec* (Violet novel: micro-readings of Québec
novels) (Montréal: Éditions Québec Amérique, 1997. 392p.).

835 **Écrire le Québec: de la contrainte à la contrariété: essai sur la
constitution des lettres.** (Writing about Québec: from constraints to
annoyance: an essay on the constitution of literature.)
Bernard Andrès. Montréal: XYZ, 1990. 225p. bibliog. (Collection
Études et Documents).

The essays contained in this work borrow from the study of narration (narratology),
institutional analysis and comparative studies; they focus on literature as an institution
in Québec. An extensive bibliography of critical works is included.

836 **Le roman québécois.** (The Québec novel.)
Réjean Beaudoin. Montréal: Éditions du Boréal, 1991. 125p.

This is a concise and pertinent text. Beaudoin sketches a brief history of the Québec
novel since the 19th century, drawing parallels with the European novel. Then follows
a thematic classification of particular works, which links the concepts of the individual,
the group, territory and space. Finally, Beaudoin tackles the field of criticism and
studies the place occupied by the novel in the publishing industry.

837 **Anthologie de la poésie des femmes au Québec.** (An anthology of
Québec poetry written by women.)
Edited by Nicole Brossard, Lisette Girouard. Montréal: Éditions du
Remue-Ménage, 1991. 400p.

The first anthology of Québec women's poetry. Poems are organized according to the
generation of the authors. On average, two or three poems follow a short biography of
each author. This collection is comprehensive and includes poems by many lesser-
known poets.

838 **Une société, un récit: discours culturel au Québec, 1967-1976:
essai.** (One society, one account: cultural discourse in Québec,
1967-76: an essay.)
Micheline Cambron. Montréal: L'Hexagone, 1989. 201p.

Cambron remarks that contemporary Western society has an essentially paradoxical
vision of the narrative. She explores the complexity of this paradox within Québec
society. Various narratives are analysed, such as songs by Beau Dommage, plays by
Michel Tremblay and a novel by Réjean Ducharme. Influenced by Jean-François

Lyotard, the author of *La condition postmoderne* (The post-modern condition) (Manchester, England: Manchester University Press, 1984), Cambron probes the narrative as a social and critical phenomenon in the post-modern vein.

839 **L'âge de la prose: romans et récits québécois des années 80.**
(The age of prose: Québec novels and texts from the 1980s.)
Edited by Lise Gauvin, Franca Marcato-Falzoni. Rome: Bulzoni;
Montréal: VLB Éditeur, 1992. 229p. (Quattro Continenti, no. 10).

The studies in this compilation deal with the decade bounded by two major historical events: the rejection of the Referendum sovereignty proposals in 1980 and the failed Meech Lake Accord in 1990. The diversity and heterogeneity of these studies, by authors and professors from both Québec and Italy, reflect and espouse the variety in Québec's literature during this decade: the overlap between genres; the recurring role of the author as a character in the novel; and the evolution of language as a literary vehicle reflecting a modern literary climate.

840 **Le voleur de parcours: identité et cosmopolitanisme dans la littérature québécoise contemporaine.** (Crossing distances: identity and cosmopolitanism in contemporary Québec literature.)
Simon Harel. Longueuil, Québec: Le Préambule, 1989. 309p.

Harel's essay studies cosmopolitanism in Montréal and the representation of the foreigner in the Québec novel since 1960. All the novels studied grapple with the problem of identity. This essay can be considered to be the 'construction' of the future of the Québec identity as projected by the study of a few key novels. The foreigner is also observed as a constructed representation. A Freudian psychoanalytical approach is used in this interpretation.

841 **Critique et littérature québécoise. Critique de la littérature/littérature de la critique.** (Criticism and Québec literature. Criticism of literature/literature of criticism.)
Edited by Annette Hayward, Agnès Whitfield. Montréal: Éditions Triptyque, 1992. 422p.

A compilation of papers presented at a colloquium entitled 'Critique de la littérature/Littérature de la critique' (Criticism of literature/Literature of criticism), held at Queen's University, Kingston, in November 1990. Twenty-eight specialists in Québec literature look at questions such as: how literary criticism is defined; what role it has played within the Québec literary establishment; how the impact of historical conditions on its practice can be evaluated; whether creative writing and criticism are incompatible; and how future paths are envisaged. The questions and reflections presented are probing, insightful, dynamic and contemporary. They incite the reader to pursue this debate through creative and critical reading. See also Nicole Fortin's *Une littérature inventée: littérature québécoise et critique universitaire, 1965-1975* (An invented literature: Québec literature and university criticism, 1965-75) (Sainte-Foy, Québec: Presses de l'Université Laval, 1994. 353p.).

842   **Le roman québécois de 1960 à 1975: idéologie et représentation littéraire.** (The Québec novel from 1960 to 1975: literary ideology and representation.)
Jósef Kwaterko.   Montréal: Éditions du Préambule, 1989. 268p. bibliog.

A study of the relationship between the ideological and the literary discourses during a transitional period in which both ideology in Québec and the field of literature underwent profound transformations. The methodology adopted here is largely defined by sociocriticism. In the first section, the author studies the conditions surrounding the publication of novels in Québec between 1960 and 1975. In the second section, he analyses the discourse in six novels by five Québec novelists: Gérard Bessette, Hubert Aquin, Jacques Godbout, Marie-Claire Blais and Jacques Ferron. A very extensive bibliography is included, which is especially good in the areas of general critical theory and studies in Québec.

843   **En quête du roman gothique québécois, 1837-1860: tradition littéraire et imaginaire romanesque.** (In search of the gothic novel in Québec, 1837-60: literary tradition and imagination in the novel.)
Michel Lord.   Québec: Université Laval, Centre de Recherche en Littérature québécoise, 1985. 155p.

Lord studies the gothic tradition insofar as it infiltrated the novel of Lower Canada between 1837 and 1860. His methodological approach of studying the 'archetypology' of the decor and the characters in novels is influenced by Northrop Frye – *The anatomy of criticism* (Harmondsworth, England: Penguin, 1957). Lord studies: the problem of the hero; the problem of the villain, and the extent to which he is linked to his surrounding environment; the archetypes of the victim; and how the works studied, which adhere to the gothic tradition, actually respond to a deep cultural need. This work includes a very useful glossary of critical terms, which helps the reader to understand the technical analysis.

844   **La logique de l'impossible: aspects du discours fantastique québécois.** (The logic of the impossible: aspects of the Québec fantastic discourse.)
Michel Lord.   Montréal: Nuit Blanche Éditeur, 1995. 360p.

The main question that Lord attempts to answer is: 'What makes a text fantastic?'. After outlining the history of the genre, the author analyses short stories written by contemporary Québec writers and then proposes a functional model of the fantastic text. This analysis provides a clear explanation of the narrative and descriptive systems which define the genre. The fantastic text is described as a written construction of the appearance of a strange phenomenon, which would be improbable according to the principle of reality. This essay is a very interesting theoretical study of a literary genre.

845   **Ouvrir le livre: essais.** (Opening the book: essays.)
Laurent Mailhot.   Montréal: L'Hexagone, 1992. 354p.

A collection of essays on diverse forms and aspects of Québec literature, which have already appeared in other books or reviews. Topics studied include poetry, the novel since 1960, the genre of the essay, the development of theatre and the foreign reception of Québec literature.

846   **The American dream in nineteenth-century Québec, ideologies and utopia in Gérin-Lajoie's 'Jean Rivard'.**
Robert Major.   Toronto: University of Toronto Press, 1996. 272p.

This study of Antoine Gérin-Lajoie's novel, *Jean Rivard*, explores two dimensions of the profound American nature which it reveals. Major analyses the ideology of the American utopia or 'success story' insofar as it is a theme animating this novel. The second stage of the analysis explores the actual representation of the American story through the novel. In this second stage of the study, Major considers this novel as an American success story, which by definition 'acts out' and represents the theme. Throughout this literary analysis, the author looks at the historical climate surrounding the novel, as well as various American references. On the relationship of the Québec novel with American society see Jean-François Chassay's *L'ambiguité américaine: le roman québécois face aux États-Unis* (The American ambiguity: the Québec novel and the United States) (Montréal: XYZ, 1995. 197p.).

847   **Littérature et circonstances: essais.** (Literature and circumstances: essays.)
Gilles Marcotte.   Montréal: L'Hexagone, 1989. 350p.

In the first section of this series of essays, Marcotte studies the emergence of various ideologies in Québec, explores the concept and impact of the institution of literature, and examines major themes in Québec novels. In the second section, he looks at several Québec writers and their personal literary endeavours. These essays cover both general and specific topics.

848   **Une littérature qui se fait. Essais critiques sur la littérature canadienne-française.** (A literature in progress. Critical essays on French Canadian literature.)
Gilles Marcotte.   Montréal: Bibliothèque Québécoise, 1994. 348p.

An updated edition of a book which was first published in 1962. It is a collection of critical essays on the poetry and novels of Québec which, during the Quiet Revolution, were considered to represent an impoverished literature compared to the literature of France. Nevertheless, Marcotte chose Québec literature as the object of his study, to glorify its so-called imperfection and value its 'testimonial' quality. Through his study, Marcotte is able to enter into a sort of dialogue with this literature. Attitudes in Québec and beyond towards Québec literature have changed, but that of Gilles Marcotte has never faltered. This book remains an innovative critical study which recognizes and appreciates the literary talent of Québec.

849   **Le roman à l'imparfait: la 'Révolution tranquille' du roman québécois: essais.** (The imperfect novel: the 'Quiet Revolution' of the Québec novel: essays.)
Gilles Marcotte.   Montréal: L'Hexagone, 1989. new, updated ed. 257p.

Marcotte studies novels written by five Québec authors in the 1960s and 1970s: Gérard Bessette, Réjean Ducharme, Marie-Claire Blais, Jacques Godbout and Jacques Ferron. Taking a modern innovative approach, Marcotte considers the 'imperfect novel' as a novel which is written in the past tense, and which is a major form of Western writing, and as the novel which is not perfect, incomplete or interminable.

His analysis focuses on both the literature and the impact of the social conditions during the period of the Quiet Revolution.

850 **Le roman québécois depuis 1960: méthodes et analyses.** (The Québec novel since 1960: methods and analyses.)
Edited by Louise Milot, Jaap Lintvelt. Sainte-Foy, Québec: Presses de l'Université Laval, 1992. 318p.

Each study in this compilation outlines a specific methodology and then applies it to an analysis of a Québec novel published after 1960. Approaches centred around the text include the thematic, the semiotic and the stylistic. Other approaches focus on the reader's point of view, namely deconstruction and feminist reading. Finally, an approach which concentrates on the historical context is sociocriticism. This compilation offers a panorama of studies which showcase, in an accessible manner for students, diverse and contemporary forms of literary analysis.

851 **L'écologie du réel: mort et naissance de la littérature québécoise contemporaine: essais.** (The ecology of reality: the birth and death of contemporary Québec literature: essays.)
Pierre Nepveu. Montréal: Éditions du Boréal, 1988. 243p.

These essays offer a re-reading and a re-evaluation of key authors in Québec literary history: Octave Crémazie (1827-79), Émile Nelligan (1879-1941), Saint-Denys Garneau (1912-43), and Alain de Grandbois (1900-75). Nepveu also looks at the more recent literary past, including poetry and novels from the 1960s and 1970s by writers such as Jacques Godbout (b.1933) and Hubert Aquin (1929-77). His re-reading of works from these two eras in Québec literature is carried out from a modern perspective, that of the 1980s. Nepveu looks back on key figures from modern Québec literature with the intention of capturing the conceptual dynamics of the particular time in which they were writing. In this sense, the modern perspective comes into contact with tradition, creating a certain 'dialogue'. The diversity of the essays in this book contributes to the 'dialogue' effect intended by the author.

852 **Postmodernism and the Québec novel.**
Janet M. Paterson, translated by David Homel, Charles Phillips.
Toronto: University of Toronto Press, 1994. 168p.

This book was first published in 1990 in French, as *Moments postmodernes dans le roman québécois* (Ottawa: Presses de l'Université d'Ottawa, 1993. 142p.), and won the Gabrielle Roy Prize for the best work of Québec literary criticism. The theoretical perspective of this book is influenced by the work of Jean-François Lyotard, author of *La condition postmoderne* (The post-modern condition) (Manchester, England: Manchester University Press, 1984). Paterson sets out to answer the following questions in her study of contemporary Québec fiction: whether there is a post-modern Québec novel; if there is, what forms it takes; and what aspects of history does it challenge. She analyses post-modern textual strategies in terms of discourse, intertextuality, the representation of the writer in fiction, the process of history, and feminist expression. Authors studied include: Hubert Aquin, Madeleine Ouellette-Michalska, Jacques Godbout, Gérard Bessette, Yolande Villemaire and Nicole Brossard.

853 **Un projet de liberté. L'essai littéraire au Québec, 1970-1990.**
(A project of liberty. The literary essay in Québec, 1970-90.)
Janusz Przychodzen. Québec: Institut québécois de Recherche sur la
Culture, 1993. 213p. bibliog.

Przychodzen examines the development of the literary genre of the essay in Québec
from 1970-90. The author proposes an analysis of the Québec essay in terms of a
'transnational text', in which the vision of reality as prescribed by the genre appears
more open to the idea of exploring other cultures, thus crossing new boundaries.
Through a study of three categories of the Québec essay, the socio-political, the personal
and the feminist, the author shows how the quest for freedom in the Québec essay
over the period covering 1960-70, instilled in the essay during the following two
decades the struggle for independence. This book, which won the 1993 Edmond-de-
Nevers Prize, includes an extensive bibliography of the literary essays published in
Québec from 1970-90. See also Pierre Milot's *Le paradigme rouge: l'avant-garde
politico-littéraire des années 1970* (The red paradigm: the political-literary avant-garde
of the 1970s) (Candiac, Québec: Éditions Balzac, 1992. 291p.).

854 **A certain difficulty of being: essays on the Québec novel.**
Anthony Purdy. Montréal; Kingston, Ontario: McGill-Queen's
University Press, 1990. 176p. bibliog.

This book, written in English, offers an account of some of the most interesting
narrative problems that mark the development of the Québec novel. Purdy applies a
contemporary narratological approach to each study. He leads the reader to an understanding of how the novels examined function on a narrative level, each in its own
socio-historical context. Each chapter is animated by his concern with Québec's
historical 'difficulty of being' as it affects the narrative endeavours of the novels in
question: Félix-Antoine Savard's *Menaud, maître-draveur* (Menaud, master of the
river); Gabrielle Roy's *Bonheur d'occasion* (The tin flute); André Langevin's
Poussière sur la ville (Dust on the city); Hubert Aquin's *Prochaine épisode* (The next
episode) (see item no. 865); and Anne Hébert's *Kamouraska* (see item no. 880).

855 **French Canadian and Québécois novels.**
Ben-Zion Shek. Toronto: Oxford University Press, 1991. 151p.
(Perspectives on Canadian Culture).

This literary survey examines the following periods and phenomena in French
Canadian and Québec novels (most of which are available in English): 'The long
gestation of the novel, 1837-1937'; 'The modern novel, 1938-59'; 'The sixties'; 'The
emergence of the feminist I'; and 'The last twenty years'. What makes this book
unique is its discussion of translation challenges in the very field of Québec novels. A
list of novels available in English translation is included.

856 **Fictions de l'identitaire au Québec.** (Fictions surrounding the
identity construct in Québec.)
Sherry Simon et al. Montréal: XYZ, 1991. 185p.

The four studies in this book question the idea of identity as a construct ('identitaire').
Each of the four authors analyses the idea of constructing or carving out an identity, in
light of the heterogeneous character of identity, mainly in the Québec literary context.
The articles concern: the 'genealogy of ethnicity'; the questioning of identity in

contemporary literary writing; the contact of discourses on homosexuality and on the nation; and the probing of the construction of identity in Jacques Ferron's short stories. The diverse analytical approaches and diverging topics dealt with in this work contribute to a more profound understanding of the concept of the identity construct as it applies to Québec and beyond.

857   **Le trafic des langues.** (The traffic of languages.)
       Sherry Simon.   Montréal: Éditions du Boréal, 1994. 228p.

This study intricately weaves together three areas of research: Québec literature, translation and intercultural relations. In examining the relationships between these three fields, Simon explores the idea of cultural identity in Québec literature and the diverse forms taken by other cultures, brought to light through the act of translation. The author studies actual Québec literary works. Simon's examination of these texts gives rise to a discussion on translation as a form of 'interlinguistic and cultural negotiation', or a dialogue between the English and French languages in Québec. This is a very interesting interdisciplinary study for researchers or students interested in literary translation insofar as it relates to a cultural, linguistic and literary exploration.

858   **Villages imaginaires: Édouard Montpetit, Jacques Ferron et Jacques Poulin.** (Imaginary villages: Édouard Montpetit, Jacques Ferron and Jacques Poulin.)
       Pamela Sing.   Saint-Laurent, Québec: Fides, 1995. 272p. bibliog. (Nouvelles Études Québécoises).

Sing examines the theme of the village in Québec literature, demonstrating the persistence of the village experience as manifested in works by Édouard Montpetit, Jacques Ferron and Jacques Poulin.

859   **Mythes et symboles dans la littérature québécoise.** (Myths and symbols in Québec literature.)
       Antoine Sirois.   Montréal: Éditions Triptyque, 1992. 154p.

Throughout this collection of essays, Sirois studies the presence of Greek myths and biblical symbols in several works by Québec and French Canadian novelists, including Anne Hébert, Gabrielle Roy, Philippe Ringuet, Michel Tremblay and Jacques Ferron. He demonstrates how myths 'inspire a contemporary work and anticipate a modern plot'.

Feminist criticism

860   **Paroles rebelles.** (Rebellious statements.)
       Edited by Marguerite Andersen, Christine Klein-Lataud.   Montréal: Éditions du Remue-Ménage, 1992. 334p.

Written by women in honour of women, this book offers a diverse collection of articles. The feminine identity is studied in a Québec context, as well as in the contexts of France and Algeria. The first four chapters constitute historical studies of French female authors from the 16th to the 19th centuries. The fifth chapter studies the link between feminism and revolutionary ideas. The sixth chapter explores the struggles of the first feminists in Québec. The seventh chapter expands the perspective of the 'francophone space' to look at the feminist problem as encountered by Algerian women. The eighth chapter provides an overview of modes of expression in feminist cinema. The ninth chapter analyses the subversion of writing by contemporary Québec feminists. Finally, the last chapter unveils various statements made by present-day women. The analyses in this book demonstrate a celebration of modern feminist polyphony in Québec, France and other French-speaking societies.

861   **Un matriarcat en procès. Analyse systématique de romans canadiens-français, 1860-1960.** (A matriarchy in process. A systematic analysis of French Canadian novels, 1860-1960.)
Janine Boynard-Frot.   Montréal: Presses de l'Université de Montréal, 1982. 236p. bibliog.

Analyses the role and the place of women in the traditional Québec novel. The author aims to show that each novel contained important ideological messages, in an effort to demonstrate that many of these novels attempted to legitimize the dominant groups in Québec society. The author also discusses the effect of changing social structures and dominant ideological discourse on the subject matter of Québec novels. This work includes a comprehensive bibliography.

862   **Le roman québécois au féminin, 1980-1995.** (Women's novels in Québec, 1980-95.)
Edited by Gabrielle Pascal.   Montréal: Éditions Triptyque, 1995. 197p.

Approximately twenty female writers from Québec are analysed in this diverse panorama of studies. Approximately half of the studies deal with the feminine identity, while the other half examine the themes of the body, childhood and passion. The main themes emerging from the studies are the search for the self, love and death, sexuality and writing, and a recognition of differences.

863   **L'autre lecture: la critique au féminin et les textes québécois.** (The other reading: feminist criticism and Québec texts.)
Edited by Lori Saint-Martin.   Montréal: XYZ, 1992-94. 2 vols.

The first volume consists of fourteen articles whose object of analysis is female Québec writers from the beginning of Québec literature until 1970. This is the first anthology of readings of women's literature in Québec. Underlying the articles is a new (female) vision of Québec literature. The second volume covers feminist writing and criticism in the 1970s, during which time the ideological climate of feminism was dramatically changing. For the first time, women were taking a stand and speaking out as women, and insisting on the collective dimension of their unique experience. The three areas covered in this book are the general theory of women's creative writing, an analysis of essential texts, and studies of significant trends. A great variety of topics is tackled in both volumes.

864 **Writing in the father's house: the emergence of the feminine in the Québec literary tradition.**
Patricia Smart. Toronto: University of Toronto Press, 1991. 300p.

The analyses of Québec literary texts carried out in this book have been undertaken with a strong awareness of gender difference. Patricia Smart uncovers new dimensions in the question of representation by studying the relationship between the literary text, its cultural context and the gender of the writer. She probes 'her-story' so as to include it in, and often correct, the traditional 'his-story'.

Classics

865 **Prochain épisode.** (The next episode.)
Hubert Aquin, translated by Penny Williams. Toronto: McClelland and Stewart, 1972. 126p. (New Canadian Library, no. 84).

This novel marked a new way of relating literature with reality and history in Québec literature. Aquin created a form of writing in the first person which resulted in an ambiguity between the author and the narrator. This novel relates the story of a psychiatric patient who writes a novel about a revolutionary whose mission is to assassinate a member of the Canadian secret service. Referring to the Canadian political situation of the 1960s, *Prochain épisode* had a tremendous impact on an entire generation of nationalists. Other novels by the same author include: *Blackout*, translated by Alan Brown (Toronto: Anansi, 1974. 168p.); *The antiphonary*, translated by Alan Brown (Toronto: Anansi, 1973. 196p.). See also Élaine Cliche's *Le désir du roman: Hubert Aquin, Réjean Ducharme* (The desire of the novel: Hubert Aquin and Réjean Ducharme) (Montréal: XYZ, 1992. 214p.).

866 **Canadians of old.**
Philippe Aubert de Gaspé, translated by Jane Brierley. Montréal: Véhicule Press, 1993. 329p.

Discusses the theme of remorse. *Les anciens Canadiens* describes the relationship between two friends, a Canadian and an orphaned Scot, who fight against each other during the Conquest. This novel is marked by nostalgia for the French regime and by the desire of the author to maintain the traditions of the original French settlers. This is a useful novel for gaining an understanding of the impact of the Conquest on the French Canadian inhabitants.

867 **Race de monde.** (Race of the world.)
Victor Lévy Beaulieu. Trois-Pistoles, Québec: Éditions Trois-Pistoles, 1996. 193p. (Oeuvres Complètes, no. 2).

Novelist, publisher, and television drama writer, Beaulieu is certainly among the most prolific authors in Québec. His work is both a reflection of Québec society and of the art of writing, presented in an autobiographical narrative style. *Race de monde*, the first volume of *La vraie saga des Beauchemin* (The real saga of the Beauchemins), describes the life of a Québec family through the eyes of Abel Beauchemin, a cynical man who dreams of writing a novel one day. The family does not constitute a theme in the novel per se; rather, it is used as a backdrop to a situation in which social determinism marks the life of the different characters.

868   **A season in the life of Emmanuel.** (Une saison dans la vie d'Emmanuel.)
       Marie-Claire Blais, translated by Derek Coltman.   Toronto: McClelland and Stewart, 1992. 138p. (New Canadian Library).

This is Marie-Claire Blais' most famous novel, winner of the Prix Médicis. A young boy, Jean Le Maigre, searches for 'authentic' values to replace those of the corrupt society in which he lives. This novel projects a grim vision of the family, Québec society, the future and the Catholic religion (which governs every element of society); and this very vision is generated by the Quiet Revolution, which coincides with the publication of the novel. Sordid images circulate throughout the novel to combine vice and virtue, reality and the imagination. This powerfully poetic novel has been considered 'a forerunner of the change of ideological codes' in Québec. The whole of her Romanesque work is published in a pocket-book collection and includes: *Anna's world*, translated by Sheila Fischman (Toronto: Lester & Orpen Dennys, 1985. 176p.); *Nights in the underground: an exploration of love*, translated by Ray Ellenwood (Don Mills, Ontario: Musson Book Co., 1979. 199p.); and *Soifs* (Thirst) (Montréal: Éditions du Boréal, 1995. 313p.). She received the Athanase-David Award in 1982 for her work.

869   **Anthologie.** (An anthology.)
       Arthur Buies, edited by Laurent Mailhot.   Saint-Laurent, Québec: Bibliothèque Québécoise, 1994. 391p.

Considered the father of Québec journalism, Arthur Buies was recognized as an important 19th-century pro-secular writer. Deeply inspired by French luminaries, Buies was an ardent polemicist who denounced church intervention in public and cultural affairs. He was also a traveller who wrote wonderful descriptions of various North American regions. This edition has been edited by Laurent Mailhot and presents a critical selection of Buies' works.

870   **Let us compare mythologies.**
       Leonard Cohen.   Toronto: McClelland and Stewart, 1966. 76p.

First published in the poetry papers of McGill University where Cohen was studying, *Let us compare mythologies* was written during Cohen's teenage years. The book is full of references to Montréal and Judaism, religious rituals, and the rituals of life. Cohen emphasizes the inhumanity and loneliness of the modern urban world. In this novel, the writer of the song, *Susanne*, and *Take this waltz* (Ste-Anne-de-Bellevue, Québec: The Muses' Co., 1994. 189p.), already presents love as a palliative for disenchantment with the world. Other titles by this author include the avant-garde novel *Beautiful loser* (Toronto: McClelland and Stewart, 1991. 76p.).

871   **Un simple soldat.** (A simple soldier.)
       Marcel Dubé.   Montréal: Éditions de l'Homme, 1967. 142p.

Dubé is an important figure in the evolution of theatre in Québec. At a time when the Québec scene was divided between the interpretation of French classics and creating original popular works, Dubé was seen as one of the first modern Québec writers of tragedy. Marked by disillusion, Dubé's characters are victims of the conventions of their social classes. In *Un simple soldat*, Joseph Latour comes back from an army recruiting camp without having realized his goal; i.e., participation in the Second World War. For Latour, his personal achievement is seen as a way to break with the weakness and the fear represented by his father. A metaphor of the situation of contemporary French Canadians, *Un simple soldat* demonstrated the futility of their predicament. Dubé was honoured in 1973 by the Athanase-David Award. Other works by the same author include: *Zone*, adapted into English by Aviva Ravel (Toronto: Playwrights Canada, 1982. 84p.); *Florence* (Montréal: Leméac, 1970. 150p.); *Les beaux dimanches* (Beautiful Sundays) (Montréal: Leméac, 1968. 185p.); and *The white geese*, translated by Jean Remple (Toronto: New Press, 1972. 106p.).

872 **Swallower swallowed.**
Réjean Ducharme, translated by Barbara Bray. London, Ontario: Hamilton, 1968. 237p.

Written by the mysterious Réjean Ducharme, an author who never appeared publicly following the launch of his first book in 1966, this novel (whose French title is *L'avalée des avalés*) begins, 'Tout m'avale' (Everything is devouring me). The novel presents the narrator's fantasy of being devoured by the world he lives in. In addition to being a testament to Ducharme's ability as a writer, this book is a testament to Ducharme's scholarship; he makes frequent allusions to the works of Émile Nelligan, Corneille and the Bible. This story of revolt is a marvellous introduction to Ducharme's universe; one of young dreamers who refuse to accept the conditions of daily life. Other titles by the same author include: *Le nez qui voque* (Paris: Gallimard, 1967. 274p.); *L'hiver de force* (The winter of strength) (Paris: Gallimard, 1973. 282p.); *Dévadé* (Paris: Gallimard; Montréal: Lacombe, 1990. 257p.); *Va savoir* (Going to find out) (Paris: Gallimard, 1994. 266p.). For a criticism of Ducharme's work, see *Paysages de Réjean Ducharme* (Landscapes of Réjean Ducharme), edited by Pierre-Louis Vaillancourt (Montréal: Fides, 1994. 319p.).

873 **The juniberry tree.**
Jacques Ferron, translated by Raymond Y. Chamberlain. Montréal: Harvest House, 1975. 207p.

A man of many talents during his lifetime, Jacques Ferron was at once general practitioner, short-story writer, and founder of the Rhinoceros Party (a fringe political party established to contest federal politics). His medical work among the poor and his involvement in politics were translated into a profound appeal for liberty and fantasy in his writing. *L'amélanchier* (The juniberry tree), which has been compared to Antoine de St-Exupéry's *The little prince* and Lewis Caroll's *Alice in Wonderland*, is a wonderful novel about innocence and the fantasy of youth. The story centres around a girl, Tinamer, who, in a poetic way, tells the story of her youth. *L'amélanchier* also has nationalist undertones, as does much of Ferron's work; Tinamer's decision to return to her 'origins' can be interpreted as a metaphor for the necessity of Quebecers to retain contacts with their origins. Other titles by the same author include: *The penniless redeemer* (*Ciel de Québec*), translated by Ray Ellenwood (Toronto: Exile Editions, 1984); *Tales from an uncertain country* (*Conte du pays incertain*), translated by Betty Bednarski (Toronto: Anansi, 1972); *The cart: a novel* (*La Charrette*) (Montréal: Bibliothèque Québécoise, 1994); and *Le salut de l'Irlande* (Ireland's good-bye) (Outremont, Québec: Éditions Lanctôt, 1997). For a critical analysis of Ferron's work, see Pierre L'Hérault's *Jacques Ferron, cartographe de l'imaginaire* (Jacques Ferron, cartographer of the imagination) (Montréal: Presses de l'Université de Montréal, 1980) and Jean-Pierre Boucher's *Jacques Ferron au pays des amélanchiers* (Jacques Ferron in the country of the juniper trees) (Montréal: Presses de l'Université de Montréal, 1973).

874 Tit-Coq.
Gratien Gélinas, translated by Kenneth Johnstone. Toronto: Clarke & Irwin, 1967. 84p.

The creation of this play in 1947 was the beginning of contemporary theatre in Québec. The principal character, Tit-Coq, is an illegitimate child who falls in love with Marie-Ange, a young girl who represents the possibility of a real family. After Tit-Coq leaves for the war, Marie-Ange is forced to marry a man chosen by her family. This play represents both the French Canadian quest for identity and their feeling of weakness. Gélinas is also the author of *Bousille et les justes* (Bousille and the righteous ones) (Québec: Institut Littéraire, 1960. 203p.).

875 Jean Rivard le défricheur suivi de Jean Rivard économiste. (Jean Rivard the pioneer followed by Jean Rivard the economist.)
Antoine Gérin-Lajoie. Montréal: Leméac, 1993. 480p.

This volume contains the text of *Jean Rivard le défricheur* and its sequel, which were first published in 1862 and 1864 respectively; the former tells the story of a poor young boy who decides, in spite of his intellectual abilities, to work on the land. His choice will result in success and, with the development of the township (described in the sequel), he finds himself able to participate in the development of the region in which he lives. According to the author, these are realist novels, and they provide an apology of simple, rural life. If the novels do not possess great literary qualities, they nonetheless provide a good picture of the rural ideology of 19th-century Québec.

876 Marie-Calumet.
Rodolphe Girard, translated by Irène Currie. Montréal: Harvest House, 1976. 167p.

Originally published in 1904 by the Lieutenant-Colonel and playwright, Rodolphe Girard, this novel was considered to be scandalous due to the disrespectful tone used by the author when writing about religion. Set in Saint-Ildefonse, Québec, in around the year 1860, the novel ends with the marriage of the priest, Narcisse Boisvert, to the maid of the presbytery.

877 Hail Galarneau!
Jacques Godbout, translated by Alan Brown. Don Mills, Ontario: Longman Canada, 1970. 131p.

Entitled *Salut Galarneau!* in French, the form of this novel was revolutionary in nature. It is based around the character of a loveable snack-bar owner, François Galarneau, who continually seeks mental release from his unsatisfying environment, and is constantly writing as a means of escape. Experimenting with language and poetic form, he gradually builds a wall of language around him. He invents a word which defines his very existence: 'vécrire', composed of the verbs 'to live' and 'to write'. Among the different interpretations of Godbout's work, readers should consult Jacques Pelletier's

Le roman national: Godbout, Beaulieu, Major (The national novel: Godbout, Beaulieu, Major) (Montréal: VLB Éditeur, 1991. 237p.).

878   **Un homme et son péché.** (A man and his sin.)
      Claude-Henri Grignon.   Montréal: Presses de l'Université de
      Montréal, 1986. 256p. (Bibliothèque du Nouveau Monde).
This novel presents Séraphin Poudrier, a character which has become famous in
Québec's collective imagination. Séraphin is a landlord so obsessed with money that
he imposes particularly cruel living conditions on his wife, Donalda, who ultimately
dies of malnutrition. If the author does not set out to vindicate the rural world, he
nonetheless demonstrates the consequences of forgetting its traditional values.

879   **The outlander.**
      Germaine Guèvremont, translated by Eric Sutton.   Toronto:
      McClelland and Stewart, 1978. 290p. (New Canadian Library, no. 151).
Along with Ringuet's *Thirty acres* (see item no. 889), *Le survenant* (The outlander)
marks the end of an idealistic and nationalist vision of the rural world. The author
presents a humanized vision of the intersection between the rural and the urban world.
The novel relates an encounter between the Beauchemin family, a family of farmers,
and a stranger who represents the urban vision of Québec society. This novel of love
and liberty sets out to reveal to the people of rural Québec the possibility of a new
existence. Germaine Guèvremont received the Anathase-David Award, the Duvernay
Award and the Sully-Olivier de Serres Award granted by l'Académie Française
(French Academy).

880   **Kamouraska.**
      Anne Hébert, translated by Norman Shapiro.   Toronto: Musson
      Book Co., 1973. 250p.
This novel was qualified by many critics as 'one of the greatest popular French novels
of the 20th century'. The story begins with a woman, Élisabeth d'Aulnières, sitting up
in the bed of her sick, second husband; reliving her past and her first marriage with a
violent man. This novel contains the traditional themes found in Anne Hébert's work:
passion and death in a closed universe where human weakness breaks individuals and
their passions. Hébert demonstrates the way the individual is oppressed by traditional
values. Another title by the same author is *Les fous de Bassans* (The insane people of
Bassans) (Paris: Éditions du Seuil, 1982).

881   **Maria Chapdelaine.**
      Louis Hémon, translated by Alan Brown.   Montréal: Tundra Books,
      1989. 93p.
Originally published in 1923, as *Maria Chapdelaine. Récit du Canada français* (Maria
Chapdelaine. An account of French Canada), this novel has gradually come to symbolize
the family, the homeland (France) and religion; it is an allegory for a people whose
main task is to preserve values received by the motherland. Since it was first published, it has been considered by many critics as a bible of national survival and an
'account of the Canadian miracle'. See also Nicole Deschamps, Raymonde Héroux
and Normand Villeneuve's *Le mythe de Maria Chapdelaine* (The myth of Maria
Chapdelaine) (Montréal: Presses de l'Université de Montréal, 1980. 263p.).

882   **The madman, the kite and the island.**
       Félix Leclerc, translated by Philip Stratford.   Ottawa: Oberon Press,
       1976. 153p.

Félix Leclerc, a popular songwriter, was certainly one of the most appreciated artists in Québec. Prior to this, however, he was a writer. This book, whose original French title is *Le fou de l'île*, describes life on a small island where a stranger is washed onto the beach by the tide. His presence divides the island population between those who accept his presence and those who see him as a threat to the community. Similar to Leclerc's other works, this novel emphasizes the psychological development of the characters rather than focusing on plot. A well-known singer and poet, Leclerc was also an important figure in Québec's literature. Other works from Leclerc include: *Le calepin d'un flâneur* (Notebook of a drifter) (Montréal: Fides, 1961. 170p.); *Moi, mes souliers* (Me and my shoes) (Montréal; Paris: Fides, 1960. 214p.); and *Pieds nus dans l'aube* (Barefoot in the dawn) (Montréal; Paris: Fides, 1947. 242p.).

883   **The town below.**
       Roger Lemelin, translated by Samuel Putnam.   Toronto: McClelland
       & Stewart, 1961. 284p. (New Canadian Library, no. 26).

Lemelin's first novel, this work depicts urban morals and deals with French Canadian identity. The community described appears as a microcosm of Québec society on the road towards urbanization and industrialization. This novel is a chronicle of everyday life, of workers and teenagers trapped in their suburbs. Despite its formal conservatism, *Au pied de la pente douce* represents a precursor of the novel of the 1960s, manifested in the brutal realism animating the narration.

884   **Two solitudes.**
       Hugh McLennan.   Toronto: Collins, 1945. 370p.

The defining novel on race relations in Canada. Though McLennan has been criticized for what has been deemed by some as a stereotypical portrayal of French Canadian culture, his work has nonetheless helped to determine the way Canadians think of their country and themselves. First published in 1945, it has since become a Canadian classic.

885   **La Sagouine.**
       Antonine Maillet, translated by Luis de Céspedes.   Toronto: Simon &
       Pierre, 1985. 183p.

A book comprising sixteen monologues. La Sagouine is an original character in French Canadian literature. A seventy-two-year-old Acadian from Prince Edward Island, this character relates the major and difficult events in her life: her youth, her wedding, and her life in the city. This book describes the evolution of Acadian society through the eyes and the original language of a poor woman. Other works by Maillet include *Pélagie-la-Charette*, translated by Philip Stratford (Toronto: General Pub., 1983. 251p.).

886   **Earth and embers: selected poems.**
       Gaston Miron, translated by D. G. Jones, Marc Plourde.   Montréal:
       Guernica, 1984. bibliog. (Essential Poets, no. 18).

From one of Québec's greatest poets, this significant book (whose original title is *L'homme rapaillé*) has won many prizes, including the Guillaume-Appolinaire Award and the Anathase-David Award. Miron's poetry is divided into two kinds: the poetry of love, in which Miron expresses his sensitivity, especially in 'La marche à l'amour' (The walk towards love); and his better known political poetry, in which he denounces the cultural and economic oppression of Québec's population and argues in favour of Québec's sovereignty. The political aspects of Miron's poetry have caused him to be compared with other national poets, such as Pablo Neruda. This book also includes Miron's essays on literature and language. In addition, it contains a bibliography of Miron's work and a short biography of his life. This edition is bilingual; each poem is printed in French and English.

887   **The complete poems of Émile Nelligan.**
Émile Nelligan, translated by Fred Cogswell.   Montréal: Harvest House, 1983. 120p. (French Writers of Canada).
Nelligan is certainly the most famous poet in Québec. His poetry has deep similarities with the French symbolism of the late 19th century. Nevertheless, in rejecting the old nationalist poetry, Nelligan's work is one of Québec literature's first steps towards modernity. From 'Soir d'hiver' (Winter evening) to 'La romance du vin' (The romance of wine), Nelligan explores the torments of the soul and of the heart with a deep accent on rhythm and emotion. See also Paul Wyczynski's *Nelligan* (Montréal: Fides, 1987. 632p.).

888   **The apprenticeship of Duddy Kravitz.**
Mordecai Richler.   Boston, Massachusetts: Little, Brown & Co., 1959. 377p.
By virtue of this work, Mordecai Richler not only embedded himself in Canada's literary fabric, but he also became an indelible part of Montréal's historical landscape, describing the downtown city, its inhabitants and the surrounding countryside with a detached clarity true to the period. *The apprenticeship of Duddy Kravitz* relates the story of a young Jew living in Montréal during the post-war period, committed to following his own convictions. This book is a wonderful story of the contradictions of the modern world, as revealed in Duddy's own character: naive yet calculating, rebellious but uneasy, simultaneously hard and vulnerable.

889   **Thirty acres.** (Trente arpents.)
Ringuet.   Toronto: McClelland and Stewart, 1989. 306p. (New Canadian Library).
First published in 1938, this novel marks the end of the predominance of the land and the rural world in Québec. The city occupies a large place in this novel, as it did in Québec during the period depicted. Through the character of the farmer Euchariste Moisan, Ringuet portrays the social transformations taking place in Québec. The land constitutes the main 'character' in the novel and reaches mythical proportions.

890   **The tin flute.** (Bonheur d'occasion.)
Gabrielle Roy, translated by Hannah Josephson.   Toronto: McClelland and Stewart, 1969. 274p. (New Canadian Library, no. 5).
First published in 1945, this novel focuses on a working-class community in Montréal. Major themes animating the novel are the difficulties of adapting to urban life, solitude, the lack of communication within the family and within the couple, evasion

261

and the ideal of human fraternity. Through its insistence on the problems of urbanization in Québec, this novel marks an original event in French Canadian literature.

891 **Master of the river.**
Félix-Antoine Savard, translated by Richard Howard. Montréal: Harvest House, 1976. 135p. (French Writers of Canada).

Beginning with several extracts from Louis Hémon's *Maria Chapdelaine* (see item no. 881), *Menaud maître-draveur*, as this novel is originally entitled, relates the story of Menaud, an old raftsman who maintains a profound animosity towards the anglophone strangers who have come into possession of the land. After the death of his only son Joson, Menaud becomes possessed by feelings of revenge which ultimately lead him to his death. Savard's novel not only presents a highly lyrical portrait of rural life, but it also describes the core value of French Canadian nationalism: national survival and loyalty to tradition. Savard won the 1939 Anathase-David Award for this novel.

892 **Agaguk.**
Yves Thériault, translated by Miriam Chapin. Toronto: Ryerson Press, 1967. 229p. (Ryerson Paperbacks, no. 16).

A novelist of solitary and marginal characters, Yves Thériault was one of Québec's first professional writers. *Agaguk*, which has been translated into more than twenty languages, describes the life of an Inuit who kills a man who stole from him. With the help of his wife, Iriook, Agaguk slowly develops a more humane vision of the world. Also see Thériault's *N'Tsuk*, translated by Gwendolyn Moore (Montréal: Harvest House, 1971. 110p.).

893 **Les belles-sœurs.** (Sisters-in-law.)
Michel Tremblay, translated by John Van Burek, Bill Glassco. Vancouver: Talonbooks, 1991. 111p.

This landmark in Québec theatre, first published in 1965, provides an insight into the life of fifteen proletarian women from East Montréal. The action is limited to one scene: a stamp-pasting party in the kitchen of the winner of a million Gold Star stamps. Within the sparse scenery of the four walls, a series of very provocative and dramatic monologues and dialogues reveals the individual and the collective frustrations of these women who are trapped in their narrow microcosm of Québec society. Presented in 'joual' (the idiomatic, slang, 'street' French of Québec), this play offers a realistic vision of Québec society.

Poetry

894 **Les gens du fleuve: anthologie.** (The people of the river: an anthology.)
Victor Lévy Beaulieu. Montréal: Stanké, 1993. 252p.

Beaulieu aims to provide a general idea of the development undergone by the Québec poet. Through the eyes of the (fictitious) character/poet Philippe Couture, we observe

the predominant theme of water. The poems in this work, written by Beaulieu/
Couture, contain traces of European literary influences (for example, Flaubert and
Mallarmé) and reflect the work of Québec poets such as Gaston Miron and Paul-Marie
Lapointe. This is a very creative anthology which integrates fiction and non-fiction.

895 **De Villon à Vigneault: anthologie franco-québécoise de poèmes à
forme fixe.** (From Villon to Vigneault: Franco-Québec anthology of
fixed-form poems.)
Compiled by Louise Blouin. Saint-Laurent, Québec: Éditions Pierre
Tisseyre; Trois-Rivières, Québec: Écrits des Forges, 1994. 142p.

Forty-seven poets from Québec and France, whose poetry is written following fixed
forms (sonnets, ballads, odes, etc.), and who respect the rules of prosody, are listed in
this book. A chronological format, respecting the birth date of the authors, allows the
reader to observe the evolution of writing (from the Middle Ages to the 20th century),
as well as the coinciding evolution of subjects. This anthology aims to present to
young readers poems which are considered to be famous and classic.

896 **Passions du poétique: essais.** (Passions of the poetic: essays.)
Joseph Bonenfant. Montréal: L'Hexagone, 1992. 232p.

Bonenfant shares with the reader his interpretations of his personal experiences of
teaching Québec poetry. He discusses, in a very accessible fashion, thematic, semiotic
and pragmatic analyses which represent his own intellectual growth within the literary
field. The second section of the book presents a survey of important poetic works in
Québec history, accompanied by analyses. The third section deals with the teaching of
poetry at the college and university levels. See also Claude Beausoleil's *Motif de
l'identité dans la poésie québécoise: 1830-95* (Identity in Québec poetry: 1830-95)
(Montréal: Estuaire, 1996. 262p.).

897 **Poésie québécoise: évolution des formes.** (Québec poetry: the
evolution of forms.)
Hélène Dame, Robert Giroux. Montréal: Éditions Triptyque, 1990.
213p.

The studies in this book adopt a semiotic approach to the analysis of poetic discourse.
Three analyses aim to describe the evolution of the Québec poetic corpus since
Nelligan. Giroux traces the evolution of poetic forms, referring to representative
examples from Nelligan to Nicole Brossard. Dame studies two 'modern' poets, Jean-
Aubert Loranger and Anne Hébert.

898 **Québec suite: poems for and about Québec.**
Edited by Endre Farkas. Ste-Anne-de-Bellevue, Québec: The Muses'
Co., 1995. 141p.

An anthology of poems from fifty-four of Canada's most prominent poets, both past
and present, including: F. R. Scott, A. M. Klein, Louis Dudek, Irving Layton, Al
Purdy and Margaret Atwood. Most of the works selected have a distinct political
resonance. More than this, however, the authors urge the reader to look beyond the
'two solitudes' (the division of Québec into English and French Canadians) and
acknowledge the sensory and spiritual nature of Québec.

899 **Poétiques de la modernité, 1895-1948: essais.** (Poetics of modernity, 1895-1948: essays.)
Claude Filteau. Montréal: L'Hexagone, 1994. 382p.

Filteau examines the notion of modernity in Québec poetry. He examines such elements as rhythm, language and genre in many poems, in order to grasp the strategic issues in the debates surrounding the question of modernity in Québec from 1895 to 1948.

900 **Oeuvres.** (Works.)
Hector de Saint-Denys Garneau. Montréal: Presses de l'Université de Montréal, 1971. 1,320p.

The publication in 1937 of *Regards et jeux dans l'espace: suivi de Les solitudes* (Perspectives and games in space: followed by Les solitudes) by Saint-Denys Garneau (Montréal: Bibliothèque Québécoise, 1993. 231p.) marks an important moment in the history of Québec's poetry. The author wrote poetry in a form razed of traditional conventions. He also introduced themes like the importance of subjectivity, the opposition between the force of evil and the force of good, and personal distress in front of death.

901 **Les textes poétiques du Canada français, 1606-1867.** (Poetic texts from French Canada, 1606-1867.)
Jeanne d'Arc Lortie, Pierre Savard, Paul Wyczynski. Montréal: Fides, 1987-96. 12 vols.

Reproduced in these twelve volumes are all the poems, written during the period 1606-1867, which could be collected from journals, reviews, collections and archives. The objective of these volumes is to render this corpus accessible to students, professors and specialists. The texts are annotated.

902 **La poésie québécoise des origines à nos jours: anthologie.** (Québec poetry past and present: an anthology.)
Edited by Laurent Mailhot, Pierre Nepveu. Montréal: L'Hexagone, 1986. new ed. 642p. bibliog.

An updated edition of an anthology which appeared in 1981. This edition offers readers a complete and diverse panorama of Québec poetry from the 17th century to the mid-1980s. It organizes the poets, their biographical notes and their poetry in chronological order. A fifty-page bibliography of poetry and critical texts concerning poetry is also included.

903 **La poésie moderne québécoise: poésie et société au Québec, 1970-1989, introduction 1970-1989.** (Modern Québec poetry: poetry and society in Québec, 1937-70, introduction, 1970-89.)
Axel Maugey. Montréal: Humanitas-Nouvelle Optique, 1989. 280p.

This book offers an illuminating study of ideologies in Québec society since 1945 and the role that poetry has played and continues to play. Maugey looks at ten poets and demonstrates the bond uniting Québec to its poets. He pays particular attention to the 'mission' undertaken by many of these individuals in their work to support and reflect Québec as a distinct society. He discusses various methodological approaches to poetry analysis before applying one in particular, which gives his approach a rich perspective.

904 **La poésie au Québec: revue critique, 1990.** (Poetry in Québec: a critical review, 1990.)
Trois-Rivières, Québec: Écrits des Forges, 1991. 213p.
This review covers the subject of poetry in Québec during the year 1990. It is divided into the following sections: Québec poetry; essays on poetry; collections and anthologies; foreign poetry published in Québec; interviews and essays on poets; and the list of the ten most stimulating works of Québec poetry for the year 1990. This unique issue of this journal is very clear, informative and well organized.

905 **La contradiction du poème: poésie et discours social au Québec de 1948 à 1953.** (The contradiction of the poem: poetry and social discourse in Québec from 1948-53.)
Pierre Popovic. Candiac, Québec: Balzac, 1992. 455p.
This study aims to situate poetry in the context of social discourse and to determine poetry's social function. The first part of the book looks at social discourse: its main discursive forms occupying the Québec scene between the 1930s and the 1950s, and literary criticism in the social sciences. The second part is devoted to applied analyses of poetry by Anne Hébert, Claude Gauvreau and Gaston Miron. See also François Dumont's *Usages de la poésie: le discours des poètes québécois sur la fonction de la poésie, 1945-1970* (The uses of poetry: the discourse of Québec poets on the functions of poetry, 1945-70) (Québec: Presses de l'Université Laval, 1993. 239p.).

906 **101 poètes en Québec.** (101 poets in Québec.)
Edited by Sylvain Rivière. Montréal: Guérin, 1995. 441p.
This anthology presents unique impressions of Québec as seen through the work of a selection of poets. Rivière's choice of poems is personal and instinctive. This work gives the reader a unique and subjective insight into contemporary Québec poetry. Bio-bibliographical notes precede each section of poems.

907 **Introduction à la poésie québécoise: les poètes et les œuvres des origines à nos jours.** (An introduction to Québec poetry: poets and works past and present.)
Jean Royer. Montréal: Bibliothèque Québécoise, 1989. 295p. bibliog.
Royer studies the various eras of poetry in Québec from its origins to the present. In each of the five periods defined, the author explores the evolution of themes, movements, significant poems and the authors themselves. A very extensive bibliography on poetic and critical works is included.

Arts

Reference

908 **Les arts et les années 60.** (The arts and the 1960s.)
Edited by Francine Couture. Montréal: Éditions Triptyque, 1991. 170p.

Parallel with the political changes occurring in Québec during the 1960s, the artistic community also experienced an explosion of creativity and transformation. This book describes the changes and innovations that occurred in Québec in the visual arts, architecture, song, dance, cinema, literature, music and theatre. Written for a popular audience, it explains who the important people and events were, in addition to their significance relative to the greater social changes taking place.

909 **La nouvelle culture régionale.** (The new regional culture.)
Edited by Fernand Harvey, Andrée Fortin. Québec: Institut québécois de Recherche sur la Culture, 1995. 255p.

Once considered parochial by critics in urban centres, the arts and culture outside of Montréal have gained considerable respect since the mid-1970s. This book reveals the increasing autonomy enjoyed by Québec's regional art sector and the sector's growing capacity for self-renewal and development. Particular attention is paid to the province's museums, publishing houses, theatre companies, and film and music festivals. This collection of scholarly essays charts the growing institutionalization of culture in the many regions of Québec illustrating the diversity that exists within Québec.

910 **Marionnettes: art et tradition.** (Marionettes: art and tradition.)
Micheline Legendre. Montréal: Éditions Leméac, 1986. 193p.

This work explores and situates the art of the marionette in Québec and throughout the world. The author shows how the evolution of this puppeteering art has been due to diverse geographical and cultural influences. The text is well illustrated with sketches and photographs. It includes an interesting and extensive history of marionettes in Montréal.

911 **Parachute.**
Montréal: Artdata, 1975- . quarterly.
A contemporary art magazine dealing with modern 20th-century art.

912 **Les arts sacrés au Québec.** (Sacred art in Québec.)
Jean Simard, photographs by François Brault. Boucherville, Québec:
Éditions du Mortagne, 1989. 319p.

The art historian, Jean Simard, and film-maker, François Brault, have produced this visually provocative and historically enlightening work on sacred and religious art in Québec. Reproduced in this book are prints, accompanied by explanations, of places and objects inspired by the religious belief in a 'higher' world governed by beauty and order.

913 **Le Cirque du soleil.**
Edited by Véronique Vial, Hélène Dufresne. Montréal: Productions
du Cirque du soleil, 1993. 144p.

This visually captivating book commemorates the tenth anniversary of the Cirque du soleil (Circus of the Sun). Brilliant photographs showcase some of the best moments of this theatre company's annual tour over the past ten years. Assorted captions punctuate the layout of the book, describing aspects of the industry such as the participants, the drama involved in the show's preparation, and the final performance. Poetic anecdotes reflecting on the Cirque du soleil are also included in the book.

Visual arts

914 **La peinture au Québec, 1820-1850: nouveaux regards, nouvelles
perspectives.** (Painting in Québec, 1820-50: new glimpses, new
perspectives.)
Edited by Mario Beland. Québec: Musée du Québec, Publications
du Québec, 1991. 624p.

This book accompanied the exposition which took place during the opening year of the Musée du Québec (Québec Museum) in 1992. The book truly espouses the mandate of the Musée du Québec, which is to 'promote and conserve Québec art from all periods'. It lists 267 works by 70 artists, accompanied by exhaustive annotations. This rich catalogue not only provides an illustration of the most beautiful works from Québec's artistic heritage, but it is also a veritable portrait of Québec and Canadian society during the period between 1790 and 1860.

915 **Les lieux de mémoire. Identité et culture modernes au Québec, 1930-1960.** (The places of memory. Modern identity and culture in Québec, 1930-60.)
Marie Carani. Ottawa: Presses de l'Université d'Ottawa, 1995. 239p.

A collection of essays which focuses on the artistic production of the 1930-60 period in Québec as entering a modern era or 'modernity'. The essays look at how the question of identity and modernity influenced artists such as Jean-Paul Lemieux, Paul-Émile Borduas, and Arthur Villeneuve.

916 **Les arts graphiques.** (Graphic arts.)
Ervin A. Dennis, John D. Jenkins. Montréal: Éditions Saint-Martin, 1990. 376p.

This manual describes in detail the graphic art process, providing explicit illustrations. The explanations are written in a simple and pedagogical style. This is an informative book for both students and professionals in this field.

917 **Montréal, métropole du Québec: images oubliées de la vie quotidienne, 1852-1910.** (Montréal, Québec's metropolis: forgotten images of everyday life, 1852-1910.)
Edited by Michel Lessard. Montréal: Éditions de l'Homme, 1992. 303p.

Rather than offering an objective history of Montréal, this book constitutes one impression of an era, communicated through photographs of everyday life. The images in each thematic section are organized following a somewhat loose chronology. Some of the themes displayed in this visually appealing work are: the urban system, business and industry, religion and teaching, and architectural eclecticism.

Music

Reference

918 **La chanson québécoise: de la Bolduc à aujourd'hui.** (The Québec song: from Bolduc to the present.)
René Chamberland, André Gaulin. Québec: Nuit Blanche Éditeur, 1994. 593p. bibliog.

This anthology views the written song as a powerful literary object. The aim of the anthology is to expose and make known the lyrics to Québec songs, and it therefore constitutes a significant repertory. The songs are divided into four periods (1930-59, 1960-68, 1969-78, and 1979 to the present), each section beginning with a description of the period. Biographical notes and bibliographies of the authors are found at the end of the anthology. Madame Bolduc (a.k.a. Mary Travers) of the title sang variants of old French songs during the Depression years. Her songs inevitably represented a conservative bent according to some critics, encouraging people to remain in the country rather than move to the city.

919 **Circuit.**
Montréal: Presses de l'Université de Montréal, 1991- . 2 issues per year.
A scholarly review that addresses issues of musical and artistic creation in contemporary Québec, North America and elsewhere. It contains English résumés.

920 **Les 101 blues du Québec: 1965-1985.** (101 blues songs from Québec: 1965-85.)
Gérald Côté. Montréal: Éditions Triptyque, 1992. 247p.
The author takes the marginal character of the blues as a starting-point for his study. Through rigorous textual and musical analyses, the author compiles discourses and circumscribes common themes, which allow him to establish a parallel between the need felt by blacks to exorcize centuries of slavery, and the similar desire among Quebecers, often referred to as 'nègres blancs d'Amérique' (white blacks of America), to escape from the yoke of the colonizer. The author analyses various dimensions of the blues: the socio-economic context; its expression; and the music itself. He then discusses the blues in Québec, and reproduces the lyrics of 101 blues songs in Québec.

921 **Dictionnaire de la musique populaire au Québec, 1955-1992.** (A dictionary of popular music in Québec, 1955-92.)
Robert Thérien, Isabelle D'Amours. Québec: Institut québécois de Recherche sur la Culture, 1992. 580p. bibliog.
This dictionary alphabetically lists bio-discographies of individuals involved in Québec's popular music industry between 1955 and the summer of 1992. 'Popular' music is defined as all music which is not classical, folk, jazz or country. The criteria respected in this selection of 351 singers, groups, songwriters, producers and composers of popular music are as follows: importance of the record production, hit success, duration of career, distinctions received, and cultural impact. Each of the decades in the period covered are succinctly discussed in the first section of the dictionary. There is, however, complimentary information on artists who were not selected. A useful bibliography of general, specific and biographical works is to be found at the end of the volume.

General

922 **Chanson et politique au Québec: 1960-1980.** (Songs and politics in Québec: 1960-80.)
Jacques Aubé. Montréal: Éditions Triptyque, 1990. 135p. bibliog.
This work first maps out a short historical synthesis of francophone songs of a political nature from the beginning of the French regime until the end of the 1960s. The author then studies the political involvement of the authors, composers and singers of these francophone songs in Québec in the period 1970-80. Finally, he explores the relation between songs and politics. An extensive bibliography of studies on this subject is included.

923 **Les nuits de la "Main". Cent ans de spectacles sur le boulevard Saint-Laurent, 1891-1991.** (Nights on the Main. A century of shows on Saint-Laurent boulevard, 1891-1991.)
André-G. Bourassa, Jean-Marc Larrue. Montréal: VLB Éditeur, 1993. 361p. bibliog.

Familiarly called 'the Main', Saint-Laurent boulevard continues to animate and represent Montréal's essence. Unique throughout North America, this street is the oldest major artery in Montréal and extends from the old fortifications to the north of the island. This book charts the cultural importance of the Main between the Saint-Lawrence River and Mount-Royal Avenue between 1891 and 1991, relating the birth of Canadian cinema, the emergence of Québec theatre, and the apogee of Chinese and Yiddish opera, among other defining events.

924 **Le guide de la chanson québécoise.** (A guide to the Québec song.)
Robert Giroux, Constance Harvard, Roch Lapalme. Montréal: Éditions Triptyque, 1996. 2nd ed. 180p.

Organized like a dictionary, and divided into different historical periods, this volume presents the principal members of the musical community in Québec. The book contains a short biography of each person listed, in addition to a critical analysis of his or her work. The book also includes a good introductory essay on the development of music in Québec. See also Giroux's *Poses et profils de la chanson* (Outlines of songs) (Montréal: Éditions Triptyque, 1993).

925 **Parcours: de l'imprimé à l'oralité.** (The path from the printed word to oral expression.)
Robert Giroux. Montréal: Éditions Triptyque, 1990. 485p.

This book is divided into two sections, literature and song. The author's reflections in both of these sections touch on culture as a whole. This is a very innovative study of both written and verbal discourses.

926 **Parodie-chanson: l'air du singe.** (Parody songs: like a monkey.)
Jacques Julien. Montréal: Éditions Triptyque, 1995. 182p.

An essay which explores parody in the contemporary popular song in Québec and France. The author studies parody as a means of producing new cultural creations and of provoking and translating social changes. He describes various subjects tackled by selected songs, and then analyses the way in which these songs deal with the subjects. This unique study contributes to the criticism of contemporary Québec culture.

927 **Musiciens traditionnels du Québec, 1920-1993.** (Traditional musicians in Québec, 1920-93.)
Gabriel Labbé. Montréal: VLB Éditeur, 1995. 272p.

This is the expanded and revised edition of Gabriel Labbé's first book, *Les pionniers du disque folklorique québécois (1920-1950)* (Pioneers of folk records in Québec, 1920-50) (Montréal: L'Aurore, [1977]. 216p.). An indispensable tool for researchers and musicians, this book presents pertinent information on approximately 100 Québec musicians through short biographies accompanied by discographies. The author correlates the historical/ideological/social climate with that of traditional music, following different time periods within the seventy-three years in question. This book is an important contribution to the knowledge of Québec's living heritage.

928 **L'OSM, les cinquante premières années.** (The MSO, the first fifty years.)
Gilles Potvin. Montréal: Stanké, 1984. 204p.

Winner of many Grammies and internationally known for the quality of its recording, the Montréal Symphony Orchestra (MSO) is a source of pride for Montréalers. This book, written both in French and English, describes the evolution of the orchestra from its creation in 1934 by Anathase David to the arrival of Charles Dutoît as its director. The book includes many pictures of the Orchestra's important figures and leaders. Also see Agathe de Vaux's *La petite histoire de l'Orchestre symphonique de Montréal* (A short history of the Montréal Symphony Orchestra) (Verdun, Québec: Louise Courteau Éditrice, 1984. 190p.).

Dance

929 **Dancing in Montréal: seeds of a choreographic history.**
Iro Tembeck, translated and revised by the author. Madison, Wisconsin: Society of Dance History Scholars, 1994. 146p. Periodical issue.

This work first appeared in French bearing the title, *Danser à Montréal: germination d'une histoire choréographique* (Sillery, Québec: Presses de l'Université du Québec, 1991. 335p.). Drawing upon her expertise as a dance historian and choreographer, Tembeck traces the historical evolution of theatrical dance in Montréal from 1930 to the present. Alternating between classical ballet and modern dance, various choreographic traditions and the novelty of experimentation, the author exposes us to the institutions, individuals and masterpieces which have marked the artistic dance scene in Montréal.

Theatre

930 **La Nouvelle Compagnie théâtrale. En scène depuis 25 ans.** (The New Theatrical Company. On stage for the last twenty-five years.)
Jean-Luc Bastien, Pierre MacDuff. Montréal: VLB Éditeur, 1988. 316p.

Relates the history of one of Québec's most popular theatre production companies. The book is divided into five sections, each representing a five-year period; within each of these sections are thematic articles on some of the productions which highlighted the period. The book also lists all the productions the NCT (Nouvelle Compagnie théâtrale – New Theatrical Company) has produced.

931 **A sociocritique of translation. Theatre and alterity in Québec, 1968-1988.**
Annie Brisset.   Toronto: University of Toronto Press, 1996. 272p.
This study examines the translation of plays carried out in Québec over a period characterized by a quest for identity. The concept of alterity or otherness animates the activity of translation which must take into account the cultural contexts of other languages. The author explains that works by Shakespeare, Molière or Tchekhov, for example, become materials to be reused, and thus reformed by Québec playwrights. Brisset's analysis emphasizes how language is a culturally infused entity and that the translation of a text will embody not only the original text, but also tensions inherent in the very language being translated into, or the target language. The phenomenon of the cultural recycling of classics thus reflects the tensions troubling Québec society. The author demonstrates how translation participates in the development of a national dramatic art.

932 **Cahiers de Théâtre. JEU.** (Theatre Booklets. PLAY.)
Montréal: Éditions Quinze, 1976- . quarterly.
A specialized journal containing articles on 20th-century French Canadian drama, including history and criticism.

933 **Essays on modern Québec theatre.**
Edited by Joseph Donohoe, Jonathan Weiss.   East Lansing, Michigan: Michigan State University, 1995. 254p.
This book contains a collection of essays either written in, or having been translated into, English. The essays attest to the complexity and elusiveness of theatre in Québec. They aim to continue a tradition of critical analysis of Québec theatre by gathering together ideas from Québec, English-speaking Canada, the United States and France. This collection of essays does not exhaust all periods of theatre; the essays reflect a wide range of interpretative techniques and theories. The texts testify to the rich imagination and innovative techniques possessed by Québec playwrights and directors.

934 **La culture contre l'art: essai d'économie politique du théâtre.**
(Culture against art: an essay on the political economy of theatre.)
Josette Féral.   Sillery, Québec: Presses de l'Université du Québec, 1990. 341p.
This essay examines the development of theatre in Québec over the last thirty years. The author integrates this development into the study of the role of various public institutions, in an effort to establish the current socio-economic situation of theatre in Québec. The author, very perceptive concerning ideological movements, emphasizes the fundamental role of art and theatre in modern society. Numerous graphs and tables illustrate financial patterns in the development of theatre.

935 **Théâtre québécois I & II.** (Theatre in Québec, volumes I and II.)
Jean-Cléo Godin, Laurent Mailhot.   Montréal: Bibliothèque
Québécoise, 1988. 2nd ed. 2 vols. bibliog.
A comprehensive introduction to the most prominent playwrights in Québec. The first
volume, originally published in 1970, encompasses the years between 1940 and 1970,
focusing on the works of such writers as Michel Tremblay, Réjean Ducharme and
Marcel Dubé. The second volume, first published in 1980, places emphasis on the
years 1970-80. Together the volumes function as a history of both the dramatists and
the theatrical arts in Québec.

936 **Fred Barry et la petite histoire du théâtre au Québec.** (Fred Barry
and the short history of Québec theatre.)
Philippe Laframboise.   Montréal: Éditions Logiques, 1996. 227p.
Known as the dean of Québec artists, especially of comics, Fred Barry remains a
popular figure in the world of Québec theatre. Written by a former journalist, this book
is divided into two sections. The first relates the life and times of Fred Barry, while
the second contains brief summaries of the careers and lives of thirty-one of his
contemporary comedians, actors and actresses. Written for the general public, this
book provides a good description of the people involved in Québec theatre and comedy
during, and prior to, the Quiet Revolution.

937 **Le théâtre au Québec: 1825-1980: repères et perspectives.**
(Theatre in Québec: 1825-1980: landmarks and perspectives.)
Renée Legris et al.   Montréal: VLB Éditeur; Société d'Histoire du
Théâtre du Québec; Ministère des Affaires culturelles; Bibliothèque
nationale du Québec, 1988. 205p.
Presents a general view of the history of theatre in Québec, focusing on three periods:
1825-1930, 1930-65, and 1965-80. This fascinating trilogy of studies, which includes
many photographs, was commissioned by the Historical Society of Québec Theatre.

938 **Theatre and politics in modern Québec.**
Elaine Frances Nardocchio.   Edmonton, Alberta: University of
Alberta Press, 1986. 157p.
The author's primary goal in this very accessible essay is to underline the political
influence on Québec theatre. More generally, this work provides readers with an
informative and accessible guide to 300 years of Québec theatre. It demonstrates the
powerful force of colonization, and documents the vitality and diversity of Québec
theatre in the years following the death of Maurice Duplessis.

939 **French-Canadian theater.**
Jonathan M. Weiss.   Boston, Massachusetts: Twayne, 1986. 179p.
A very clear introduction to Québec theatre. Weiss focuses exclusively on dramatic
literature rather than performance. He studies the historical development of theatre in
Québec from the 1800s up to the 1980s. His analyses of the texts are always well
situated within the social and political context.

Film

Reference

940 **Cinémas: Revue d'Études Cinématographiques.** (Cinema: Journal of Cinematographic Studies.)
Montréal: Université de Montréal, Département d'Histoire de l'Art, 1990- . 3 issues per year.

An academic journal on various aspects of the film industry, such as marketing and cinematic techniques. Articles emphasize the history of Québec cinema and the current state of the industry. Published three times a year, this journal is interesting for those who want to explore the many faces of cinema in Québec.

941 **Dictionnaire du cinéma québécois.** (A dictionary of Québec cinema.)
Edited by Michel Coulombe, Marcel Jean. Montréal: Éditions du Boréal, 1991. 603p.

Many of the entries in this dictionary concern individuals who have contributed to the production of films in Québec; these biographical articles are listed alphabetically. The dictionary also contains a list of functions, which includes only those jobs relating to the cinema. This list, as well as that of filmographies, is not exhaustive, but remains very extensive nonetheless. This is a very useful resource.

942 **Discographie du cinéma québécois: 1960-1990.** (Discography of Québec cinema: 1960-90.)
Les Rendez-vous du Cinéma québécois. Montréal: Association des Cinémas parallèles du Québec, 1991. 29p.

The first discography of Québec cinema, this constitutes a stimulating acknowledgement of the field. The following criteria were used in the selection of titles: the films must be Québec productions or co-productions; the music must have been composed solely for film; and it must be available on record, cassette or compact disc. Included in this work is the discography itself, an index to composers and a film index. This is not an exhaustive directory.

943 **24 images.**
Longueuil, Québec: Le Préambule, 1979- . 5 issues per year.

The best magazine on Québec cinema. It publishes interviews with important directors in Québec, reviews of the latest productions both in Québec and in other societies, and well-documented articles on the various challenges facing the industry. For reviews of Québec's latest film productions, the reader can also consult *Séquences* (Sequences) (Montréal: Service d'Éducation cinématographique de l'Office diocésain des Techniques de Diffusion de Montréal, 1955- . bi-monthly).

General

944 **Le cinéma québécois à l'heure internationale.** (Québec cinema at
the international hour.)
Marie-Christine Abel, André Giguère, Luc Perreault. Montréal:
Stanké, 1990. 340p.

This book combines photographs and descriptions of not only the major 'contributors'
to Québec cinema, but of the photographic directors, musical score composers, artistic
directors, makeup artists, etc., in order to provide a comprehensive view of the team
effort involved in the film industry in Québec. Around sixty entries are included,
comprising a representative mosaic of Québec cinema on the international stage today.

945 **Le déclin de l'empire américain.** (The decline of the American
empire.)
Denys Arcand. Montréal: Éditions du Boréal, 1986. 173p.

The script of one of the most important Québec films in terms of its international
recognition. Written and directed by Denys Arcand, *Le déclin de l'empire américain*
relates the growing cynicism of a group of bourgeois historians living in a cottage in
the Eastern Townships. Substituting their youthful dreams with a disproportionate
obsession with sex, the characters brilliantly symbolize the discouraging attitudes prevailing in Québec society following the 1980 referendum. See also Arcand's *Jésus of
Montréal* (Montréal: Éditions du Boréal, 1989. 188p.), which was nominated for best
foreign picture at the Oscars.

946 **Dans l'ombre des projecteurs: les femmes dans le cinéma au
Québec de 1896 à 1969.** (In the shadow of projectors: women in
Québec cinema from 1896 to 1969.)
Jocelyne Denault. Montréal: Presses de l'Université du Québec,
1996. 245p.

This book offers one view of the presence (and absence) of women in the history of
cinema insofar as it is seen as a social institution in Québec. The author examines film
production and all the activities which have allowed cinema in Québec to become not
only an important recreational activity, but also an educational activity and consequently an agent of social integration. An annex contains an extensive list of films by
women who participated in film production in Québec before 1970.

947 **Essays on Québec cinema.**
Edited by Joseph I. Donohoe Jr. East Lansing, Michigan: Michigan
State University Press, 1991. 194p. bibliog.

This book contains essays divided into four sections. In the first section, Esther
Pelletier analyses the growing importance of pre-production procedures in the industry,
especially in the preparation of the scenario. The second section is composed of
commentaries from two leading filmmakers (Pierre Perrault and Jean-Pierre Lefebvre)
on film. The third section deals with individual directors and themes. Finally, the
fourth section offers interpretations of individual films. Following the essays is a
biographical dictionary containing career summaries of thirty-five of the most important
directors, writers and producers in the history of Québec cinema. A concise bibliography
of critical works in this area is included in the work.

948   **Le cinéma québécois.** (Québec cinema.)
       Marcel Jean.   Montréal: Éditions du Boréal, 1991. 123p. bibliog.
       (Collection Boréal Express, no. 2).

A brief history of film production in Québec. Jean endeavours to examine the aesthetics of the main creators and the themes animating their films. The author tackles such subjects as the essential role of the documentary in the production of a film based on fiction, the role of state agencies in the development of the film industry, and feminist cinema.

949   **Le cinéma au Québec. Essai de statistique historique, 1896 à nos jours.** (Cinema in Québec. Historical statistical essay, 1896 to the present.)
       Yvan Lamonde, Pierre-François Hébert.   Québec: Institut québécois de Recherche sur la Culture, 1981. 481p.

This is a quantitative history of the cultural phenomenon of cinema. This unique study focuses on the very evolution of the cinemas themselves, their clientele, and business-related competition in the industry. The study is not exhaustive, but explores the subjects in question in great depth.

950   **Histoire générale du cinéma au Québec.** (A general history of Québec cinema.)
       Yves Lever.   Montréal: Éditions du Boréal, 1995. 640p. 2nd ed.

This work offers a panoramic synthesis of the history of cinema in Québec. A socio-critical perspective is adopted, developed in France by Marc Ferro, Jean-Pierre Jeancolas, Pierre Sorlin and Edgar Morin. Lever examines the climates of production, distribution, criticism and legislation in each of the following periods: 'The silent film in Québec (1896-1938)'; 'The quiet dreams of French Canadians (1939-55)'; 'The cinema of the Quiet Revolution (1956-68)'; and 'The maturation period (1969-94)'. Lists of awards and associations are included in the annexes.

951   **Les 100 films québécois qu'il faut voir.** (The 100 Québec films that must be seen.)
       Yves Lever.   Montréal: Nuit Blanche Éditeur, 1995. 283p.

The 100 films listed in this detailed guide (containing the name of the film, the director, the film length, etc., followed by a two-page description) already are, or will eventually become, classics of Québec cinema. Although the selection of titles is quite subjective, Lever has make an effort to represent each aesthetic tendency.

952   **Cinéma de l'imaginaire québécois: de La petite Aurore à Jésus de Montréal.** (Cinema of the Québec imagination: from *La petite Aurore* [Little Aurore] to *Jésus de Montréal* [Jesus of Montréal].)
       Heinz Weinmann.   Montréal: L'Hexagone, 1990. 270p.

The author examines the dual role of Québec cinema as both catalyst and product in the development of Québec's national identity. This essay explores the individual and collective dreams of Quebecers insofar as the cinema projects these dreams to the public. Heinz Weinmann analyses eight key films which reveal the obsessions of, and changes in, the Québec psyche, oscillating between its destiny and its decline. This essay is informative on cultural, sociological and historical levels.

Folklore

953 **Héritage de la francophonie canadienne.** (French Canadian heritage.)
Jean-Claude Dupont. Sainte-Foy, Québec: Presses de l'Université Laval, 1986. 269p.

This important book presents a very good overview of the oral tradition in French-speaking Canada. The authors present the different customs and beliefs, legends, tales and songs of the various regions in Canada. Moreover, the authors pay attention to the divergence in the same stories across different regions. The book also contains a very good introduction on the evolution in Québec and Canada in the research on oral traditions.

954 **Le légendaire de la Beauce.** (Legends of the Beauce.)
Jean-Claude Dupont. Montréal: Leméac, 1978. 200p. bibliog.

Located on the south shore of the Saint-Lawrence River near Québec City, the Beauce region has a rich oral tradition. The author describes some of the main themes of this tradition, which include the nocturnal spirit, the devil, and sorcery. Based on 100 interviews with people of the region, Dupont outlines these legends. The author also makes comparisons with other oral traditions in Québec. The book contains a lexicon and photographs of objects associated with the various legends described.

955 **Légendes de l'Amérique française.** (Legends of French America.)
Jean-Claude Dupont. Sainte-Foy, Québec: Le Secrétariat permanent des Peuples francophones, 1985. 66p. bibliog.

This brief work presents the legends of French-speaking people from different states and provinces in both Canada and the United States. Each story is accompanied by a picture of the author. This book is part of a larger collection written by the author, a well-known ethnologist, on the legends of different regions and on various themes in Québec's social imagination. Other works by the same author which examine the legends of various regions in Québec in more depth include *Légendes du coeur du Québec* (Legends from the heart of Québec) (Sainte-Foy, Québec: J. C. Dupont, 1985. 63p.) and *Légendes du Saint-Laurent* (Legends of the Saint-Lawrence) (Sainte-Foy, Québec: Légendes du Saint-Laurent, 1985. 2 vols.).

956 **Mélanges en l'honneur de Luc Lacoursière: folklore français d'Amérique.** (Essays in honour of Luc Lacoursière: French folklore of America.)
Jean-Claude Dupont et al. Montréal: Leméac, 1978. 486p. bibliog.

Luc Lacoursière is one of Québec's pioneers in the study of French American folklore. This volume of essays, in his honour, highlights some of the main themes of his work: ethnography, the preservation of historical documents, popular songs, and legends. A significant amount of information is provided not only on Luc Lacoursière's work but also on the general evolution of the study of Québec folklore and French-speaking Canada. The volume includes an extensive bibliography on Lacoursière's publications.

957   **De Ker-Is à Québec: légendes de France et de Nouvelle-France.**
(From Ker-Is to Québec City: legends from France and New France.)
Fernand Grenier, Rémi Clark.   Québec: La Galerie le Chien d'Or,
1990. 108p.

Grenier reproduces prints by the painter Rémi Clark in an effort to pay tribute to the folklore and heritage of France and New France. Clark's paintings indicate a creativity inspired by the gothic and the mythical, by a powerful mythological universe. The images are inspired by French and Québec legends. The author situates each print, displaying particular legends, in an appropriate context. Historical and geographical explanations accompany the prints, and a lexicon can be found at the end of the book. Grenier aims to translate the emotion and fantasy of Québec's legendary heritage through the representation and explanation of the work of Rémi Clark.

958   **Contes et sortilèges des quatre coins du Québec.** (Tales and magic
spells from the four corners of Québec.)
Edited by Nicole Guilbault.   Québec: Documentor, Cégep
François-Xavier-Garneau, 1991. 162p.

This book presents forty-three legends and tales which have been gathered by students for a course on Québec folklore. The texts are arranged according to the main themes of these literary genres, such as the devil, extraordinary beings, children, and wonders and miracles. A lexicon found at the end of the book greatly facilitates the reading of these texts.

959   **Antiquités du Québec.** (Québec antiquities.)
Michel Lessard.   Montréal: Éditions de l'Homme, 1995. 380p. (Objets
Anciens).

The historian and author, Michel Lessard, devotes this volume to material objects relating to Québec's social and cultural life. He includes prints and descriptions of articles of clothing, recreational objects, and devices used for the means of communication, among others. This illustrated work tells the story of Québec through an examination of antique objects.

960   **Contes à raconter et à écouter: 12 contes du Canada français.**
(Tales to read aloud and listen to: twelve tales from French-speaking
Canada.)
Jani Pascal.   Montréal: Guérin, 1988. 294p.

The author has reproduced a series of amusing and phonetically catchy stories to be read out aloud. She defines the 'tale' as a magical story, amusing in nature, which has been passed down from generation to generation. These stories are presented in an effort to draw attention to the spirit of the collective imagination and Québec's cultural heritage on the one hand, and to amuse both adults and children alike, on the other.

961 **La chasse-galerie, de la légende au mythe: la symbolique du vol magique dans les récits québécois de chasse-galerie.** (The flying bark canoe, from the legend to the myth: symbolism of the magical flight in Québec texts of the Chasse-galerie.)
Brigitte Purkhardt.   Montréal: XYZ, 1992. 207p.

This study explores the symbolic system of the magical flight of Québec's legend of the chasse-galerie (flying bark canoe). The transformation of the legend to the myth is the focus of the study; the 'chasse-galerie' characterizes Québec on a basic level initially, but the countless mythical traces in its discourse inscribe Québec within a much vaster legendary discourse. The analysis focuses on four exemplary stories by Damase Potvin, Wilfred-Hidola Girard, Honoré Beaugrand and Marie Caroline Watson Hamelin. The analysis profiles not only '*how*' the chasse-galerie flies into Québec's imaginary sky, but *why*'.

962 **La danse traditionnelle au Québec.** (Traditional dance in Québec.)
Robert Lionel.   Sainte-Foy, Québec: Presses de l'Université du Québec, 1986. 184p.

Traditional dances were frequently associated with important events in Québec. In this interesting book, Séguin presents the kinds of dance that were performed in various circumstances; in this way, he reveals Québec's customs and traditions.

963 **Conteurs québécois: 1900-1940.** (Québec storywriters: 1900-40.)
Edited by Adrien Thério.   Ottawa: Presses de l'Université d'Ottawa, 1988. 229p. bibliog.

The first anthology of Québec storywriters covering the years from 1900 to 1940, a period which is not very well known in Québec literary history, especially in the genre of the novel. This anthology introduces the reader to approximately thirty fables from this time. These texts are often moving – in a comical or tragic way – and centre around family life in a rural or village setting. Each story is preceded by a short biography and bibliography of each author.

964 **La danse traditionnelle dans l'Est du Canada: quadrilles et cotillons.** (Traditional dance in Eastern Canada: quadrilles and cotillions.)
Simonne Voyer.   Sainte-Foy, Québec: Presses de l'Université Laval, 1986. 509p. maps.

The author presents an exhaustive description of the quadrilles and cotillions from Québec, along with illustrations to facilitate interpretation. The extensive terminology section at the end of the book is extremely informative.

Sport and Leisure

Reference

965 **Dictionnaire La Presse des sports du Québec.** (*La Presse* dictionary of sports in Québec.)
Patrice Fontaine.   Montréal: Éditions Libre Expression, 1996. 348p.

A dictionary of all the major athletes and sports organizations in the history of Québec. It provides statistical and biographical information on the different athletes.

966 **Géo Plein Air.** (Geo Outdoors.)
Montréal: Géo plein air, 1992- . bi-monthly.

A well-produced magazine on the various outdoor activities in Québec, such as climbing, country skiing and hiking. The magazine also presents portraits of athletes who participate in these activities. It also includes a very good section on the quality of new equipment on the market.

967 **Guide Plein Air du Québec.** (Outdoor Guide to Québec.)
Montréal: Traffic communication, 1989- . 2 issues per year.

Published twice a year, this guide details information on the varied outdoor activities that can be practised in Québec. It includes information on the location of outdoor sites, equipment needed for various activities, and other pertinent information for the interested amateur. See also *Fêtes Populaires au* Québec (Popular Holidays in Québec) (Montréal: Société des Festivals populaires du Québec, 1987-).

968 **Loisir et sport au Québec.** (Leisure and sport in Québec.)
Sainte-Foy, Québec: Québec dans le monde, 1993.

An index of the different organizations associated with sport and leisure activities in Québec.

969   **Magazine Tourisme Jeunesse.** (Young Tourist Magazine.)
       Montréal: Tourisme jeunesse, 1995- .

Formerly known as *Temps Libre* (Free Time), this magazine provides important information for those interested in youth tourism in Québec. The magazine suggests
destinations and activities that would appeal to young people. It also provides valuable
tips for those who plan to travel to other parts of the world. The descriptions of personal travel experiences of different people are often very interesting.

970   **Society and Leisure = Loisir et Société.**
       Sainte-Foy, Québec: Presses de l'Université du Québec, 1978- .
       quarterly.

A bilingual scholarly journal devoted to the scientific study of leisure in various
societies.

General

971   **Les pratiques culturelles des québécois. Une autre image de
       nous-mêmes.** (Quebecers' cultural practices. Another image of
       ourselves.)
       Edited by Jean-Paul Baillargeon.   Québec: Institut québécois de
       Recherche sur la Culture, 1986. 394p.

A series of essays on the role and significance of the major cultural and leisure activities
of Quebecers between 1971 and 1985.

972   **L'église et le loisir au Québec avant la Révolution tranquille.**
       (The Church and leisure in Québec before the Quiet Revolution.)
       Michel Bellefleur.   Sainte-Foy, Québec: Presses de l'Université du
       Québec, 1986. 221p. bibliog.

The Church was a major actor in Québec society before the Quiet Revolution. One
of the areas in which it played an important role was in the organization of leisure
activities. The author describes the social milieu in which the clergy had to assume the
leadership of organizing leisure activities in order to maintain control of moral codes
of behaviour. This book not only provides an excellent description of the development
of leisure activities in Québec, but also a very good portrait of Québec during the first
half of the 20th century. It includes an extensive bibliography.

973 **Du loisir à l'innovation: les associations volontaires de personnes retraitées.** (From leisure to innovation: the volunteer associations of retired people.)
Marie-Marthe T. Brault.   Québec: Institut québécois de Recherche sur la Culture, 1987. 176p. bibliog. (Documents de Recherche, no. 15).

The author explores the reasons behind the rise in number of senior citizens' groups. Brault argues that these associations have become a means of socializing for a new generation of retired people. Moreover, she argues that these associations are providing new forms of community solidarity. The question of intergenerational contact in leisure activities is also discussed in the book. It includes a comprehensive bibliography.

974 **Les Expos. Du parc Jarry au Stade olympique.** (The Expos. From Jarry Park to the Olympic Stadium.)
Denis Brodeur, Daniel Caza.   Montréal: Éditions de l'Homme, 1996. 301p.

Relates the evolution of the Expos, the major league baseball team in Montréal. Brodeur, the well-known sports photographer, and Caza include pictures of the important events and players in the history of the club.

975 **Baseball's fabulous Montréal Royals. The minor league team that made major league history.**
William Brown.   Montréal: Robert Davies Publishing, 1996. 192p.

Relates the history of the Montréal Royals, Montréal's famous junior league baseball team. In the course of their fifty-five seasons in the International League, the Royals won nine pennants, seven league championships and three Junior World Series titles; they broke the colour barrier in professional baseball with the signing of Jackie Robinson; and they started the careers of such greats as Chuck Connors, Roy Campanella, Tommy Lasorda and Roberto Clemente. This chronological look at the team's defining moments also contains game accounts, player profiles and anecdotes. Among other titles on Montréal's contribution to baseball is Maury Allen's biography of Jackie Robinson, Montréal's most famous player, entitled *Jackie Robinson, a life remembered* (New York: Franklin Watts, 1987. 260p.). On the Montréal Expos, the current National League team, William Humber's *Cheering for the home team: the story of baseball in Canada* (Erin, Ontario: Boston Mills Press, 1983) contains a section on the team's history.

976 **Les meilleurs sites d'observation des oiseaux au Québec.** (The best observation sites in Québec for birdwatching.)
Normand David.   Sainte-Foy, Québec: Presses de l'Université du Québec, 1990. 300p.

This guide presents the best observation sites in the different regions of Québec. The author details the types of birds that can be found at each site and lists some important information related to the location of the sites. The book includes an index.

977 **The game. A thoughtful and provocative look at a life in hockey.**
Ken Dryden. Toronto: Macmillan, 1983. 248p.
Written by one of the Montréal Canadians' best goalkeepers, this is the story of nine days in the life of a hockey legend during the 1970s. While other stars have written their memoirs, Dryden's literate and articulate style, combined with the insight he brings to understanding the game of hockey, sets this book apart. *The game* is an essential read for all those interested in coming closer to understanding Canada's foremost game and its impact on society. Other Québec hockey legends have also written sports memoirs. Among the better ones is Jean Béliveau's *My life in hockey* (Toronto: McClelland and Stewart, 1994. 308p.).

978 **L'histoire du hockey au Québec: origine et développement d'un phénomène culturel.** (The history of hockey in Québec: origins and development of a cultural phenomenon.)
Donald Guay. Chicoutimi, Québec: JCL, 1990. 293p.
The game of hockey has profoundly marked Québec society. This book relates the history of the game and its evolution. The book is well documented and brilliantly introduces the controversies of the hockey world: players' salaries, violence, and the future of French-speaking Quebecers in the sport. The book also includes many pictures of important players in the history of hockey in Québec.

979 **Introduction à l'histoire des sports au Québec.** (An introduction to the history of sport in Québec.)
Donald Guay. Montréal: VLB Éditeur, 1987. 294p. (Collection Études Québécoises).
An introduction to the history of the establishment and development of thirteen different sports in Québec. The author delves into the first manifestations of each sport, the important sporting events in Québec, and describes how they were organized in the 19th century. Among the sports included are baseball, boxing, hockey and swimming. The author demonstrates that the establishment of different sports is essentially the result of the British influence and British culture following the waves of immigration from the British Isles. The author mainly uses newspapers as his principal source of information. See also Gilles Janson's *Emparons-nous du sport: les Canadiens français et le sport au XIXe siècle* (Grabbing hold of sport: French Canadians and sport during the 19th century) (Montréal: Guérin, 1995. 239p.).

980 **Loisir et culture au Québec.** (Leisure and culture in Québec.)
Roger Levasseur. Montréal: Éditions du Boréal Express, 1982. 192p.
Various institutions have attempted to influence Quebecers' leisure time in an effort to preserve Québec's distinct culture. This book examines leisure and cultural activities as a means to understanding Québec society. Levasseur charts the evolution of leisure in Québec from the first attempts to organize playing fields in 1929 to the creation of the Department of Culture in 1979. This book reveals how the Church was slowly replaced by the Québec state as the principal organizer and defender of culture. Levasseur's research illustrates the importance of institutions in the protection of Québec's national culture.

981   **La chasse au Québec.** (Hunting in Québec.)
Paul-Louis Martin.   Montréal: Éditions du Boréal, 1990. 408p.
bibliog.

A very detailed essay on the history of hunting in Québec from the *ancien régime* to the contemporary period. The author describes different hunting techniques, the arms used, categories of game, and their uses. The book includes many pictures and a comprehensive bibliography.

982   **Loisir et société: traité de sociologie empirique.** (Leisure and society: an empirical sociological treatise.)
Gilles Pronovost.   Sainte-Foy, Québec: Presses de l'Université du Québec, 1993. 347p.

Argues that the evolution of a society can be explained by studying the population's leisure activities. The author begins with a comprehensive theoretical discussion, introducing the reader to the main debates in this particular field of sociology. The remainder of the book describes the change in activities, in actors, and in the role of socializing institutions in Québec.

983   **Randonnée pédestre au Québec.** (Hiking in Québec.)
Yves Séguin.   Montréal: Ulysse, 1996. 180p. 2nd ed.

A very well-written and researched guide to hiking in Québec. In the first section of the book, the author provides important information on the equipment necessary in Québec's climate, on the type of difficulties that people may face while hiking, and on the particularities of hiking in Québec. The remainder of the guide is devoted to the different sites across Québec. Information on the physical aspects of the sites and how to reach them by car is another useful feature of this guide. Other Ulysse guides include: *La motoneige au Québec* (Ski-dooing [snowmobiling] in Québec) (Montréal: Ulysse, 1995); *Randonnée pédestre Montréal et environs* (Hiking in and around Montréal) (Montréal: Ulysse, 1996); and *Ski de fond au Québec* (Cross-country skiing in Québec) (Montréal: Ulysse, 1994).

984   **Les Glorieux: histoire du Canadiens de Montréal en images.**
(The Glorious Ones: a history of the Montréal Canadians through photographs.)
Réjean Tremblay, Ronald King, with a foreword by Maurice Richard.
Montréal: Transcontinental, 1996. 167p.

An excellent illustrated history of the most successful sports franchise (professional sports club) in North America. Related works include Line Bonneau and Taïeb Hafsi's *Sam Pollock et le Canadien de Montréal* (Sam Pollock and the Montréal Canadians) (Sainte-Foy, Québec: Presses de l'Université du Québec, 1996), which focuses on the management of the hockey club during the mid-1960s when the expansion of the league changed the game. See also Claude Mouton's *Toute l'histoire illustrée et merveilleuse du Canadien de Montréal* (A comprehensive illustrated account of the marvellous history of the Montréal Canadians) (Montréal: La Presse, 1986).

Libraries and Museums

985   **Musée de la civilisation. Concept and practices.**
Ronald Arpin.   Québec: Musée de la Civilisation, 1992. 155p.
Describes the museological choices and the management practices of the Musée de la civilization (Museum of Civilization) in Québec City, which opened in October 1988. Written for readers involved in museum administration, this book at once describes the principal foundations of the museum's mission in addition to illustrating this mission using concrete examples. This book is accessible to non-museum specialists who want to know more about this particular museum.

986   **Museological trends in Québec.**
Edited by Marcel Côté.   Montréal: Société des Musées québécois, 1992. 154p.
Comprises the proceedings of the Third Forum of the Museum Association held in Québec City, reuniting a dozen museum professionals. This book will be of interest and use to museum specialists eager to learn about how Québec museums have attempted to build bridges between their institutions and society.

987   **L'archivistique: son histoire, ses acteurs depuis 1960.** (Archiving: its history and its principal animators since 1960.)
Louise Gagnon-Arguin.   Sainte-Foy, Québec: Presses de l'Université du Québec, 1992. 229p.
Describes the evolution of the archivist profession in Québec since 1960. The author draws parallels between the evolution of the profession and the modernization of state and society in Québec. The book also contains a good chapter on the place archivists occupy in Québec society.

988 **Les librairies agréées: 1983 à 1992.** (Accredited bookstores: 1983 to 1992.)

Gaétan Hardy, Jean-Paul Sylvestre. Québec: Ministère de la Culture et des Communications, 1994. 76p.

This work provides a portrait of the evolution of the library industry since 1983. Among the themes examined are those of the numbers, sales and revenues of libraries. While the study is primarily statistical in nature, the authors also explain market changes in the industry.

989 **Pointe-à-Callière.**

François Megendie. Montréal: Section b, 1994. 115p.

Awarded the Grand Prix d'Architecture (Grand Prize for Architecture) from the Order of Québec Architects in 1993 and the Governor General's Award for excellence in architecture in 1994, the Pointe-à-Callière, Montréal's museum of archaeology and history, is one of the city's most innovative and singular monuments. This book contains a description of the museum's conception and design, and of the museum itself. Aside from the technical drawings, and the illustrations, the majority of the volume is dedicated to an interview with the museum's principal architect, Dan Hanganu. This book will be of interest to those curious as to the way the museum's design is intended to reflect its central mission of transmitting Montréal's archaeological and historical heritage.

The Publishing Industry

990 **Du texte à l'image: le livre illustré au Québec.** (From text to images: illustrated books in Québec.)
Silvie Bernier. Sainte-Foy, Québec: Presses de l'Université Laval, 1990. 335p.

In examining the way books have been illustrated in Québec, Bernier reveals the different aspects of both the linguistic and iconographic heritages in Québec. Different editions of Québec classics, like *Maria Chapdelaine* (see item no. 881), are compared in order to demonstrate the divergence and convergence between text and illustration. A chapter dedicated to a publishing house specializing in popular books demonstrates the way in which the editorial and environmental contexts affect the relationship between text and image. Overall, this study of books published between 1910 and the 1950s allows the reader to witness the different artistic styles, such as naturalism, symbolism, cubism and surrealism, as they were applied to book illustration. Rather than situate book illustrations within greater artistic movements, Bernier suggests that each work studied bears witness to its historical origins as well as indicating the position its illustrator occupied in the art industry.

991 **L'édition littéraire au Québec de 1940 à 1960.** (Literary publishing houses in Québec from 1940 to 1960.)
Silvie Bernier. Sherbrooke, Québec: Université de Sherbrooke, 1985. 217p. bibliog.

The significant impact of ideas on the history of Québec is revealed in this book which devotes several chapters to particular publishing houses which emerged in the 1940s, namely Erta, Fides, Valiquette, and Variétés. By relating the flurry of publishing activity during these two decades to the social conditions of the times, these essays convey the manner in which publishing was intimately linked to the evolution of society. The book concludes with a comprehensive bibliography of works concerning publishing during this period.

992   **Bibliographie du Québec.** (Bibliography of Québec.)
Québec: Bibliothèque nationale du Québec, 1968- . monthly.

This series, published at monthly intervals since April 1972, lists all titles published in Québec or received by Québec's National Library for the month in question. An annual index covers the entire year and directs the reader to the appropriate monthly issue. The types of material covered include books, brochures, microforms, printed music, serials, maps, electronic documents, and musical recordings. Titles in each issue are presented according to the Library of Congress cataloguing scheme. From April 1969 to January/March 1972, the guide was published three times a year, and prior to that it was published annually.

993   **L'édition au Québec.** (Publishing in Québec.)
Ignace Cau.   Québec: Ministère des Affaires culturelles, 1981. 229p.

Examines the publishing industry as a cultural phenomenon, highlighting the impact publishing has had on the development of Québec society since the 1960s. Cau takes a positive view of government intervention in this sector and describes how government support has, in part, helped create a dynamic and prosperous industry.

994   **Pour que vive la lecture: littérature et bibliothèque pour la jeunesse.** (So that reading might come alive: literature and libraries for the young.)
Edited by Hélène Charbonneau.   Montréal: ASTED, 1994. 241p.

Québec possesses a reputation of excellence in the industry of children's literature. This very good and comprehensive collection of essays on the state of children's literature and public libraries in Québec also demonstrates the passion Québec youth has for reading. In the first section, different authors present the main characteristics of Québec children's literature. The second and third sections explain how the institutions and the different actors in this sector can encourage reading among youth.

995   **Livre et lecture au Québec, 1800-1850.** (Books and reading in Québec, 1800-50.)
Claude Galarneau, Maurice Lemire.   Québec: Institut québécois de Recherche sur la Culture, 1988. 270p.

Examines the continuity of relations between France and Québec in the realm of book publishing. This investigation of the publishing industry reveals the continued cultural ties between France and Québec despite the fact that Upper and Lower Canada were under British control after 1760. The connections between the English-speaking and French-speaking communities are examined within the various classes in Québec. The book also describes the role played by important religious orders and institutions, such as the Sulpicians and Parliament, in the dissemination of printed material. The authors suggest that, contrary to popular belief, printed materials, such as newspapers and periodicals, were widely read among both the French-speaking and English-speaking elites and popular classes. This book stems from a colloquium held in Québec City in May 1987 which brought together scholars from both Québec and France.

996 **Livre et politique au Bas-Canada, 1791-1849.** (Books and politics in Lower Canada from 1791 to 1849.)
Gilles Gallichan. Sillery, Québec: Éditions du Septentrion, 1991. 519p. bibliog.

Linking the development of political and judicial institutions with the growth and development of the publishing industry, Gallichan illustrates the degree to which publishing was one of the most important cultural instruments in the development of Lower Canada. Following a brief chapter describing the social and cultural aspects of Québec City, five chapters reveal the links between politicians and publishers, and between the press and political parties. Gallichan further demonstrates the role played by the press in the daily execution of the government's functions. The last two sections of the book examine the parliamentary library and its contents. A selected bibliography and index will aid interested readers in locating further information.

997 **L'industrie du livre.** (The book industry.)
Gaétan Hardy. Québec: Ministère de la Culture, 1993. 3 vols.

A quantitative study of three institutions of the book industry in Québec: the publishing house, the library and the book fair. A complete overview is provided of the current state of the industry in Québec.

998 **L'imprimé au Québec: aspects historiques, 18e-20e siècle.** (Printed matter in Québec: historical characteristics, 18th-20th centuries.)
Edited by Yvan Lamonde. Québec: Institut québécois de Recherche sur la Culture, 1983. 370p. (Collection Culture Savante. no. 2).

A collection of essays which broadly examines the nature of printed matter in Québec and related social phenomena such as illiteracy. Specifically, the relationships between writer and publisher, society and books, and the government and publishing, are examined. Allan Greer critically assesses the validity of the traditional perception of Québec as 'pathologically illiterate', concluding that Québec society was no worse off in comparison to other developed countries. Other authors examine the cultural and literary societies which paved the way for the establishment of public libraries. The libraries of private individuals are also examined. Together, these essays chart the development of the groups and institutions at the heart of the transformations in the publishing industry.

999 **Éditeurs transatlantiques.** (Transatlantic publishing houses.)
Edited by Jacques Michon. Montréal: Éditions Triptyque; Sherbrooke, Québec: Éditions Ex Libris, 1991. 245p.

A study of six publishing houses active during the 1940s and their role in the diffusion of a progressive literature in Québec. The authors of the book argue that their openness to foreign and alternative literature was among one of the important triggers of the Quiet Revolution. The publishing houses under study are: Éditions Lucien Parizeau; L'Arbre; Serge; Mangin; Fernand Pilon; and B. D. Simpsons.

1000 **L'édition du livre populaire.** (Popular publishing houses.)
Edited by Jacques Michon. Sherbrooke, Québec: Éditions Ex Libris, 1988. 204p.

A study of four publishing houses which have specialized in popular books since 1920, namely Édouard Garand, Éditions de l'Étoile, Éditions Marquis, and Granger Frères. This study covers the social, economic, and literary factors which gave rise to the emergence of these publishers. Overall, these essays will provide the reader with a general understanding of how this particular part of the publishing industry started and how it developed.

1001 **Ces livres que vous avez aimés. Les best-sellers au Québec de 1970 à aujourd'hui.** (The books you have loved. Québec bestsellers from 1970 to the present.)
Denis Saint-Jacques, Jacques Lemieux, Claude Martin, Vincent Nadeau. Québec: Nuits Blanches, 1994. 223p.

Four experts examine the phenomenon of bestsellers: their creation; their history; their audience; and what they tell us about society in general. Tables and graphs complement their study. The first section examines the jobs involved in the distribution and editing of books. The second looks at the bestseller lists. The third section looks at where these books come from as well as the changes in the types of books which make the bestseller lists. The last section attempts to identify the motivations of buyers and their purchasing habits.

1002 **Lettres d'un libraire.** (Letters from a librarian.)
Henri Tranquille. Montréal: Leméac, 1976. 2 vols.

A collection of letters written by a well-known Québec polemicist and librarian, which deals principally with Québec literature.

1003 **Lasting impressions. A short history of English publishing in Québec.**
Bruce Whiteman. Montréal: Véhicule Press, 1994. 98p.

Provides a history of English publishers from the arrival of the first printers in Québec City in 1764. Written by the curator of the Rare Books and Special Collections at McGill University, this short book benefits from his expertise in addition to being accessible to the non-specialist. In his own words, this book is an attempt to highlight some of the printing industry's successes and 'to view them within a lightly drawn cultural context'.

Mass Media

1004   **La pub. Trente ans de publicité au Québec.** (The ad. Thirty years of advertising in Québec.)
Jean-Marie Allard.   Montréal: Éditions Libre Expression; Publicité-Club de Montréal, 1989. 228p.

One of the first books on the evolution of publicity in Québec. The book does not provide a deep analysis of the contents of publicity but focuses on major events: prizes; the foundation of the Publicité-Club; and instances of government intervention.

1005   **La presse québécoise: des origines à nos jours, index cumulatif, 1764-1944.** (The Québec press: from its origins to the present day, cumulative index, 1764-1944.)
André Beaulieu.   Sainte-Foy, Québec: Presses de l'Université Laval, 1987. 6 vols.

A guide to all newspapers that have existed in Québec and Lower Canada. The author provides information on the papers' circulation and ideological stance. Also see John Hare and Jean-Pierre Wallot's *Les imprimés dans le Bas-Canada, 1801-1810. Bibliographie analytique* (Lower Canadian newspapers, 1801-10. Analytical bibliography) (Montréal: Presses de l'Université de Montréal, 1967. 381p.).

1006   **Les quotidiens montréalais de 1945 à 1985.** (Daily newspapers in Montréal between 1945 and 1985.)
Jean de Bonville.   Québec: Institut québécois de Recherche sur la Culture, 1995. 223p.

A comparative analysis of Montréal's newspapers between 1945 and 1985 on the bases of their physical appearance, their content, and their writing style. The author principally employs quantitative data in his analysis, which distinguishes his work from typical analyses which focus on the ideological aspects of Québec's media. His work includes many tables. The author also published a work on the origins of mass media in Québec, entitled *La presse québécoise de 1884-1914. Genèse d'un media de masse* (The Québec press from 1884 to 1914. The emergence of a mass media) (Sainte-Foy, Québec: Presses de l'Université Laval, 1988. 416p.), in addition to an analytical bibliography on Québec journalism, entitled *La presse québécoise de 1764 à 1914: bibliographie analytique* (The Québec press from 1764 to 1914: an analytical bibliography) (Sainte-Foy, Québec: Presses de l'Université Laval, 1995. 351p.).

1007   **Les journalistes dans les coulisses de l'information, 2e édition.**
        (Journalists behind the news.)
        Paul-André Comeau et al.   Montréal: Éditions Québec Amérique,
        1980. 421p. bibliog.

A collection of essays written by well-known Québec journalists, including Lysiane Gagnon, Joan Fraser, and Gilles Lesage, on the different challenges that faced journalists at the beginning of the 1980s. Among the challenges discussed in this book are the media's manipulation of the public, labour relations issues, and the future of the anglophone media in Québec. Several contributions are still relevant today. The work includes a comprehensive bibliography.

1008   **Le Devoir: un journal indépendant, 1910-1995.** (*Le Devoir*: an
        independent newspaper, 1910-95.)
        Edited by Robert Comeau, Luc Desrochers.   Sainte-Foy, Québec:
        Presses de l'Université du Québec, 1996. 368p. (Les Leaders du
        Québec Contemporain, no. 8).

This book distinguishes itself from other histories of Québec's most important intellectual newspaper by casting aside the rose-tinted glasses which are too often used in eulogizing the singular achievements of this Québec institution. This book is the product of a symposium on *Le Devoir*. Following four brief essays written by current and former editors, the other essays are classified into the following thematic chapters: *Le Devoir* as a business enterprise; the paper's role as an intellectual force; the modernization of Québec; nationalism and identity; culture and the arts; the international scene; and *Le Devoir* today. Overall, this book provides one of the most balanced and global analyses of this newspaper and its unique place in Québec.

1009   **Le Devoir.** (The Duty.)
        Pierre-Philippe Gingras.   Montréal: Éditions Libre Expression, 1985.
        295p.

Written by a former employee of *Le Devoir*, this book does not provide a deep analysis, but relates a series of events and obstacles that the newspaper faced in its history. The book also discusses the place occupied by *Le Devoir* and its members in political debates in Québec and Canada.

1010   **L'information-opium: une histoire politique du journal *La Presse*.**
        (Information-opium: a political history of *La Presse*.)
        Pierre Godin.   Montréal: Parti Pris, 1972. 469p.

Describes the history of the newspaper, *La Presse*, in relation to its political role. While the focus is on one particular newspaper, the issues discussed in this work can be easily applied to the industry at large: media concentration; the links between politicians and newspapers; and journalists' working conditions. This study includes tables.

1011   **Commission royale sur les quotidiens = Royal Commission on Newspapers.**
Tom Kent.   Ottawa: Commission, 1981. 323p.

Created in response to the increasing concentration of ownership in the Canadian press industry, this Royal Commission provided a very good report in 1981 not only on the financial aspects of newspapers but also of their role and place in Canadian society. The Commission concluded that the increasing concentration of ownership in the newspaper industry was having a direct impact on editorial content. Moreover, the Commission found that journalists were not always free to carry out their daily tasks. The Commission proposed the drafting of legislation to regulate ownership in addition to a bill of rights protecting journalists.

1012   *Le Devoir*: **reflet du Québec au 20e siècle.** (*Le Devoir*: a reflection of 20th-century Québec.)
Edited by Robert Lahaise, with a foreword by Lise Bissonnette, and an afterword by Guy Rocher.   LaSalle, Québec: Éditions Hurtubise HMH, 1994. 504p.

Le Devoir is certainly one of the most influential newspapers in 20th-century Québec. This collection of essays on its influence is divided into two sections. The first part describes the general evolution of the newspaper since its foundation in 1910 until 1993. The second section focuses on more specific aspects, describing the manner in which *Le Devoir* has reported on issues such as the economy, the arts, feminism, modernity and political questions throughout its time. This is the most wide-ranging study that has been written on the changing face of *Le Devoir*.

1013   **Les communications au Québec.** (Communications in Québec.)
Edited by Alain Laramée.   Montréal: Éditions Saint-Martin, 1993. 246p.

This collection of essays focuses on the cultural importance of communications in Québec and the need to develop political tools to manage this sector. Against the backdrop of the increasing ease with which new technology renders political borders invisible, this collection of essays examines the communications industry in Québec sector by sector, reveals the major socio-economic and cultural challenges, and proposes avenues of intervention to face these challenges. This work focuses on the political and cultural issues associated with each sector.

1014   **Communication et culture.** (Communication and culture.)
Jean-Paul Lemaire, with a foreword by Fernand Dumont.
Sainte-Foy, Québec: Presses de l'Université Laval, 1989. 296p.

Written for the general public, this book aims to make the reader aware of the important link between culture and communications in Québec. Moreover, the author's multidisciplinary approach reveals the extent to which both culture and communications mutually influence each other. While the first half of this work discusses the theoretical relationships between culture and communications, the rapid changes in communications technology, and the impact of these changes, the second half of the book examines their concrete manifestations: five essays analyse the discourse in television and print media, and two essays discuss communications as the meeting place of different cultures.

1015 **Recherches québécoises sur la télévision.** (Québec research on television.)
Edited by Annie Méar. Montréal: Éditions coopératives Albert Saint-Martin, 1980. 210p.

A series of scholarly articles which assess the impact of television on Québec culture and society. The work is organized into five sections: programming; advertising; audience analysis; the economics of television; and the future of Québec television.

1016 **Le Canada de Radio-Canada: sociologie critique et dialogisme culturel.** (Radio-Canada's Canada: critical sociology and cultural dialogism.)
Greg Marc Nielsen. Toronto: Éditions du GREF, 1994. 202p. bibliog.

Using the theory of the critical sociology of culture, this comparative work describes the role of both linguistic sections (anglophone and francophone) of Radio-Canada and their similarities with the populations they serve. This book provides a good analysis of the sociological differences between the English- and French-speaking populations in Canada. It includes a comprehensive bibliography.

1017 **La presse québécoise des origines à nos jours.** (The Québec press: from its origins to the present.)
Québec: Presses de l'Université Laval, 1973-90. 10 vols.

An annotated list of newspapers and periodicals (both French- and English-language) published in the province. This work includes bibliographical references, brief historical notes and library locations in Québec and Ontario.

1018 **Les médias québécois: presse, radio, télévision, câblodistribution.** (Québec media: the press, radio, television and cable.)
Marc Raboy. Boucherville, Québec: Gaëtan Morin Éditeur, 1992. 280p.

An introduction to the structure, organization, and operation, of mass media in Québec. A structuralist approach is employed to describe and analyse this industry. In discussing the political economy of the media, the role of regulatory bodies and finally the role of journalists, Raboy successfully highlights the public debates which have taken place in Québec involving the media. The production and reception of media content is also discussed. Overall, this book will be welcomed by the non-specialist.

1019 **Movements and messages: media and radical politics in Québec.**
Marc Raboy, translated by David Homel. Toronto: Between the Lines, 1984. 165p. bibliog.

Raboy studies the relationship of different types of communications media to the social and political movements of the 1960s and 1970s. He looks at how these movements have shaped their own communications strategies in opposition to the state. Alternative publications are discussed, such as *Parti Pris*, *Québec Presse* and *Bulletin Populaire*.

1020   **25 ans de télévision au Québec.** (Twenty-five years of television in
       Québec.)
       Pierre Richard.   Montréal: Québécor, 1986. 374p.
A study of television productions between 1960 and 1985. The author presents the
concepts, public reviews and artists of some of the most popular shows in Québec's
history.

1021   **Le "30".** (The '30'.)
       Montréal: Fédération professionnelle des Journalistes du Québec,
       1976- . [monthly].
The official organ of the Professional Federation of Québec Journalists, this periodical
presents articles which deal with the practice of journalism in Québec. Among the
subjects frequently studied are media concentration, the power of television, and
journalistic ethics. The articles are well written and the journal objectively presents
the different opinions in the industry.

1022   **Les industries de la culture et des communications au Québec et
       au Canada.** (The cultural and communications industries in Québec
       and Canada.)
       Edited by Gaëtan Tremblay.   Sillery, Québec: Presses de
       l'Université du Québec; Sainte-Foy, Québec: Télé-Université, 1990.
       429p. (Communication et Société).
An excellent collection of essays on the state of the different cultural and communications
industries in Québec. If some of the legislation and economic conditions have changed
since the publication of this book, it nevertheless provides important information on
the influential institutions in the industries of film, music, radio, television, and on the
legal framework that exercises control over them. The last section of the book deals
with particular case-studies of selected companies.

1023   **La population face aux médias.** (The public and the media.)
       Lina Trudel.   Montréal: VLB Éditeur, 1992. 223p.
Provides the necessary background information to enable readers to take a more critical
view of the media and its influence on democracy and public opinion. Trudel's main
objective is to discuss the media's place in society, how it operates, and the legal and
ethical regulations which guide and control the media.

General Periodicals

1024 **L'Actualité.** (Current Affairs.)
Montréal: Maclean Hunter, 1976- . bi-monthly.
Published bi-monthly since 1990, this magazine is the most widely read current affairs magazine in Québec. While it does cover international affairs, its content focuses on issues relating to Québec culture and politics. This is an important publication for those wishing to keep up with current issues in Québec.

1025 **Châtelaine.**
Montréal: Maclean Hunter, 1928- . monthly.
A women's magazine which includes articles on fashion, family relations, health tips, and interviews with popular figures in Québec's artistic community.

1026 **Le Devoir.** (The Duty.)
Montréal: L'Imprimerie Populaire, 1910- . daily.
Published six times a week, this is Québec's most important broadsheet newspaper despite its deceptively low circulation. Founded by Henri Bourrassa in 1910, *Le Devoir* has always involved itself in the public debate on political and cultural issues. Its editors, therefore, are respected not only as journalists but also as opinion leaders. *Le Devoir* makes no apologies for its left-of-centre, and often nationalist, editorial stands. This newspaper is an essential read for anyone interested in Québec politics.

1027 **The Gazette.**
Montréal: Southam, 1785- . daily.
The Gazette is Québec's oldest newspaper. Originally established in 1785 as a bilingual publication, it is now the English-speaking community's largest circulated broadsheet daily paper.   *The Gazette* covers international, national and local news, in addition to topics of special interest, although international and national news is typically culled from wire services. Its editorial positions have become increasingly hard-line federalist and radical, and its local news coverage falls prey to political bias at times. Nevertheless, this newspaper is the anglophone community's mouthpiece and

should be read by anyone who wishes to understand the English-speaking community in Québec.

1028 Hour.
Montréal: Communications Voir Inc., 19- . weekly.

One of the two alternative, weekly English-language tabloids in Montréal. Its news coverage is marginal, while its advertising content is high, but it offers one of the most complete listings of Montréal's cultural events, cinema, theatre and art shows. *Hour* is published by the same company as *Voir* (see item no. 1032).

1029 Mirror.
Montréal: Quebecor, 1980- . weekly.

Montréal's oldest alternative, English-language, weekly tabloid newspaper. Similar to *Hour* (see item no. 1028), its news coverage is local and sparse. Nevertheless, it offers the most comprehensive set of listings, reviews and articles on Montréal's cultural events.

1030 La Presse. (The Press.)
Montréal: La Presse Ltd., 1884- . daily.

The French-language broadsheet newspaper with the largest circulation in North America. Published seven days a week, *La Presse* covers local, national and international news. It includes general interest sections such as arts and entertainment, sports and business. *La Presse's* editorial stand tends towards the federalist point of view on national issues.

1031 Le Soleil. (The Sun.)
Québec: Division du Groupe Unimédia, 1896- . daily.

Québec City's largest circulating, and most serious, newspaper. *Le Soleil* was originally the provincial Liberal Party's organ. Today, it is an excellent, non-Montréal-based complement to the political analysis of *Le Devoir* (see item no. 1026). Other regional newspapers of note are: *Le Nouvelliste* (The Newsman), *La Tribune* (The Tribune), *Le Quotidien de Chicoutimi* (The Chicoutimi Daily), *La Voix de l'Est* (The Voice of the East), and *The Record*.

1032 Voir. (Light.)
Montréal: Communications Voir Inc., 1986- . weekly.

Voir is Montréal's French-language alternative tabloid weekly newspaper. As is the tradition in the French press, its editorial stands receive somewhat more attention than *Voir*'s English-language equivalent, *Hour* (see item no. 1028). In common with *Hour* and the *Mirror* (see item no. 1029), *Voir* provides a complete guide to cultural events; the major difference is its more comprehensive listing of francophone events and its larger classifieds section.

General Reference Works

1033   **Bibliographie du centre du Québec et des Bois-Francs.**
(A bibliography on central Québec and the Bois-Francs.)
Yves Beauregard.   Québec: Institut québécois de la Recherche sur la
Culture, 1986. 495p. maps. (Documents de Recherche, no. 9).
Contains over 3,100 items relating to central Québec and the Bois-Francs.

1034   **Bibliographie du Québec 1821-1967.** (A bibliography on Québec,
1821-1967.)
Montréal: Bibliothèque nationale du Québec, 1980- .
When completed, this multi-volume set will provide an inventory of all titles, excluding
government publications, published in Québec between 1821 and 1967.

1035   **Francophonie nord-américaine: bibliographie sélective.**
(French-speaking North America: a selective bibliography.)
Edited by Michel Brûlé.   Québec: Secrétariat permanent des Peuples
francophones, 1991. 192p.
Contains 400 monographs on French-speaking North America, arranged by subject
and region.

1036   **Canadian Periodical Index = Index de Périodiques Canadiens.**
Toronto: Globe and Mail, 1986- . monthly.
An index of articles published in Canadian periodicals.

1037   Catalogue de la Bibliothèque nationale du Québec: revues
       québécoises. (The Bibliothèque nationale du Québec [Québec
       National Library] catalogue: Québec journals.)
       Montréal: Bibliothèque nationale du Québec, 1981. 3 vols.

Arranged alphabetically by title, this catalogue is very inclusive for 19th-century and
contemporary material.

1038   **Bibliographie de la Gaspésie.** (A bibliography on the Gaspé.)
       Marc Desjardins.   Québec: Institut québécois de la Recherche sur la
       Culture, 1987. 436p.

An inventory of 4,395 works relating to the Gaspé published before 1986. This is the
most wide-ranging and accessible bibliography of published works about the Gaspé
available. University theses relating to the region are also included.

1039   **Bibliographie des Îles-de-la-Madeleine.** (A bibliography on the
       Magdalen Islands.)
       Marc Desjardins.   Québec: Institut québécois de Recherche sur la
       Culture, 1987. 281p. map. (Documents de Recherche, no. 13).

An inventory of published works, media, film, and resources relating to the region.
This is the most wide-ranging and up-to-date bibliography on this fascinating region
and covers works published up to 1985. Seventeen thematic sections list the 1,413
titles catalogued in this book. The only selection criteria used is subject matter.
General works which discuss this region only tangentially were excluded. Public
documents were only included if they were of an official nature and were widely
circulated.

1040   **Dictionnaire de l'Amérique francaise.** (A dictionary of French
       America.)
       Charles Dufresne, Jacques Grimard, André Savard, Gaëtan Vallières.
       Ottawa: Presses de l'Université d'Ottawa, 1988. 386p.

Provides short biographies, and brief entries on places, names, institutions, events and
major themes of French-speaking North America.

1041   **Bibliographie de Charlevoix.** (A bibliography on Charlevoix.)
       Serge Gauthier, Martine Néron, Marc-André Bluteau, Dominique
       Dufour, Yves Lefrançois.   Québec: Institut québécois de la
       Recherche sur la Culture, 1984. 316p. maps. (Documents de
       Recherche, no. 3).

Contains 1,810 references, classified according to over 10 themes ranging from
politics and geography to culture and famous personalities, relating to the Charlevoix
region, which is defined by the intersection of the Laurentians and the Saint-Lawrence
Seaway. A list of various archives and their contents is also included.

1042 **Bibliographie de l'Abitibi-Témiscamingue.** (A bibliography on
Abitibi-Témiscaminque.)
Benoit B. Gourd. Rouyn, Québec: Direction des Études
Universitaires, 1973. 270p.

Despite its date of publication, over 6,000 items classified according to 7 major
themes make this work one of the most thorough and complete bibliographies of the
region.

1043 **Bibliographie de la Mauricie.** (A bibliography on the Mauricie.)
René Hardy, Guy Trépanier. Québec: Institut québécois de la
Recherche sur la Culture, 1991. 294p. maps. (Documents de
Recherche, no. 27).

Lists over 3,400 items relating to the Mauricie region, classified by theme. The
authors have also included an inventory of local archives, a section listing historical
monographs published by municipal authorities, and a section on well-known regional
personalities such as famous writers, journalists and politicians.

1044 **Bibliographie de la Côte-du-Sud.** (A bibliography on the South
Shore.)
Yves Hébert. Québec: Institut québécois de Recherche sur la
Culture, 1986. 339p. maps. (Documents de Recherche, no. 8).

An inventory of 1,979 references relating to Québec's South Shore which extends
from Beaumont to Rivière-du-Loup. A list of university theses is included, in addition
to a section of useful addresses which provides the reader with a guide to social,
educational, justice and media services in the region.

1045 **Le manuel de la parole. Manifestes québécois.** (The manual of the
speech. Québec manifestos.)
Daniel Latouche, Diane Poliquin-Bourassa. Montréal: Éditions du
Boréal Express, 1971, 1978, 1979. 3 vols.

An anthology of manifestos in three volumes, covering the periods from 1760 to 1899,
1900 to 1959 and 1960 to 1980. The editors have chosen manifestos which help to
explain the evolution of Québec society in the last 200 years, including the Patriots'
manifestos and the manifestos of the FLQ (Front de Libération du Québec). Each
manifesto is accompanied by a series of annotations which help to elucidate the context
in which they were written.

1046 **Bibliographie des Laurentides.** (A bibliography on the Laurentians.)
Serge Laurin, Richard Lagrange. Québec: Institut québécois de
Recherche sur la Culture, 1985. 370p. maps. (Documents de
Recherches, no. 7).

The Laurentians is among the more well-known regions in Québec since it plays
host to a multitude of vacationing Montréalers and tourists. More precisely, the
Laurentians is the name François-Xavier Garneau, Québec's first historian, gave to the
mountain range which runs parallel to the Saint-Lawrence along its northern shore.
This work classifies over 2,000 items.

1047 **Livres d'Ici.** (Books From Québec.)
Montréal: Société de Promotion du Livre, 1982- . monthly except
July and August.
This trade publication offers comprehensive information about the Québec publishing
world.

1048 **Les livres disponsibles canadiens de langue francaise = Canadian
French Books in Print.**
Montréal: Bibliodata, 1987- .
Provides author, title and subject access to over ninety per cent of the non-governmental
titles in print. This work includes books and periodicals from Québec and from
French-language publishers in other provinces.

1049 **French Québec. Imprints in French from Québec 1764-1990 in
the British Library.**
D. J. McTernan.   Bury St Edmunds, England: The British Library,
1992. 2 vols.
This two-volume catalogue indicates the French works held by the Humanities and
Social Sciences Division, Collection Development, of the British Library. Maps,
manuscripts, music, prints and drawings are therefore excluded. Moreover, the other
selection criteria are that works included in this catalogue must have been printed in
Québec and must have been written mainly in French. The first volume attempts to
present French Québec's perception of itself through its artistic and philosophical
works while the second deals with Québec's social and political institutions, history,
and geophysical features.

1050 **Bibliographie de la Rive-Sud de Québec: Lévis-Lotbinière.** (A
bibliography on Québec's South Shore: Lévis-Lotbinière.)
Françoise de Montigny-Pelletier, Andrée Raiche-Dussault.   Québec:
Institut québécois de Recherche sur la Culture, 1989. 263p.
(Documents de Recherche, no. 19).
Contains just over 2,000 references to items on Québec's South Shore, namely Lévis-
Lotbinière. The eastern and western extremities of this region overlap slightly with the
regions of previously published bibliographies in this series, namely *Bibliographie de
la Côte-du-Sud* (see item no. 1044), and the *Bibliographie du Centre du Québec et des
Bois-Francs* (see item no. 1033).

1051 **Bibliographie du Haut-Saint-Laurent: sud-ouest de la
Montérégie.** (A bibliography on the Upper Saint-Lawrence:
southwest Montérégie.)
Monique Perron, Luc Boisvert, Roland Viau.   Québec: Institut
québécois de la Recherche sur la Culture, 1990. 318p. maps.
(Documents de Recherche, no. 24).
Lists over 3,000 items relating to the region of the Upper Saint-Lawrence. This region,
often eclipsed by the better-known regions of the Montérégie and Montréal, comprises
the counties of Châteauguay, Vaudreuil, Soulanges, Beauharnois, and Huntingdon.

1052   **Point de repère: index analytique d'articles de périodiques québécois et étrangers.** (Point of reference: an analytical index to Québec and foreign articles and periodicals.)
Montréal: Centrale des Bibliothèques, Bibliothèque nationale du Québec, 1984- . available on microfiche and online. updated bi-monthly.

Provides author, title, and subject, access to the content of major Québec periodicals and other selected periodicals of the French-speaking world. It is available online and on microfiche, and is updated bi-monthly.

1053   **Bibliographie de la Côte-Nord.** (A bibliography on the North Shore.)
Gaston Saint-Hilaire, Andrée Raiche-Dussault.   Québec: Institut québécois de Recherche sur la Culture, 1990. 340p. maps.
(Documents de Recherche, no. 26).

Sparsely populated, the North Shore's history is defined both by the aboriginal presence in the interior and by small fishing posts along the shore. More recently, technological advancements have permitted the development of the region's forestry and hydro-electric resources. This bibliography contains over 3,900 items classified according to different themes. Information on local services and archives are also included.

1054   **A reader's guide to Québec studies: 1988.**
André Senécal.   Québec: Gouvernement du Québec, 1988. 2nd ed. 145p.

This work identifies 1,200 important titles (both monographs and periodicals) of key sources related to Québec. Works in the areas of the humanities and social sciences are arranged by broad categories.

1055   **Bibliographie de Lanaudière.** (A bibliography on Lanaudière.)
Daniel Tessier, Denis Chabot, Josée Masse, Christian Morissonneau, Réjean Olivier.   Québec: Institut québécois de Recherche sur la Culture, 1987. 270p. maps. (Documents de Recherche, no. 14).

A bibliography of over 1,600 items relating to the Lanaudière region, one of Québec's youngest administrative regions. No place, whether natural or man-made, bears the name Lanaudière. The region is better known for the municipal agglomerations found therein such as Assomption and Joliette. This region extends north from the Saint-Lawrence and is delimited on the east by the Laurentians, and by Mauricie on the west.

1056   **Catalogue collectif des impressions québécoises, 1764-1820.** (A catalogue of Québec prints, 1764-1820.)
Milada Vlach, Yolande Buono.   Québec: Direction générale des Publications gouvernementales, 1984. 195p.

A descriptive catalogue listing 1,115 titles of Québec works published prior to 1820 found in the major libraries in Québec. It includes an index of English equivalents for the French subject and genre terms, and an appendix listing the holdings of each library.

Indexes

There follow three separate indexes: authors (personal or corporate); titles; and subjects. Title entries are italicized and refer either to the main titles, or to other works cited in the annotations. The numbers refer to bibliographical entry rather than page number. Individual index entries are arranged in alphabetical sequence.

Index of Authors

311

312

Index of Titles

314

322

Q

335

Index of Subjects

339

350

Map of Québec

This map shows the more important features.

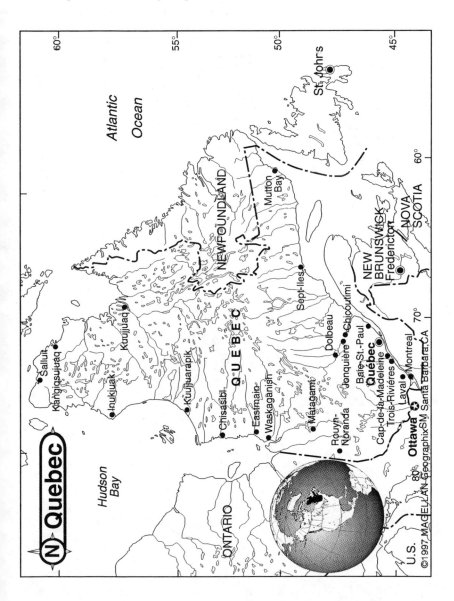

ALSO FROM CLIO PRESS

INTERNATIONAL ORGANIZATIONS SERIES

Each volume in the International Organizations Series is either devoted to one specific organization, or to a number of different organizations operating in a particular region, or engaged in a specific field of activity. The scope of the series is wide-ranging and includes intergovernmental organizations, international non-governmental organizations, and national bodies dealing with international issues. The series is aimed mainly at the English-speaker and each volume provides a selective, annotated, critical bibliography of the organization, or organizations, concerned. The bibliographies cover books, articles, pamphlets, directories, databases and theses and, wherever possible, attention is focused on material about the organizations rather than on the organizations' own publications. Notwithstanding this, the most important official publications, and guides to those publications, will be included. The views expressed in individual volumes, however, are not necessarily those of the publishers.

VOLUMES IN THE SERIES

1 *European Communities*, John Paxton

2 *Arab Regional Organizations*, Frank A. Clements

3 *Comecon: The Rise and Fall of an International Socialist Organization*, Jenny Brine

4 *International Monetary Fund*, Anne C. M. Salda

5 *The Commonwealth*, Patricia M. Larby and Harry Hannam

6 *The French Secret Services*, Martyn Cornick and Peter Morris

7 *Organization of African Unity*, Gordon Harris

8 *North Atlantic Treaty Organization*, Phil Williams

9 *World Bank*, Anne C. M. Salda

10 *United Nations System*, Joseph P. Baratta

11 *Organization of American States*, David Sheinin

12 *The British Secret Services*, Philip H. J. Davies

13 *The Israeli Secret Services*, Frank A. Clements